From Bassermann to Bebel

From Bassermann to Bebel

The Grand Bloc's Quest for Reform in
the Kaiserreich, 1900–1914

Beverly Heckart

Yale University Press,   New Haven and London

1974

Published with assistance from the
foundation established in memory of
Philip Hamilton McMillan of the class of 1894, Yale College

Designed by John O. C. McCrillis
and set in Times Roman type.
Printed in the United States of America by
The Murray Printing Co., Forge Village, Mass.

Published in Great Britain, Europe, and Africa by
Yale University Press, Ltd., London.
Distributed in Latin America by Kaiman & Polon,
Inc., New York City; in Australasia and Southeast
Asia by John Wiley & Sons Australasia Pty. Ltd.,
Sydney; in India by UBS Publishers' Distributors Pvt.,
Ltd., Delhi; in Japan by John Weatherhill, Inc., Tokyo.

To my great-aunt Zora

Contents

Acknowledgments

No book is solely the product of its author. This author particularly could not have begun or completed this work without the encouragement of her mentors and colleagues. For his persistent interest, continuous intellectual stimulation and patient help, I owe especial thanks to Dietrich Gerhard. He read and commented upon the several versions of the manuscript, and through his broad experience and imagination expanded my own knowledge and insights. My friends and colleagues at the Max Planck Institut für Geschichte and at the University of Göttingen will always occupy a special place in my memory for their detached explanations of German society and politics. Without them, I should never have gained a valuable perspective on German history. On this side of the Atlantic, my colleagues at Central Washington State College more than shared in the preparation of this book both by reading it several times and by allowing me to vent my many frustrations with it upon them. I am also indebted to Henry A. Turner, Jr., for his understanding and constructive criticism.

When publishing a history, it would be fitting for the author to mention as collaborators all those librarians and archivists who sorted, suggested, ordered, and delivered the materials necessary for filling his or her pages. My list of names would be very long, but it would include the librarians at the University of Göttingen, the archivists and staff at the *Bundesarchiv* in Koblenz, at the *Deutsche Zentralarchiv* in Potsdam, at the *Badische Generallandesarchiv* in Karlsruhe, and at the International Institute for Social History in Amsterdam. I am particularly grateful to the staff at the Social Democratic party archives in Bonn for making my work there a personally warming as well as a scholarly rewarding experience. To Dr. Fritz von Bülow for granting me permission to use the Prince von Bülow's papers, a special word of thanks.

The financial contribution made to this project by the Fulbright Fellowship program, the Washington University Research Fellowship program, and the Central Washington State College Faculty Research Committee, should and will be acknowledged, not with thanks, but by this author's appropriate encouragement of their continued support for future scholars and authors.

Last, but not least, my great-aunt Zora deserves more than the one line of dedication that appears at the beginning of this book. Throughout my life, she has been a constant source of inspiration and support. No words could ever express what I owe her. This dedication is merely a small token of my appreciation.

B. H.

Abbreviations

Bassermann remnant, 303 — Bassermann Papers, Bundesarchiv Koblenz

Briefwechsel — Viktor Adler, *Briefwechsel mit August Bebel und Karl Kautsky,* ed. Friedrich Adler (Vienna, 1954)

DZAP, FVP — Deutsches Zentralarchiv Potsdam, Akten der fortschrittlichen Volkspartei

Freisinniger Parteitag, 1905 — *Der Sechste Parteitag der freisinnigen Volkspartei* (Wiesbaden, 1905)

Freisinnige Volkspartei — *Die Freisinnige Volkspartei, ihr Programm und ihre Organisation* (Berlin, 1909)

Kürschners, 1907 — *Kürschners deutscher Reichstag, Biographisch-Statistisches Handbuch, 1907–1912,* ed. Herman Hillger, 3rd ed. (Berlin and Leipzig, no date)

NL Akten, R 45 1/1 — Akten der nationalliberalen Partei, Bestand R 45 I, Bundesarchiv Koblenz

NL Baden — Akten der nationalliberalen Partei Badens, Generallandesarchiv Karlsruhe

NL Vertretertag, 1906 — *Neunter Allgemeiner Vertretertag der nationalliberalen Partei am 6. und 7. Oktober in Goslar* (Berlin, 1906)

NL Vertretertag Preussens, 1913	*Vierter preussischer Vertretertag der nationalliberalen Partei am 6. April. 1913 in Hannover* (Berlin, 1913)
Schulthess, 1907	Heinrich Schulthess, ed., *Europäische Geschichtskalender* (Nördlingen, 1871 et seq.)
SPD Fraktionsprotokolle	*Die Reichstagsfraktion der deutschen Sozialdemokratie, 1898 bis 1918,* ed. Erich Matthias and Eberhard Pikart, 2 vols. (Düsseldorf, 1966)
SPD Parteitag, 1898	*Protokoll über die Verhandlungen des Parteitages der sozialdemokratischen Partei Deutschlands* (Berlin, 1898)
SPD Württembergs, 1907	*Bericht des Landesvorstandes, der Landtagsfraktion, und Protokoll der Landesversammlung, 1907,* ed. Sozialdemokratische Partei Württembergs (Stuttgart, 1907)
Vereinigung Parteitag, 1906	*Erster Delegiertentag des Wahlvereins der Liberalen zu Berlin am 17. und 18. Februar. 1906* (Berlin, 1906)
Verhandlungen des Reichstages	*Stenographische Berichte der Verhandlungen des deutschen Reichstages* (1871 et seq.)
Verhandlungen Baden	*Verhandlungen der zweiten Kammer der Stände-Versammlung des Grossherzogtums Baden* (Karlsruhe, 1819 et seq.)
Verhandlungen Preussens	*Stenographische Berichte über die Verhandlungen des preussischen Hauses der Abgeordneten* (Berlin, 1850 et seq.)

Part I: The Reorientation of the Parties

1

Demokratie und Kaisertum

The "mastering of the past" (*Bewältigung der Vergangenheit*) has pre-occupied many German historians who in some way experienced or suffered from the recent "catastrophe" of German history. Two historians who attempted to analyze the roots and development of National Socialism were Gerhard Ritter and Friedrich Meinecke, and both attributed its power to the German failure to achieve a satisfactory political balance between nationalism and liberal democracy. In the course of German history, one of these movements always suffered at the expense of the other. When nationalism and national unity were in the ascendant, liberal democracy declined; when liberal democracy achieved its goals, national integrity suffered an eclipse. Part of the reason for this fatal dichotomy lay in an equally harmful division of Germany's political forces. Those groups most interested in national unity and integrity were never enthusiastic about liberal-democratic ideals; and those who wanted the "sovereignty of the people" deemphasized the "sovereignty of the nation." The two groups never successfully ac-commodated each other even though reflective Germans realized that this accommodation was necessary for the survival of a united German state in the modern world. One of those reflective Germans was Fried-rich Naumann. During his lifetime, he was actively involved in a political scheme to combine the forces of nationalism and democracy, and he greatly influenced the generations to which Ritter and Meinecke belonged. Both historians later recalled his plans, and Meinecke idealized them as the regrettable missed opportunity in German history.[1] The story of that opportunity, its setting, its development, and its political implications is the purpose of this book.

1. Gerhard Ritter, *The German Problem: Basic Questions of German Political Life, Past and Present* (Columbus, 1965), pp. 126–128; Friedrich Meinecke, *The German Catastrophe: Reflections and Recollections* (Boston, 1963), p. 19.

Friedrich Naumann was born in a small Saxon town in 1860.[2] Like many other famous Germans he was the son of an Evangelical pastor and grew up in a pious and conservative home. As a young man he was urged to follow in his father's footsteps by training for the ministry. Had he been a less sensitive and imaginative person living in less troubled times, nothing would have disturbed this traditional pattern, and Naumann would never have made his mark in German politics and history. However, the period in which Naumann grew to manhood saw substantial changes in German society. During the first thirty-five years of Naumann's life, Germany experienced that nationalistic revival which united the nation under Prussia and made it the strongest military and industrial power on the European continent. Under the impetus of this new power, German commerce and capital penetrated to all parts of the world, and eventually Germany acquired colonies in Africa and the Pacific. The German merchant marine became the second largest in the world, and a fledgling fleet began to enhance and protect the new position of Germany in Europe and the world. Most Germans of Naumann's generation felt a more or less intense patriotic pride in all these recent achievements, and most supported the policy of *Weltpolitik* espoused by Kaiser Wilhelm II and begun by the German government at the turn of the century. This meant an increase in all the trappings of national and global strength: the army, the navy, the colonies, and industrial production. Most Germans of the time were willing to make the political and economic sacrifices that contributed to these accretions in national power, and they voted for political parties that adopted these national causes. Ultimately they identified with German world power, and this accounted for the great popularity of German nationalism and imperialism.

Naumann shared the national pride and aspirations of his contemporaries, but his moral and intellectual sensitivities also made him keenly aware of certain flaws in Germany's development. The industrial growth which made German Weltpolitik possible was also accompanied by the same poverty, socioeconomic adjustment, and psychological hardship produced by industrialization everywhere.

After his initial theological training, Naumann accepted a position at the *Rauhes Haus* in Hamburg, a home and school for destitute children founded by the pioneer Christian social worker Johann Wichern and his

2. Subsequent biographical data for Friedrich Naumann are taken from Theodor Heuss, *Friedrich Naumann* (Stuttgart, 1937).

son Johannes. The work of the Wicherns included an "Inner Mission" to the workers of Hamburg, and here Naumann directly experienced the "social question." This problem continued to bother him when he accepted the pastorate in a church in the small Saxon town of Lang-enberg, where many of his parishioners sometimes suffered from the impoverishing effects of Saxon industrialization. The more he learned about the social problems of his time, the more attracted he was to their solution, and he eventually became director of the Inner Mission in Frankfurt. His experiences with the urban workers he served gradual-ly convinced him that social work would not solve all the problems he confronted; some sort of social reform was also necessary. At first Naumann thought such reform could be achieved through established and respected political channels, and he joined the Christian Social movement founded by the erstwhile court preacher, Adolf Stoecker, and participated in its annual Evangelical Social Congresses. This movement had close ties with the politically dominant Conservative party and sought to influence the party toward social legislation.

The reasoning behind Naumann's choice was theoretically sound. The Conservative party primarily represented the Prussian Junker aristocracy with its traditions of noblesse oblige and ideals of Christian charity. This group worked to counteract the economic hardships and social dislocations accompanying industrialization, and the leading Junker statesman, Chancellor Otto von Bismarck, initiated the first national social insurance in Europe. The Conservative party also had strong ties with Kaiser Wilhelm II, who publicly proclaimed his interest in alleviating the lot of the industrial worker. In 1889, he personally intervened in favor of the workers in a miners' strike in the Ruhr, and in 1890 he dismissed Bismarck in part for opposing progressive social policies.[3] The alliance between the "social" kaiser and the Conservatives backed by the Christian Socialists should have guaranteed progressive social legislation. However, social legislation tended to strengthen the working classes economically and increase their political power in the state. For various reasons, neither Conservatives nor kaiser could countenance this development, and their attitude toward social legisla-tion cooled considerably during the 1890s.

As representatives of the traditional land-owning Prussian aristocracy,

3. Norman Rich, *Friedrich von Holstein,* 2 vols. (Cambridge, 1965), 1: 260–279. Cf. J. C. G. Röhl, *Germany without Bismarck: The Crisis of Government in the Second Reich, 1890–1900* (Berkeley and Los Angeles, 1967), pp. 34–55.

the Conservatives were accustomed to wielding and influencing power
in the state. They supported the German monarchical system because
the crown, whether Prussian king or German kaiser, traditionally
adhered to conservative political principles. Neither German unification
nor industrialization had changed this relationship. Although the
Conservatives feared a loss of influence after Bismarck unified Germany,
their political supremacy in Prussia, the dominant state in the new
German empire, insured their continued exercise of power. The Prussian
king was German kaiser, the Prussian prime minister was German
chancellor, and the Prussians held the most seats in the *Bundesrat*, or
German upper house. Thus unification posed no threat to the Con-
sevatives as long as they maintained their power in Prussia through the
Prussian three-class suffrage, which allowed wealthy citizens more representatives than poorer ones and assured the Conservatives almost
half the seats in the Prussian legislature. In the last analysis, however,
neither the federal arrangements of Germany nor the Prussian franchise
endangered the Conservatives as long as they retained their special
arrangement with the monarch. In the constitutional monarchy of
Prussia-Germany, the king and kaiser, not the parliament, held ultimate authority; he appointed and dismissed the chancellor and other
ministers of state; their policies were his policies and vice versa.

Yet the special relationship between the crown and its ministers on the
one hand and the Conservatives on the other hand was endangered in
the last decade of the nineteenth century. The elections of 1890 decreased
Conservative representation in the Reichstag, and the new Caprivi
government unwittingly followed a course inimical to the Conservatives.
The new chancellor attempted to cultivate interests that directly opposed
or challenged the position of the Conservatives. He initiated a series
of reciprocal trade treaties which improved the market for Germany's
industrial goods and lowered grain tariffs in consonance with the
liberal principle of free trade, but Caprivi's action also threatened the
prices received by Conservative Junker grain farmers. He reduced the
military service period and shortened the term of the military budget in
deference to long-standing Centrist and liberal demands, but he thereby
endangered the traditional Conservative, aristocratic domination of
military policy and personnel. None of these policies intended to alienate
the Conservatives; rather they sought to expand the base of government in recognition of the groups which contributed to Germany's

strength and which constituted important voting blocks in the Reichstag and in the Prussian *Landtag*. Yet the Conservatives opposed
any measures that detracted from their political or economic dominance. In protest against Caprivi's economic policies, they formed the
Agrarian League, a powerful pressure group, which agitated bitterly for
more favorable policies toward grain farmers and became the rallying
point for Conservative opposition to the government. Conservative
opposition eventually forced the dismissal of Caprivi in 1894, and for
a while, at least, the kaiser's government ruled in accordance with the
Conservatives' desires and principles.[4]

Yet this Conservative pattern could not continue forever in unaltered
form. As Max Weber demonstrated, the policies of Caprivi aroused the
Conservatives because they reflected a new economic situation. In an
industrial society, an aristocracy that relied on agriculture would lose
the economic underpinnings of its political power. To retain power in
the state, the aristocracy had two choices. It could compromise with
the new society by acquiring an industrial interest through investments,
or it could turn against the industrial system and attempt to maintain
political power through artificial economic measures. The latter was the
method chosen by the Conservative Prussian aristocracy. At the same
time, the Conservatives also rejected such accompaniments to industri-
alism as concessions to middle- or working-class parties, suffrage reform, or social legislation.[5]

The Conservative choice disappointed Friedrich Naumann and
eventually led to his disillusionment with the conservative Christian
Social movement and the Evangelical Social Congresses. During his
short term as pastor in Saxony, Naumann began to study Marx and
Germany's Marxian Social Democratic party. Later, he decided that
this party was the only one capable of granting urban workers the

4. J. Alden Nicols, *Germany after Bismarck: The Caprivi Era, 1890–1894* (Cambridge,
Mass., 1958). Cf. Röhl, *Without Bismarck*, pp. 75–117.

5. Hans Booms, *Die Deutsch-Konservative Partei: Preussische Charakter, Reichsauf-
fassung, Nationalbegriff* (Düsseldorf, 1954), pp. 24–43; Andreas Dorpalen, "The German
Conservatives and the Parliamentarization of Imperial Germany," *Journal of Central
European Affairs* 11 (July 1951) : 184–199. For the relationships between the Conservatives
and the Agrarian League, see S. R. Tirrell, *German Agrarian Poltics after Bismarck's Fall:
The Formation of the Farmers' League* (New York, 1951), and Hans-Jürgen Puhle, *Agrarische
Interessenpolitik und preussischer Konservatismus im wilhelminischen Reich, 1893–1914:
Ein Beitrag zur Analyse des nationalismus in Deutschland am Beispiel des Bundes der Land-
wirte und der Deutsch-Konservativen Partei* (Hanover, 1966).

reforms they needed and deserved. Having reached this conclusion, Naumann at first tried to develop a greater tolerance for Social Democracy within the Christian Social movement. But the Christian Socialists had no desire to sever their ties with the Conservatives, and as their antiindustrial, antireform bias became ever more apparent, Naumann finally left the movement in 1894—in the same year as Caprivi's dismissal. In that year, he also founded the famous weekly, *Hilfe*, which was dedicated to persuading others to "help" in the task of social reform and legislation.

Naumann's failure to steer his Evangelical brothers toward Social Democracy reflected the strength of the dominant attitudes of his generation. For most of German society, the Social Democrats were anathema. They originally became a separate party in response to the same abuses that attracted Naumann to social reform.[6] More importantly, the Social Democrats were the descendants of the liberal democrats of mid-century who attempted to create a German democratic regime during the revolution of 1848. As inheritors of the revolutionary tradition, they opposed the unification of Germany under Prussia because they correctly believed it would diminish the chances for a true German democracy. After unification, the Social Democrats continued to oppose the new state by refusing to vote funds for the army, for colonial ventures, and later for the navy. In an age when most Germans enthusiastically supported such symbols of national strength, the Social Democrats were extremely unpopular. Moreover, they added to this unpopularity by perpetuating the revolutionary and republican ideals of 1848. They refused to give the *Hoch* to the kaiser which opened and closed every session of the Reichstag, and their leader, August Bebel, proclaimed the Paris Commune as the herald of future revolutionary events. At a time when grave social adjustments confronted all of Europe and resulted in such radical and unpopular movements as anarchistic terrorism and the International Workingmen's Association,

6. General histories of Social Democracy in this early period are Frolinde Balser, *Sozial-Demokratie 1848/49–1863: die erste deutsche Arbeiterorganisation "Allgemeine Arbeiterverbrüderung" nach der Revolution*, 2 vols. (Stuttgart, 1962); Roger Morgan, *The German Social Democrats and the First International, 1864–1872* (Cambridge, 1965); Vernon Lidtke, *The Outlawed Party: Social Democracy in Germany, 1878–1890* (Princeton, 1966). Cf. Horst Lademacher, "Zu den Anfängen der deutschen Sozialdemokratie, 1863–1878: Probleme ihrer Geschichtsschreibung," *International Review of Social History* 4 (1959); and Ernst Schraepler, *August Bebel: Sozialdemokrat im Kaisserreich* (Göttingen, 1966).

German society genuinely feared that Social Democracy would act on its antinational prejudice and its revolutionary promises. Indeed, Social Democracy was seen as the chief source of weakness in the new German state. When two attempts on the life of Kaiser Wilhelm I occurred in 1878, the government was able to exploit the popular psychology that linked Social Democracy, anarchism, revolution, and national disunity to pass discriminatory legislation against the Social Democratic party. Its clubs were disbanded, its newspapers suppressed, its leaders harassed. The only political activity allowed it, at the behest of the liberal and Centre parties, was representation in the Reichstag.

Antinationalism and the threat of revolution, however, were not the only reasons for discrimination against the Social Democrats. Their very raison d'être endangered the sinews of German society. Their demands for popular sovereignty sounded unreasonable to a society not far removed from the conservative feudal concept of a hierarchy in which the working class worked and left the business of government to its social superiors. Since the rest of German society modeled itself on the dominant aristocratic Conservatives, the working-class Social Democrats, who insisted on their right to influence government because of their inherent dignity and value as workers, were out of tune with most of their contemporaries.[7] Relegated to the bottom of the scale socially, legally, and politically, the Social Democrats reacted by adopting a singularly uncooperative attitude toward German parliamentary life. They rationalized their stand by claiming that the Reichstag, though elected by universal suffrage, was merely a chimera of self-government since it had no power to appoint the ministry and could always be overruled by the Bundesrat. Although they were right about these limitations, they overlooked the considerable power of the Reichstag to influence or change legislation introduced by the government. Their negativism became more pronounced after the antisocialist laws were passed, and until their repeal in 1890, Social Democrats in the Reichstag refused to vote even for legislation that partially agreed with their demands. Though they continued to sit in the Reichstag, for

7. For the feudal, aristocratic tone of German society, see Hajo Holborn, "Der deutsche Idealismus in sozialgeschichtlicher Bedeutung," *Historische Zeitschrift* 174 (1952) : 364; and Ernst Kohn-Bramstedt, *Aristocracy and the Middle Classes in Germany* (London, 1937), pp. 228–230; Peter Molt, *Der Reichstag vor der improvisierten Revolution* (Cologne, 1963), p. 74. Also Lamar Cecil, "The Creation of Nobles in Prussia, 1871–1918," *American Historical Review* 75 (1969–70): 757–795. Cf. Lidtke, *Outlawed Party*, p. 6.

them it remained a symbol of the rape of democracy that occurred through Prussian unification of Germany.

Given Social Democracy's aims and attitudes and its reputation as the nation's political pariah, the Christian Socialist refusal to accept and understand it was natural. Even Naumann had reservations about its antinationalistic and antimonarchical bias. But he was convinced that its demands for democracy and social reform were justified and necessary for the health of German politics, and after his break with the Christian Socialists, he began to search for ways to reconcile democracy with the German monarchy and German nationalism. In 1896, he founded a new political club, the *Nationalsoziale Verein*, which mostly consisted of educated middle-class reformers like himself who had deserted the Christian Social movement. This middle-class nucleus, through its program of social democracy, eventually hoped to attract the support of enough working-class elements to create a new party strong enough to compete successfully with Social Democracy. Unlike Social Democracy, the Nationalsoziale Verein would support both the monarchy and the German policy of Weltpolitik. Despite these good intentions, however, the new party never really had a chance in German politics. At election time, it had to compete with eight other well-established parties, and the vote cast for the Verein was pitifully small.[8] In the Reichstag elections of 1898, not one of its candidates succeeded, and conflict among the leadership weakened the party from within. Misfortune and conflict often inspire a new approach to an old problem, and the apparent failure of the Nationalsoziale Verein goaded Naumann toward a new method of combining German nationalism and democracy.

In this endeavor, he was greatly influenced by Max Weber, with whom he became friends at the Evangelical Social Congresses. Like Naumann, Weber shared the enthusiasm of the age for German achievements, and his initial sociological researches, which resulted in the famous Freiburg Inaugural Address, were concerned with maintaining and increasing national power. In his study of the waning economic and social powers of the agricultural aristocracy of East Elbia, he con-

8. Martin Wenck, *Die Geschichte der Nationalsozialen von 1895 bis 1903* (Berlin-Schöneberg, 1905). Also see Dieter Düding, *Der Nationalsoziale Verein, 1896–1903: Der gescheiterte Versuch einer parteipolitischen Synthese von Nationalismus, Sozialismus und Liberalismus* (Munich, 1972).

cluded that its continued exercise of political power, embodied in the Conservative party, was obsolete. According to Weber, the nation's elite should have consonant economic and political power. In an industrial age, the dominance of the agriculturally based Conservatives was unhealthy for the German body politic; instead, the middle classes, who based their wealth on a growing commercial and industrial power, should become the nation's new political leaders. But this new elite could not function alone; it needed the support of the working classes who oiled the wheels of Germany's new industrial strength. Democracy was the form that guaranteed this support; democracy would strengthen, not weaken, the state, and a strong middle-class party that espoused both nationalism and democracy should take the place of the Conservatives in German politics. Thus, Weber criticized the Nationalsoziale Verein because he thought that a new working-class party did not fulfill contemporary political needs, and Naumann's idea of combining both middle-and working-class elements in one party was unrealistic because it ignored the fact that modern political parties were based on the concrete and separate economic interests which created modern classes.[9]

Naumann's answer to these criticisms was a new method of combining nationalism and democracy. The new method was unveiled in a book, first published in 1900, which eventually ran into several editions and stirred the imagination of socially conscious patriots like Meinecke. The name of the book was *Demokratie und Kaisertum*, and although its ideas were couched in vague and enthusiastic rhetorical phrases (a clue to Naumann's great appeal as a speaker), they reflected the Weberian theme of the interrelationship among national, industrial, and popular power. Naumann no longer expected a new political party to synthesize nationalism, democracy, and the interests of the middle and working classes. Instead he suggested a new course of action based on existing parties, interests, and institutions.

When Naumann analyzed German politics in *Demokratie und Kai-*

9. Reinhard Bendix, *Max Weber: An Intellectual Portrait* (New York, Anchor edition, 1962), pp. 14–41; Wolfgang Mommsen, *Max Weber und der deutsche Politik, 1890–1920* (Tübingen, 1959), chapters 2–5, for his influence on Naumann, pp. 138–151. Cf. Peter Gilg, *Die Erneuerung des demokratischen Denkens im wilhelminischen Deutschland* (Wiesbaden, 1965), pp. 178–185, 188–189. For an analysis which attacks the ideas of Naumann and Weber as elitist, see Walter Struve, *Elites against Democracy: Leadership Ideals in Bourgeois Political Thought in Germany, 1890–1933* (Princeton, 1973).

sertum, he particularly stressed the need for democracy in a modern German state. Indeed, "democracy" was the most frequently used word in the whole first part of the book. In connection with this democratic necessity, Naumann revived his old idea of tolerance for and accommodation with the Social Democrats; he even deemphasized their revolutionary traditions in favor of more cooperative and pacific tendencies recently revealed by the party.[10] The problem was to change their antinational and antimonarchical bias and to eliminate the prejudice of German society against them. In order to achieve this goal, the monarchy would have to become democratic. By making this demand, Naumann knew that he was flying in the face of all German conventions, but he reasoned its possibilities quite persuasively. Since the adoption of the undemocratic Prussian king as German kaiser had offended the Social Democrats, it was necessary to show that the kaiser did not have to impose his Prussian traditions on the German Reich. Rather, Naumann argued that the united Germany was a new phenomenon, and by virtue of this fact, the *Kaisertum* was also new. By accepting the new office of kaiser, the Prussian king had severed his links with the past. The Kaisertum itself was the symbol of the new German conditions: its military strength, its industrial power, its Weltpolitik. Since democracy was also a facet of Germany's new strength, the kaiser could adopt it as part of the national achievement.[11] Thus, nationalism and the monarchy could be reconciled with democracy and the Social Democrats.

By postulating the novelty of the German Kaisertum, Naumann hoped to break the traditional relationship between the crown and the Prussian Conservatives. This would free the kaiser to rely on other parties for support and enable him to make concessions to them. Although this was his ultimate goal, Naumann realized that neither the kaiser nor the Conservatives would voluntarily sever the link between them. Rather, the kaiser would have to be forced to turn to other parties. This could best be done by depriving the Conservatives of the alliance

10. Friedrich Naumann, *Demokratie und Kaisertum: Ein Handbuch für innere Politik* (Berlin-Schöneberg, 1900), pp. 1–98. The "rebirth" of the Prussian monarchy as a result of the birth of the Reich was a favorite liberal idea during the Wilhelminian period. See Rudolf Vierhaus, "Kaiser und Reichstag zur Zeit Wilhelms II," *Festschrift für Hermann Heimpel zum 70. Geburtstag am 19. September 1971,* 2 vols. (Göttingen, 1971), vol. 1.

11. Naumann, *Demokratie und Kaisertum,* pp. 150–159, 173, 223.

with the national parties that gave them support outside Prussia. According to Naumann, these parties, the Centre and the National Liberals, represented two other aristocracies; the clerical and the industrial. All three groups formed a governmental bloc because of common political and economic interests and common support of the crown. But at the time that Naumann wrote *Demokratie und Kaisertum*, the interests of the industrial aristocracy were beginning to differ from those of the other two. Its industrial nature conflicted particularly with the agricultural Conservatives. In order to further its own interests, the National Liberal industrial aristocracy would eventually be forced to seek new political allies. The most natural ally would be the working-class Social Democrats because their interests too were furthered by the maintenance of the industrial system. The necessity of this economic alliance would eventually convert the National Liberals to democracy. Having made the conversion, they would be able to gain Social Democratic support for the national monarchy. The National Liberals were most suited to this task of persuasion since they were the most enthusiastic supporters of national strength. Since they became a separate liberal party in order to support unification, their own existence was linked with nationalism. They were the chief adherents of Welt-politik since the new imperium both reflected and extended their own industrial power. Influential National Liberals were important members of various nationalistic organizations such as the Army, the Navy, and Colonial Leagues. For political and economic reasons, they were the best candidates for challenging the domination of the Conservatives and effecting a reconciliation between *Demokratie und Kaisertum*.[12]

This reconciliation involved a complex political process. When Naumann published his book, the National Liberals had already become aware of their differences with the Conservatives. Many of them opposed the Conservative stand on tariffs and agricultural policy, and all supported the naval bills in the face of Conservative opposition. National Liberals were also developing a small tolerance for Social Democracy. Twice in the decade before 1900, they voted against a renewal of legislation to suppress or harass Social Democratic activities. Yet in Naumann's scheme this tolerance must lead to cooperation with the Social Democrats in opposing the government and in passing legisla-

12. Ibid., pp. 81–128.

tion favorable to both parties. Ultimately, the National Liberals had to commit themselves firmly to democracy. In return, the Social Democrats must emerge from their "egg shell" and agree to cooperate with the monarchy and the National Liberals. Naumann censured the Social Democrats for failing to see the interrelationship among power politics, industrialization, and the welfare of the working classes. If power politics and capitalism mutually supported one another, and if capitalism was the prerequisite for socialism as the Social Democrats claimed, then Naumann's logic demanded that power politics and socialism were also interdependent. In Naumann's view, the "unintelligent" course of intransigent opposition to a "national" policy, followed by the Social Democrats, forced the kaiser and his government to rely on the right rather than the left. Once Social Democracy supported a strong national monarchy, its demands for democratic concessions would be doubly commanding, and it would gain the support and leadership of the National Liberals.[13] Thus the simultaneous conversion of Social Democracy to nationalism and the National Liberals to democracy would lead to an alliance based on mutual interests.

Naumann thought that cooperation between liberals and Social Democrats would first lead to a leftist bloc opposed to the government in the manner of England's loyal opposition. Indeed he pointed to England's two-party system as a model for German politics. When this leftist opposition achieved a majority in the Reichstag, the kaiser's government would have to cooperate with it in order to govern effectively and maintain national strength. The government's need for the majority's support would force it to make liberal and democratic concessions such as parliamentarisation and suffrage reform.[14] The link between kaiser and Conservatives would then be broken, and the monarchy would become democratic. The conflict between nationalism and democracy, between German society and the Social Democrats would be resolved.

The originality of *Demokratie und Kaisertum* lay in its new combination of existing attitudes and institutions. Several of Naumann's contemporaries, as we shall see, attacked the same problem from the point of view of the monarchy or from that of the various parties and

13. Ibid., pp. 8–18, 150, 173, 182–185, 223.
14. Ibid., pp. 42, 49, 55–56, 65–80, 128–130, 194–205. Cf. Gilg, *Erneuerung demokratisches Denkens,* pp. 192–199, 204–211, 214–215.

interest groups. Few had seen the possibilities of weaving the separate strands together. Fewer yet had seen the possible long-range effects of changes already occurring in German politics: the interest of Kaiser Wilhelm II in nationalism, the altered position of the Conservatives, the discontent of the National Liberals, the new freedom of the Social Democrats, the emergence of Germany as Europe's foremost industrial power. Naumann's vision of a new political constellation, indeed a new political system, was a daring mixture of these developments. By 1900, the former conservative seminary student with an interest in social reform had become a political figure preaching a new social system. The rest of Naumann's life would be devoted to achieving his new ideas and persuading others to adopt them. Thus we must turn to that wider society in which Naumann lived and worked after the publication of *Demokratie und Kaisertum*.

2

From Bassermann to Bebel

At the party congress of the Nationalsoziale Verein in 1901, Naumann reiterated the plan he had outlined in *Demokratie und Kaisertum*. There he coined the phrase which became one of the famous bywords for a bloc of the left; in order to achieve a national, democratic Germany all the parties from "Bebel to Bassermann" must work together.[1] In the future this slogan was used in either its original or its reversed form; supporters of Naumann's idea talked about a majority from "Bebel to Bassermann" or a bloc "from Bassermann to Bebel." The alliteration of the phrase, which helped it to gain currency, derived from the happy coincidence that Bassermann and Bebel were the respective leaders of the National Liberal and Social Democratic parties. Through the use of their names, Naumann's slogan embodied his whole idea. Moreover, the phrase implicitly included a third group necessary to the creation of a bloc of the left which Naumann had not explicitly mentioned in *Demokratie und Kaisertum*. These were the Left Liberals, and in their political attitudes and demands, they fell between the National Liberals and Social Democrats. Thus, there were really three groups necessary for the creation of a bloc from Bassermann to Bebel, and we must understand their politics at the turn of the century in order to see why Naumann considered them capable of building a majority of the left.

THE SOCIAL DEMOCRATS

In 1900, the Social Democrats were paradoxically the most promising recruits for some sort of majority of the left. First of all, they had never completely severed their former connections with the liberal movement. In many cases, their program demands coincided with those of the

1. Friedrich Naumann, *Werke,* 4 vols. (Cologne, 1964), 4 : 215–236.

16

liberals, and in the decade before 1900 they voted with the liberals for Caprivi's trade treaties and for minor social legislation. This limited cooperation was a partial positive reaction to the repeal of the anti-socialist laws. Once legal discrimination ceased, the Social Democrats felt freer about parliamentary participation. Moreover, Social Democracy often supported the liberals in the Reichstag elections. The feature of German electoral law which required a majority for every winning candidate to the Reichstag and to the various state legislatures or Landtage meant that Social Democratic candidates participated in the general election in order to determine their general popular appeal, but if they failed to reach the runoff election, held between the two top candidates in the district, they often threw their weight behind the liberal parties. Usually, Social Democrats supported Left Liberals, but they could also favor an occasional National Liberal.[2] Unfortunately this procedure seldom worked in reverse; liberals did not vote for Social Democrats. In addition to this support for the liberals at election time, Social Democracy, despite its declarations to the contrary, showed an increasing tendency toward accommodation with existing society as its candidates were elected in increasing numbers to various state legislatures and local councils. In 1901 there were 75 Social Democrats in state legislatures and 20 in town and borough councils, and, as one Social Democrat expressed it, the small meeting room of a town or borough council was hardly conducive to "declarations of a fight to the death with bourgeois society."[3] Actually Social Democrats had always tended toward cooperation in non-Prussian and nonnational legislatures. Those delegates who sat in the Saxon *Landtag* under the antisocialist laws took their oath to the king and initiated and voted for legislation along with the delegates of the other parties.[4] Thus flamboyant revolutionary rhetoric was often accompanied by quiet, moderate parliamentary work. Bebel might glorify the Paris Commune, but he did so in a German parliament and not from the top of a German barricade.

2. Thomas Nipperdey, *Die Organisation der deutschen Parteien vor 1918* (Düsseldorf, 1961), pp. 311–314. Support for the liberal parties usually occurred in non-Prussian states.

3. Gerhard A. Ritter, *Die Arbeiterbewegung im wilhelminischen Reich* (Berlin-Dahlem, 1959), p. 232; *SPD Fraktionsprotokolle*, 1: Anlage B, pp. *clxiii–clxxxv*. Also Carl Severing, *Mein Lebensweg,* 2 vols. (Cologne, 1950), p. 150.

4. Vernon Lidtke, *The Outlawed Party: Social Democracy in Germany, 1878–1890* (Princeton, 1966), pp. 222–228.

It is one of the ironies of modern political life that no one wholly believes the promises of respectable politicians, yet everyone believes that a self-proclaimed revolutionary will make good his promise of revolution. And so it was with German society at the end of the nineteenth century. The only Germans who did not believe the socialist revolutionary rhetoric were the Social Democrats themselves. The party's original Gotha program explicitly committed the party to legality, and only the antisocialist legislation of the 1880s forced the party to disseminate literature and organize clubs clandestinely. When repressive legislation was repealed in 1890, the Social Democrats returned to legal activities. It was true that both Bebel and Friedrich Engels publicly expected the fulfillment of their revolutionary hopes in the near future, but they hardly expected a violent revolution in the old style; Bebel once admitted that revolutionary rhetoric was only a tactic for creating the party's popular appeal. Moreover, the party's leading Marxist theoretician, Karl Kautsky, described the revolution as an evolutionary process; and since he was noted for his aversion to the rough-and-tumble of the regular party congresses,[5] he was hardly capable of leading a revolutionary phalanx. The party's Erfurt program, formulated in 1891, did not even advocate the overthrow of the existing government, and in the same year, the revolt of a group of young activists who wanted the party to withdraw from parliamentary work in order to devote itself to agitation was promptly quelled by the leadership. In addition the party's official newspaper, *Vorwärts*, and the official magazine, *Neue Zeit*, were acidly critical of German and bourgeois politics, but they studiously refrained from clarion calls to revolt.

In the same year that the Erfurt program was formulated and the activist revolt quelled, passive legality was given further emphasis by the advent of a movement that came to be called reformism. The most

5. For ambiguity of and ambivalence toward the idea of revolution in German Social Democracy, see Susanne Miller, *Das Problem der Freiheit im Sozialismus* (Frankfurt / Main, 1964), pp. 110–120. Also Ritter, *Die Arbeiterbewegung,* pp. 89–90, and Peter Gilg, *Die Erneuerung des demokratischen Denkens im wilhelminischen Deutschland* (Wiesbaden, 1965), pp. 62–64. For Bebel and Kautsky, see Erich Matthias, "Kautsky und der Kautskyanismus. Die Funktion der Ideologie in der deutschen Sozialdemokratie vor dem ersten Weltkriege," *Marxismus-Studien,* 2nd series, ed. I. Fetscher, *Schriften der evangelischen Studiengemeinschaft* (Tübingen, 1957), 5 : 151–197; and Walter Holzheuer, *Karl Kautskys Werk als Weltanshauung: Beitrag zur Ideologie der Sozialdemokratie vor dem ersten Weltkrieg* (Munich, 1972), pp. 35–43.

prominent spokesman of the movement was a southerner named Georg von Vollmar. Vollmar was the only son of a Bavarian civil servant and last in a line which traced its noble ancestry to the fourteenth century. He was the only aristocrat to join the Social Democrats during the Second Reich. Having begun his career as an official in the Bavarian government, Vollmar volunteered for service in the Franco-Prussian War and was severely wounded in January 1871. Crippled and incapacitated by his wounds, he devoted the next three years to an intensive study of national economy, politics, and philosophy—a study which led to his espousal of Social Democracy. After the repeal of the antisocialist laws, Vollmar settled permanently in Bavaria—where he represented Munich both in the Reichstag and in the Landtag—and introduced reformism with the famous Eldorado speeches of 1891.[6] The Eldorado speeches not only reinforced the Social Democratic trend toward parliamentarism, they also urged the party to forsake that revolutionary rhetoric which so much offended official German society. Vollmar argued that the Social Democrats, twenty years after the fact, could hardly change the means or the fact of German unification, and they ought to cease their criticism of the state and work to change its disagreeable features. Moreover, Social Democrats should stop harping on revolution as a means of change and admit that they hoped to "shape the future" through "slow, organic development."[7] In other words, Vollmar wanted the party to halt its screeching, vocal opposition to the Prusso-German nation-state and make its rhetoric consonant with its practice.

In time, the entire southern wing of the party which included Bavaria, Baden, Württemberg, and Hesse came to accept Vollmar's reformism. It has often been argued that reformism came more easily to the south than to the north because the south was less industrialized, socioeconomic conflicts were less harsh, and the party more dominated by a petit bourgeois mentality. While the rise of radical, antireformist Social Democratic organizations in rapidly growing southern industrial cities like Nuremberg or Stuttgart would seem to support this argument, in reality it was most probably the liberal, non-Prussian political atmosphere of the south which fostered reformism. The socioeconomic argu-

6. *Deutsches Biographisches Jahrbuch* (Berlin, 1929), 4 : 276–289.
7. Wilhelm Mommsen, *Deutsche Parteiprogramme* (Munich, 1960), pp. 336–337.

ment for reformism loses credence from the fact that the trade unions, as well as the southerners, supported reformism. Although trade-union leaders were as capable as party leaders in making revolutionary statements, Carl Legien, the Chairman of the General Commission of the Free Trade Unions, was as outspoken as Vollmar in his emphasis on "the quiet course of society's development."[8] In the heavily industrialized Ruhr area, Otto Hué, editor of the *Bergarbeiter Zeitung* and a prominent leader of the miners' union, openly advocated reformism, and shortly after the publication of *Demokratie und Kaisertum*, he organized a lecture tour through the Ruhr for Friedrich Naumann.[9] Since Hué also occasionally argued the benefits of imperialism for the working class, one could only conclude that he agreed with Naumann's ideas on democratic nationalism. Sociological information relating to the Social Democratic electorate also belies the socioeconomic argument for reformism. While the great masses of party members were from the working class and conceivably susceptible to radicalism, and while it is true that many industrial urban areas were Social Democratic strongholds at election time, there were many people classified as lower middle class or as farmers who lived in small towns and rural areas, in the north as well as the south, who enlarged the total Social Democratic electorate.[10] Although these people may have suffered from certain adjustments to industrialization which attracted them to certain economic demands in the socialist program, they could also have found a remedy for these ills in the programs of other parties. The one thing that the Social Democratic party supported which the others did not was the demand for democracy and opposition to the long-standing political and social discrimination connected with the Prussian suffrage and the dominant aristocratic ideals of German society. The desire for equality was shared by the lower middle class, small landholders, and

8. Gilg, *Erneuerung demokratisches Denkens*, p. 145.

9. Johann Fritsch, *Eindringen und Ausbreitung des Revisionismus im deutschen Bergarbeiterverband* (Leipzig, 1967), pp. 18–19, 33–34.

10. See Robert Michels, *Political Parties*, trans. Eden and Ceder Paul (New York, 1915), p. 270, for party membership. For voters, R. Blank, "Die soziale Zusammensetzung der sozialdemokratischen Wählershcaft Deutschlands," *Archiv für Sozialwissenschaft und Sozialpolitik* 20 (1905) : 527–533, estimated that in cities having a population over 100,000, the middle class may have cast one-third of the Social Democratic votes. In counting the votes of all cities having a population over 10,000, some of which had a small working class, Social Democracy polled 48.3 percent of the vote. In predominantly agricultural areas like Mecklenburg, Social Democracy received one-third of all votes cast.

agricultural laborers with the urban working class. This pattern was the same all over the Reich, in both the north and the south. Thus, southern leaders were reformist, not because of the complexion of their support, which merely reflected conditions in the nation as a whole, but because many demands of the northerners such as the equal suffrage, the secret ballot, close cooperation between the ministries and the legislature had already been achieved in the south. For this reason, southerners could expect to realize other parts of the Social Democratic program more easily than their northern colleagues, and they could afford to be less strident in their rhetoric and more conciliatory in their actions.

But the southerners and the trade unions were not the only practitioners of reformism. It increasingly became the practice of the entire party throughout the 1890s. In the Reichstag, Social Democrats voted for measures designed to help the working class, and they also began to show some interest in nationalistic projects such as the army and the colonies. The reformist Wolfgang Heine argued, in a vein similar to Naumann's, that the Social Democrats should support military legislation in return for democratic concessions,[11] and although the party was hardly ready for such a drastic step at the turn of the century, it did become involved in colonialism. While it criticized imperialism for its costliness and brutality, it also claimed that a peaceful extension of Western culture to underdeveloped areas would have a civilizing effect. In this connection, the Social Democrats appointed themselves the tribunes of the colonized peoples in the German Reichstag in order to diminish the governmental brutality which they deplored. While such activities hardly equaled the active support of the "bourgeois" parties for imperialism, they represented a small compromise with existing imperialistic policies. Another small compromise with the existing state, taken by a party congress at the turn of the century after almost thirty years of abstinence in protest against the Prussian suffrage, was the decision to participate as a party in the Prussian elections.[12]

11. Milorad Drachovitch, *Les Socialismes français et allemand et le problème de la guerre, 1870–1914* (Geneva, 1953), p. 256. Cf. Raymond Blum, "German Social Democracy in the Reichstag, 1890–1914" (unpublished doctoral diss., University of Minnesota, 1962), pp. 140–142.

12. Hans-Christoph Schröder, *Sozialismus und Imperialismus: Die Auseinandersetzung der deutschen Sozialdemokratie mit dem Imperialismusproblem und der Weltpolitik vor 1914,* Part I (Hanover, 1968), pp. 142–181. On the Prussian elections, see Ritter, *Die Arbeiterbewegung,* p. 182.

This trend toward reformism sparked the theoretical movement called revisionism which Eduard Bernstein presented in his *Voraussetzung des Sozialismus* in 1899. Naumann thought enough of Bernstein's ideas to send him the galley proofs of *Demokratie und Kaisertum* in a bid for a favorable review.[13] Although Bernstein reviewed the book critically in the *Sozialistische Monatshefte*, a monthly magazine founded to air reformist and revisionist views, there were points of agreement between him and Naumann. Bernstein wanted the Social Democratic party to admit in theory as well as in practice that it wanted to reform rather than revolutionize German politics. He wanted it to renounce those revolutionary pretensions which hindered its successful integration into German political life. In addition, he advocated Social Democratic cooperation with the liberals in order to achieve various democratic goals.[14] In this respect too, he merely wanted Social Democracy to espouse explicitly, and as a matter of policy, a long-standing practice. Thus Bernstein's revisionism not only reflected Social Democratic reformism, it also corresponded with Naumann's schemes for a bloc of the left.

Social Democracy's increasing participation in German politics motivated both Bernstein and Naumann to publish their respective works at the turn of the century. Yet just as it appeared to Bernstein that Social Democracy was ready to abandon its revolutionary theory and to Naumann that Social Democracy was ready to join an alliance with other nonrevolutionary parties, a radical movement began within the party's ranks that retarded the achievement of both men's goals. Essentially, this radical movement wanted to reinforce Social Democracy's isolation from German life and to reemphasize its revolutionary traditions. Led by Rosa Luxemburg, it began with an attack on Bernstein's revisionistic theories and eventually introduced a new revolutionary tactic, the mass strike, into Social Democracy's political repertoire.[15] At the time, this movement served to rivet the attention of German society on Social Democratic radicalism. Indeed, since its advent, much Social Democratic and even German history has been written from the viewpoint of the radicals. Yet in the mainstream of

13. Schröder, *Sozialismus und Imperialismus,* p. 17, n. 40.
14. Gilg, *Erneuerung demokratisches Denkens,* pp. 159–161.
15. For the best presentation of Rosa Luxemburg's role in the German party, see J. P. Nettl, *Rosa Luxemburg,* 2 vols. (Oxford, 1966).

Social Democratic development, the radical program was a temporary diversion. To be sure, it eventually led to a damaging split in the socialist movement as a whole, but it did not influence the permanent, legalistic policies of the party. For a time, however, the radicals under Rosa Luxemburg succeeded in postponing the total acceptance of reformist and revisionist ideas. Their success was due to their temporary alliance with the earlier radical strain which proclaimed Social Democracy's opposition to the existing state. Curiously enough, the issue of cooperation with the liberal parties formed the backbone of the alliance and led to the famous fight over revisionism during the party congress at Dresden in 1903.

At this congress, it was Bebel himself who led the attack on revisionism. In the Social Democratic archives in Bonn, there is a portrait of a black-suited August Bebel painted when he had already acquired the silver hair, the gnarled hands, and the peculiar thinness which often accompanies old age. Yet the magnetic blue eyes still reflect the fighting spirit and the obstinacy of youth. The spirit was learned in a hard school. Born in 1840 as the son of a Prussian noncommissioned officer, Bebel grew up in desperately straitened circumstances. The family was always poor; his father, his stepfather, and his mother all died of consumption while he was still a boy, and Bebel left school to learn the trade of a woodturner. After several *Wanderjahre*, he settled down and opened a shop in Leipzig, where he began his political career. At first, he participated actively in the liberal workers' educational societies and through them became acquainted with German socialism of the Lassallean stripe. His early battles with Lassallean socialism colored all his subsequent career as a liberal and a democrat; he never understood how to make his peace with the Prussian state and all it symbolized. This opposition to Prussia-Germany and everyone who accommodated it was the source of August Bebel's radicalism. When he emerged as leader of the Social Democrats under the antisocialist laws, he imposed his brand of radicalism on his compatriots, and his leadership accounted for the party's antagonism to revisionism.[16]

For Bebel, Bernstein's denial of Social Democracy's revolutionary traditions struck at the heart of its opposition to the existing system.

16. August Bebel, *Reminiscences,* trans. Ernest Untermann (New York, 1911). Cf. Ernst Schraepler, *August Bebel* (Göttingen, 1966) and Lidtke, *Outlawed Party,* pp. 32–38.

Opposition and revolution went hand in hand until the system was changed. By the same token, those who said they wanted reform were already part of the system. Bebel refused to say he would compromise with the existing state, and this refusal explains his quarrel with the revisionists. Since neither Bernstein nor his supporters were as skillful as Bebel in a political scrap, his victory was complete. In response to Bernstein's suggestion that the Social Democrats utilize their election victory of 1903 (they became the second largest party in the Reichstag) to seek the vice-presidency of the Reichstag, all cooperation with bourgeois parties was banned; the prohibition included election agreements, articles in bourgeois newspapers, and participation in parliamentary praesidia.[17] In this matter, the old radical Bebel teamed up with the new radicals under Rosa Luxemburg to preserve the party's tradition of opposition to Prussia-Germany.

The defeat of revisionism in 1903 led Rosa Luxemburg to believe that the party was truly revolutionary, and two years later she suggested the mass strike as a means of attaining revolutionary ends in a revolutionary way. Yet the proposal for mass strikes signaled the end of the alliance between old and new radicals. The Social Democratic leadership, which included Bebel and the party's executive committee, was always uncomfortable about mass demonstrations, and it never encouraged the annual May Day celebrations of international labor. The attitude of Bebel and the executive committee was aptly expressed in the phrase: "General strike is general nonsense."[18] The resolution drafted by the executive committee for approval by the party congress of 1905, where the issue was discussed, reflected this attitude; the mass strike could be used to prevent a reactionary breach of the constitution, but it would not be used for offensive or revolutionary purposes.[19] From 1905 onward, Bebel and the party leadership grew more conservative as the new radicals became more insistent on a "revolutionary" course. In its fight against these new radicals, the leadership tended to lean increasingly on the support of the reformists and revisionists. This

17. *SPD Parteitag, 1903,* pp. 392–395, 418–419; cf. Carl Schorske, *German Social Democracy, 1905–1917: The Development of the Great Schism* (Cambridge, Mass., 1955), pp. 23–24.

18. The phrase coined by Ignaz Auer, general secretary of the party, Drachovitch, *Les Socialismes,* p. 202.

19. For this and subsequent description of trade-union and party conflicts and cooperation see Schorske, *Social Democracy,* pp. 36–58; also Nettl, *Rosa Luxemburg,* 1 : 306 ff.

process began soon after the party congress of 1905. When mass suffrage demonstrations swept Germany in the wake of the curtailment of the Hamburg suffrage and aroused fears of a general strike, the party executive took steps to decrease the proportions of any future strike. It concluded a secret agreement with the notoriously reformist trade unions whereby it promised to discourage a mass strike and relieved the unions of any financial responsibility should a strike occur without their approval. This agreement, when it finally leaked out to the radicals, caused a long, bitter, and unsuccessful floor fight at the party congress of 1906. The majority of the congress resolved to recognize the trade unions as partners of the party with a right to consultation in common problems.

Prior to 1906, the party and trade unions were two different entities; although the union leadership belonged to the party, many union members did not, and the leaders tried not to embroil the unions in party affairs. However, the trade unions had just seen one of the worst years in their history—a spate of unsuccessful strikes and successful lockouts—which depleted their treasuries and decreased their effectiveness. The reason for this bad year lay in the increasing tendency of employers to organize against the trade unions, and the leadership feared that any future mass strike would only lead to mass sanctions against the unions which would ruin them financially and organizationally. Thus, the unions wanted a partnership with the party in order to prevent the damages of "revolutionary" activity. Since their membership and hence their fighting force was always larger than the membership of the party, the partnership implied the victory of reformism within Social Democracy.

In 1905 and 1906, few people saw the implications of the decisions made at the party congresses. Social Democrats saw that the mass strike was approved for the first time in party history; they only vaguely realized that its use was restricted to defense against an unlikely governmental coup d'état. The rest of German society, alarmed by the first street demonstrations since the revolution of 1848, was convinced of Social Democracy's revolutionary nature. Also, since trade unions were almost as offensive to German society as Social Democracy, few people grasped the conservative nature of the decisions made at the congress of 1906. It is even doubtful whether the old radical Bebel realized that he had significantly undermined his own position as the proclaimer, but not the practitioner, of revolution. Henceforth, the party, in its fight against the revolutionary radicals, would veer even more toward the right, and this direction would increase the possibility of cooperation with other parties and particularly with the liberals.

THE LEFT LIBERALS

The liberals with whom the Social Democrats could best cooperate were not specifically mentioned in *Demokratie und Kaisertum*. They were a motley and relatively disorganized group of parties collectively called the Left Liberals. If, to follow Naumann's pattern, we were to attach a class label to them, we would have to call them the representatives of commerce and finance, members of the *Grossbürgertum* or upper middle class. They were very strong in coastal cities like Bremen, Danzig, and Stettin which depended for their prosperity on foreign trade. Their representatives in the Reichstag had close connections with the great banks of Berlin, which depended, to a certain extent, on the free flow of capital between nations. Yet they also represented the lower strata of the middle class: small businessmen and farmers, teachers, lawyers, and lower civil servants.[20] The latter were drawn into the Left Liberal movement because they all had an interest in free trade, and the Left Liberals were the most undiluted proponents of laissez-faire in Germany. The protective tariffs, export premiums, and agricultural subsidies favored by the Conservatives hindered the trade of commercial and financial circles in the coastal cities and Berlin and squeezed the small businessman or farmer in areas like Saxony, Schleswig-Holstein, or Oldenburg.

20. For the influence of bankers, see Hans Jaeger, *Unternehmer in der deutschen Politik, 1890–1918* (Bonn, 1967), p. 122. Also for the Left Liberal appeal to farmers see Gerhard Stoltenberg, *Politische Strömungen im schleswig-holsteinischen Landvolk, 1918–1933* (Düsseldorf, 1962), pp. 16–17, and Rudolf Heberle, *Landbevölkerung und Nationalsozialismus: Eine soziologische Untersuchung der politischen Willensbildung in Schleswig-Holstein, 1918–1932* (Stuttgart, 1963), pp. 13–29. Also Konstanze Wegner, *Theodor Barth und die Freisinnige Vereinigung: Studie zur Geschichte des Linksliberalismus im wilhelminischen Deutschland, 1893–1910* (Tübingen, 1968), pp. 99–101; and Ludwig Elm, *Zwischen Fortschritt und Reaktion: Geschichte der Parteien der liberalen Bourgeoisie in Deutschland, 1893–1918* ([East] Berlin, 1968), pp. 13 ff. Assuming that the occupations of delegates reflect the occupations and socioeconomic interests of their constituents, Peter Molt, *Der Reichstag vor der improvisierten Revolution* (Cologne, 1963), p. 78, reports that between 1893 and 1914, the most frequently represented occupations were: 11 large estate owners, 12 medium or small farmers, 18 merchants or bankers *(Gewerbliche Grossbürgertum)*, 17 medium or small businessmen, 29 liberal professionals, 20 teachers or professors.

The Left Liberals shared their interest in free trade with the Social Democrats since both felt that protective economic policies raised the cost of living for the working man. The Left Liberals' interest in the working class derived from their loose connection with a small group of trade unions called the Hirsch-Duncker *Gewerkvereine*. Founded by the two Progressives whose names they bore, these unions were some of the oldest in Germany, but like the Left Liberals themselves, they had been superseded in numbers and power by the Social Democratic "free" trade unions. In 1900, their membership was approximately one-eighth that of the "free" trade unions. Although they originally rejected the strike as a means of coercing employers, they occasionally joined the socialists in industrial disputes and finally adopted the strike as an official part of their program. Because of their weakness, they never influenced the Left Liberals to the same extent that the "free" unions influenced the Social Democrats, but the desire to retain their support certainly accounted for increasing Left Liberal attention to social reform and social legislation.[21]

Yet socioeconomic policies were not the only ones drawing Left Liberals and Social Democrats together. Both had a common history in the liberal Progressive parties of mid-century, and hence both favored a liberalization of German politics. Left Liberal voters suffered from the same type of political and social discrimination as the Social Democrats, and in some districts, such as Berlin and the coastal cities, a certain overlapping of the Left Liberal and Social Democratic electorate occurred. Many Left Liberals shared, for the same reasons, the Social Democratic prejudice against the monarchy and against Prussian unification of Germany, and they too voted against military and colonial bills. They too were counted as an antinational and antigovernmental group, and if they escaped the opprobrium reserved for the Social Democrats, it was only because they did not share its revolutionary ethic. German society lumped the Left Liberals together with the Social Democrats as "the left." For these reasons, we could expect the two groups to be well

21. Wegner, *Theodor Barth,* pp. 32, 35n.35; Heberle, *Landbevölkerung;* Karl Erich Born, *Staat und Sozialpolitik seit Bismarcks Sturz* (Wiesbaden, 1957), pp. 72–74; Alfons Gornik, *Die Entwicklung der nichtsozialdemokratischen Arbeiterbewegung in Deutschland* (doctoral diss., Halle, 1909), pp. 3 ff. Left Liberal interests also coincided with those of some National Liberals, Helga Nussbaum, *Unternehmer gegen Monopole: Ueber Struktur und Aktionen antimonopolistischen bürgerlicher Gruppen zu Beginn des 20. Jahrhunderts* ([East] Berlin, 1966), pp. 152–154, 158.

disposed toward one another and to form a nucleus for the bloc from Bebel to Bassermann.[22]

The possibility of an alliance first occurred when individual Left Liberals began to recognize the basic legitimism and emerging reformism of Social Democracy. In 1892, the year after Vollmar's Eldorado speeches, Ludwig Bamberger, a dogmatic economic liberal, wrote that Social Democracy was becoming a more moderate movement.[23] Later, the most important Left Liberal to discern and seize upon the political possibilities of Social Democratic reformism was the colorful and courageous Theodor Barth. As the Bremen delegate to the Bundesrat, he had won his political spurs by casting the single opposing vote against Bismarck's protective tariffs. Thereafter, he founded a weekly magazine, the *Nation,* to serve as a forum for general liberal opposition to Bismarck's policies. After Bismarck's dismissal, Barth used the pages of the *Nation* to revive the traditional liberal demand for responsible parliamentary government in Germany in the hope that the new chancellor, Caprivi, would be more amenable to the pleas of the left. The dismissal of Caprivi and the conservatism of the 1890s forced him to abandon this hope and, instead of looking for concessions from above, he, like Naumann, began to look to pressure from below as a means of achieving liberal concessions. In this quest, he began to develop an idea which had been anathema to liberal parties for over two decades: a liberal alliance with the Social Democrats. In recognition of the common Left Liberal–Social Democratic fight against conservatism, Barth suggested a "red" *Kartell* which, in contrast to the previous Kartell or alliance of the right, would be an alliance of the left.[24] Though for

22. For the overlapping of the electorate, compare charts of runoff elections in Wegner, *Theodor Barth,* pp. 144–147. For the general policies of the Left Liberals, see Ludwig Bergsträsser, *Geschichte der politischen Parteien in Deutschland,* 10th ed. (Munich, 1960); Felix Rachfahl, "Eugen Richter und der Linksliberalismus im neuen Reich," *Zeitschrift für Politik* 5 (1912); A. Rubinstein, *Die Deutsch-Freisinnige Partei bis zu ihrem Auseinanderbruch, 1884–1893* (doctoral diss., Basel, 1935); H. E. Matthes, "Die Spaltung der national-liberalen Partei und die Entwicklung des Linksliberalismus bis zur Auflösung der deutsch-freisinnigen Partei" (unpublished doctoral diss., Kiel, 1953). For a dubious analysis of the Freisinnige Partei before the split of 1893, see Gustav Seeber, *Zwischen Bebel und Bismarck: Zur Geschichte des Linksliberalismus in Deutschland, 1871–1893* ([East] Berlin, 1965).

23. Ludwig Bamberger, "Die Krisis in Deutschland und der deutsche Kaiser," *Gesammelte Schriften,* 5 vols. (Berlin, 1892–1897) 5: 419–439. Cf. Gilg, *Erneuerung demokratisches Denkens,* p. 135.

24. Georg Gothein, "Theodor Barth;" E. Feder, *Theodor Barth und der demokratische Gedanke* (Gotha, 1919). Also Rubinstein, *Die Deutsch-Freisinnige,* pp. 30–34; Wegner,

different reasons, Barth's ideas came very close to Naumann's scheme for a leftist opposition.

When Theodor Barth advocated his "red" Kartell, he belonged to a small, loosely organized Left Liberal party called the *Freisinnige Vereinigung* (Radical Association). The leadership of this group was drawn from the upper middle class. They were bankers, such as Georg von Siemens, Karl Mommsen, and Wilhelm Kaempf, and exporters like Hermann Frese, and their economic roles accounted for their liberalism and for their increasing willingness to compromise with Social Democracy. They were people who, by and large, could afford to take an independent political stand. In addition, after 1903, they were in less electoral competition with the Social Democrats than their radical liberal colleagues. In contrast to other Left Liberals, they increasingly deviated from their former dogmatic economic liberalism in favor of social welfare and trade unionism. Their close connections with financial and industrial circles may also explain their increasing sympathy for nationalistic policies. They broke with other Left Liberal groups by voting for Caprivi's military reform, and toward the end of the century the Freisinnige Vereinigung supported an expansion of the German navy and the acquisition of territory in China. Thus it began to combine those characteristics of nationalism and democracy which were so important to Naumann's bloc of the left.[25]

These qualities eventually attracted Naumann to the Freisinnige Vereinigung when he dissolved the Nationalsoziale Verein in 1903, and his group helped to promote and popularize Barth's plan for a red Kartell. In recognition of the combined efforts of the two men, the idea of a liberal alliance with the Social Democrats was known as the "Barth-Naumann tactic." The popularization of this tactic did not mean, how-

---

Theodor Barth, pp. 8–10, 51–60, 112–115; Gilg, *Erneuerung demokratisches Denkens,* pp. 109–110, 133–135; Elm, *Zwischen Fortschritt und Reaktion,* pp. 39 ff.

25. On electoral competition with the Social Democrats, see Wegner, *Theodor Barth,* pp. 17–24, 99–100, 144–147. Arthur Dix, *Die deutschen Reichstagswahlen 1871–1930 und die Wandlungen der Volksgliederung* (Tübingen, 1930), p. 16; and Dirk Stegmann, *Die Erben Bismarcks: Parteien und Verbände in der Spätphase des wilhelminischen Deutschlands* (Cologne, 1970), p. 79. Martin Wenck, *Geschichte der Nationalsozialen von 1895 bis 1903* (Berlin-Schöneberg, 1905), p. 111, discusses the Vereinigung's interest in social reform; but Düding, *Der Nationalsoziale Verein,* pp. 166, 181–84, refutes Wenck's view by revealing the resistance of the leadership to a revised social program. Both Elm, *Zwischen Fortschritt und Reaktion,* pp. 64–66, 74–77; and Eckart Kehr, *Schlachtflottenbau und Parteipolitik, 1894–1901* (Berlin, 1930), pp. 124–25, 140, 307, examine the problem of Weltpolitik.

ever, that it was immediately accepted even within the Vereinigung itself. Although these liberals accepted Social Democratic support in runoff elections, voted with them on occasional legislative measures, and incurred the wrath of all other bourgeois parties by joining the Social Democrats in a Reichstag demonstration against the tariff bill of 1902, they still regarded a full-fledged "red" Kartell with suspicion. When Barth suggested that the Vereinigung support Social Democrats in the Prussian elections of 1903 in hopes of increasing the mandates of the left, he aroused much opposition within the party. The rank and file objected strongly, and Barth's proposal alienated his own election district. In all fairness to the voters, because of the Prussian public ballot, the Left Liberals had to exhort their local clubs to find electors with enough civic courage to cast a vote for their own party; a public vote for Social Democracy could result in economic and social boycott in the elector's district. Nevertheless, in 1903, the party congress of the Vereinigung courageously voted, 300 to 20, to negotiate agreements with the Social Democrats in those districts where neither party could gain an electoral victory without mutual support. The party reviewed the issue again in 1905—this time as a matter of general policy and not in the isolated instance of one Prussian election—and decided to conclude reciprocal election agreements with the Social Democrats as part of its fight against conservatism. With this decision, the Vereinigung committed itself firmly to an alliance of the left. In the future, it was to pursue this policy with missionary zeal.[26]

An alliance of liberals and Social Democrats was only one part of the Barth-Naumann tactic. The other part called for unity among the various liberal groups in order to create that strong middle-class party which Max Weber suggested. In 1903 there existed, in addition to the Freisinnige Vereinigung, two other Left Liberal parties: the *Süddeutsche Volkspartei* (the South German Peoples' party) and the *Freisinnige Volkspartei* (Radical Peoples' party). The Süddeutsche Volkspartei seceded from the mainstream of liberalism at the same time as the Social Democrats and for much the same reasons; it believed in more

---

26. For the 1902 demonstration, see Wegner, *Theodor Barth,* pp. 40–41. For the resistance to the move to the left, see Nipperdey, *Organisation,* p. 226; Hermann Pachnicke, *Führende Männer im alten und im neuen Reich* (Berlin, 1930), pp. 23–24; Gothein, "Theodor Barth," p. 355. On the Prussian ballot, see *Hilfe* 13 (1907) : 659. And on the 1905 decision, see Wilhelm Kulemann, *Zusammenschluss der Liberalen* (Dresden, 1905), pp. 26–27.

political and social democracy than most liberals were willing to permit at the time. Like the Social Democrats, it was vigorously opposed to Prussian unification of Germany. After unification, it remained a party with a narrow base in southwestern Germany, particularly in Württemberg, and it was led, in 1903, by two Swabians: Conrad Haussmann, who became the chairman of the Interparty Caucus (*Interfraktioneller Ausschuss*) during World War I, and Friedrich von Payer, who later became vice-chancellor of Germany under the wartime Hertling government. The Freisinnige Volkspartei was the main competitor of the Vereinigung in the north. It shared the same political and economic liberalism and appealed to the same socioeconomic groups. Its main difference from and opposition to the Vereinigung stemmed from its refusal to compromise with Weltpolitik and its almost rabid opposition to Social Democracy. Much of its obstinacy was due to its doctrinaire leader, Eugen Richter, who ruled the party with an iron hand. Yet this division and the resultant bickering between the Left Liberal parties led to a serious weakness at election time; in 1903, they lost over 20 per cent of their seats in the Reichstag. Both Barth and Naumann, as well as many others, hoped that Left Liberal unification would help it to regain its strength.[27]

In the same year as the disastrous Reichstag elections and the Vereinigung's decision to cooperate with the Social Democrats, a movement to unite the Left Liberals finally began. The group that initiated the movement for unity was the small, regional Süddeutsche Volkspartei. At its party congress in 1903, it passed a resolution calling for a "closer union of the bourgeois left in order to combat more energetically . . . the increasing reaction" in the nation. The resolution recommended such initial methods of liberal cooperation as election agreements and a common parliamentary *Fraktion;* it also advocated cooperation with the Social Democrats. The resolution was warmly greeted by the Vereinigung, but the Freisinnige Volkspartei was more restrained. Only its weak, southern branch showed a genuine willingness for Left Liberal

27. The only book devoted entirely to the Süddeutsche Volkspartei is Klaus Heger, *Die deutsche demokratische Partei in Württemberg und ihre Organisation,* Heft 24, *Leipziger rechtswissenschaftliche Studien* (Leipzig, 1937). Cf. Oscar Stillich, *Die politischen Parteien in Deutschland,* 2 vols. (Leipzig, 1908–1911), 2 : 284–285. For biographical material on Conrad Haussmann, see *Deutsches biographisches Jahrbuch* 4 (1922) : 90–95. For Friedrich von Payer, *Mein Lebenslauf,* included in his personal papers. For the failure to gain votes, see Dix, *Die Reichstagswahlen,* p. 21.

cooperation. Despite the lack of enthusiasm on the part of the northern Volkspartei, the local Left Liberals in Frankfurt am Main, a southern city, took the initiative of calling together representatives of the three Left Liberal groups to discuss ways and means of unification. This Frankfurt meeting created an unofficial standing committee to act as an ambassador of unity.[28]

The outstanding achievement of the standing committee was the formulation of a program which renounced the outworn shibboleths of nineteenth-century Manchester liberalism and signaled the advent of modern, liberal democracy: the Frankfurt Minimal Program of 1905.[29] This program not only provided a theoretical base for future Left Liberal unification, it also brought the Left Liberals closer to the ideals and purposes of Social Democracy. Its advocacy of an equal and direct suffrage coincided with the Social Democratic demand for a democratic suffrage in Prussia, Saxony, and other German states. Its demand for a progressive income tax and expanded social legislation repeated the Social Democratic desire to benefit the working class. Its call for the maintenance and extension of the right of association not only recognized the rights of political parties, it also capitulated to the rights of those trade-union organizations represented by Social Democracy. Thus the Frankfurt program strongly departed from the old liberal ideals of a limited suffrage and laissez-faire and embraced the new ideals of political and social democracy.

This new program had a mixed reception. As expected, both the Vereinigung and the Süddeutsche Volkspartei accepted it.[30] However, the large and orthodox Freisinnige Volkspartei approached the program and its prospect of unity more gingerly. When a delegation from the southwest formally moved for more cooperative efforts with the other Left Liberal parties at the party congress of 1905, the discussion that followed made it clear that both traditional, liberal views *and* a disinclination to accept the Social Democrats played a great role in its objection to unity. Certain delegates objected particularly to the figure of Naumann, who was sure to play an important role in any unified liberal

28. On the resolution, see Kulemann, *Zusammenschluss,* p. 31. For other efforts toward Left Liberal unity, see Carl Funck, *Lebenserinnerungen* (Frankfurt/Main, 1921), p. 25; Wilhelm Kulemann, *Erinnerungen* (Berlin, 1911), pp. 197–199. Cf. Wegner, *Theodor Barth,* pp. 105–106.

29. Kulemann, *Zusammenschluss,* pp. 87–89.

30. *Nation* 24 (1908) : 65.

party, since his ideas embodied the very departure from orthodox liberalism that the party had long espoused. The resolution adopted at the end of the discussion allowed for friendly cooperation with the Vereinigung but rejected any cooperation with the Nationalsoziale Verein.[31] Since Naumann's group, to all intents and purposes, was one with the Vereinigung, the two parts of the resolution effectively negated each other. But despite the resolution of 1905, many desired a change within the Freisinnige Volkspartei. As long as Richter lived, there was only a strong minority opposed to liberal dogmatism, but Richter himself had long been sick and inactive, and when he died in March 1906, an altered policy within the party and the acceptance of Left Liberal unity became much easier. In the winter of 1906, members of the Volkspartei met with representatives of the other two Left Liberal parties and tentatively accepted the Frankfurt Minimal Program. In May of the same year, the business committees of all three parties agreed to cooperate in the coming Reichstag election; the election committee began its meetings in the middle of November 1906.[32] After three years of bickering, the Left Liberals began the slow process of unification with which they hoped to strengthen the liberal movement.

THE NATIONAL LIBERALS

The Left Liberals' unification and their alliance with Social Democracy were not the only processes necessary for a realization of the Barth-Naumann tactic. Because of their previous role as the "industrial aristocracy" participating in governmental majorities, the National Liberals carried the most weight with the government, and their cooperation with the left would thus be needed to gain liberal or democratic concessions. Yet it would be difficult to persuade them to join such an opposition. Part of the difficulty naturally lay in their monarchical, liberal-conservative traditions that originally made them a governmental party. Another difficulty lay in a latent conflict of interests between them and the other parties of the proposed bloc from Bassermann to Bebel. Naumann's use of the phrase "industrial aristocracy" to describe the National Liberals was apt because it implied that sense of elitism which accompanies wealth, ownership, and power; as a self-

31. *Freisinniger Parteitag, 1905*, pp. 21–36.
32. *Nation* 24 (1908): 97; *Freisinnige Volkspartei*, pp. 24–28; *Vereinigung Parteitag, 1910*, p. 14.

conscious elite, striving to identify itself more and more with the old hereditary aristocracy, the National Liberal "industrial aristocracy" could not easily accommodate itself to groups whose demands challenged its long-established position.

For the National Liberals, elitism was particularly strong in the economic realm, where the party had close ties with heavy industry and its pressure group, the *Centralverband deutscher Industrieller* (Central Association of German Industrialists). This group was founded shortly after the onslaught of the great European depression of the last quarter of the nineteenth century to protect, as it said, "national labor." Actually, this phrase meant the protection of the profits of the iron industry through protective tariffs. When the Centralverband allied with the aristocratic agricultural interests of East Elbia, who were also adversely affected by the depression, the result was the introduction of Bismarck's protective economic policies and a political alliance between National Liberals and Conservatives.[33] When the Conservatives formed the radical Agrarian League for the promotion of agricultural interests, they attracted the support of National Liberal farmers[34] and forged a further link between the two parties. An aversion to trade unions and their political representatives, the Social Democrats, formed another bond between the National Liberal heavy industrialists and the Conservatives. The Conservatives abhorred the democratic demands of the Social Democrats; the Centralverband feared the activities of Social Democracy's trade unions. It refused to recognize collective bargaining; it pressured the government for legislation suppressing strikes; and when this failed, it created employers' organizations designed to utilize the same kind of collective action against the unions that the unions themselves used in industrial conflicts. These employers' organizations proliferated faster than the trade unions and in some branches of industry, such as metal and textiles, they soon covered more workers than did the trade unions. Moreover, in 1904 and 1905 two national groups, the Society of German Employers' Organizations and the

33. Ivo Lambi, *Free Trade and Protection in Germany, 1868–79,* Beiheft 44, *Vierteljahrschrift für Sozial-und-Wirtschafts-geschichte* (Wiesbaden, 1963). Also Hartmut Kaelble, *Industrielle Interessenpolitik in der wilhelminischen Gesellschaft* (Berlin, 1967), pp. 190 ff.

34. Party policy was, however, more anti-League than pro-League, Hans-Jürgen Puhle, *Agrarische Interessenpolitik und preussischer Konservatismus im wilhelminischen Reich, 1893–1914* (Hanover, 1966), pp. 193 ff. Also S. R. Tirrell, *German Agrarian Politics after Bismarck's Fall: The Formation of the Farmers' League* (New York, 1951), pp. 214–215.

Central Office of German Employers' Organizations (the latter under the auspices of the Centralverband), were formed with headquarters in Berlin to coordinate antiunion activities.[35] The effectiveness of these organizations partially accounted for the trade-union fear of defeat in the event of a mass strike.

The link between heavy industry and the National Liberals and hence between them and the Conservatives was strongest in Prussia, where the important industrial area of Rhineland-Westphalia contained the coal, iron, and steel complex of the Ruhr Valley and where the Centralverband dominated National Liberal politics. Yet the Centralverband did not limit its political activities to Rhineland-Westphalia. It elected its own men to the Prussian Landtag and attempted to influence policies through pressure on the party and the Fraktion. Nationally it supported a *Sammlungspolitik,* or a combination of all the nonsocialist parties, to combat the growing power of the Social Democrats at the polls and in the Reichstag. Both government and Conservatives supported this tactic, and the Prussian National Liberals could use their considerable influence over the party as a whole to press for its adoption as an alternative to any alliance with the left.[36]

Despite these difficulties, Naumann claimed that the interests of the "industrial aristocracy" were similar to those of the middle and working classes, and there was some evidence to support this view. When Naumann implied that the National Liberals were the "industrial aristocracy," he consciously oversimplified the situation. While it was true that more businessmen sat in the Reichstag for the National Liberals than for any other party,[37] they were a very heterogeneous group. They not only represented the heavy industrial interests incorporated in the Centralverband, they also represented light industrialists, small business-

---

35. Roswitha Leckebusch, *Entstehung und Wandlungen der Zielsetzungen, der Struktur und der Wirkungen von Arbeitgeberverbände* ([East] Berlin, 1966), pp. 16–50, 89–90, 144–145; Arnold Heidenheimer and Frank Langdon, *Business Associations and the Financing of Political Parties* (The Hague, 1968), pp. 18ff. Cf. Kaelble, *Industrielle Interessenpolitik,* pp. 68–80; and Stegmann, *Die Erben Bismarcks,* pp. 26, 32ff.

36. Kaelble, *Industrielle Interessenpolitik,* p. 223. Also Theodor Eschenburg, *Das Kaiserreich am Scheideweg: Bassermann, Bülow und der Block* (Berlin, 1929), p. 112. For the formulation and progress of the *Sammlungspolitik,* see Stegmann, *Die Erben Bismarcks,* pp. 63ff.

37. In 1896, the percentage of businessmen in the National Liberal Fraktion was 65.1 percent, in 1903, 56.9 percent. Thereafter it declined considerably, Jaeger, *Unternehmer,* p. 51.

men, and middle-sized farmers in middle and southern Germany. For instance, one of the strongholds of National Liberalism was the province of Hanover, which was relatively untouched by industry and dotted with small towns and middle-sized dairy farms that depended on the imports of cheaper grain feeds. Because their activities depended on imports and cheaper goods, protective tariffs and indirect taxes were not always as beneficial to them as to the dominant groups in the Centralverband and the Agrarian League. Indeed the first bitter clash between the National Liberals and the Agrarian League occurred in Hanover[38] even before Naumann published *Demokratie und Kaisertum*. Among these various groups, the light industrialists first took the lead in opposing the Centralverband and its promotion of an alliance with the Conservatives. First of all, they objected to the close relationship between industry and agriculture because of the increasing enmity of the Agrarian League to all economic policies advantageous to industry. Secondly, they resented the cartelization of much of heavy industry, which, in its pricing and distributing policies, hurt the small producer. Since light industry was much more vulnerable than heavy industry to trade-union activities, it favored more accommodation to union pressures and began to recognize collective bargaining against the opposition of the Centralverband. Light industrialists also favored more social legislation since it relieved them of the sole responsibility for their workers' welfare. For all these reasons, the light industrialists broke with the Centralverband in 1895 and formed their own association: the League of Industrialists (*Bund der Industriellen*).[39]

Since the National Liberals depended on both groups of industrialists for financial and political support, the split between them resulted in a political schizophrenia within the party. The schizophrenia was exhibited in the split of the Reichstag Fraktion over Caprivi's trade treaties, over antisocialist measures, and antiunion laws. One group voted for, one group voted against these measures. The pressure of the light industrialists and other groups, notably the farmers of Hanover, resulted in a breach with the Agrarian League which weakened the ties between National Liberals and Conservatives. Yet the various splits were not due entirely to economic causes; there was also an ideological source of

38. Puhle, *Agrarische Interessenpolitik*, pp. 193ff.
39. Kaelble, *Industrielle Interessenpolitik,* pp. 164ff; Stegmann, *Die Erben Bismarcks,* pp. 33–34.

division. There were many people within the party who objected to the increasing conservative emphasis of National Liberal politics. During the years of the Reichstag Kartell between National Liberals and Conservatives, several members of the Fraktion resolved to create an intra-party organization devoted to a revival of liberal policies. Not many of these men were reelected after the dissolution of the Kartell, but their sentiments lived on within the party.[40]

The man who incorporated both the change of economic interest and the revival of liberal sentiment within National Liberalism was Ernst Bassermann. In contrast to Bebel's Prussian birth and northern background, Bassermann came from the southern state of Baden, where state government was liberal and politics dominated by the National Liberals. He belonged to a famous Baden family whose ancestors had been active in Baden politics since the beginning of the nineteenth century. Trained as a lawyer, he was also influential in commercial and financial circles in his position as board member for various corporate enterprises—none of them directly involved in heavy industry. His rise in the Reichstag Fraktion and in the party itself during the 1890s was due as much to the lack of any other strong leading figure as to his own hard work in the legislature. His main claim to distinction was his persistent opposition to measures designed to limit the constitutional guarantee of individual political freedom; in 1895 and 1899, he opposed government bills directed against the Social Democrats even though heavy industry and a large part of the Fraktion supported it. In addition to his support of the "liberal constitution," Bassermann was socially progressive and endorsed measures to improve the material condition of workers and to diminish conflicts between employer and worker. His liberal stance in constitutional matters and social legislation did not mean that he denied the monarchy or nationalism, nor did it indicate an interest in the democratic ideas enjoying a revival at the turn of the century; rather Bassermann's liberalism tried to reinvoke the liberal traditions of his party.[41]

40. J. Alden Nichols, *Germany after Bismarck* (Cambridge, Mass., 1958), pp. 149, 294–295; Karola Bassermann, *Ernst Bassermann* (Mannheim, 1919), pp. 82, 101. For the failure of the liberals to be reelected, see Wilhelm Kulemann, *Politische Erinnerungen* (Berlin, 1911), pp. 153–154.

41. For subsequent biographical material see Karola Bassermann, *Bassermann,* pp. 73–88, 96–103, and Elisabeth von Roon, *Ernst Bassermann, Eine politische Skizze* (Berlin, 1925). Both ladies were his daughters. Cf. *Neue Deutsche Biographie,* 1: 623. For his business

When Bassermann became leader of the National Liberal party, there was a group of Young Liberals within the party who wanted to revive its liberal traditions. The first Young Liberal club was founded in Cologne in reaction to the Conservative victory in the Prussian elections of 1898, and it was therefore one of the most explicit manifestations of the nascent divergence of interest between National Liberals and Conservatives. From Cologne, the movement spread throughout the Rhineland and southern Germany, and by 1900, it included 2,500 members, mostly between the ages of 21 and 35, enrolled in Young Liberal clubs throughout the country; significantly, most of its members were professional people who were only indirectly connected with industry. In 1901, the growth of the movement resulted in the foundation of a nationwide association called the *Reichsverband der Nationalliberalen Jugend* (National Association of National Liberal Youth). These Young Liberals wanted "to work as a ferment" inside the party, and they called for a reform of the "constitution, legislation, and administration in a free and popular sense."[42] Officially, the Young Liberals stood far to the left of Bassermann, and many had succumbed to the appeal of Naumann's ideas. One young southerner claimed that Naumann "had forged . . . the . . . ideas of a liberal-thinking, modern man into a secure formula."[43] and Gustav Stresemann, in his early political career, progressed from the Nationalsoziale movement to the Young Liberals and then to the National Liberal party.[44] It was Naumann's combination of the national and the democratic ideal which attracted Young Liberals. It led to their agitation for an equal suffrage in the various German states, for more progressive social legislation, for a more liberal school policy, for constitutional reform. Hence, the Young Liberals not only wanted to reemphasize the party's old liberal tradition, they wanted to infuse it with democracy. Moreover, the Young Liberals also subscribed to Max Weber's ideal of a large middle-class democratic party. They revived the memory of a time when the liberal movement had been united and strong, and from the turn of the

involvement, see Nussbaum, *Gegen Monopole*, p. 192, n. 161. For his interest in social legislation, see Ernst Brandenburg, *50 Jahre nationalliberalen Partei* (Berlin, 1917), pp. 27–28.

42. Kulemann, *Zusammenschluss*, pp. 27–28, 42.

43. Quoted in Gilg, *Erneuerung demokratisches Denkens*, p. 233.

44. Donald F. Warren, *The Red Kingdom of Saxony: Lobbying Grounds for Gustav Stresemann, 1901–1909* (The Hague, 1964).

century onward, the Young Liberals became "the pioneers of liberal unity."[45] For them, unity would be achieved through more cooperation between National and Left Liberals.

In the years after the founding of the Young Liberal organization, more political contacts between National and Left Liberals did occur. Yet the Young Liberal schemes would have come to naught had they not served National Liberal interests. Those light industrialists and small farmers who revolted against the Centralverband and the Agrarian League shared common social and economic concerns with the middle classes who voted for the Left Liberals, and Bassermann's leadership tended to emphasize the political traditions that the National Liberals shared with the Left Liberals. Moreover, the National Liberals began to lose ground in several state legislatures after the turn of the century, and in order to regain the strength of liberalism in general, they began to cooperate with the Left Liberals in election campaigns. For a while this cooperation was unofficial, but at the National Liberal party congress of 1905, Bassermann proclaimed it as part of party policy. Thus the National Liberals moved toward liberal cooperation at the same time that the Left Liberals began their process of unification.[46]

Liberal cooperation did not mean the unification of National and Left Liberals, and Bassermann explicitly made this distinction in 1905. It did, however, imply a National Liberal drift toward the left consonant with the Barth-Naumann tactic. This drift did not include cooperation with the Social Democrats; traditional antisocialist prejudice and stiff competition with the Social Democrats in urban and rural areas prevented that strategem. Yet liberal cooperation might include that opposition to the government which Naumann prophesied in *Demokratie und Kaisertum*, and this issue was raised at the National Liberal party congress held at Goslar in 1906. The immediate cause for questioning the party's traditional support of the government was the vote of the Reichstag Fraktion for higher indirect taxes in the legislative session of 1906. At the time there was a slight economic recession, and in Saxony, the center of light industry, and other urban areas National

45. Stillich, *Die politischen Parteien,* 2 : 319.
46. *Politisches Handbuch der nationalliberalen Partei* (Berlin, 1908), p. 361; *Hilfe* 9, no. 43 (1903): 3, outline the cooperation. Cf. Wolfgang Hofmann, *Die Bielefelder Stadtverordneten* (Lübeck and Hamburg, 1964), p. 64. The official recognition is recorded in *NL Vertretertag, 1905,* 2 : 30–31.

Liberals bitterly complained that the vote misrepresented their business interests.[47] This dissatisfaction combined with the general malaise represented by the Young Liberals, and their organization opened the more general attack on the party's policies. Since they verbalized the feelings of other party members, their specific complaints and proposals are worth a detailed discussion.

The Young Liberal complaints involved the practices, the program, and the organization of the National Liberal party. First of all, they scored the Reichstag Fraktion for persistently supporting the government "under all circumstances" and paying no attention to the interests of the voters. Secondly, they claimed the party program was deficient in expressing liberal principles and the will of the voters, and Hermann Fischer, the Young Liberal chairman, called for its "further development." Both the former and the latter complaints correctly saw the interrelationship between the National Liberal role as a governmental party and the conservatism of the National Liberal program. In fact, the party had reformulated its program along conservative lines in 1884 in order to harmonize its demands with the wishes of the government.[48] Thus, any reemphasis of the party's liberalism would involve opposition to the government. Yet before this could happen, some changes were also necessary in the party's organization. Fischer decried the "rather lamentable role" that party congresses and even the executive committee played in party policy, and he demanded that future delegates to the Reichstag be held accountable to the party program by the party congress. Here, Fischer put his finger on one of the main sources of difficulty within the party. Up until 1899, German law prohibited a network of interregional political clubs,[49] and this meant that the National Liberals, who were primarily organized for political purposes in contrast to the Social Democrats, the Centre, and the Conservatives, who used their economic and cultural associations as a screen for political activity, had a very weak organizational structure.

47. *NL Vertretertag, 1906*, pp. 31–32, 41–42.
48. Fischer is quoted from *Nationalliberale Jugend* 6 (1906): 149. Ludwig Bergsträsser, *Geschichte der politischen Parteien in Deutschland,* 11th ed. (Munich, 1965), pp. 146–147, explains the 1884 shift.
49. Helga Nussbaum, "Zum sozialökonomischen Hintergrund der Gegensätze in der nationalliberalen Partei zwischen 1900 und 1914," *Wissenschaftliche Zeitschrift der Friedrich-Schiller Universität Jena, Gesellschafts-und-Sprachwissenschaftliche Reihe* 14 (1965) : 267.

Party congresses met, but because of the lack of a regular communications network, the delegates could hardly develop a strategy for challenging the party notables. These notables were usually a few propertied and cultured men in each district who selected National Liberal candidates for the legislature according to their docility in serving the interests of the selection committee. When the ban on nationwide political clubs was lifted, the new party organization institutionalized the notables in the central committee (*Zentralvorstand*) which selected the executive committee and determined the agenda of party congresses. The same men also continued to select candidates for the legislature, and hence they continued to control the party's legislative policy. The Young Liberals' desire to revise the party's program and to increase the power of the party congresses was directed against the influence of these conservative local leaders; in effect the Young Liberals wanted to democratize the party as well as the country. The best example of this goal was the proposal to create new local election committees which would include Young Liberals as well as older National Liberals. In this way, the Young Liberals, with the support of other factions, intended to steer the party in a more liberal and democratic direction.[50]

At the party congress of 1906, the most vocal support for the Young Liberal position came from the Rhineland and from a young Saxon who was emerging as a promising national politician. From the Rhineland, Bernhard Falk, a delegate from Cologne, told the party leadership "it would be a self-delusion" to "conceive that [Young Liberal] opinions [were] limited to the circles of youth alone," and a representative from Elberfeld, Hintzmann, told the congress that the older gentlemen in his club shared many of the youth's misgivings about the party's policy.[51] But the most articulate supporter of the youth was Gustav Stresemann. Under the influence of the Nationalsoziale movement and the Young Liberals and disillusioned by the conservative National Liberals in his adopted town of Dresden, he and his friends had founded

50. In 1913, the occupational groups most represented on the Zentralvorstand were merchants and bank directors, 13; factory owners and directors of industrial enterprises, 19; judges and high officials, 25; professionals (lawyers, doctors), 32; Nipperdey, *Organisation*, pp. 80ff, 103–104. Also see *Von Bassermann zu Stresemann: Die Sitzungen des nationalliberalen Zentralvorstandes, 1912–1917*, ed. Klaus-Peter Reiss (Düsseldorf, 1967), pp. 16–21; Stegmann, *Die Erben Bismarcks*, p. 27. The Young Liberals' proposal is from *Kölnische Zeitung*, September 10, 1906, no. 967.

51. *NL Vertretertag, 1906*, pp. 84, 46.

a new, independent, and more progressive National Liberal Dresden club. By 1906, he had graduated into the ranks of the older National Liberals, had become the director of the Saxon branch of the League of Industrialists, and was actively engaged in drumming up support for a reform of the Saxon suffrage.[52] The young Stresemann was no democrat; but he did think that a reassertion of liberal principles was a necessary task of the National Liberal party. He echoed the Young Liberal accusation that the National Liberals had become an unreflective, governmental party, and he attacked its lack of liberal courage and determination:

> It is always said that we are not so significant quantitatively as to make our will felt. Have you so little esteem for the party that you assess it according to the numbers of its representatives? I believe the Chancellor and the government are far too smart . . . to burden themselves with the odium of constantly dealing with the Centre and the Conservatives. They know very well . . . that [our party] is seen . . . in Germany and other places as the representative of property and culture, and therefore they . . . wish it to participate in making legislation; . . . therefore . . . the National Liberal party could place much greater demands for consideration upon the government.[53]

This entire speech implied that the National Liberals had liberal principles worth asserting and that opposition to the government on behalf of these principles would be justified. In other words, Stresemann suggested the tactic outlined by Naumann in *Demokratie und Kaisertum.*

This bid for a new liberal direction revealed a fundamental split in the National Liberal party. In 1906, the split was not yet severe, but many speakers in favor of a new policy explicitly or implicitly mentioned two intraparty currents. The conservative Prussian wing, whose views prevailed at the party congress, strongly opposed the new direction favored by the Young Liberals and their supporters. Its leader, Robert Friedberg, summarized its position:

52. Warren, *Red Kingdom.*
53. *NL Vertretertag, 1906,* p. 53.

> The gentlemen presume us, in total opposition to all National Liberal traditions, to be solely a party of opposition and negation. . . . We will retain tradition, it makes no difference whether we will be a small or a large party in the future. . . . We have to apply ourselves in the direction of the founders of our party in positive cooperation in the tasks of the empire. We do not want to let ourselves encroach on this principle from any direction. . . .[54]

Thus there would be no new program, no new organization, and no new bickering with the government. The National Liberals would retain their former official conservatism. Having affirmed the status quo, the congress ended with the passage of several resolutions reasserting the unity of the party and urging everyone to cooperate in the coming national elections.[55] The meeting's finale, however, could not conceal that the party was on the verge of change. The Young Liberals' agitation for reform, Bassermann's determination to hold a moderate, liberal line, the decision to cooperate with the Left Liberals, all pointed to a new departure in National Liberal politics.

At the end of 1906, the majority of the left sketched out in *Demokratie und Kaisertum* was not yet a reality. Yet the three necessary participants in such a bloc had experienced important transformations since the book's initial publication. The Social Democrats moved closer to reformism; the Left Liberals espoused democracy and unity; the National Liberals revived their liberal ideals. All three were searching for a new and more effective policy, and this search increased the possibilities of their cooperation. Seemingly, they needed a catalyst to bring them more closely together. This spark was provided by a political thunderstorm which arose at the end of 1906.

54. Ibid., pp. 122–123.
55. Ibid., pp. 144–146.

3

The Bülow Bloc: Transition of the Liberals

The political crisis which arose in December 1906 concerned that important preoccupation of Germans in the decade before World War I: the maintenance and extension of national power. For over two years, the government had been embroiled in a rebellion in southwest Africa, and as the costs of fighting the natives rose, the government turned to the Reichstag to authorize additional military credits for the African war. Had the credits involved merely an addition to Germany's regular standing army, they would not have aroused any particular emotions. However, since they were destined for a "warring" purpose, they were considered necessary "to save German lives in Africa." Yet a majority of the Reichstag refused to approve the credits! Faced by this frustration of a clearly defined national purpose, the government dissolved the Reichstag and called for new elections. These elections, which occurred in January, were accompanied by so much propaganda on the part of the government and by such nationalistic fervor that one historian has called them the "national" elections of 1907.[1] The election campaign was ruthless in dealing with those parties that dared to reject monies needed for the safety of German fighting men. Social Democracy, consistent with its antinationalist and antiimperialist program, was one of these parties. Their negative vote was expected. Yet the other bloc of naysayers was the usually reliable, governmental Centre party. Its vote was most important for the defeat of the military credits, for the dissolution of the Reichstag, and for the crisis of 1906.

THE CENTRE

The Centre party[2] was an anomaly in German politics. Organized as a national party at the time of unification in order to protect the rights

1. George Crothers, *The German Elections of 1907* (New York, 1941).
2. The most comprehensive, though somewhat old-fashioned, history of the Centre party

of Catholics in the new Reich, it had, for a while, occupied an outcast position similar to that of Social Democracy. Catholic opposition to Bismarck's policies and Catholic insistence on a conservative, religiously oriented cultural and educational policy had alienated both the government and the liberals and resulted in the famous *Kulturkampf*. As a representative of Catholic interests, the Centre party shared in the prejudice and discrimination directed at the church and its members. When Naumann referred to the Centre as the "clerical aristocracy" in *Demokratie und Kaisertum,* he reflected both a Protestant religious and a national-liberal political bias. He believed that the privileged and honored position of the church in European and German society, with its hierarchical organization and traditional domination of many aspects of life, militated against its recognition and acceptance of democracy. In this respect, Naumann mistakenly confused the church with the Centre party. Although some priests sat in the party's Reichstag Fraktion, its policies were separate from and sometimes contradictory to the desires of the hierarchy.[3] In 1900, however, it was difficult to define its political status. It was probably the only party that represented the entire spectrum of German society and therefore had to accommodate internally all the economic and political interests separately embodied in the other German parties. For a time, it was dominated by influential Catholic aristocrats whose political and economic interests dovetailed with those of the Prussian Conservatives. These landowning aristocrats and the sizable Catholic peasantry enabled the party to ally with the Conservatives and the National Liberals on the matter of protective tariffs, and their interests were partially responsible for that governmental majority of "aristocracies" described by Naumann. Moreover, the strong Catholic social movement, similar to that of the Evangelical Social Congresses and the Inner Mission, inclined the Centre to the same kind of paternalistic social reform espoused by

---

is Karl Bachem, *Vorgeschichte, Geschichte, und Politik der deutschen Zentrumspartei,* 8 vols. (Cologne, 1927–1931); also see George G. Windell, *The Catholics and German Unity, 1866–1871* (Minneapolis, 1954).

3. For Naumann's assessment, see Friedrich Naumann, *Demokratie und Kaisertum: Ein Handbuch für innere Politik* (Berlin-Schöneberg, 1900), pp. 81ff. For the disparity between policy and interests, see S. R. Tirrell, *German Agrarian Politics after Bismarck's Fall: The Formation of the Farmers' League* (New York, 1951), p. 184. Cf. John K. Zeender, "German Catholics and the Concept of an Interconfessional Party, 1900–1922," *Journal of Central European Affairs* 23 (1964) : 427.

Conservatives. In addition, although the Centre originally opposed nationalistic and imperialistic ventures, it usually voted for such bills in the Reichstag after 1890. It is important to remember, however, that the Centre always retained a traditional abhorrence of extreme nationalism even when it supported an increase of military, naval, and colonial power. Also, despite its antiliberal inclinations, the party could support those liberal demands that furthered its interests: equal rights for all, limited parliamentary responsibility, and even an equal suffrage in states where Catholics had a majority. Lastly, the Centre, like all the other German parties, wanted to augment its own political power at the expense of the Conservatives.[4]

This last desire explains its vote against the colonial bill of 1906. Although its vote partially stemmed from its objection to abuses in colonial administration recently exposed by the Centre deputy, Matthias Erzberger, it was also a bid for governmental recognition of the Centre's growing political power. As a well-organized broadly based party, it had been the largest in the Reichstag for well over a decade, and this fact forced both government and Conservatives to consider its wishes. In the years before 1906, no major legislation could be passed without its approval, and it was truly a pivotal party.[5] For a time, this influence had not disturbed the government, but certain developments occurring at the turn of the century were changing the party's passive political stand and the government's attitude toward it. First of all, the aristocratic, conservative wing ceased to dominate the party, and control of its policies passed to a group of middle-class Catholics involved in commerce, finance, and industry who wanted to exert political power consonant with their economic power. These changes in party leadership led to strong admonitions against the Agrarian League,[6] which

4. For the Catholic social movement, see Lorenz Zach, *50 Jahre Zentrum: Wirtschafts- und-Sozialpolitik in Reichstag, 1871–1921* (Berlin, 1921), pp. 17–137; and Dirk Stegmann, *Die Erben Bismarcks: Parteien und Verbände in der Spätphase des wilhelminischen Deutschlands* (Cologne, 1970), pp. 29–31. Cf. Bachem, *Vorgeschichte,* 4 : 81–86. For antinationalism, see Hans Spellmeyer, *Deutsche Kolonialpolitik im Reichstag* (Stuttgart, 1931), pp. 16–41; Bachem, *Vorgeschichte,* 5 : 13ff., 50ff., 455ff. For interest in liberal demands, see Peter Gilg, *Die Erneuerung des demokratischen Denkens im wilheliminischen Deutschland* (Wiesbaden, 1965), pp. 238–240.

5. Arthur Dix, *Die deutschen Reichstagswahlen, 1871–1930* (Tübingen, 1930), p. 21. Cf. Friedrich Naumann, *Die politischen Parteien in Deutschland* (Berlin-Schöneberg, 1910), pp. 132–133; and Hans Müller, "Der deutsche Katholizismus, 1918–19," *Geschichte in Wissenschaft und Unterricht* 27 (1966) : 522.

6. Tirrell, *German Agrarian Politics*, p. 184; Zeender, "German Catholics," pp. 426–

could only alienate the Conservatives, and to another kind of campaign that eventually disturbed other groups as well. Catholics in Germany were a minority and therefore subject not only to Protestant and liberal prejudices but to a certain discrimination suffered by minorities everywhere. A report published at the turn of the century revealed that Catholics occupied a proportionately lower number of higher administrative posts than did Protestants, and consequently they were the second most underrepresented group in this category; only the working class suffered more from the same type of discrimination. The middle-class campaign to end this discrimination resulted in a Protestant reaction. Anti-Catholic propaganda increased between 1900 and 1906, and even the kaiser and court fell prey to its power. Thus there was heavy pressure on the government to cease its cooperation with the Centre in the Reichstag.[7]

In addition to the inconvenience caused the government by leading middle-class Catholics, there was a more dangerous but weaker movement within the party: democracy. The democratic movement was stimulated by the party's interest in the social problem, and many Centrists experienced the same transformation that Naumann did in the decade before *Demokratie und Kaisertum*. Ironically, the very elements tending toward Social Democratic reformism also encouraged Centrist democracy. The Christian trade-union movement, founded to combat the "atheistic" Social Democratic unions, supported the Centre, and in order to compete with the Social Democrats the party had to recognize some of the unions' political and economic demands. At the same time, the southern wing of the party, nurtured in a liberal political atmosphere, became increasingly democratic as it fought to

---

427. Hans-Jürgen Puhle, *Agrarische Interessenpolitik und preussischer Konservatismus im wilhelminischen Reich, 1893–1914* (Hanover, 1966), pp. 190ff.; also Herbert Gottwald, "Zum Verflechtungsprozess des politischen Katholizismus mit dem Imperialismus vor dem I. Weltkrieg," *Wissenschaftliche Zeitschrift der Friedrich-Schiller Universität Jena, Gesellschafts-und-Sprachwissenschaftliche Reihe* 14 (1965) : 251ff.

7. On discrimination, see Bachem, *Vorgeschichte,* 6:7–9. Cf. John R. Gillis, "Aristocracy and Bureaucracy in Nineteenth-Century Prussia," *Past and Present* 41 (December, 1968): 123, 126; J. C. G. Röhl, "Higher Civil Servants in Germany, 1890–1900," *Journal of Contemporary History* 2 (1967) : 109–110. For more evidence of discrimination, Lamar Cecil, "The Creation of Nobles in Prussia, 1871–1918," *American Historical Review* 75 (1970) : 768. Bernhard von Bülow discusses the pressure to cease cooperation in *Memoirs,* trans. G. Dunlop and F. A. Voigt, 4 vols. (Boston, 1931–32), 2 : 282–283. Cf. Bachem, *Vorgeschichte,* 6 : 318–326, 375; and Zeender, "German Catholics," p. 427.

gain power in southern legislatures by means of the universal, equal suffrage.[8] Matthias Erzberger, who bitterly attacked the government's colonial policy in 1906, was a southern deputy from Württemberg. In a sense, Erzberger was Naumann's Catholic counterpart; he believed in many liberal and democratic reforms desired by Naumann, and he also ardently supported the nationalistic Weltpolitik. Though sometimes rash and abrasive in his personal and political encounters, he realized the necessity of maintaining unity by conciliating the various groups within the party. It was particularly necessary to consider the much more conservative wishes of the Prussian Centrists. The Prussian right wing prevented the Centre from playing a wholly democratic role within the Reich, but the potential for such a role was important. Democratic tendencies within the Centre would later lead the party into an alliance with the left, and in 1906 these tendencies made the government uneasy. If the party's left wing became dominant, if the party retained its strength in the Reichstag, and if the government continued to cooperate with it, then democracy could threaten the conservative imperial system. In order to avoid such a situation, the government wanted to diminish the influence of the Centre in the Reichstag, and the party merely gave it the opportunity by voting against a "national issue."[9]

When the Reichstag was dissolved in 1906, the chancellor of Germany was Bernhard von Bülow. The son of a Mecklenburger nobleman who served the Danish king before the wars of unification and the Prussian king thereafter, he had illustrious aristocratic and patrician genealogies on both sides of the family. As a young man, he entered the diplomatic corps and served in minor posts at the embassies in Rome, Saint Petersburg, Vienna, and Paris before his appointment as minister to Rumania and eventually ambassador to Italy. From this post, he was called to be secretary of foreign affairs in the midst of a crisis over

8. Karl Buchheim, *Geschichte der christlichen Parteien in Deutschland* (Munich, 1953), pp. 313–316; *The Programm and Organisation of the Christian Trade Unions of Germany* (Geneva, 1921), p. 3; Thomas Nipperdey, *Die Organisation der deutschen Parteien vor 1918* (Düsseldorf, 1961), pp. 280–281; cf. Gilg, *Erneuerung demokratisches Denkens*, pp. 240–245.

9. On Erzberger, see Klaus Epstein, *Matthias Erzberger and the Dilemma of German Democracy* (Princeton, 1959), pp. 10–12, 62ff. For the Prussian Centrists, see Buchheim, *Geschichte der christlichen Parteien*, p. 306; Zeender, "German Catholics," p. 428. For the government's reaction, see Bülow to Count zu Stolberg-Wernigerode, November 20, 1909, Bülow Papers; Crothers, *German Elections*, p. 102; Epstein, *Erzberger*, p. 56.

naval expenditures in the Reichstag in 1897. One of his first tasks as foreign secretary was the solution of this crisis, which he achieved together with the newly appointed secretary of the navy, Admiral von Tirpitz. Their work resulted in the passage of Germany's first great naval bill in 1898. At the same time, Bülow continued and intensified the program of Weltpolitik. Germany occupied and leased Kiaochow, pressured England for Samoa, and led the troops that quelled the Boxer Rebellion. In 1900, another naval bill passed the Reichstag, and in that same year, Bülow became chancellor.[10] His own career therefore was linked with and reflected an increase in German power at home and abroad; it also revealed some of the weaknesses of that power. The chief fault of German foreign policy in this era was its failure to realize the effects of German strength on other European powers. Hence, Germany failed to achieve an understanding with England; it heedlessly provoked the first Moroccan crisis and was forced to suffer the subsequent diplomatic defeat at Algeciras. Algeciras was an acute embarrassment for the government, and nationalistic and commercial circles attacked it for causing the loss of German "prestige." Adding to this humiliation, Erzberger and the Centre impugned German honor from another direction by exposing administrative abuses in the colonies and refusing to vote the credits for a colonial war. This recalcitrance occurred just as the kaiser was bitten by anti-Catholic propaganda and began to complain about Bülow's increasing reliance on the Centre. Beset by enemies at home and abroad, Bülow badly needed a political victory to bolster the reputation of his government and the dignity of the nation. Thus he dissolved the Reichstag and called for the "national" elections of 1907.

THE BÜLOW BLOC: LIBERAL SUPPORT OF THE GOVERNMENT

When Bülow dispensed with Centre support, he had to find or create a new combination of parties for a Reichstag majority. This new majority eventually became the Bülow Bloc: an alliance of Conservatives, National Liberals, and Left Liberals. These parties had voted for the colonial funds of 1906, and the government planned and fought the election campaign on the basis of the "national" loyalty of these three parties. It was not surprising that the Conservatives and National Liberals, by virtue of their national loyalty, should combine in a

10. Bülow, *Memoirs,* vol. 4.

governmental bloc. It was, however, the first time that Left Liberals had voted en masse for an important colonial bill, and it was the first time that they were either asked or consented to participate in a governmental majority. At the time, their cooperation was seen as a significant Left Liberal transformation,[11] yet it was the result of a long evolution. Although Left Liberals traditionally opposed the acquisition of colonies because colonial ventures were both costly and nationalistically motivated, they had always supported the maintenance of the colonies when they devolved into German possession. Moreover, since 1893, Left Liberals had gradually espoused various parts of the nationalistic program, including colonialism. It that year, the Freisinnige Vereinigung split with the Freisinnige Volkspartei because it believed that a vote for Caprivi's military bill would encourage liberal concessions from the government. Thereafter, the party increasingly supported national, imperial bills on their own merits. At the turn of the century it voted for the new naval program and the acquisition of Kiaochow because of the benefits to German economic interests. When Naumann's group merged with the Vereinigung, he and his national-social colleagues injected their firm belief in German imperialism into the party. Meanwhile the Freisinnige Volkspartei also experienced a change of heart regarding nationalism. It too supported the naval program, and in 1902, contradictory to all its former beliefs in laissez-faire, it voted for the nationalist, protective tariff. In 1904 and again in 1906 it voted war credits for southwest Africa and approved a bill for the construction of colonial railroads.[12] When the Bülow Bloc was formed, it was not difficult for the Left Liberals to step into the "nationalist" camp. Though they were hesitant about joining a governmental bloc because of their liberal ideals, Bülow courted them with the promise of liberal concessions[13] and renewed the old hope, held by Barth, Naumann, and others, of liberal influence in German government. Moreover, participation in the Bülow Bloc furthered the new desire for liberal unity by enforcing the cooperation of Left Liberals and National Liberals in elections and in the Reichstag.

11. Crothers, *German Elections*, p. 53.

12. Spellmeyer, *Deutsche Kolonialpolitik*, pp. 15–97 passim. Cf. Konstanze Wegner, *Theodor Barth und die Freisinnige Vereinigung* (Tübingen, 1968), pp. 69ff., and Ludwig Elm, *Zwischen Fortschritt und Reaktion: Geschichte der Parteien der liberalen Bourgeoisie in Deutschland, 1893–1918* ([East] Berlin, 1968), pp. 62–64, 78–81, 90–94, 146–151.

13. *Freisinnige Zeitung*, January 22, 1907, no. 18; Pachnicke, *Führende Männer*, p. 85. Cf. Crothers, *German Elections*, pp. 156–157.

Liberal unity also suited the peculiar conception of German politics that influenced Bülow's formation of the Bloc and incidentally explained, in a negative way, why a book like *Demokratie und Kaisertum* necessarily had such great appeal. Bülow saw German politics as the adjustment of a desirable feudal arrangement to modern times. King and country existed at the heart of this feudal arrangement, and they were indissolubly allied with their staunchest supporters, the aristocratic Conservatives. At times, the interests of king and country were served by an alliance with the "clerical" Centre, but this combination was increasingly difficult because the Centre's mass support inclined it toward democracy. Moreover, modern conditions ruled out the crown's exclusive reliance on the Conservatives and Centre as updated versions of the feudal estates of "nobility and clergy." Modern life required some "essence and spirit" (*Natur und Geist*); and in Bülow's scheme of things, the liberals or third estate would supply the new ingredients.[14] Bülow thus intended to renew an alliance attempted ever since the era of Caprivi: the Reichstag should have a "collective" majority of Conservatives and liberals, of the aristocracy and the middle classes allied against the democratic working classes. In proposing this alliance, Bülow was not really reactionary; indeed he was more liberal than many men of his background. He understood the value of the Reichstag for a strong German state, and his desire to include the liberals in a parliamentary majority attempted to strengthen the hand of the government vis-à-vis its detractors at home and abroad. Yet Bülow was a firm believer in the existing constitution; he had no plans for parliamentarization nor for a responsible ministry, even when he later admitted the feasibility of appointing liberals to important administrative posts.[15] In 1906, his concepts embraced only the liberal spirit of the third estate; he had little sympathy for democratic forces.

While Bülow was willing to admit the middle-class liberals to positions of power and influence within the German state, he was not prepared to recognize the working class or fourth estate. As he revealed in a letter written a short time before 1907, the new political combination was directed against it:

> Certainly it is not excluded that a legislative interference vis-à-vis Social Democracy can, with time, turn out to be necessary. As

14. Bülow to Stolberg-Wernigerode, November 20, 1909, Bülow Papers.
15. Bülow, *Memoirs,* 2 : 572.

practical politicians we must wish however, that such an interference only occurs if the National Liberals and the Centre also
see the dira necessitas of such an act so that a measure against
Social Democracy would not be paralyzed by a fight between the
bourgeois parties among themselves or by a conflict between the
government and the bourgeois parties. Therefore I recognize . . .
the necessity to shield the bourgeois parties from one thing; that
when they do not hold together, the dilemma could arise: victory
of the revolution or coup d'état with absolutism. I have preached
this cohesiveness of the bourgeois parties again and again. . . .

I am of the opinion that the fight against Social Democracy and
also the parliamentary fight should not be . . . left up to the
government, but that it must be waged by the parties of order.
. . .[16]

Although Bülow, in this analysis, envisioned more repressive legislation
such as the antisocialist laws or the attempted legislation of the nineties,
the Bülow Bloc would include those parties whose support for such
legislation was hardest to achieve. In 1907, neither he nor the liberals
had any scruples about a government-sponsored, hard-hitting campaign
against the Social Democrats. Their vote against the colonial funds was
played up; the Centre vote was played down. Election propaganda
emphasized the unpatriotic nature of Social Democracy, and candidates
of the Bülow Bloc received support from the propagandistic Association
against Social Democracy, a group founded three years before which
represented agrarian and heavy industrial interests. The result of this
antisocialist campaign was the decimation of the Social Democratic
mandates in the Reichstag and the establishment of a majority for the
Conservatives and liberals of the Bülow Bloc. Though not a part of the
Bloc, even the Centre gained seats at the expense of Social Democracy.[17]

While Bülow triumphed over the Centre and Social Democracy, his
"marriage of conservative and liberal spirits" was less than a happy one.
The liberals were willing to cooperate with the Conservatives for a

16. DZAP, Reichskanzlei, Parteien 1/4, 1, no. 1395/1, Bülow to Stolberg-Wernigerode,
January 7, 1904. Cf. Dieter Fricke, "Der deutsche Imperialismus und die Reichstagswahlen
von 1907," *Zeitschrift für Geschichtswissenschaft* 9 (1961), pp. 539–541.

17. On propaganda, see Crothers, *German Elections,* pp. 144ff; for the government's
role in the elections, see DZAP, Reichskanzlei, Reichstag 2/2, 1–4. Cf. Stegmann, *Die
Erben Bismarcks,* p. 47. For the Centre's advance, see Dix, *Die Reichstagswahlen,* p. 21.

variety of reasons. The National Liberals, as former members of the Kartell, disliked losing their once important position in the Reichstag to the Centre and wished to regain their influence with the government; if liberal policies were implemented thereby, so much the better. The Left Liberals, never a governmental party, hoped to regain their credibility with the German voter and thus recoup some of their former strength at the polls. Yet they regarded liberal reform as essential to their support in Bülow's Bloc. Although they were willing to vote together with Conservatives and government when matters of defense and imperial policy were at stake, they were apprehensive about domestic issues. Even though Bülow enticed them into the Bloc with promises of liberal concessions, the Left Liberals especially feared a continuation of the same conservative policy that had governed Germany for the past three decades. A portent of their real weight and influence within the Bloc occurred immediately after the elections. The liberals had won more seats than the Conservatives in the Reichstag, and many felt that the new Reichstag president should be a liberal. Bülow and the Conservatives insisted on electing a Conservative president.[18] Less than a month after the praesidium elections, von Payer, the leader of the small Süddeutsche Volkspartei, reported a very unsatisfactory interview with Bülow:

> . . . . [W]e approached everything sensitively, but the man doesn't want to know anything about practical politics, and he must not have thought much about his liberal program yet . . . ; he couldn't even indicate to me how he imagines the cuts and simplifications of the tax system . . . [H]e even wrote down that he must speak with [Secretary of the Interior] Posadowsky about the *Vereinsgesetz.* . . . I made clear to him the consequences of parting without his offering something to liberalism. He finally countered . . . with the phrase: "You think then that it does not suffice to announce the dinner without at least serving the fish and the soup." I heartily supported him [in that viewpoint].[19]

But von Payer left the interview with no promise of liberal concessions. These fears of a conservative policy were not limited to the radical

18. Theodor Eschenburg, *Das Kaiserreich am Scheideweg: Bassermann, Bülow und der Block* (Berlin, 1929), pp. 60–65.
19. Payer to Haussmann, March 6, 1907, Haussmann Papers.

Left Liberals; even the National Liberals feared a continued conservatism. Bassermann, although he publicly supported the Bloc, had serious private misgivings. As far as he could tell, Bülow intended to reward the liberals very little for their support of the government:

> The basis of the Bülow policy is a good relationship with the Conservatives and Agrarians—he knows that if he does not have this backing, he will fall. . . . The influence of the Conservatives remains dominant; . . . the liberals will have to be satisfied with crumbs, and that will finally mean the end of [the] Bloc . . . [T]here will be no consideration of liberalism since it must support the Chancellor in the fight against the Centre.[20]

To be sure, the liberals supported the government's military, naval, and imperial policies, but a parliamentary partnership with the Conservatives was only viable if the liberals received some concessions.

THE PRUSSIAN SUFFRAGE

The most important anticipated concession was Prussian suffrage reform. For the liberals and for the nation, the Prussian suffrage was "the German problem." Constituted on a three-class basis in 1850, its unchanged, antiquated provisions clearly benefited the Conservatives and discriminated most against the Social Democrats. In the last Prussian election held before the formation of the Bülow Bloc, the Conservatives won 47 per cent of the representation in the Landtag compared with 21 per cent representation in the Reichstag. The contrast was even sharper when comparing seats with votes cast. Whereas the Conservatives received 300,000 votes for 203 seats in the Landtag, the Social Democrats, with approximately the same number of votes, elected not a single representative. In the same year, 31 Social Democrats were elected from Prussian constituencies to the Reichstag.[21] The Landtag was a partial source of the heavy Conservative influence in the Prusso-German state, and any fair reform of the suffrage would have to decrease Conservative representation there. Hence if the liberals were

20. Quoted in Eschenburg, *Das Kaiserreich*, p. 77.

21. These figures reflect the total percentage for the Deutschkonservative Partei and the Deutsche Reichspartei, both of whom participated in the Bülow Bloc, Dix, *Die Reichstagswahlen*, p. 21; *Zeitschrift des königlichen preussischen statistischen Landesamt*, Ergänzungsheft 23: *Die preussischen Landtagswahlen* (Berlin, 1905), pp. 40–41. For the Reichstag's composition see *Kürschners, 1907–1912*.

to insist on reform, they could count on stiff opposition from the Conservatives. But hope for this very reform had lured them into the Bloc, and the liberals determined to press their advantage.

Shortly after the formation of the Bloc, Naumann, as one of the chief proponents for wringing liberal and democratic concessions from the government, wrote an article in the *Berliner Tageblatt* advocating the introduction of the Reichstag suffrage, as the only truly liberal one, into Prussia. For him, the question of the Prussian suffrage was the "question of the life or death of the Bloc and Bülow's chancellorship." Should the chancellor encounter opposition from the Conservatives, he should dissolve the Landtag and use governmental influence against them in the new elections.[22] Naumann thereby proposed both a radical suffrage (for Prussia at least) and a radical method for achieving it; yet not even his fellow liberals supported his radicalism wholeheartedly.

The Left Liberal attitude toward suffrage reform was much more ambivalent than Naumann's article. Theoretically, they supported the equal, direct, and secret Reichstag suffrage for Prussia, and throughout the 1890s they introduced motions to this effect into the Prussian Land-tag. In 1905 they incorporated this demand into the Frankfurt program. On the other hand, they realized that the introduction of the equal suffrage into Prussia could be disadvantageous to their own position both in the Landtag, where they were overrepresented, and eventually in local communities, where the three-class suffrage gave them a majority in town and borough councils. At the party congress of 1906, one of the members of the Freisinnige Vereinigung objected to a resolution in support of the equal suffrage because of its adverse consequences for the liberals in the Hanseatic cities. In 1907, an influential member of the Freisinnige Volkspartei wrote to Bülow that although it would not be "beneficial" to the politics of the Bloc if another Prussian election were held under the existing three-class suffrage, the Volkspartei was willing to postpone its insistence on the equal suffrage in deference to a less radical government bill. At the time, the most immediate Left Liberal demands were the secret ballot and a new system of districting, and these overlapped with the demands of the National Liberals.[23]

22. *Hilfe* 13 (1907) : 502.
23. For the Left Liberals' theoretical support, see Walter Gagel, *Die Wahlrechtsfrage in der Geschichte der deutschen liberalen Parteien, 1848–1918* (Düsseldorf, 1958), pp. 143–144. For the Hanseatic liberals' objections, see *Vereinigung Parteitag, 1906*, p. 22. The extent to

The National Liberals did not even theoretically advocate the Reichs-tag suffrage for Prussia. They stood firmly by the traditional German liberal view that only the "propertied and the educated" should bear political responsibility. Furthermore, they feared the encroachment of the Centre and Social Democrats on their own mandates. Accordingly, they advocated the transformation of the three-class into a plural suffrage based on age, income, and education; but this advocacy was no hard and fast demand. The minimum demands of the National Liberals were threefold: the introduction of direct election, the secret vote, and a system of just districting. The desire for just districting was important because it later became an intricate bone of contention between liberals and Conservatives. It countered the existing system of dividing each individual precinct, rather than the wider area of the dis-trict, into voting classes according to the proportion of taxes paid. The effect of the existing system, particularly in the large cities, was that a man paying 20 to 30 RM in taxes might vote in the first class in a rel-atively poor precinct, whereas a man paying 2,000 to 3,000 RM might vote in the second or third class in a well-to-do precinct. The object of the existing system of division was the reduction of the "plutocratic character" of the suffrage, and it was precisely the heavy industrial plutocrats in the Rhenish-Westphalian cities who objected to it. They felt "disenfranchised" by the system, and since they supported the National Liberal party, the National Liberals made the revision of districting one of their own demands. Like the Left Liberals, the National Liberals defended their own interests, but they aimed at reform all the same.[24]

Bülow's proposals for reform, announced publicly on January 10, 1908, ignored these liberal demands. They provided neither for a direct suffrage nor for the secret ballot. For many liberals, the proposals were

which the Left Liberals would compromise is indicated in DZAP, Landtag 2/1, 2, no. 1070, Schmidt-Elberfeld to Bülow, September 25, 1907; cf. Wegner, *Theodor Barth*, p. 130.

24. For the districting reform, see Eugen Schiffer, "Blockpolitik, Wahlreform in Preussen, Schulpolitik, u. a., Rede gehalten in Magdeburg am. 18. Oktober, 1907," *Nationalliberale Schriften* 9 (Berlin, 1907). Also Eschenburg, *Das Kaiserriech*, pp. 79–80; and Gagel, *Die Wahlrechtsfrage,* pp. 163–164. The effect of the existing system of districting can be found in a speech of Richard Fischer in *Verhandlungen des Reichstages*, 231 : 2622–2631. For the plutocracy's objections, see DZAP, Reichskanzlei, Landtag, 2/1, 3, no. 1071, newspaper clipping from the *Westfälische Politische Nachrichten, Nationalliberale Korrespondenz für Westfalen,* April 6, 1910.

no solution to the German problem, and their disappointment coincided for once with Social Democratic outrage. When Bülow announced the government's intentions, the Social Democrats launched a series of protest demonstrations all over Prussia. At the same time, they called on the Left Liberals to abandon the Bülow Bloc. This appeal fell on the sensitive ears of a group already in serious disagreement about continued support of the government. The Freisinnige Volkspartei, "caught in the paddle-wheel of the Bloc" wanted to remain, and since it was the most numerous and powerful Left Liberal group, its attitude dominated the actions of the others. In the ranks of the Vereinigung, there was open rebellion. Barth and his supporters wanted to desert the Bloc while Naumann and others favored remaining as a means of furthering liberal unity through cooperation with the Freisinnige Volkspartei. As for the South Germans, they too had serious misgivings. Haussmann, the co-leader of the party, wanted to leave the Bloc; his colleague, von Payer, also thought that withdrawal was the most democratic course. On the other hand, they did not want to destroy the embryonic Left Liberal unity. In the end, both Vereinigung and South Germans decided to remain in the Bülow Bloc and ignore their disappointments.[25]

The ease with which the majority of Left Liberals ignored the crisis did not satisfy a man like Theodor Barth; his patience with Bülow was exhausted. Barth knew, even before January 10, that the government would grant no concrete reform,[26] and he resumed his previous efforts for cooperation with Social Democracy. At the beginning of January, he contacted Eduard Bernstein in hopes of instituting a joint Left Liberal–Social Democratic suffrage committee on the basis of the Social Democratic program and in agreement with Social Democratic methods. Bernstein, who agreed with Barth's ideas on cooperation, accepted his offer and informed other interested party members. Bebel himself discussed the plan with Barth, but fearing to dampen the Social Democrats' fire with liberal water, he opposed cooperation. At one point, both Bebel and Singer, the party's co-leader, opposed cooperation so much that they considered an open break with their reformist comrades

25. *Protokoll über die Verhandlungen des Parteitages der sozial-demokratischen Partei Preussens* (Berlin, 1908), pp. 3–7. The "paddle wheel" phrase was used in a letter from von Payer to Haussmann, December 21, 1907, Haussmann Papers. Haussmann's sympathies are reported in *Vorwärts*, January 10, January 15, January 17, January 26, 1908; his reservations, in von Payer to Haussmann, January 18, 1908, Haussmann Papers.

26. DZAP, Naumann Papers, Barth to Naumann, January 2, 1908.

who favored it. Bebel doubted the capability of any "castrated" bourgeois party to act effectively, and he finally obtained on official edict
from the executive rejecting a joint committee.[27]

However, the Social Democratic leadership was not the only obstacle
to cooperation. The liberal rank and file, as always, lagged just behind
its own leadership and balked at an alliance with the Social Democrats.
In February, Barth embarrassedly informed Stampfer, his Social Democratic contact in Breslau, that a joint protest meeting could not take
place there because "his friends [the Vereinigung] . . . first wanted to
make an attempt to cooperate with the Volkspartei. . . . " Stampfer was
understanding: "I believe that the Breslauers mean well, only they
suffer from the same evil as most of their spiritual comrades in the
country; they're frightened out of their wits. . . ." Stampfer thought the
best course for the Social Democrats was patience, propaganda, and
hope for renewed efforts at cooperation. He did not want "to let the
temporarily frustrated plan with Barth out of sight"; perhaps he could
yet succeed in achieving it.[28] Yet this episode in Breslau reflected the
reluctance of the liberal middle classes to associate themselves with the
so-called "red revolutionaries." They were as psychologically unpre-
pared as the Social Democrats for a common front against the government.

This failure to achieve an alliance with the Social Democrats did not
deter Barth and his supporters from forming their own liberal suffrage
movement. Throughout Prussia and South Germany during February
and March, 1908, they participated in a series of protest meetings. Even
the less enthusiastic Freisinnige Volkspartei held assemblies protesting
Bülow's betrayal of the liberals. The result of this Left Liberal agitation
in 1908 was the creation of a liberal committee to propagandize the
injustices of the Prussian suffrage and persuade the non–Social Democratic electorate of the need for reform through brochures, pamphlets,
and speakers. Although these activities were certainly a pale imitation
of the stirring street demonstrations of the Social Democrats, the events

27. For Barth's attempt at cooperation, see DZAP, Barth Papers, Bernstein to Barth,
January 16, 1908. Also see Eduard Bernstein, "Das Werk des Preussentages und der Wahl-
rechtskampf," *Sozialistische Monatshefte* 12 (January 9, 1908), pp. 10–17. For Bebel's final
rejection, see DZAP, Barth Papers, Bebel to Barth, February 2, 1908; Molkenbuhr Diaries,
February 8, 1908; Bebel to Adler, February 1, 1908, *Briefwechsel,* p. 483.
28. DZAP, Sammlung Löbe, Stampfer to Löbe, February 8, 1908.

of the late winter exhibited hopeful signs of progress toward a majority of the left. Despite reservations on both sides, some Left Liberals had wanted to cooperate with the Social Democrats in extraparliamentary agitation, and their overtures met with a favorable response.[29]

THE *Vereinsgesetz*

The denial of substantial reform of the Prussian suffrage was not the only disappointment facing the liberal parties at the beginning of 1908. The second liberal condition for joining the Bülow Bloc was the ultimate passage of a *Vereinsgesetz* (law of association) guaranteeing the freedom to combine in political clubs and assemble in political meetings. Although the constitution of the Reich provided for legislation unifying the various state laws (mostly dating from the period of reaction after the revolution of 1848), the repeated attempts of the liberals to achieve not only a unified, but a liberal, law had failed due to the opposition of both the government and the Conservatives. The liberals, in advocating a national law regulating the right of combination, hoped to eliminate restrictions and abuses in Prussia and Saxony, and the government was willing to meet them halfway. Under the impetus of a Left Liberal resolution passed in the Reichstag during the early period of the Bloc, the government introduced a bill in the first half of December 1907.[30] From the first, it was clear that both Conservatives and National Liberals basically agreed with the government's bill. The Left Liberals, for their part, immediately expressed dissatisfaction with certain provisions, and their complaints coincided with the principal objections of the Social Democrats who, together with the Centre, supplied the chief opposition to the bill. The Left Liberals' stance placed them in a peculiar position vis-à-vis the other parties of the Bülow Bloc, and their opposition to the Vereinsgesetz was, in a sense, the first breach of the unstable coalition.

The Left Liberals, the Social Democrats, and the Centre chiefly objected to paragraph 7, which sought to make the use of the German language mandatory in all *public meetings*. This provision was part of the whole program of Germanizing the non-German minorities of Prussia and the Reich which had begun in the 1870s. Although it affected the French and the Danes, the program principally applied to the Poles and sought to diminish and eventually eliminate Polish

29. *Hilfe* 14 (1908) : 33, 103, 118, 135.
30. *Verhandlungen des Reichstages,* 248: Drucksache no. 482, 13–18.

nationalism.[31] The Left Liberals granted the dangers of Polish nationalism to the integrity of the German state. However they considered paragraph 7 an "exceptional" provision—a violation of the liberal principle of equal justice for all—and they warned that previous "exceptional laws" directed against the Centre and the Social Democrats had never diminished the popular appeal of these two parties. An exceptional provision against the Polish language had very little chance of preventing Polish nationalism; it would only drive the Polish movement underground and create martyrs whose memory would enhance the movement's appeal.[32] The Social Democrats and the Centre, with their considerable trade-union support, saw the problem in another light as well. Paragraph 7 not only discriminated against the Poles in Polish Prussia, it also discriminated against Polish and other foreign workers in Rhenish Prussia. Inasmuch as trade-union meetings were public, the exclusion of foreign languages for use in public meetings would hamper the organization of foreign workers into trade unions and would harm both their own welfare and that of their fellow German workers. The Left Liberals agreed with the opposition on this point; the *Berliner Tageblatt* even suggested that the Rhenish-Westphalian industrialists had instigated paragraph 7 with the aim of preventing the trade-union organization of foreign labor.[33] Therefore when the bill went into committee in the middle of December 1907, the Left Liberals had their job cut out for them. Their task was to change paragraph 7 and to wring as many other liberal concessions as possible from the government, the Conservatives, and the National Liberals. The achievement of these concessions was imperative to protect them from Social Democratic attacks as well as to preserve their own liberal honor.

The Left Liberals actually did succeed in preserving a large part of their honor. First of all, in order to prevent the continuation of chicanery by the police and the courts in the administration of the law, they exacted a clarity of language which plugged the loopholes incorporated

31. Richard Tims, *Germanizing Prussian Poland: The H-K-I Society and the Struggle for the Eastern Marches in the German Empire, 1894–1919* (New York, 1941), pp. 50ff; and Hans-Ulrich Wehler, "Die Polenpolitik im deutschen Kaiserreich, 1871–1918," *Politische Ideologien und nationalstaatliche Ordnung: Studien zur Geschichte des 19. und 20. Jahrhunderts: Festschrift für Theodor Schieder zu seinem 60. Geburtstag,* ed. Kurt Kluxen and Wolfgang J. Mommsen (Munich, 1968), pp. 297–316.
32. Ernst Müller-Meiningen in *Verhandlungen des Reichstages,* 229 : 2133–2134.
33. Wolfgang Heine in *Verhandlungen des Reichstages,* 229 : 2120.

from existing laws into the proposed bill. Secondly, they won exemptions for election campaigns from the otherwise strict regulations for notifying the police about political assemblies. Finally, and most important, they added a provision that the law apply only to specifically *political* clubs and meetings in contrast to the government's plan to apply the law to any clubs or assemblies of a *public* nature.[34] This additional provision excluded most trade-union activities from police surveillance and benefited the unions affiliated with the Social Democrats and the Centre.

Paragraph 7 proved a tougher nut to crack. At first, the Left Liberals attempted to preserve the use of foreign languages for *all* public meetings. The government, however, refused to accept this condition, and it threatened to withdraw the bill entirely if the Left Liberals remained obstinate. Finally the National Liberals, true to their liberal alliance, suggested a compromise that all the parties of the Bloc eventually accepted. In areas where the non-German inhabitants constituted more than sixty percent of the population, as in Polish Prussia, the foreign language would remain the public language for the next twenty years; thereafter German was compulsory. This compromise relieved the pressure on areas with large minorities, but since the Left Liberals never succeeded in making the distinction in paragraph 7 between political and public activities that they achieved in the other provisions of the bill, it did not affect the cheap Polish and foreign labor so vital to union leaders in West Germany, where a German majority prevailed. Paragraph 7 therefore became an "exceptional" provision against the trade unions who would have to use German in addressing foreign workers, and the government explicitly indicated that the law would apply particularly to Social Democratic trade unions. Clearly, in light of existing political conditions, the Left Liberals had won a victory, but their victory was almost Pyrrhic:

> That is the hard-pressed situation of the Left Liberal Fraktion
> . . . The German Vereinsgesetz remains in its misery and confusion
> if the opportunity is now lost. That is one side of the matter. On
> the other hand, the mutilated remains of paragraph 7 are . . . so
> dumb and ignorant that it is truly no small presumption [to expect
> us] to swallow it . . . The Poles in the Rhenish-Westphalian areas
> and in districts with large minorities . . . will be most affected.

34. Ernst Müller-Meiningen in ibid., 332 : 4564–4565.

The Left Liberals realized that paragraph 7 was a disfiguring blemish to the law; but without paragraph 7, there would be no Vereinsgesetz.[35]

When the bill finally emerged from committee in April, 1908, all parties of the Bloc agreed to vote for it, and its acceptance in the Reichstag was assured. The deliberations in plenum were merely a formality— a game in which the opposition parties could air their grievances in public and attack those whose political behavior disappointed them. During this game, there developed a curious dialogue between the Left Liberals and the Social Democrats. Müller-Meiningen, the chief spokesman for the Left Liberal *Fraktionsgemeinschaft* (joint delegation), opened the dialogue by praising the "great progress" that the bill represented and by enumerating its merits. He then turned to the Social Democratic opposition and apologized for the deficiencies of paragraph 7:

> . . . [W]e too regret, that we had to renounce some just demands . . . in consideration of the distribution of strength in this High House. . . . We too maintain, even today, that the whole [system] of surveillance is superfluous. However, it is completely clear to us and . . . also to you that this law, in spite of everything, means a considerable progress in the exercise of political rights and freedoms . . . [and its] miscarriage would be an irresponsible folly on our part.[36]

In the issue of paragraph 7, circumstances had forced the Left Liberals to dilute their honor with prudence.

According to the Social Democrats, this prudence had sullied Left Liberal honor. They accused the Left Liberals of "sacrificing intellect and conviction, not to speak of more serious things."[37] Carl Legien, the most famous and responsible of the trade-union leaders, complained of the disastrous effects of paragraph 7 on trade-union organization. If, according to their own utterances, the Left Liberals agreed with the Social Democrats about the consequences of the bill, they had no other choice but a rejection of the whole law. He alluded to all the foreigners

35. For government threat and the Left Liberals' indignation, see *Hilfe*, 14 (1908) : 56, 145, 201; for the National Liberals' mediating role, see Eschenburg, *Das Kaiserreich*, p. 100. The text of the compromise as well as its intended application by the government can be found in *Verhandlungen des Reichstages,* 246: Drucksache no. 819, Anlage 1: 4902–4903, and in the speech of Adolf Gröber, 232 : 4794, 4797.

36. *Verhandlungen des Reichstages,* 232 : 4564–4565.

37. Wolfgang Heine, ibid., 232 : 4558.

brought to Germany by industrial enterprisers–not only Poles, but Italians, Czechs, Hungarians, and Letts—and turned angrily on his Left Liberal colleague:

> Herr Müller-Meiningen, if you do not wish to take away the possibility of the workers organized in unions to defy this procedure, then take care that we can make ourselves understood, in their mother tongue, to these strikebreakers hauled in from abroad— and in public meetings as well![38]

Legien's outrage was understandable: before 1908, no language clause existed in any of the laws of association and although Social Democratic trade unions suffered from official chicanery, they could at least expect to apprise cheap foreign labor of its rights so as not to undermine previously gained victories of German workers. Trade-union organization of foreign labor was so important to the Social Democrats that they even momentarily abandoned their stubborn opposition to the Bülow Bloc and the proposed law. In their desperation, they attempted a small compromise:

> [T]here has to be no special declaration from my side that my Fraktion will decide against paragraph 7 under any circumstances; however, we will vote for the amendment, which would introduce a certain mitigation, whereby the prohibition against foreign languages would be valid only for political assemblies.[39]

Thus the Social Democrats were willing to abandon their absolute opposition to a language clause if the public meetings of the trade unions were exempted. They were even prepared to cooperate with the bourgeois parties in this effort. Yet their appeal was already too late. Any compromise with the Social Democrats was unpalatable to the government and to the other parties of the Bloc. If the bill were to pass, the Left Liberals had to cooperate with the Conservatives and the National Liberals.

The Left Liberals freely admitted that their votes were necessary for the passage of the bill, and they set about defending their position

---

38. In the first reading of the bill, ibid., 229 : 2179–2180. Hans-Ulrich Wehler, *Sozialdemokratie und Nationalstaat* (Würzburg, 1962), p. 182, argues that in its concern for trade-union activities, Social Democracy ignored the integral nationalistic tendencies of paragraph 7.

39. Karl Legien in *Verhandlungen des Reichstages,* 232 : 4657–4658.

against the Social Democrats. Wearied by Social Democratic needling about principles, both Müller-Meiningen and von Payer stressed that they were engaged in the art of the possible. The Social Democrats understood this art well enough when they themselves temporized in state legislatures and municipal councils. Müller-Meiningen even accused the Social Democrats of depriving the Left Liberals of valuable support in their duel with the government.[40] In the matter of the Vereinsgesetz, the pattern of Left Liberal politics emerged in its full dilemma. Caught between their liberal principle and their desire to influence the course of events, pulled between the right and the left, the Left Liberals felt themselves attacked from all sides. If they aligned themselves with the government and a majority of the right, they were accused of renouncing principle. But if they opposed the government and allied with democratic forces, they isolated themselves and accomplished nothing.

Crisis in the Left Liberal Ranks

The Left Liberals voted for the Vereinsgesetz in order to achieve a more liberal policy in the Reich even though it did not satisfy their ultimate demands. Yet this accomplishment threatened that Left Liberal unity which had been strengthened by participation in the Bülow Bloc and was conceived to be absolutely essential for winning concessions from the government. Unity would provide power, and during the years of the Bülow Bloc, the Left Liberals made important strides toward forming a single party. In 1907, the three groups had formed a Fraktionsgemeinschaft in the Reichstag and an extraparliamentary political committee for the discussion and solution of differences of opinion among them. In the same year they held their first joint assembly.[41] The existence of these unified organizations created the superficial impression that harmonious relations progressed from day to day, but insiders knew that Left Liberal unity was not as complete as it seemed. The Freisinnige Volkspartei particularly found it difficult to cooperate with its more radical partners, and it continually stressed its right to an independent course of action. Such assertions disturbed the formulation of a common policy. Meanwhile, there were differences of opinion over the tactics of the Prussian suffrage movement and over the

40. Ibid., 232 : 4659, 4671.
41. *Freisinnige Volkspartei*, pp. 24ff.

passage of the Vereinsgesetz. Ultimately, the differences over the Vereinsgesetz led to a decisive crisis of the Left Liberal Fraktionsgemeinschaft and hence to a crisis of Left Liberal unity.

The difficulty was caused by the deepening dissatisfaction of Barth and his supporters with Left Liberal participation in the Bülow Bloc. At the party congress of 1907, Barth voiced violent objections to the Bloc on the grounds that it promised little in the way of democratic progress. Playing upon a simile once used by the chancellor himself, Barth said that Bülow was like the host who showed his hungry guests the menu and then placed it back in his pocket. The defeat in the Prussian suffrage reform and the Pyrrhic victory of the Vereinsgesetz merely proved that there wasn't even any menu, and Barth began to urge the Left Liberals to leave the table. As a result, a new crisis developed at the beginning of February 1908. At a meeting of the Vereinigung's executive committee, both Barth and Helmuth von Gerlach, his colleague in opposition, resigned from that venerable body and increased their acrimonious public criticisms of their colleagues. While the Fraktionsgemeinschaft prepared to accept the compromise over paragraph 7, Barth circulated a petition against it. When the Left Liberals finally decided to vote for the law, Barth labeled the decision a "collapse of character." His criticisms became so sharp and the unrest within the party so great that the Freisinnige Vereinigung finally called the party congress that Barth demanded.[42]

Although the passage of the Vereinsgesetz was the immediate cause of the congress and many local clubs introduced motions representing either a pro or con position, the discussion quickly boiled down to two interrelated issues: (1) Whether or not to remain in the Bülow Bloc; and (2) thereby insure or endanger the Fraktionsgemeinschaft and with it the future of a united Left Liberal party. If the Vereinigung broke with the Bloc, it also broke with the two other liberal parties and thereby retarded or even ruined the chances of consummating the proposed Left Liberal unity. In the debate on this issue, there were three principal viewpoints.

Barth argued ardently for separation from the Bloc. The willingness of the Vereinigung to acquiesce in the violation of liberal principles contained in paragraph 7 of the Vereinsgesetz stemmed from its partic-

42. For Barth's increasing dissatisfaction, see *Vereinigung Parteitag, 1907*, pp. 66–70; *Hilfe* 14 (1908): 68, 99; Barth to Gothein, March 19 and 23, 1908, Gothein Papers, 16.

ipation in the liberal Fraktionsgemeinschaft and its obligation to cooperate with and submit to the Freisinnige Volkspartei as the largest and strongest Left Liberal party. The Volkspartei was drifting more and more to the right, and this direction led it further and further away from an ideal liberal-democratic development. In fact, the policy of the Bloc was a battle against democratic developments in the nation: "Up until now, I have assumed that our . . . [party] had set itself the task of making sure that a bourgeois democratic party also exists alongside Social Democracy so that the necessary democratisation of Germany does not depend on Social Democracy alone."[43] If the Fraktionsgemeinschaft could not supply such democratic direction, it should be abandoned despite its contribution to Left Liberal unity and strength. Implicit in this argument was the choice of alliance with the left. If the Vereinigung could not achieve liberal democracy in coopera- tion with other liberals, then perhaps it should seek a better alliance with the Social Democrats.

The sharpest answer to Barth came from his more conservative enemy, Hermann Pachnicke. Pachnicke believed that a withdrawal from the Bloc would mean a disastrous loss of votes. Liberal voters were tired of endless opposition, and they now desired some liberal power mani- fested by some sort of influence in the legislative process. Of course the Vereinsgesetz was not ideal, but it and the Bloc represented the practical policy demanded by the voters. Barth's continual harping on coopera- tion with the Social Democrats only created dissension within the party, and the voters would no longer stand for it. As for the Freisinnige Volkspartei, Pachnicke refused to believe that it would tolerate all manner of offense to the principle of equality under the law. For the present, however, the Volkspartei found the continuous criticism of Barth and his supporters incompatible with a spirit of cooperation. Its leaders demanded that the Vereinigung create discipline and unity within its ranks, and the Vereinigung intended to do so.[44] For Pachnicke therefore, the issue was not democracy but the maintenance of the tradition, the strength, and the unity of liberalism. For him, the mood of the voters dictated an orientation to the right practiced within the framework of the Bülow Bloc.

The most moderate and sympathetic answer to Barth came from

43. *Vereinigung Parteitag, 1908*, pp. 30–33.
44. Ibid., pp. 35–38.

Naumann. Naumann's temperament and his friendly relationship with Barth prevented his making a sharp attack. As he traced his political biography from the Nationalsoziale Verein to 'the Freisinnige Vereinigung, he remembered that it was Barth who attracted him to liberalism. At that time, Barth had two appealing ideas: the necessity of a firm liberal unity and the development of liberal contacts with the Social Democrats in order to create a new German left. This "Barth-Naumann tactic" still had validity. The main difficulty was that such a tactic had meaning only if a strong liberal-democratic party existed. Barth's desire to breach the Fraktionsgemeinschaft merely endangered the fruition of his earlier strategy. The party should not abandon its ideal of cooperation with the Social Democrats, but that was a task for the future. The "psychological disposition" for such an alliance did not yet exist either within liberalism or Social Democracy. Until such a disposition did exist, the liberals had to increase their own strength and unity. It would only endanger unity to withdraw from the Gemeinschaft, and since the other Left Liberal parties chose to remain in the Bloc, the Vereinigung must remain also.[45]

In arguing for continued participation in the Bülow Bloc, Naumann applied a lesson he had learned from the failure of his Nationalsoziale Verein. A small group, attempting to steer an independent course, was doomed to failure between the giant millstones of right and left. Naumann had joined the Vereinigung in the search for a larger, more effective organization. He realized that organization, similar to that of the Centre and the Social Democrats, was the only competitive means in the fight against reaction, and Left Liberal unity provided this competitive organization. Naumann's emphasis on unity, as opposed to Barth's emphasis on democracy, again reflected the influence of Max Weber, who had long urged a "closed phalanx of the liberal bourgeoisie" against the Conservatives. In 1908, Weber explicitly approved Naumann's position in the crisis over the Vereinsgesetz.[46] The decision to remain in the Gemeinschaft was the decision to create the "closed phalanx" necessary for fighting the forces of reaction. Ultimately, a united Left Liberal party could expect to exercise more political power

45. Ibid., pp. 46–53.
46. Wolfgang Mommsen, *Max Weber und die deutsche Politik* (Tübingen, 1959), pp. 151–152. Cf. Wegner, *Theodor Barth,* pp. 96–97; and Nipperdey, *Organisation,* pp. 229–230.

with both National Liberals and Social Democrats. In fact, a united Left Liberal party was a necessity for the development of Naumann's dream of a national-democratic left. Therefore the crisis of Left Liberal participation in the Bloc involved much more than a disagreement of principle over the Vereinsgesetz; it involved the life or death of the embryonic bloc from Bassermann to Bebel. For Naumann, the choice was an obvious, if difficult, one; the Vereinigung should continue to participate in the Bülow Bloc until all three Left Liberal parties decided en bloc to desert it.

Such reasoning also dominated the majority of the party. Barth's supporters had introduced a censure motion against the vote for the Vereinsgesetz; the congress of the Vereinigung rejected the motion. Instead it urged continued participation in the Fraktionsgemeinschaft, expressed the hope that the Gemeinschaft would represent a "decisive liberalism," and chastised the critics by urging them to "remain conscious of the necessity of cooperation" with the other parties. The vote confronted Barth's radicals with the choice of regimenting themselves to the majority of the congress or leaving the party, but they had made their decision long before the congress convened. Immediately after the vote on the censure motion, they declared their withdrawal from the Vereinigung; altogether three local clubs and nineteen important members withdrew—among them Barth, his friend and longtime editor of the *Nation*, Paul Nathan, and two members of Naumann's original organization, von Gerlach and Rudolf Breitscheid, who later became a Social Democrat.[47] But this secession did not endanger the life of the party; the majority remained to await the fulfillment of unity.

THE SOCIAL DEMOCRATS AND THE NATIONAL QUESTION

Despite Left Liberal participation in the Bülow Bloc and the mutual recriminations between them and the Social Democrats over the Vereinsgesetz, Naumann's speech during the Left Liberal crisis indicated that cooperation between liberals and Social Democrats was still a long-range goal. As we have seen, the previous contacts between the two groups were maintained during the period of the Bloc, and the 1907 election campaign itself demonstrated the impossibility of erecting a hard and fast barrier between them. In the Rhineland and in Baden,

47. *Vereinigung Parteitag, 1908*, pp. 67–69, 91; DZAP, Broemel Papers, meeting of the executive committee, May 5, 1908.

liberal sentiment inclined more against the Centre than against the Social Democrats. Even the National Liberals attempted to conclude agreements with the Social Democrats for the runoff election in these areas, but the Social Democrats refused to cooperate. The government itself recognized the special situation in Baden and urged that very Left Liberal candidates be placed in several districts to attract socialist voters. It even considered ceding them their urban strongholds, Mannheim and Karlsruhe, in order to win their support in other areas against the Centre. The Social Democrats themselves realized the desirability of supporting Left Liberal candidates. Their slogan for the runoff election expressly sanctioned a Social Democratic vote for a Left Liberal, and they helped to elect thirteen Freisinnige candidates.[48] A major reason for supporting the liberals was the extremely defensive position of the socialists. Heine, a revisionist, wrote to Vollmar describing the Social Democratic dilemma: "In 1903 one could consider whether and to what extent the Freisinnige should be allowed to lose in order to teach them a lesson. This time we don't even have that choice. The danger of a considerable gain of the Conservatives is very great . . . ."[49] Even though they disagreed with the liberals' support of the government, the Social Democrats were driven to support them in order to combat the Conservatives.

An example of the fighting, but disappointed, psychology of the Social Democrats was pointedly acted out in Württemberg. Because of the sudden dissolution of the Reichstag in 1906, the previously scheduled Württemberg Landtag elections coincided with the Reichstag elections. This coincidence caused the peculiar situation in which the Left Liberal Süddeutsche Volkspartei allied *with* the Social Democrats for the Landtag elections but fought *against* them in the Reichstag elections, where, according to the national pattern, they allied with the National Liberals. The general liberal agreement in Württemberg cost the Social Democrats at least three mandates in the Reichstag elections. Added to this loss was the confusion of the voters caused by two concurrent contradictory election campaigns. By the time the Social Democrats

48. For the National Liberals' proposed deal, see Eschenburg, *Das Kaiserreich,* pp. 55–56; Josef Schofer, *Grossblock-Bilanz: Zeitgemässe politische Erinnerungen* (Freiburg i. Breisgau, 1913), pp. 31–33. For the government's strategy, see DZAP, Reichskanzlei, Reichstag 2/2, 1, 71. For the Social Democratic cooperation, see *Schulthess, 1907,* p. 17; Crothers, *German Elections,* p. 173.

49. Heine to Vollmar, January 26, 1907, Vollmar Papers.

in Württemberg sat down to discuss the Reichstag runoff election, they badly needed a scapegoat. Their natural course would have been outright rejection of all Left Liberals. However there were two prominent Left Liberals standing for the election in Württemberg: Conrad Haussmann, the co-leader of the Süddeutsche Volkspartei, and Friedrich Naumann. The Social Democrats decided to distinguish between the two. The onus of perfidy fell on Haussmann for negotiating the election contract with the National Liberals; Social Democratic voters were strictly admonished to abstain from voting in Haussmann's district and from throwing their weight to a political traitor. On the other hand, Naumann was a perfectly acceptable candidate; and the reasons for supporting him were significant. First of all, the Social Democrats hoped that support for Naumann would bring Left Liberal reciprocity in other districts. Secondly and most important, they throught that Naumann's ideas had significance for the nation as a whole and not for Württemberg alone. His election to the Reichstag would be a good chance to test his ideas on the national stage.[50] No one explicitly mentioned which of Naumann's ideas were most promising, but the Württemberg leadership was notoriously reformist, and it probably supported his plans for a liberal–Social Democratic rapprochement.

Elsewhere, the Social Democrats expressed grave disappointment with the Left Liberals in the elections of 1907. Hermann Molkenbuhr, a member of the Social Democratic executive committee whose copious diaries indicate many significant thoughts that were not expressed publicly, believed they had deserted their principles entirely by helping to elect thirty Conservatives to the Reichstag. According to him, they had abandoned "the possibility of creating a majority of the left" and had sold their souls to the government and the Conservatives, both of whom would cast them aside at the first opportunity.[51] Molkenbuhr's private remarks reflected two things. Whatever they might say publicly about bourgeois parties, many Social Democrats privately counted on some vague future cooperation with the Left Liberals. Left Liberal participation in the Bülow Bloc made the necessity of cooperation apparent, and the liberal turn to the right left the Social Democrats with a keen sense of isolation. Previously, the Left Liberal opposition

50. *SPD Württembergs, 1907*, pp. 19–20, 82, 93.
51. Molkenbuhr Diaries, January 2 and 5, 1907.

to the government, although separate from that of the Social Democrats, had provided them with moral support. The formation of the Bülow Bloc deprived the Social Democrats of their last bulwark against total political ostracism.

In addition, the desertion of the Left Liberals made the Social Democrats the only truly nonnational party at the same time that the election of 1907 indisputably proved the force of the "national question." Bebel had never been blind to the fact that reversals in German foreign policy negatively affected the government's policies toward the Social Democrats, but the decimation of the party in the Reichstag and the defection of the Left Liberals were an unexpected shock. The shock may have contributed to a partial rethinking of the party's stand on the national question. Within the Fraktion at least, a subtle change was noticeable. Soon after the formation of the Bülow Bloc, Eduard David, an acknowledged revisionist from Hesse, led a thorough discussion of the Fraktion's tactics in which Bebel frankly agreed with David. Although the minutes of the Fraktion's meeting did not pinpoint the exact tactical problems discussed, Gustav Noske later provided a clue in the Reichstag when, directly after a speech by Bülow warning about the dangers of encirclement, he forcefully stressed Social Democracy's willingness to defend the Fatherland against any attack.[52]

This speech was the subject of a heated debate at the party congress of 1907. There, the Social Democratic radicals claimed that it implied support for the existing reactionary, nationalistic system instead of adherence to socialist internationalist, democratic ideals. As Kautsky so aptly stated: "The German proletariat [should be] at one with the French proletariat and not . . . with the German firebrands and Junkers." In opposition to the radicals' emphasis on socialist principles, Noske's supporters revealed a preoccupation with the political advantages of support for the "national" question. Vollmar strongly applauded the speech and attacked the radicals' antimilitaristic views; a delegate from Kassel bluntly pronounced that Noske's speech had greatly helped Social Democratic recruitment in the provinces, and David pointed out similarities to previous statements of Bebel. If one

52. Bebel relates to Adler the effect of foreign policy in letter of September 16, 1905, *Briefwechsel*, p. 468. For Bebel's agreement with David, see *SPD Fraktionsprotokolle*, 1 : 183. For Noske's speech see *Verhandlungen des Reichstages*, 228 : 1098–1099.

criticized Noske, then one must also criticize Bebel. Bebel himself rose
to the challenge. After a short defense of Noske's speech, he addressed
himself to the main problem of the defense of the Fatherland:

> If we ever really must defend the Fatherland, we will defend it
> because it is our Fatherland, the earth on which we live, whose
> language we speak, whose customs we possess, because we want to
> make our Fatherland into a land which exists nowhere else in the
> world in such perfection (*Vollkommenheit*) and beauty. We defend
> this Fatherland not for but against [the existing regime]. . . .[53]

This spirited declaration of patriotism and national fervor was significant in its timing as well as its contents.

At least two radicals, Klara Zetkin and Karl Liebknecht, considered
Noske's speech a reaction to the defeat in the elections, and they argued
that the party should ignore the reversal at the polls and continue to
emphasize its international character.[54] Bebel and other supporters of
Noske avoided any discussion of the elections, but they also avoided
reiterating the standard internationalist phrases. This omission was a
clear indication that the Social Democrats had begun to forsake, if
they had not already forsaken, their former rigid stance in "national"
issues. In addition, the significant debate on Noske's speech occurred
after the German Social Democrats had disavowed the use of the mass
strike for preventing war and had opposed an anticolonialist resolution
at the International Congress of 1907.[55] This trend toward support for
or acceptance of nationalism was never reversed. The party had learned
its lesson in the elections of 1907, and later events proved that if a
choice had to be made between the party's popularity and the "national
question," popularity was the greater consideration.

The Social Democratic swing to the right followed hard on the heels
of the Left Liberal transformation into a national party. Thus one more
difference between the two parties was eliminated. Social Democratic
affirmation of national solidarity, its small bid for compromise in the
Vereinsgesetz, its repeated exhortations to the liberals to abandon the

53. The relevant portions of the debate can be found in *SPD Parteitag, 1907,* pp. 235,
247–250, 254–257, 262.
54. Ibid., pp. 247–250.
55. Carl Schorske, *German Social Democracy, 1905–1917: The Development of the Great
Schism* (Cambridge, Mass., 1955), pp. 79–85.

Bloc, all showed a desire to achieve a rapprochement with the liberals. In 1907, however, the Left Liberals were too preoccupied with the possibilities of political power to cultivate their previous partners in opposition. Despite their reservations about participation in the Bülow Bloc, they needed a thorough disappointment to renew their orientation toward the left. As we have seen, the events of 1908 increased their dissatisfaction with the government, but they continued to support the policy of the Bloc. Only at the end of 1908 did the Daily Telegraph Affair cause their first dissociation from support of the government and its policies.

LIBERAL OPPOSITION TO THE GOVERNMENT

In addition to Prussian suffrage reform and the Vereinsgesetz, there was an unspoken and deliberately undefined domestic issue that had existed since unification: the introduction of responsible parliamentary government. Unexpectedly, this issue appeared on the political scene in the aftermath of the Daily Telegraph Affair. In October, the English newspaper, the *Daily Telegraph*, printed an article combining several different conversations of the kaiser with his English "friends" which compromised Anglo-German relations and aroused great consternation throughout Germany. When questioned in the Reichstag, Bülow refrained from admitting that the article had appeared through his own administrative neglect, and the whole affair increased the existing dissatisfaction with the kaiser's "personal regime" and led to a constitutional crisis over the chancellor's responsibility. In order to prevent a future "affair," the chancellor had to be given more responsibility for the kaiser's political acts. Irresponsibility on the chancellor's part could be avoided if the Reichstag were to assume more control over his exercise of office. Such steps would necessitate a change in the imperial constitution and, because of the implication of parliamentary responsibility, would alter the political direction of the Reich.

Parliamentary responsibility was an ideal shared by all the German parties except the Conservatives. After unification, the Social Democrats were too weak and too isolated to achieve the ideal, and both Centre and liberals had not actively pursued it since the formulation of the German constitution. Bismarck's chancellorship was too strong to challenge, and since his replacement by weaker men, no single crisis or series of crises was serious enough to provoke the non-Conservative parties against

the chancellor. Yet the Daily Telegraph Affair and Bülow's neglect
provided such a crisis, and the Left Liberals decided to reactivate their
old demand for parliamentary responsibility. By doing so, they broke
with the government and the Bülow Bloc for the first time since 1907.
Their motivation is unclear, but their disappointment over the government's treatment of their liberal demands during 1908 probably contributed to their independence from the Bloc. In pressing for parliamentary responsibility, the Left Liberals once again combined with
their old partners on the left, the Social Democrats.

In order to prevent another "affair," both parties wanted to change
both the imperial constitution and the parliamentary rules of the Reichstag. The constitution provided only for the legal, not the political,
responsibility of the chancellor, and even this provision was so vaguely
worded that it did not state to whom the chancellor was responsible.
It made no provision for the Reichstag to check the chancellor in case of
a miscarriage of office. In addition, the Reichstag's parliamentary rules
made no provision for a censure of the chancellor. Only the kaiser, who
appointed the chancellor, could officially charge him with irresponsibility or imprudence. The Left Liberals and Social Democrats wanted to
remedy this state of affairs by changing the constitution to state explicitly that the chancellor was responsible for all actions of the kaiser
and that the Reichstag had the right to indict him before a high court
for "acts against the constitution . . . or the welfare of the Reich."
In the matter of the parliamentary rules, they agreed in principle that
censure motions could be attached to interpellations of the chancellor
in the Reichstag. The Social Democrats wanted to take the more
radical step of demanding the responsibility of the chancellor to the
Reichstag and its right to demand his dismissal, but the Left Liberals
recognized that this demand was too extreme for the existing situation.
They refused to support it, and the Social Democrats eventually accepted the Left Liberal limitation.[56]

The Social Democratic willingness to support the moderate Left
Liberal motion for constitutional and procedural change indicated two
different attitudes: they were willing to cooperate with the bourgeois

56. For the Social Democrats' motion, see *Verhandlungen des Reichstages,* 250: Drucksachen no. 1036, no. 1039, no. 1040, no. 1063, no. 1064; for their cooperation with the Left
Liberals, Ernst Müller-Meiningen and Georg Ledebour in ibid., 233 : 5905, 5920.

parties when the achievement of their program was at stake; and they accepted even a moderate or limited realization of this program. Nevertheless, the Social Democrats publicly doubted the Left Liberals' sincerity and willingness to risk their position in the Bülow Bloc by firmly opposing the government.[57] Stung by this suspicion, the Left Liberals answered that even were they to refuse their cooperation with the government in the pending tax legislation for the sake of constitutional reform, they could not count on Social Democratic support because party resolutions prohibited a Social Democratic vote for money bills. Until such time as the Social Democrats were ready to cooperate unequivocally in the work of the parliament, Left Liberal participation in the Bülow Bloc was the only possible course for the accomplishment of liberal purposes.[58] This exchange between the Left Liberals and the Social Democrats over the best way to achieve liberal, constitutional reform was very similar to the dialogue that accompanied the Vereinsgesetz. At the same time that the two parties spoke for their own members and the larger public, they seized the opportunity to upbraid the other for its failure to contribute to the country's liberalization. However, between the passage of the Vereinsgesetz and the demands for constitutional reform, a change in the position of both parties had occurred. By espousing an independent motion, the Left Liberals announced their increasing estrangement from the Bülow Bloc, and the Social Democrats recognized and encouraged this estrangement by supporting the Left Liberal posture.

Although the Left Liberals and Social Democrats agreed on constitutional reform, they needed the support of both Centre and National Liberals if they hoped to specify the responsibility of the chancellor. The Centre, though it agreed with constitutional reform in principle, wanted to avoid offending both government and Conservatives in the fall of 1908 in order to regain the influence it had lost since the formation of the Bülow Bloc. Nevertheless, it offered weak support to the leftist parties by introducing its own motion for a law (*not* a constitutional change) "to regulate . . . the responsibility of the Chancellor."[59] Given this loose agreement between left and Centre, the position of the

---

57. Georg Ledebour and Paul Singer in ibid., 233 : 5920–5921, 5951.
58. Friedrich Naumann in ibid., 233 : 5945.
59. Ibid., 250 : Drucksache no. 1037.

National Liberals became important because of the prestige they enjoyed with the government and because they would play a decisive role in any future decision to expand the powers of the Reichstag.

The National Liberals, and especially Bassermann, disliked the "personal regime" of Wilhelm II, and their consternation over the Daily Telegraph Affair inclined them toward change. Parliamentary responsibility was an old liberal demand, and the National Liberals had only discarded it at Bismarck's insistence.[60] Thus their liberal traditions, now in the process of revival, dictated some sort of support for the Left Liberal motion. Yet their devotion to the monarchical system and the need to consider their conservative right wing made them resistant to any far-reaching constitutional reform. While publicly warning the Left Liberals against endangering the Bloc, privately they debated the matter seriously. On November 25, a member of the party's left wing, Johannes Junck, presented the problem to the Fraktion. He himself favored some form of ministerial responsibility to the Reichstag and thought it consonant with the liberal traditions of the party, but he did not allow personal sentiments to influence his political judgment. In his eyes, the time was ripe for a law making the chancellor liable for impeachment in case of *unconstitutional* activities, but he thought that the government would hardly permit the Reichstag to influence his impeachment or dismissal in "political" matters. In other words, the Reichstag was not yet strong enough to force the resignation of a chancellor simply because it thought his policies detrimental to the "welfare of the Reich." At least it was not possible to achieve this change through specific laws or constitutional amendments. Junck argued that such an increase of parliamentary powers would result only in response to gradual pressures exerted by the Reichstag on the government. These considerations influenced the Fraktion in its decisions. The National Liberals followed Junck's advice inasmuch as they supported the Left Liberal motion making the chancellor responsible for the acts of the kaiser and endorsed a change in the parliamentary rules, but they rejected the idea of impeachment altogether. The National Liberals were not yet ready to question the powers or the wisdom of the monarchy.[61]

60. Ludwig Bergsträsser, *Geschichte der politischen Parteien in Deutschland,* ed. W. Mommsen, 11th ed. (Munich, 1965), p. 106.
61. For Junck's argument, see Fraktion meeting, November 25, 1908, NL Akten, R 45

In 1908 this reluctance hardly affected the course of events. The motions for change were referred to the Reichstag's Rules Committee, where they presumably died under pressure from the government. The incident was important only because it showed the National Liberals' willingness to consider gradual constitutional change. It also showed the impact of the drive to "reliberalize" the party that had occurred since the turn of the century. National Liberal arguments and actions, particularly those of the left wing, agreed considerably with the radical aims of the Left Liberals and even with the Social Democrats. Moreover, their willingness to cooperate with the parties of the left, to the exclusion of the Conservatives, also implied their own growing dissatisfaction with the Bülow Bloc.

TAX REFORM

This hint of National Liberal dissatisfaction was portentous for an important measure facing the Bülow Bloc in 1909: tax reform. In the years before the turn of the century, the needs of the central government had increased to such an extent that it resorted to more and more loans in order to meet these needs. It was the need to redeem these loans and find additional revenue in the first decade of the twentieth century that led to tax reform. Until 1906, the central government's revenue consisted of indirect taxes levied on consumer goods such as beer, tobacco, and liquor, and contributions, determined by the size of the population, by the several states (*Matrikularbeiträge*). Although it was not explicitly denied the central government in the imperial constitution, the right of direct taxation was assigned to the states, and they defended this right with vigor. Nevertheless, the situation by 1906 was so pressing that the tax reform of that year introduced, for the first time, a direct, imperial inheritance tax levied on individual bequests of the deceased. Although this tax provided financial relief at the time, it was clear that the central government needed to tap more sources of revenue in the future. It was the kind of tax—direct or indirect—that posed the problem.

The problem arose because of the severe differences among the German parties and particularly among the parties of the Bülow Bloc over taxation. The Conservatives opposed a direct, imperial tax because it infringed on states' rights. This Conservative objection

1/9; for result, see Fraktion meeting, December 1, 1908, NL Akten, R 45 1/9.

was not important in principle; it was necessary to protect their constituents' interests. Once the principle of direct imperial taxation were admitted, the Reichstag, increasingly dominated by liberal and democratic financial, commercial, and industrial elements, would supersede the taxing power of the Prussian legislature where Conservative agricultural interests still had the upper hand.[62] Thus the problem of taxation reflected the conflict between the old and new economic interests described in another context by Weber and Naumann. Because its members represented both sides of the conflict, tax reform would be the most exacting task faced by the Bülow Bloc.

These internal problems were further exacerbated by the position of the Centre. In 1906, the Centre, with an eye to its trade-union support, had insisted on the direct inheritance tax as a substitute for higher indirect taxes. But since the formation of the Bülow Bloc, the Centre had resented the displacement of its influence by the liberals, and the divergence between Conservatives and liberals over taxation gave it a chance to recoup its former loss. Because the Centre's landed interests also desired to protect agriculture from additional direct taxation, the Centrists could easily accommodate the Conservatives in 1908/09.

Here the anomaly of the Centre appears once again. Although its industrial elements urged a policy aligned with the left in matters such as the Vereinsgesetz, its landed aristocrats and large peasant constituency favored an alignment with the right in fiscal issues. As the representative of the broad spectrum of German society, the Centre could pivot back and forth between right and left. In 1908 the desire for power dictated a swing to the right. If the Centre supported the Conservative stand on taxation, it could regain its importance in German politics.[63] As a result, a majority of Conservatives and Centre would be ranged against the liberals and the Social Democrats, all of whom favored some sort of direct, national tax.

62. A good modern account of the Reich's financial history and the conflict over tax reform in the years before 1908–09 is Peter-Christian Witt, *Die Finanzpolitik des deutschen Reiches von 1903 bis 1913: Eine Studie zur Innenpolitik des wilhelminischen Deutschlands,* vol. 415 of *Historische Studien,* ed. W. Berges et al. (Lübeck and Hamburg, 1970), pp. 17ff. Also Wilhelm Gerloff, *Die Finanz-und-Zollpolitik des deutschen Reiches* (Jena, 1913), pp. 399–401, 427–428, 439; and Edwin R. A. Seligman, *Essays in Taxation,* 10th rev. ed (New York, 1925), pp. 343, 473–480, 499–500.

63. Witt, *Die Finanzpolitik,* pp. 123–131, 231, 234. Also for the Centre's importance both in the tax reform and the strengthening of the Reichstag, Manfred Rauh, *Föderalismus und Parlamentarismus im wilhelminischen Reich* (Düsseldorf, 1973), pp. 245 ff.

The National Liberals, who had faithfully voted the taxes needed by the government for over two decades, had received such stinging criticism for their approval of indirect taxes in 1906 that they had changed their party program the next year to include a demand for direct taxes. This change then posed another problem: what kind of direct tax should be levied? The rural, landed members of the National Liberal party objected to any extension of the inheritance tax that would affect agricultural capital. The Young Liberals, in close agreement with the Social Democrats, demanded a national income tax as the most equitable for a modern state. The leadership, including both Bassermann and Friedberg, favored a general tax on property which would affect both landed and industrial wealth equally and thereby balance the claims and the interests of the National Liberal constituency.[64] In demanding a tax on property, the National Liberal leadership agreed substantially with the Left Liberal position. The Left Liberals had always opposed indirect taxes because they interfered with freedom of trade and burdened consumers, and they favored a tax on property because of its elasticity. In supporting direct taxation the liberals veered leftward toward the Social Democrats, who advocated direct taxation and were equally well-disposed toward an inheritance, property, or income tax.[65] Thus in the matter of the tax reform the liberals and the Conservatives held diametrically opposing views, and if no compromise between the two were found, the days of the Bülow Bloc were numbered.

The situation was particularly unfavorable for the Bloc since its members had known from the very beginning that tax reform presented an obstacle to their cooperative effort. The secretary of the treasury, Sydow, aware of the conflict between liberals and Conservatives over taxes, accepted the task of preparing the reform bill only if he had absolute freedom in acquiring a majority for the passage of the bill. In September 1908, during the bill's preparation, Sydow invited the Centre to discuss its wishes for reform with the government[66] and thereby implicitly informed the liberals that their cooperation with the Con-

---

64. Ilse Hennicke, *Die Rolle der Erbschaftssteuer in der Steuerpolitik der grossen politischen Parteien* (doctoral diss., Heidelberg, 1929), pp. 41–42; Curt Köhler, *Der Jungliberalismus* (Cologne, 1912), p. 35. Cf. Eschenburg, *Das Kaiserreich,* pp. 85, 97, 195.

65. Hennicke, *Die Rolle der Erbschaftssteuer,* pp. 86–89, 106ff.

66. DZAP, Broemel Papers, Vereinigung's executive committee meeting, September 24, 1908.

servatives and the government, at least in the tax reform, had become dispensable. The government's attitude may also have determined the liberals' actions during the Daily Telegraph Affair. Certainly there were frequent references to the tax reform in the debates on constitutional change. Also, the Left Liberals were the first to take the hint that the government no longer needed or depended on the Bülow Bloc, and they decided, as early as September, not to regard tax reform as an integral part of the policy of the Bloc.[67] This decision signified their willingness to abandon the Bloc entirely unless their demands on taxation were met. They determined that their main concern was not the maintenance of the Bloc, but the security of the embryonic Left Liberal unity. As for the National Liberals, even their conservative leader, Friedberg, informed the government that the National Liberals would refuse cooperation unless a direct tax were included.[68] This nascent liberal opposition to the government signaled the impending collapse of the Bloc. But the government was not yet ready to proclaim the Bloc a corpse; Bülow had staked his chancellorship on the passage of a direct tax, and he fully intended to attempt a compromise between the liberals and Conservatives.

Yet the government bill made the task of compromise among the parties of the Bloc even more difficult. It called for a total yearly income of 500 million RM; 80 per cent would come from indirect taxes and 20 per cent from an inheritance tax on entire estates instead of a tax on individual inheritances. The government had chosen an inheritance tax in deference to the Bundesrat, which opposed the property tax suggested by the National Liberals because it would deprive the states of an important source of revenue.[69] Initially the Left Liberals were the only Bloc members who indicated any willingness to go along with the government's plan. The Conservatives continued to oppose any direct national tax including the estate tax. The National Liberals therefore became the pivotal party in the tax reform: would they compromise or would they persist in demanding a property tax?

67. The conflict over tax reform, not only among the participants of the Bülow Bloc, but also between the Reich and the individual states, and between himself and the Prussian finance minister, Paul von Rheinbaben, had caused Sydow's predecessor, Hermann von Stengel, to resign in despair, Witt, *Die Finanzpolitik*, pp. 188, 200–201; also see Naumann to Haussmann, September 22, 1908, Haussmann Papers.

68. Eschenburg, *Das Kaiserreich*, p. 85.

69. For Sydow's preparation of the bill, Witt, *Die Finanzpolitik*, pp. 199–249; also Seligman, *Essays in Taxation*, pp. 500–502.

The National Liberals refused to compromise; they decided to insist on a general property tax, and they spoke accordingly in the Reichstag.[70] They maintained this stance during the month of February 1909 when direct taxation was finally debated in two specially created tax committees. Although the committees tried to find some compromise satisfactory to all the parties of the Bloc, by the middle of the month, all types of direct taxes had been rejected through one or the other combination of parties or by the Bundesrat. Throughout the deliberations, both Conservative and National Liberal positions hardened. The Conservatives continually rejected any national direct tax; the National Liberals firmly adhered to a national tax on property. Even when the Conservatives agreed to a direct tax on individual inheritances (in contrast to the whole estate), the National Liberals rejected it.[71] Yet despite their differences of opinion and the intransigeance of Conservatives and National Liberals, it might have been possible to work out some sort of compromise on direct taxes had there not been disagreement over the indirect taxes on liquor.

All the parties of the Bloc agreed with the government plan to raise the tax on liquor, but the Conservatives and the Centre opposed a tax that would eventually affect consumption and prove harmful to the small distillers who supported their parties. Existing law already provided for the central government's payment of a certain fixed sum (*Liebesgabe*) to distillers to compensate for the loss of business caused by the tax. This Liebesgabe acted as an agricultural subsidy and the liberals, who bitterly opposed it, wanted to decrease the amount paid. During the discussion in committee, both Centre and Conservatives voted to maintain the sum paid to distillers. The liberals voted against them.[72] At this point, the agrarian Conservatives, who found the agrarian Centre a much more agreeable partner in the matter of taxation, lost patience. Confronted with National Liberal intransigeance in the issue of direct taxes and National Liberal opposition to the Liebesgabe, the Conservative leader, Oskar von Normann, met with Bassermann on

70. Fraktion meeting, November 13, 1908, NL Akten, R 45 1/9; *Verhandlungen des Reichstages,* 233 : 5624.

71. Fraktion meetings, February 8 and 17, March 3, 1909, NL Akten, R 45 1/9. See Witt, *Die Finanzpolitik,* pp. 265–270.

72. The tax on liquor and the Liebesgabe was as much a hornet's nest as the imperial direct tax, Witt, *Die Finanzpolitik,* pp. 46–49, 97–99, 271–272; Seligman, *Essays on Taxation,* pp. 502–503; for the vote, see Fraktion meeting, February 8, 1909, NL Akten R 45 1/9; *Verhandlungen des Reichstages,* 237 : 8649–8650.

March 24 to tell him that the Conservatives no longer considered the Bloc a functioning unit for the tax reform. In effect, the Conservatives deserted the Bloc because they refused to compromise their economic interests. Thereafter they disregarded all further attempts of either the government or the liberals to find a compromise on the direct tax. Both they and the Centre high-handedly pushed a proposal through the budget committee which raised existing indirect taxes and levied a one-sided tax on nonagricultural property; and at the beginning of July, they passed their reform through the Reichstag. On July 14, Bülow resigned. His Bloc had collapsed, his tax reform was defeated, he had lost the support of the influential Conservatives, and he had failed to inspire the continued confidence of the kaiser.[73]

THE END OF THE BÜLOW BLOC

Nominally, Bülow's resignation meant the end of his attempt to combine the Conservative and liberal spirits of Germany. This experiment had failed once before, with the resignation of Caprivi, and the failure had led to a resumption of Conservative policies. Would history repeat itself? Immediately before the creation of the Bülow Bloc, the Conservatives had dominated German politics through an alliance with the Centre. We have seen that the Centre was shunted out of its advantageous position because it was too presumptuous. In 1909, the liberals were dropped for much the same reason, but their loss was the Centre's gain. The Centre had seen its opportunity to regain a modicum of influence by offering the Conservatives its support in the tax reform, and this alliance benefited the Centre's conservative agrarian wing. The old combination of Conservatives and Centre became the new governmental majority; its popular name was the Black and Blue Bloc, black for the clerical Centre, blue for the Prussian Conservatives. It would be a mistake, however, to assume that the government intended to rely completely on the "knights and the clerics." German life had become much too complex for such a simple solution to its problems, and the new Chancellor Bethmann Hollweg realized this fact too. He

73. For the Conservatives' desertion of the Bloc, see Eschenburg, *Das Kaiserreich,* pp. 215–216. On efforts at compromise, see Fraktion meetings, March 24, April 27, May 4, 1909, NL Akten R 45 1/9; *Verhandlungen des Reichstages,* 256: Drucksache no. 1455, 1–3. For the Conservative-Centrist action, see Seligman, *Essays on Taxation,* pp. 501ff; Witt, *Die Finanzpolitik,* pp. 273–299. On Bülow's resignation, see Bülow, *Memoirs,* 2 : 565ff.

was appointed first minister of the Reich in order to continue Bülow's attempt to find a resolution of Germany's political problems.[74] Thus Bülow's resignation involved a change of personalities rather than a change of policies.

Theobald von Bethmann Hollweg seemed eminently suited for the task of combining the old and new orders. His family background was neither Junker nor Catholic, and it included members of the commercial and financial circles of the free city of Frankfurt. His grandfather, Moritz August, was a constitutional liberal and Prussian *Kultusminister* during the "New Era" and had left the Prussian ministry when Bismarck became minister-president. His father, Felix, had purchased an estate in Brandenburg where his Swiss mother gave birth to Theobald. The young man, Theobald, entered the Prussian civil service in 1881 and rose swiftly through the ranks during the eras of Bismarck and Wilhelm II. His extraordinary industry and intelligence helped to single him out as a man with a promising future. In 1899 he became the youngest person ever selected as *Oberpräsident* of the Mark Brandenburg and won a reputation for skillfully mediating the conflicts among the various interest groups of that rapidly urbanizing area. In 1905, he was appointed Prussian minister of the interior and in 1907 he replaced the famous social reformer, Posadowsky, as the imperial secretary of the interior and deputy chancellor. In these positions, he was responsible for supervising the formulation of certain political and social reform bills that came before the Reichstag soon after his appointment as chancellor. As a politician and as a human being, he was more compatible with the liberals than with the Conservatives. A studious and introverted man, he possessed that quality of *Bildung* or intellectual cultivation and refinement which was most admired by certain middle-class Germans. Because this quality was manifest in his public speeches and activities, the Prussian Conservatives dubbed him the "Philosopher." Others have called him a model civil servant with the implication that he lacked the qualities of statesmanship. He has been variously described as

74. For these and subsequent data on Bethmann Hollweg, see Eberhard von Vietsch, *Bethmann Hollweg: Staatsmann zwischen Macht und Ethos* (Boppard, 1969), and Konrad Jarausch, *The Enigmatic Chancellor: Bethmann Hollweg and the Hubris of Imperial Germany* (New Haven, 1973). Also Fritz Stern, "Bethmann Hollweg and the War: The Limits of Responsibility," *The Responsibility of Power,* ed. L. Krieger and F. Stern (New York, Anchor Books, 1969), pp. 274–282, and Hans-Günter Zmarzlik, *Bethmann Hollweg als Reichskanzler, 1909–1914* (Düsseldorf, 1957).

"kind, intelligent, and honest" with a "contemplative" breadth of "vision."[75] Certainly he understood or tried to understand more about the German lower classes than any previous chancellor. He was the first chancellor ever to hold an extraparliamentary conversation with August Bebel. At the time Bebel was sick and dying, but the extraordinary event caused the Social Democratic leader to blush and give a special explanation to the visitor who witnessed it.[76] Bethmann Hollweg genuinely believed it necessary to integrate the Social Democrats into the existing political and social structure. He resembled Naumann, Barth, the Young Liberals, and others who recognized the declining radicalism of the working classes and desired more cooperation between the working classes and the rest of German society. When he became chancellor, Bethmann Hollweg was no democrat, but he himself later wrote that a continued "conservative policy in the Reich was . . . an impossibility."[77] Already as Prussian minister of the interior, he had decided that Prussian suffrage reform was the only means of ensuring the survival of Prussia and Germany. But he was not prepared to ignore Conservative influence in the determination of governmental policy. Instead he tried, as Bülow had done, to seek a modus vivendi between the old Conservatives straining to maintain their power and the "new liberal-radical" forces that challenged them. In 1909 this task demanded that Bethmann Hollweg understand the National Liberals in order to conciliate them.

Throughout the negotiations over the tax bill, the National Liberals had shown little inclination to compromise with the Conservatives. What caused them, after years of cooperation with both the government and the Conservatives, to drop their role as a governmental party and become an opposition party? Certainly part of the reason was their conviction that Bülow and the Conservatives had made few concessions to the liberals within the context of the Bloc. National Liberal disappointment began with the plans for the Prussian suffrage reform. In August 1907 Bassermann had visited Bülow at Norderney and dis-

75. Eugen Schiffer, *Ein Leben für den Liberalismus* (Berlin-Grünewald, 1951), pp. 189–191; Ernst Müller-Meiningen, *Parlamentarismus: Betrachtungen, Lehren, und Erinnerungen aus deutschen Parlamenten* (Berlin, 1926), p. 167.

76. Gustav Mayer, *Erinnerungen: Vom Journalisten zum Historiker der deutschen Arbeiterbewegung* (Munich, 1949), p. 179.

77. Theobald von Bethmann Hollweg, *Betrachtungen zum Weltkrieg,* 2 vols. (Berlin, 1919), 1: 98.

covered that the government planned only minimal liberal concessions.[78] Government officials in contact with the National Liberals immediately after this discussion reported Bassermann's reaction:

> Just now a rather deeply-rooted transformation is occurring within the National Liberal party. Bassermann is deeply upset. . . . The National Liberals will certainly never deny any national demand, . . . whether the Bloc exists or not, ... but they do not want to cooperate in Prussia any longer under any circumstances. They have had enough of playing the governmental party which has nothing to say. . . .[79]

There were others who shared Bassermann's estrangement from the government and the Bloc. One Prussian National Liberal confided to a government administrator that he was "personally offended and annoyed" by the government's handling of National Liberal interests and believed that "the chancellor does nothing for his friends." Since 1907, the government had done little to bolster the sagging hopes of the National Liberals. In the matter of the tax reform particularly, it ignored the National Liberal need to do justice to both their landed and their industrial constituency and favored the economic interests of the agrarians. At the same time relations between the National Liberals and the Agrarian League deteriorated, and this circumstance affected their cooperation with the Conservatives. During the deliberations on the tax reform, the Agrarian League launched a vigorous propaganda campaign against the National Liberals and accompanied a by-election in the rural district of Norden with slanderous polemics against them. The campaign directly influenced the National Liberal Fraktion's decision to sever the party's connections with the League, and since the League was directly connected with the Conservatives, this breach only hastened the National Liberal withdrawal from the Bülow Bloc.[80]

When the National Liberals withdrew from the Bloc, they found themselves in concert with the Left Liberals and Social Democrats, and Naumann immediately proclaimed a "future majority from Bebel to

78. Eschenburg, *Das Kaiserreich,* p. 81.

79. DZAP, Reichskanzlei, Parteien 1/3, 1, no. 1393, Privy Councillor Richard Witting to Chamberlain Paul von Roell, August 21, 1907.

80. For the National Liberals' loss of faith in the government, see DZAP, Reichskanzlei, Parteien 1/3 1, no. 1393, Roell to Privy Councillor Scheefer, August 27, 1907; Puhle, *Agrarische Interessenpolitik,* pp. 193ff ; Fraktion meeting, March 9, 1909, NL Akten, R 45 1/9.

Bassermann." Certainly the liberal and the Social Democratic stand on taxes coincided to a remarkable degree, and during the committee deliberations, the Left Liberals consulted with the Social Democrats in violation of the Bloc arrangement and with a view toward future cooperation. The Social Democrats heightened the appearance of unity by voting for a limited inheritance tax, supported by the liberals in the first two plenary readings, as a last attempt at compromise, but the Social Democrats were not particular about the type of direct tax they approved. Throughout the committee negotiations, they supported the inheritance and the property tax equally, and they never committed themselves to a positive vote for the inheritance tax in a third plenary reading. The National Liberals quickly noted this Social Democratic lack of firmness and discrimination. They wanted to avoid any hint of cooperation with the Social Democrats, and they publicly opposed the idea of a bloc from Bassermann to Bebel. The appearance of unity arose from the fact that the Social Democrats chose to identify their own position with that of the liberals. Once they decided to renounce their former opposition to all money bills, they were driven to the side of the liberals by the final Conservative refusal to negotiate an equitable direct tax. Social Democratic dependence on the liberals manifested itself clearly in their decision not to filibuster against the indirect taxes in the Reichstag because they lacked liberal support. Thus the Social Democrats, and not the National Liberals, actively increased the chances for cooperation in a bloc of the left.[81]

For their part, the National Liberals wanted to remain independent. Their leap into the opposition was a new experience which they wanted to explore and exploit alone. Bassermann wanted to change the direction of the party, but neither he nor others felt it could become purely anti-governmental. One of the most penetrating analyses of the party's position in 1909 was written in mid-December by the young Eugen Schiffer, future Weimar Democrat and justice minister, in a letter to the self-appointed liaison with the government, Hutten-Czapski:

81. For Naumann's observation, see *Hilfe* 15 (1909) : 211. The Left Liberals' cooperation is implied in letter of Payer to Wiemer, June 2, 1909, Haussmann Papers. For the National Liberals' resistance to a bloc, see Fraktion meeting, May 4, 1909, NL Akten R 45 1/9; Ernst Bassermann in *Verhandlungen des Reischtages,* 236 : 7842. The Social Democratic decision occurred at the Fraktion meeting, July 7, 1909, *SPD Fraktionsprotokolle,* 1 : 216.

I do not believe that any dominant instance of the National Liberal party would want to place the party in the sulking corner or recommend to it a policy of aggravation, of negation, or of opposition at any price. We do not think of needlessly urging the right more and more toward the Centre. . . .

This Reichstag was elected in order to promote conservative-liberal politics; it has dispensed with its inner justifications in the minds of the people since this foundation has been shattered. Misplaced is worse than unprotected trust. . . .

The reversal of the National Liberals would benefit neither themselves, the Fatherland, nor the government. [The government] only has an interest in support from a strong National Liberal party. One must, . . . in the judgment and evaluation of the entire political situation, always keep in mind that the parliament is not the people and the Fraktion is not the party. An altered attitude of the National Liberals would perhaps make it easier for the government to finish the parliamentary business, but its position in and to the people would not improve but deteriorate. . . .

The . . . Chancellor [Bethmann Hollweg] has also urged practical work in opposition to fruitless arguments over the past. I agree with him, but on the condition that it must be work which does not employ merely the Fraktionen and special interests, but the people in its breadth and depth; a work which . . . leads to a new arrangement of parties, not merely of Fraktionen."[82]

The tone of the letter had much in common with Naumann's idealism. It neither opposed nor supported the government, but it manifested a new dedication to "the people," a renewed consideration for the democratic forces which partially determine the course of any modern state. The National Liberals would not become a democratic party, but they could act with greater appreciation of democratic demands. In this case, the new direction of the National Liberals could increase the chances for cooperation with the Social Democrats and for a nebulous bloc from Bassermann to Bebel.

82. Bogdan, Graf von Hutten-Czapski, *Sechzig Jahre Politik und Gesellschaft,* 2 vols. (Berlin, 1936), 2 : 8–10.

Part II: The Grand Bloc

4

The Baden Grand Bloc

Local politics are often a testing ground for measures and tactics later adopted on a national level, and when new ideas emerge in a time of change, it is often wise to look for their initial implementation on the local level. Thus events in the small state of Baden when the Bülow Bloc collapsed merited the attention of all who hoped for a change of political direction in the Reich. As a South German state, Baden had a well-developed tradition of constitutional and parliamentary government dating back to the early nineteenth century, and its exemplary liberal politics earned it the affectionate title of *Musterländle* or model state. Most of the important issues of nineteenth-century German history—national unity, liberal government, even the Kulturkampf—had first been thrashed out in the Baden Landtag. At the time of unification, the Grand Duke of Baden had urged Bismarck to adopt a more liberal constitution, and although he failed to convince Bismarck, the Iron Chancellor did not prevent him from appointing liberal ministers in his own state who worked in real cooperation with the National Liberal majority in the Landtag.

During the decade of the nineties, however, this liberal regime was threatened by the growing power of the Centre, which began to gain more seats in the legislature and, at the same time, sponsored a popular movement for suffrage reform. In a state with a Catholic majority, the Centre reasoned that a more equitable suffrage would give it a legislative majority which would lead to the appointment of Centrist ministers and the initiation of Centrist policies. All these plans and actions were, of course, part of the wider democratic movement within the party and the desire of middle-class Catholics to counteract political and social discrimination. The corresponding movement in the Reich led, as we have seen, to the formation of the Bülow Bloc. Baden, however, was not the Reich; the Grand Duke was not the kaiser, nor were his ministers the conservative imperial government. Thus the suffrage movement found a hearing in the Baden ministries, and in 1904 a bill for direct and equal suffrage was introduced and passed through the Landtag.[1] Its passage made Baden the most liberal, democratic state in Germany. The National Liberals voted for reform, after much political soul-searching, although their affirmative vote definitely threatened the political domination of the National Liberals in the legislature and the liberal regime in force since unification. In addition, many National Liberals feared that a Centrist majority and Centrist ministers would reverse the secularization of cultural life—artistic and academic freedom, separation of church and schools—which they had gradually introduced into Baden throughout the previous thirty years.[2]. These latter fears were shared by the Left Liberals and the Social Democrats, and after the reform of 1904, the National Liberals turned toward these parties on the left for help in the fight against the Centre.

For the National Liberals in Baden, a leftward shift was no difficult task. They were probably the most democratic branch of their party and shared many political goals with the Left Liberals. In the years before the suffrage reform, their democratic attitudes were strengthened by their desire to transform themselves into a mass party, able to compete with both Centre and Social Democrats, and by the activities of the Baden Young Liberals. Although the Young Liberals had their own state organization, they were members of the local National Liberal clubs, sat on the state executive committee, and exercised considerable influence over the state party as a whole. They played a leading role in the party's adoption of suffrage reform, and they urged a united front with the Left Liberals. The Left Liberals, a small and relatively insignificant group, were receptive to liberal cooperation, and by the beginning of 1905, the National Liberals made their first alliance with the left by negotiating an election agreement that eliminated competition with the Left Liberals throughout the state.[3]

1. Friedrich W. von Rauchhaupt, *Handbuch der deutschen Wahlgesetze und Geschäftsordnung* (Munich, 1916), p. 81.

2. Josef Schofer, *Zehn Jahre badischer Schulkämpfe,* 4th ed. (Freiburg i. Breisgau, 1911). Also Karl Bachem, *Vorgeschichte, Geschichte und Politik der deutschen Zentrumspartei,* 8 vols. (Cologne, 1927–1931), 8 : 155.

3. For the National Liberals' move to the left, see Ziegler to Fröser, January 25, 1905,

Since this liberal agreement occurred in the year before the formation of the Bülow Bloc, it was the first such comprehensive cooperation between the two liberal groups. Advocates and supporters of liberal unity promptly dubbed the agreement the "Bloc" and became the first to employ the term in reference to German political arrangements. Previously, the word used to denote cooperation between parties was "Kartell," as in the Conservative–National Liberal alliance during the Reichstag of 1887–1890, and we have seen that Barth employed this term when he first advocated a rapprochement between liberals and Social Democrats. After the turn of the century, the liberals substituted the words *"Zusammengehen"* or *"Zusammenschluss"*—going or fusing together—when describing an alliance of the left, presumably because of the conservative connotations of the word "Kartell." The term "Block" first occurred in Wilhelm Kulemann's pamphlet, *Zusammenschluss der Liberalen*, which appeared in 1905 just after the conclusion of the liberal Baden negotiations. Kulemann was an older gentleman, with a long career on the left wing of the National Liberal party, who was greatly influenced by Naumann's national-democratic ideals. Later in the year, Naumann's weekly, *Hilfe*, placed quotation marks around the word "Block" in order to emphasize its relatively novel use in German politics. At the time, a bloc was the name given to French governmental coalitions, and its adoption into German was both an imitation of the French terminology and a wishful envy of the power enjoyed by the French parliamentary parties. It signified the desire of German liberals for the same kind of legislative influence enjoyed by their French counterparts. When used in reference to the liberal election agreement in Baden, it expressed the intention of further cooperation in the Landtag.[4]

In order to become a truly legislative bloc, however, the liberals had

---

NL Baden; for the Young Liberals' influence, E. Rebmann et al., *Das Grossherzogthum Baden* (Karlsruhe, 1912), p. 1099. See also the election campaign program of the Young Liberals in the minutes of the state executive committee meeting, September 20, 1903, and the record of the state committee meeting, September 27, 1903 in NL Baden. For liberal unity, see Ludwig Haas, *Die Einigung des Liberalismus und der Demokratie* (Frankfurt / Main, 1905), pp. 14–15; Wilhelm Kulemann, *Der Zusammenschluss der Liberalen* (Dresden, 1905), pp. 33–35. The copy of the agreement between the National and Left Liberals is dated December 9, 1904, NL Baden.

4. For the introduction of "Zusammengehen," see *Hilfe* 8, no. 52 (December 1902) : 1; *Die Nation* 19 (1903) : 226. Compare with Kulemann, *Zusammenschluss*, p, 38, and *Hilfe* 9, no. 29 (July 23, 1905) : 2, for the origins of "Block." For Kulemann's role in the National Liberal party, see his *Politische Erinnerungen* (Berlin, 1911), pp. 152–197.

to win elections, and this feat proved harder than they expected. In the general Baden election held on October 19, 1905, they won relatively few seats in the legislature. Only 14 National Liberals and 2 Left Liberals were elected by absolute majority, while the Centre captured 28 seats. Yet all was not lost. In Baden as in other states, the law required a runoff election in all districts where one candidate had not received a clear majority. In 1905, runoff elections were scheduled in 23 districts.[5] Although the National Liberals had lost their traditional majority and were in danger of losing control of the Landtag to the Centre, it was possible for the liberals to defeat the Centre if they included another partner in their political alliance.

Given the circumstances in Baden, the most logical partner for the liberals was Social Democracy. The Social Democrats in Baden were the least threatening to law and order of all the branches of the party. More liberal in social and political life and less industrialized than Prussia or Saxony, Baden hardly experienced the bitter social and political conflicts of the German north. Because of their differences from the north, the Social Democrats in Baden guarded their independence from the national leadership in Berlin and had already invoked its wrath by voting for the state budget. The moderation of the state's party once led the minister of the interior to say that he would "not like to miss the representatives of Social Democracy in the legislature," and even the National Liberals admitted that Social Democratic demands for the improvement of working conditions were justified. The state party's spokesman, Wilhelm Kolb, was a leading reformist, and he realized that until Social Democracy was large and strong enough to command a majority in the legislature, it would have to ally with other parties. Before the elections of 1905, he publicly declared his party's willingness to conclude an agreement with the liberals on the basis of reciprocal support. The demand for reciprocity was important. Social Democrats frequently voted for liberals in the runoff elections, but a liberal vote, and particularly a National Liberal one, for a Social Democrat was extremely rare. A reciprocal agreement therefore implied a formal recognition of an alliance.[6]

5. Josef Schofer, *Grossblock-Bilanz: Zeitgemässe politische Erinnerungen* (Freiburg i. Breisgau, 1913), pp. 6–7.

6. On the special characteristics of the Baden Social Democrats, see Carl Schorske, *German Social Democracy, 1905–1917: The Development of the Great Schism* (Cambridge, Mass., 1955), p. 25; Anton Weissmann, *Die Sozialdemokratische Gefahr in Baden* (Freiburg i. Breisgau, 1912), pp. 60–61; Kulemann, *Zusammenschluss,* pp. 33–35. For Kolb's biography,

Since an alliance with the Social Democrats violated all their traditions, the National Liberals initially balked at such a step. But under prodding from the Young Liberals, they began to consider the idea seriously. The state executive committee discussed the possibility of alliance, and although there was no precipitate rush toward the Social Democrats, by election time in 1905, the National Liberals had clearly decided to steer toward cooperation. During the general election, the liberals dampened the campaign against the Social Democrats in districts where liberal support for the Social Democrats was likely in the runoff elections. By the same token, Left Liberal candidates were also placed in those districts where Social Democratic support for the liberals in the runoff was likely. No negotiations with the Social Democrats occurred before the general election, but the liberals clearly set the scene for cooperation. On the day after the general election (October 20), three representatives of the liberal bloc unofficially visited Kolb to sound him out about an agreement for the runoff election. He gave a positive answer, and the responsible members of the bloc met together the next day to make the irrevocable decision to support the Social Democrats. On October 22, liberals and Social Democrats wrangled over terms and two days later signed the contract promising mutual election support. In five districts, the liberals withdrew their candidates in favor of the Social Democrats; in reciprocation, the Social Democrats withdrew their candidates in favor of the liberals in twelve districts; in six districts the two groups decided to fight it out. The results of this agreement proved it worthwhile; in the runoff elections on October 27 and 28, the Centre received no new mandates at all. Thereafter the Baden legislature contained 28 Centre and 3 Conservative representatives—the so-called right—and 23 National Liberals, 6 Left Liberals, and 12 Social Democrats—the so-called left. Despite the division into right and left, the real antagonists in the legislature were the Centre and the National Liberals, and the balance of mandates between the two parties was such that if the National Liberals wanted to block any proposal of the Centre, they would have to turn to the Social Democrats for help.[7]

---

see Franz Osterroth, *Biographisches Lexicon des Sozialismus*, vol. I: *Verstorbene Persönlichkeiten* (Hanover, 1960), p. 167. On the 1905 agreement, see *Hilfe* 10, no. 48 (November 27, 1904) : 2.

7. *Hilfe* 11, no. 29 (July 23, 1905) : 2 and no. 44 (November 5, 1905) : 4, reported the preparations made by the liberals prior to the election. The report is corroborated and the

Thus the National Liberals took steps to extend the cooperation established during the elections into the legislature. They formed a legislative bloc with the Left Liberals and prepared to deprive the Centre of the politically valuable post of Landtag president. In order to get their own candidate elected, the liberals once again solicited the votes of the Social Democrats, and once again, the Social Democrats insisted on reciprocity. They would vote for a liberal president if the liberals would vote for a Social Democratic vice-president. This willingness to accept a vice-presidential post was unprecedented and significant since the Dresden resolution had forbidden a Social Democrat to make the appearance at court that customarily accompanied the office. In 1905 the Baden Social Democrats had no intention of violating the Dresden resolution, and by demanding representation in the praesidium, they presented the National Liberals with the dilemma of reconciling their need for votes with Social Democracy's offensive antimonarchical principle. The National Liberals did not shy away from the bait. They posed only one important condition for their reciprocal vote: the Social Democratic vice-president must "resign himself in a tactful way to the exercise of the court duties" that accompanied the office. The operative word in this reply was "tactful," and the National Liberals never explained what it meant. The formulation was vague enough to prevent a violation of their own monarchical principle, but it also allowed for a compromise with the Social Democrats. Nevertheless, the compromise was not an easy one. The "exercise of court duties," even if performed in a "tactful way," still involved an offense against the Dresden resolution that could cause a serious altercation with the national party. After a sober caucus of the Fraktion, the Social Democrats finally agreed that their candidate, Adolf Geck, would fufilll all duties stipulated by the constitution and parliamentary procedure, and that "he would not disturb any additional contact of the other presidents with the court through any kind of demonstration."[8] Since neither the constitution nor parliamentary procedure required an ap-

---

terms of the agreement are recorded in the accounts of the state committee meeting, September 27, 1903 and the executive committee meeting, October 21, 1905, NL Baden. Cf. Schofer, *Grossblock*, pp. 7–9, 14. For the election results, see Alfred Rapp, *Die badischen Landtagsabgeordeneten: 1905–1928* (Karlsruhe, 1929), p. 105.

8. Schofer, *Grossblock*, pp. 99–100; for the Dresden resolution, see *SPD Parteitag, 1903*, pp. 418–419.

pearance at court, the decision completely evaded the obligation. Yet the National Liberals accepted the Social Democratic answer. Their candidate was elected president, and the Social Democrat, Geck, was elected second vice-president. With this election, the liberal-socialist alliance passed from the polls into the Landtag.

Although the liberals tended to see this alliance as a turning point for Social Democrats, Kolb saw it as a turning point for liberalism.[9] With regard to the situation in Baden, Kolb was probably closer to the truth. Reformists like him, and even the national leadership, had never rejected support for or from the liberals. Moreover the Baden Social Democrats certainly gave more than they got from the 1905 agreement. Its real significance lay in the role played by the National Liberals. Previously, they had hardly contemplated support for the "nonnational and revolutionary" Social Democrats. In 1905 they found that such support was necessary. Faced with the choice between the loss of political influence and compromise with the Social Democrats, they chose the Social Democrats.

This lesson was not lost on their more orthodox, traditional, and conservative northern colleagues, who accused the Badenese of aiding the enemies of the state; even Bassermann issued a sharp protest against the election agreement. These attacks may explain why the National Liberals failed to pursue their alliance with the Social Democrats in the Badenese legislature. In most important political issues, they sided with the Centre against the Left Liberals and the Social Democrats. In turn, the Social Democrats' strident and extreme demands for complete separation of church and state did not attract the National Liberals, who depended on the support of many Evangelical groups throughout the state.[10] After the "national" elections of 1907, the policy of the Bülow Bloc had a conservative effect on both parties and governments. For both National Liberals and Social Democrats, cooperation in Baden was incompatible with national politics, and subtle external pressures

9. Wilhelm Kolb, "Blocktaktik, Blockpolitik und Sozialdemokratie," *Sozialistische Monatshefte* 10 (1906) : 277.

10. For Bassermann's objections, see *Frankfurter Zeitung,* December 8, 1905, no. 340; *Vereinigung Parteitag, 1906,* p. 24. For the incompatibilities, see Wilhelm Kolb, "Das badische Blockexperiment und seine Lehren für die Sozialdemokratie," *Sozialistische Monatshefte* 10 (1906) : 1014–1020; Hannalore Schlemmer, "Die Rolle der Sozialdemokratie in den Landtagen Badens und Württembergs und ihr Einfluss auf die Entwicklung der Gesamtpartei, 1890–1914" (unpublished doctoral diss., Freiburg, 1953), p. 83.

worked against the alliance. In the spring of 1907 the minister of the interior, Karl Schenkel, who had encouraged the agreements of 1905, was forced to resign. At the same time, the railway ministry, which administered the state-owned railroads, threatened to fire a politically active railroad worker unless he resigned from the Social Democratic party.[11] Thus the Bülow Bloc cast a conservative pall over any attempts to pursue a leftist policy, and this political situation prevailed when the Grand Duke of Baden died at the end of September 1907.

The death of every head of state demands the observance of certain formalities on the part of other governmental bodies. In this case, the National Liberal president of the legislature suggested that the members of the Landtag praesidium send a declaration of sympathy to the Grand Duke's family. The Social Democratic vice-president, Geck, in accordance with the socialists' antiroyalist principles, protested that no such act was demanded by the constitution, and his name did not appear on the card sent to the family.[12] Naturally enough, the court and staunch supporters of royalty were outraged, and this outrage exacerbated the relationship between National Liberals and Social Democrats. The National Liberals could not continue their legislative partnership with the Social Democrats, no matter how superficial, without invoking the wrath of the government and their own voters.

The loss of National Liberal support threatened political isolation for Social Democracy. In an attempt to avert complete ostracism, the two Social Democratic leaders, Kolb and Ludwig Frank, attended the Grand Duke's funeral at which the kaiser was also present. Their attendance at the burial, viewed as a matter of form by the other parties, was again a violation of Social Democratic principle. It constituted formal recognition of the monarchical system, and though the Grand Duke himself was merely royal small fry, attendance at an event where the kaiser was present was, for the Social Democrats, an outrage. Even the party in Baden could not condone Kolb's and Frank's political opportunism; at a special conference at the end of October, the state executive committee, the state Fraktion, and members of the press sharply censured the two leaders.[13] Yet the censure did not solve the party's dilemma, a dilemma clearly revealed in a letter Kolb wrote to

11. *Hilfe* 13 (1907) : 517–518; cf. Bachem, *Vorgeschichte*, 8 : 149–150.
12. Schofer, *Grossblock*, pp. 101–102.
13. Ibid., p. 103; *Schulthess, 1907*, p. 150.

Vollmar about the incident. The letter explained that Kolb and Frank attended the Grand Duke's funeral with an eye on the imminent re-election of the legislature's praesidium; their attendance supposedly demonstrated that Geck's action was a mistake. Kolb frankly stated that the Badenese Fraktion was considering a change of attitude necessary to save the wavering political position of the party.

Under pressure from Bassermann and under fire from the Centre because of Geck's lack of form, the National Liberals were losing the courage to continue even the appearance of the liberal-socialist alliance. If nothing were done to regain National Liberal confidence, the consequences would be fourfold: (1) The Centre would win the presidency in the legislature; (2) consequently the election agreement "would be questioned," and the Social Democrats "would seriously have to reckon with a clerical-conservative majority"; (3) in such a case, the Social Democrats would lose their ability to tip the political scales to their own advantage; and (4) a loss of mandates would most probably be a result of the elections of 1909. Kolb's main concern was the prevention of a conservative, i.e., Centre, majority in Baden. Hence he was unwilling to sacrifice the potential influence of Social Democracy for the sake of a mere formality. If the party wanted to play a positive role in the Baden Landtag, it would have to bolster the courage and confidence of the National Liberals by firmly and openly agreeing to appear at court. Any other course was unreasonable: "As long as a monarch stands as the head of the state and is a constitutional factor in legislation, he cannot be ignored. . . . Somehow we can no longer make do with our previous tactics of 'principle' in the question of participation in the praesidium. In Baden we now stand before a momentous decision."[14] Momentous it surely was. If the Social Democrats appeared at court, they would symbolically recognize the very system they had pledged themselves to wipe out. By so doing, they would no longer be *the* revolutionaries but merely the extreme left wing of the bourgeois opposition parties.

Regardless of the Social Democratic decision, the National Liberals were clearly in a difficult position. On November 19, their state executive committee met with the Left Liberals to consider their strategy vis-à-vis the praesidium. All agreed that a Social Democratic vice-

14. Kolb to Vollmar, November 11, 1907, Vollmar Papers.

president could not be reelected without guarantees against a repetition of Geck's behavior. On the other hand, there was a serious split between the Young Liberals, who wanted a Centre president under no circumstances, and the more conservative leadership, who feared that the election of a Social Democrat would result in the loss of influence with the government and a loss of mandates. Eventually the committee decided to leave the final decision in the hands of the Fraktion but ruled Geck out as a possible candidate. The subsequent negotiations with the Social Democrats failed since they insisted on Geck's reelection, and the Centre easily won the presidency because of the liberal-Socialist conflict.[15]

During the next year, the National Liberals continued to side with the Centre in the legislature against the Left Liberals and Social Democrats. Indeed the party avoided any public identification with the Social Democrats. At the same time, the split between right and left wings, evident at the time of Geck's misbehavior, widened. The left wing, including a strong Young Liberal faction, sharply criticized the party's allegedly conservative actions. The right wing, consisting of the urban upper-middle class and the rural voters, feared a sellout to the Social Democrats. In Freiburg, the local right wing seceded and formed a Free Conservative club. The leadership of the state party changed hands in 1908, and the new leader, Rudolf Obkircher, was more conservative than the previous one. However the Baden party still had to consider its tactic for the coming state elections, and in this respect, was caught in the same dilemma as before. It dreaded losing its domination of the legislature to the Centre party, and in order to maintain its position, it had to fall back on the Left Liberals and Social Democrats.[16]

Social Democrats and the Vote for the Budget

The Social Democrats in Baden realized as well as anyone else the dilemma of the National Liberals at election time, and they believed

15. Executive committee meeting, November 19, 1908, NL Baden; Schofer, *Grossblock*, pp. 103–104.

16. For Young Liberal shift, see clipping from *Badische Landeszeitung*, November 7, 1908, no. 522 in NL Baden; also *Fortschritt* 3 (1908) : 319; for the right, Josef Schofer, *Zentrumspolitik auf dem badischen Landtage, II: 1907–08* (Baden-Baden, 1908), p. 192; for the Free Conservatives, Rebmann, *Das Grossherzogthum Baden*, p. 1101; for the new leadership, see Binz to Obkircher, September 24, 1908, NL Baden.

that by good behavior they could woo the National Liberals into another election agreement. One sign of good behavior would be a vote for the state budget in violation of all party canons. Although the Social Democrats, both in the Reichstag and the state legislatures, had long voted for specific sections of the budget designated for improvements in public education, a vote for the budget in toto was prohibited as a vote of confidence for the existing reactionary society. There were only two instances in which a vote for the budget was justified: (1) when Social Democratic approval would demonstrably benefit the working-class taxpayer; and (2) when the Social Democrats had a majority in the legislature and presumably the responsibility for the budget proposals. It was significant that Bebel himself introduced and insisted on the viability of these two exceptional cases despite the bitter opposition of the party's co-leader, Paul Singer, who feared that Bebel had opened the Pandora's box of voting exceptions.[17] Actually it was not the exceptions themselves that caused the trouble but the attitudes of southern reformists, who adopted very independent attitudes toward budget voting. At infrequent intervals in the past, both the Bavarians and the Badenese had voted for their state budgets and incurred the censure of the national party congress.[18] Yet the party was not prepared for the assault on the budget principle that occurred as reformism gathered strength.

The first sign of reformist revolt was the Württembergers' vote for the entire budget in 1907. There were a variety of reasons why they considered a vote for the budget necessary. Like the Badenese, they were striving toward a liberal-socialist alliance and thought a vote for the budget would attract the liberals. Also, the Fraktion had participated substantially in the deliberation of the budget and had succeeded in winning the respect of other members of the Landtag as well as salary increases for a number of lower-grade state officials whose support the Social Democrats either enjoyed or were trying to attract. Lastly, the Social Democrats in Württemberg had arranged the congress of the Second International in Stuttgart in 1907 and had encountered no difficulty from the state government whatsoever. The government itself had

17. Paul Kampffmeyer, *Wandlungen in der Theorie und Taktik der Sozialdemokratie* (Munich, 1904).
18. Ibid.; Reinhard Jansen, *Georg von Vollmar, Eine politische Biographie* (Düsseldorf, 1958), p. 97.

offered the first-class waiting room in the Stuttgart railroad station as a reception hall for arriving socialist dignitaries.[19]

The attitude of the Württemberg government toward the International Congress was truly remarkable. Prior to the congress, Chancellor Bülow attempted to pressure the Württemberg government into forbidding the meeting in Stuttgart. He was acting on the advice of Bethmann Hollweg, then Prussian minister of the interior, who thought the Social Democrats were testing the tolerance of the various state governments. If the non-Prussian governments accepted the International Congresses, eventually the socialists would dare to plan a meeting in Berlin. If the Prussian government then objected to the International Congress in Berlin, as would surely be the case, they would reveal a divergence of policy between the various German governments which would be detrimental to the interests of the empire. In order to prevent this dilemma, the Württemberg government ought to take steps to prohibit the meeting. These considerations pointedly demonstrated the repressive policies of the Prussian government, and the fact that a Prussian minister of the interior could attempt to influence other governments through the chancellor, who was also Prussian prime minister, again disclosed the close identification between the Prussian and the imperial governments. Yet the Württemberg ministry was proud of its "tolerantly administered state" and frankly thought the Prussians were too "*polizeilich prophylaktisch.*" It neatly sidestepped the pressures from Berlin. It refused to prohibit the International Congress unless it could publicly state that the imperial government requested the action. At this point, Bethmann Hollweg decided that a public statement would arouse unfavorable opinion abroad. The matter was dropped, and the congress went on.[20] The whole affair was another example of the differences between Prussia and the south in political action and thinking.

Although the Social Democrats had no way of knowing about Württemberg's private correspondence with Berlin, the government's public position toward the International Congress played a determining role in the decision to vote for the budget in 1907. Significantly, the

19. *SPD Württembergs, 1907,* pp. 97–99; Wilhelm Keil, *Erlebnisse eines Sozialdemokraten* 2 vols. (Stuttgart, 1947–48), 1 : 242.

20. DZAP, Reichskanzlei, Parteien 1/4, 4, no. 1395/4, Bethmann Hollweg to Bülow, December 13, 1906 and meeting of the Royal Ministry of State [Württemberg], April 27, 1907.

national party leadership also chose to ignore this infringement of socialist dogma, probably out of the same considerations. At the state party congress, however, the organization in Stuttgart, which was dominated by left-wing radicals, violently protested the vote. Given this challenge, the Württemberg reformists countered with a fairly refined defense. When the Fraktion debated the vote for the budget, it considered the following question: If rejection of the budget was a deserved vote of no-confidence in the government, were there times when such a rejection was a tactical mistake? The Fraktion had agreed that rejection would be a mistake in 1907, and it voted for the budget.[21] Yet this argument stood party principle on its head. It did not ask whether acceptance of the budget sinned against socialist principle; such a question played directly into the hands of the radicals. Instead, the Württembergers asked the question negatively: Could rejection of the budget be an error in tactics? Such a question resulted in a political riddle: Could principle tactically and temporarily err? The Württembergers' answer was "yes." In view of the special governmental treatment accorded them and their desire to court the liberal parties in 1907, a vote against the budget was obviously a tactical error. In other words, the Württemberg Fraktion determined to do the opportune thing regardless of party dogma. This reasoning of course reflected the reformism of the Württemberg party, but it also applied to other states and their Social Democratic parties.

At the beginning of 1908, a conference of South German socialists under Vollmar's reformist leadership met at Würzburg, ostensibly to discuss ways and means of reforming the Prussian suffrage. The national party congress later charged that this meeting was the first in a South German conspiracy to vote for the budget, and in view of later events,[22] it was probable that some back-room conversations on budget voting took place. Later in the same year, the South German representatives to the various state legislatures met in Stuttgart, where Vollmar openly presented the issue of budget voting and where they decided to vote for the budget as a general rule (*in der Regel*). This decision was a step beyond the previous year's Württemberg action, which had seemed like an isolated instance governed by extraordinary circumstances, and it would surely provoke objections from the national leadership. Signifi-

21. *SPD Württembergs, 1907*, pp. 98–99.
22. *SPD Parteitag, 1908*, pp. 394–395.

cantly, no member of the national executive committee was present at Stuttgart although the Bavarians had informed it of the meeting. The conference was not reported in the press, and during June and July, the lull before the storm reigned over the usually uneasy atmosphere of the party. The radicals knew the pertinent details of the Stuttgart conference in June,[23] and it seemed likely that the party executive was informed that something was in the air. Everyone, it seemed, was waiting for the events of the coming month.

At the beginning of July, the southerners began to prepare themselves to vote for the budget and the certain subsequent conflict with the national leadership. For the Bavarians, the step was not too difficult. The state budget for 1908 was an especially favorable one since it raised the allocations for civil servants (which included railway and postal workers) and corresponded to Social Democratic demands. Although there were some members of the Bavarian Fraktion who objected to a breach with party dogma, the Bavarian leadership decided to abide by the decision of the Stuttgart conference and forced through the Fraktion a unanimous vote for the budget. In Baden, there was also a conflict between the leadership and the more orthodox Social Democrats, and again the reformist leadership imposed its will on the Fraktion. As the southerners' preparations neared completion, news of their intentions reached the national executive. By the eighth of August, both Bebel and Molkenbuhr knew that the Baden Fraktion intended to vote for the budget. Molkenbuhr was scandalized but admitted that it was too late for the executive to alter the situation. To make matters worse, the national executive, early in August, bluntly asked the Baden leadership if the Fraktion intended to vote for the budget and received no reply. Finally, on the twelfth and fourteenth of August respectively, the Badenese and the Bavarians voted for their state budgets.[24]

Molkenbuhr expected a vicious opposition to the southerners' decision, and he was not disappointed. All the nonreformist sections of the party protested violently, not only because of the vote but because of the secrecy surrounding the vote. They began to prepare a general

23. Rossmann to Henke, June 2, 1908, Henke Papers.

24. Auer to Vollmar, July 4 and July 30, 1908, Vollmar Papers. Erhard Auer was the state party secretary who, as Vollmar's physical condition weakened, became the real force in the Bavarian party. When Vollmar died, he became party leader, played an influential role in the 1918 revolution, and lived through an assassination attempt in 1919. See also Timm to Vollmar, July 31, 1908, Vollmar Papers. For the Baden vote, see *SPD Parteitag, 1908,* p. 339; For the national executives' reaction, see Keil, *Erlebnisse,* 1 : 214; Molkenbuhr

condemnation of the southerners at the party congress, and the danger
of a party split was imminent. Yet as soon as he knew of the southerners'
intentions, Bebel was aware of the danger. The importance of preserving
party unity, particularly in the face of attacks from other parties, decided
the issue for him. By the middle of August, he began to calm the national
executive and to marshal his forces for the fight at the Nuremberg
party congress to be held in September. Molkenbuhr had the task of
pacifying the radical Berliners and, together with Kautsky, of drafting a
mild resolution for the congress. Other party members, interested in
party unity but certain of a northern victory, worked on the tactic of
isolating the southerners within the party. Meanwhile the South Germans did not sit idly by and await their fate. At the end of August, the
Bavarians armed themselves with the weapon of popular support by
securing the approval of the entire state congress for their controversial
action. At the same time, Kolb and Frank met in Munich with the
Bavarian leaders to decide on strategy. Above all, they resolved that a
retreat was out of the question and planned a declaration later given
at the party congress. The southerners, having heard only the battle
cries of the radicals and knowing little or nothing about the leadership's intentions, expected a party split right up until the last minute.[25]

During the third week in September, the two sides—radicals and
reformists—arrayed themselves on the battlefield at Nuremberg. Bebel
opened the proceedings with a speech which reiterated the principles of
the party and attacked the southerners' idea that positive and effective
parliamentary action was better than undying opposition and intransigeance. Social Democrats should never lose sight of their final revolutionary goal; the small attractive pebbles of social reform must be
left on the roadside and sacrificed to the final victory over the "capitalistic system."[26] After this opening volley, the South German defenders,
with Frank to the fore, raised their standards.

Ludwig Frank, next to Vollmar and Kolb, was the most prominent of

Diaries, August 8, 1908; the lack of reply, *Hilfe* 14 (1908) : 543.
  25. On the danger of split, see Molkenbuhr Diaries, August 23, 1908; Liebknecht to
Parvus, August 31, 1908, Kautsky Papers; on Molkenbuhr's attempt to avoid, see his diaries,
August 8 and 23, 1908; Bebel to Kautsky, August 22, 1908, Kautsky Papers; cf. Bebel to
Adler, September 1, 1908, *Briefwechsel*, p. 492; on the attempt to isolate the southerners see
Liebknecht to Parvus, August 31, 1908, Kautsky Papers. For the determination of the
southerners, see Auer to Vollmar, September 2, 1908, Vollmar Papers; and Frank to Leonie
Meyerhof-Hildeck, September 21, 1908 in Ludwig Frank, *Aufsätze, Reden, und Briefe*, ed.
Hedwig Wachenheim (Berlin, 1924), p. 125.
  26. *SPD Parteitag, 1908*, pp. 288–289.

the southern reformists and the youngest. When he stepped into the spotlight at the party congress in 1908, he was a handsome and rhetorically gifted man of thirty-four. The son of a small Badenese businessman, he had studied law and had established a thriving practice in the city of Mannheim. He originally won his party spurs as a legal adviser to the party press and as the founder of the party's youth movement. His socialism had a strong individualist taint derived from from his model, the moderate, non-Marxist French socialist, Jean Jaurès. Elected to the Baden Landtag in 1905 and to the Reichstag in 1907, he shared with Kolb a belief in practical politics and quickly became Kolb's right-hand man.[27]

At the beginning of his speech, Frank used the standard arguments of the reformists and revisionists. He emphasized the material gains that the budgets in question had brought to the workers, the large degree of tolerance shown to Social Democracy by southern governments, and stressed the need to call the bluff of the Social Democrats' enemies. But he also added two new dimensions to the debate. He absolutely rejected the idea of a centrally enforced party conformity. According to him, the national leadership had become the prisoner of the radical Berlin organization which lived in the politically deprived Prussian environment. The difference between Berlin and Baden was the difference in the suffrage; in Berlin, the workers were not represented in the legislature and in Baden they were. This difference meant that the orthodox stand on the budget, so revered by the Berliners, ultimately worked to the disadvantage of the workers of Baden. In reality, the radical zeal of the Berliners, who professed such concern for the workers' ultimate welfare, only negated the very aims of the party.[28] The implication of this argument was the duty of Social Democracy to exploit its representation in the legislature to the fullest.

The corollary to this argument, and the most significant one introduced by Frank, was Social Democracy's duty to cooperate with other parties. In their vote for the budget, the Badenese had considered the special parliamentary constellation in which they participated—the "so-called Grand Bloc." Participation in the "Grand Bloc" had pre-

27. Osterroth, *Verstorbene Persönlichkeiten*, p. 84. Cf. Sally Grünebaum, *Ludwig Frank: Ein Beitrag zur Entwicklung der deutschen Sozialdemokratie* (Heidelberg, 1924), pp. 10–12, 15–22.
28. *SPD Parteitag, 1908*, pp. 317–326.

vented a clerical-conservative majority in the legislature, and the Badenese intended to pursue the same policy in the future. The price for participation in the Grand Bloc was a vote for the budget in order to encourage the support and trust of the liberal partners.[29] This argument for the "Grand Bloc"—the term used for the formal cooperation be-tween liberals and socialists in Baden—was a new departure in Social Democratic politics. Indeed, Frank's speech at the congress of 1908 contained the first use of the term "Grand Bloc" in a national setting. Considering the origin of the term "Bloc "in German politics with its specific reference to French practice, to the liberal "coalition" in Baden, and its contemporary use in the governmental Bülow Bloc, Frank, by using the term "Grand Bloc" in his defense explicitly extended the idea of participation in a governmental "coalition" to the Social Democrats. It was also significant that this term, which became a byword in German politics, was first used on the national level by a Social Democrat.[30] By so doing, Frank, on behalf of his fellow reformists, served notice of their intention to become a responsible factor in the nation's political life.

Frank's arguments attacked both party tradition and the formidable Dresden resolution, and he aroused the radicals' deepest ire. Yet he and his southern colleagues received a kind of negative support from the executive committee of the party. Concerned for party unity more than anything else, it arbitrated a mild compromise resolution that merely declared the budget voters "out of step" with party principles.[31] There was no hint of condemnation, isolation, or expulsion from the party, no threat of sanctions in the future. In answer, the reformists determined to press their point. In order to proclaim their stand openly and clearly, the delegations of Baden, Württemberg, and Bavaria, together with a few northern sympathizers, penned their own declaration of independence from the national party:

> We recognize the German party congress as the legitimate repre-sentation of the entire party, as the highest authority in all matters

29. Ibid., pp. 322ff.

30. Susan Schwarz Tegel, who is currently working on a biography of Ludwig Frank, informs me that the term was used frequently in Baden after the agreements of 1905. The term also appears in the debates *SPD Württembergs, 1907*, p. 97. As far as I can determine, however, Frank was the first one to use the term at a national meeting or in a national publi-cation. The liberals first used the term in *Hilfe* 15 (1909) : 129.

31. *SPD Parteitag, 1908*, p. 189.

> of principle and tactics which affect the empire as a whole. How-
> ever . . . in all matters of state politics, the state organization is
> the appropriate . . . quarter . . . which has to determine the
> course of state politics independently according to its special
> circumstances . . . [T]he decision over the vote on the budget
> must remain the preserve of the state Fraktion . . . responsible
> only to the state organization. . . .[32]

The southerners thereby answered the resolution of the party congress
with a defiance that measured the strides made by the reformists and
revisionists within the party since Dresden. One reformist, commenting
on the outcome of the congress, noted that

> as the southerners immediately vow[ed] not to prostrate themselves
> despite the [executive's] resolution, no voice [was] raised, and all the
> rabble-rousers, who threatened so fiercely before [the congress],
> [were] seized with silence.[33]

The party congress at Nuremberg, technically a victory for the radicals,
was the first successful test of reformist strength. Ludwig Frank, back
from battle and safe in his Baden bastion, recognized this fact too.
"Nuremberg," he wrote, "was not the end, but the beginning of our
detachment from the Berlin movement."[34]

THE BADENESE EXPERIMENT

The moral victory of the southerners at the Social Democratic
congress of 1908 with its implied acceptance of Frank's argument for
the Grand Bloc occurred at an auspicious time in German politics. The
Social Democrats had already begun a cautious rapprochement with
the liberals, and the first breach in the Bülow Bloc, over the issue of
tax reform, appeared almost simultaneously with the meeting of the
Social Democratic congress in 1908. Immediately after the congress,
the Left Liberals broke with the Bülow Bloc over the constitutional
issue connected with the Daily Telegraph Affair. Thereafter the breach
widened until the National Liberals themselves followed the Left
Liberals into opposition over the issue of tax reform. When the Bülow

32. Ibid., p. 426.
33. DZAP, Heine Papers, Heine to E. Fisher, September 19, 1908.
34. Frank to Schlommer, October 23, 1908 in Frank, *Aufsätze*, p. 126.

Bloc collapsed, the liberals and the Social Democrats found themselves in the same opposing camp. Frank's argument for the Grand Bloc occurred, therefore, just as the prerequisites for such a Bloc appeared on the national level. At the same time, the favorable national atmosphere affected the nascent Grand Bloc in Baden.

The one obstacle to the Grand Bloc in Baden in 1909 was the crisis inside the National Liberal party. Its conservative elements, which had gained the upper hand in 1907, still opposed any encouragement of the Social Democrats. Moreover, 1909 was an election year, and there was even difficulty in making an election agreement with the Left Liberals—a practice which had become National Liberal policy. The best example of the difficulties involved occurred in the rural election district of Lörrach. In this district, the National Liberals had close associations with the conservative Agrarian League, and already in 1905 the Left Liberals had opposed a candidate from the conservative landowning circles of the district. At that time, the National Liberals had nominated a Young Liberal to appease their radical partners, but he had died in the interim, and his successor was the conservative chairman of the state party, Obkircher, whom the local members insisted on renominating in 1909. The Left Liberals adamantly opposed his candidacy, and this opposition cast a shadow over the entire state negotiations for an election agreement.[35] Lörrach was not the only rural district where the National Liberals and the Left Liberals failed to reach an agreement, and by July 1909, even the tentative urban agreements had come to naught. Most of the friction between the two liberal groups resulted from the objections of conservative National Liberals to the radical policies of the Left Liberals. For instance, they criticized them for making an alliance with the National Social Club, a remnant of Naumann's group, which continued to exist in the south. These criticisms were rooted in a general aversion to the Social Democratic party, and ultimately the Left Liberal willingness to cooperate with the Social Democrats caused the failure of a general liberal cooperation.[36] When

35. "Wie steht es mit dem angeblichen Bruch des Blockabkommens in Lörrach-Land?" official declaration, no date, NL Baden; "Die Stellung der nationalliberalen Partei nach dem Scheitern des Blocks," publication of the *Badische Landeszeitung,* no date; also the correspondence between National and Left Liberals, October 26, 1908 to February 7, 1909, NL Baden.

36. Confidential communication to executives of local and Young Liberal clubs, July 1, 1909, NL Baden.

the general Baden election occurred at the end of October 1909, the liberal Bloc was in shambles, and the outlook for a repetition of the Grand Bloc was very grim indeed.

The results of the general election once again proved the truth of the slogan, "United we stand; divided, we fall." Compared to the 23 mandates won by the Centre and the 10 won by the Social Democrats, the National Liberals captured only 4, the Left Liberals only one mandate, and the National Liberal domination of the legislature was threatened more than ever before. Thus they were forced to make the objectionable compromise they eschewed before the election. Hurriedly, the National Liberal executive committee met and, despite governmental opposition to the Grand Bloc, voted, with only one dissenting voice, to conclude another agreement with the Left Liberals and the Social Democrats for the runoff elections. The Social Democrats, reported one source, were so eager for an agreement that they assured the National Liberals that their own ambitions did not exceed those of the liberals, and the final agreement certainly favored the liberals more than the Social Democrats. Nevertheless the Social Democrats acquitted themselves very well. They won 20 seats; the Centre, 36 seats; while the National Liberals acquired 17 and the Left Liberals 7 seats. Whereas the National Liberals lost 30 percent of their former mandates, the Social Democrats gained 60 percent, and they were now the second largest party in the Landtag.[37]

Once again, the conclusion of the election agreement increased the prospects for a Grand Bloc in the legislature, and once again, events depended on the National Liberals. Obkircher, who lost the election in Lörrach to the Social Democrats, and also his leadership of the party, told a group of reporters to eliminate the term Grand Bloc from the press entirely; they could expect no further cooperation between the parties of the "left."[38] But the new leadership had other ideas which it revealed as northern National Liberals began to criticize all hints of a

37. Schofer, *Grossblock*, pp. 45–51; cf. clipping from the *Breisgauer Zeitung*, October 27, 1909, NL Baden. The Left Liberals either withdrew their own candidates or supported the National Liberals in 12 districts; the National Liberals did the same for the Left Liberals in 12 districts. The Left Liberals withdrew their own candidate in Lörrach-Land and abstained. The liberals either withdrew their own candidates or supported the Social Democrats in 10 districts whereas the Social Democrats supported the liberals in 18 districts! The small Conservative party had 3 delegates, Rapp, *Die Landtagsabgeordneten*, p. 105.

38. Meeting of editors from Baden liberal newspapers on November 7, 1909, NL Baden.

Grand Bloc. In November, the state party's executive secretary, Paul Thorbecke, wrote a sharp letter to the national leadership:

It would be much better if the *Korrespondenz* [the official national party paper] refrained in the future from a discussion of matters in Baden; it could also determine, if it wants to emphasize to us the principles of the party, how far and how often the Prussian National Liberals have compromised themselves by agreements with the right which were not purely electoral tactics. We shall fight such action of the central leadership . . . with all sharpness and bring this affair to discussion before the next meeting of the state party; . . . the opinion vis-à-vis the central leadership will . . . not be exactly favorable.[39]

The letter indicated that the National Liberals could imitate their Social Democratic partners very well in a fight with the national leadership and that they intended to pursue the policy of the Grand Bloc with equal obstinacy.

The decision to cooperate in a Grand Bloc loudly announced the victory of the left wing inside the Baden National Liberal party. The man who engineered this victory was the newly elected chairman of the Fraktion, Edmund Rebmann. Rebmann was Kolb's National Liberal counterpart, and his rise to leadership was meteoric. The director of the Humboldt Gymnasium in Karlsruhe and hence a state official, he won his first seat in the Landtag in 1905, and although he was chairman of the state business committee, there was little sign of his influence in the party before 1909. Originally he represented an election district in Freiburg, where the left wing was particularly strong and wherepreference for the Social Democrats had already caused a right-wing secession from the party. The victory of the left wing and Rebmann's emergence as leader were also facilitated by the absence of the two leading conservatives in the former Fraktion, Obkircher and Karl Wilckens, and the victory of predominantly left-wing candidates.[40]

Backed by a strong left wing, it was not difficult for Rebmann to persuade the Fraktion to vote for a Social Democratic vice-president of

39. DZAP, Bassermann Papers, Thorbecke to the [National Liberal] Central Office, November 3, 1909.
40. Rapp, *Die Landtagsabgeordneten*, pp. 6–48 passim.

the Landtag; the Social Democrats even received a promotion from second to first vice-president. Once again, however, the Social Democrats refused to make the customary visit to the Grand Duke, but this time the National Liberals solved the problem by persuading them to sign the guest book at the royal palace. On the other hand, the Social Democrats were no longer content with the vice-president's position as recognition of their partnership with the liberals. As the second largest party in the Landtag, they felt entitled to the chairmanship of the all-important budget committee, and they put this request to the National Liberals. This was no small demand, and the National Liberals discussed it "very earnestly since important complications could result from the chairmanship of this committee." Given the Social Democrats' traditionally negative attitude toward the public budget, the National Liberal hesitation was understandable. Tax reform was on the government's agenda, and in 1906, the Social Democrats had rejected a revision of the income tax. The National Liberals probably feared Social Democracy's fiscal "irresponsibility" once it gained the chairmanship of the budget committee, but this fear was probably unfounded considering the action of the Württembergers in 1907. Finally, despite all their hesitations the National Liberals decided to give the Social Democrats the deputy chairmanship, and Kolb eventually shared responsibility for the budget committee with Rebmann. As compensation, Frank became chairman of the almost equally important committee on justice and administration which was to debate and prepare the important and controversial reform of local government.[41] Nothing indicated more than the negotiations over these appointments the National Liberals' intention to dominate the Grand Bloc despite the Social Democratic preponderance of mandates. The Social Democrats tamely accepted this dominance since they, too, had made important gains. The vice-presidency and the deputy chairmanship of the budget committee were first events within the movement; they showed that once Social Democrats had a large enough representation in the legislature and desired to cooperate with the liberal parties, the liberals themselves would recognize the party as a worthy partner.

The partnership was formally cemented at the beginning of the

41. Fraktion meeting, November 29, 1909, NL Baden; Frank, *Aufsätze*, p. 182; Rapp, *Die Landtagsabgeordneten*, p. 99; Schlemmer, "Die Rolle der Sozialdemokratie," pp. 89–90.

Landtag of 1910. The National Liberals carefully identified the Grand Bloc as a "tactical cooperation" for the defense of liberal progress:

> It depends on the representatives of Social Democracy . . . to prove . . . that they . . . can cooperate practically in the business of the legislature. . . . If we . . . as a bourgeois liberal party want to use the opportunity to cooperate with this party in individual cases . . . without detriment to our program, then we are rendering a service to the state. . . .[42]

The Social Democrats agreed that progress was the most important issue of the day, and they desired to make a substantial contribution:

> Right now it is not a matter of establishing the socialistic state but a matter of finally . . . making Germany a truly liberal bourgeois constitutional state of stripping away the feudal fetters which still bind us even today. . . .[43]

The two parties also agreed on more than liberal progress; both were thoroughly annoyed by the Baden government's admonitions against a Grand Bloc, and both took pains to assure the government that the Bloc was not directed against it. In order to manifest his party's good will toward the government, Kolb let the minister of the interior, von Bodman, know that he considered it "his task to support the government in the immediate future."[44] In view of the fact that the government had planned the most massive reforms since the 1870s for the coming legislative session, it was doubly important that the parties of the Grand Bloc remained on good terms with one another and with the government in order to influence reform to their own advantage.

One of the most important of the new reforms concerned the Baden schools. The National Liberals expected the most support from the Social Democrats in this matter, and it was this "cultural task" that promised the most extensive cooperation. Both National Liberals and Social Democrats saw the Catholic Centre as a threat to the system of nondenominational schools that had legally existed in Baden since

42. *Amtliche Berichte über die Verhandlungen der badischen Ständeversammlung,* January 12, 1910, supplement to the *Karlsruher Zeitung,* January 14, 1910.
43. Ibid.
44. Felix Hecht to von Bodman, January 9, 1910, Bodman Papers.

1876. In a country where denominational schools were the rule rather than the exception, this nondenominational system was unidue in all of Germany, and both parties wanted to preserve and improve it. Both agreed that the only business of the clergy in the schools was religious instruction; neither the teaching nor the supervision of secular subjects by the clergy was admissible. Both agreed that the preservation of the nondenominational system depended on strict governmental control over the number of private denominational schools. But there were serious differences about the role of religion in the state schools. In line with their principle of the separation of church and state, the Social Democrats demanded the elimination of religious instruction. The National Liberals, dependent on the support of conservative Evangelical pressure groups, could not afford to advocate either the separation of state and church or the removal of religious instruction from the schools. In this matter, the Left Liberals were much closer to the Social Democrats. In any case, the Baden school reform of 1910, concerned as it was with the improvement of instruction and the welfare of the students, about which all the parties agreed, provided little scope for an argument or a compromise over these problems of Weltanschauung.[45]

There were only two instances in which the religious problem, and hence the opportunity to present a solid front against the Centre, came to the fore. The first was the matter of nondenominational normal schools. Although the nondenominational schools existed on paper and worked well in areas with a religiously mixed population, there still existed small Badenese communities of homogeneous religious faith and according to the law, these communities had the right to demand a teacher who professed their faith and went to church with them. By the same token, although Baden had three nondenominational normal schools, the state maintained three denominational ones for those desiring to attend. In the past, both Left Liberals and Social Democrats had introduced motions into the legislature for making these confessional normal schools nondenominational, but at first they had little success in finding a majority. The National Liberals originally split over the issue, but in 1910, a Social Democratic motion attained the support of

45. On nondenominational schools, see Schofer, *Schulkämpfe*. For the National Liberal policy, see Ziegler to Schmidt, February 9 and March 12, 1905 and Thorbecke to Rebmann, March 10, 1911, NL Baden. Cf. Frank, *Aufsätze*, pp. 62–63; for the 1910 agreement, see *Verhandlungen Baden*, 493 : Drucksache 33b, Anlage 2.

all the National Liberals and the Left Liberals for the elimination of
the confessional normal schools. Compared with the previous National
Liberal split on this issue, their unanimous vote represented a concession
to the Social Democrats and an affirmation of their commitment to
the Grand Bloc. Since the government and the upper house rejected the
Bloc's decision, it had little material effect on the reform;[46] it was
significant only because of the National Liberal concession to the Grand
Bloc.

The second instance of cooperation between the members of the
Bloc involved the exemption of children of religious dissidents from
religious instruction. Both Social Democrats and Left Liberals introduced a proposal exempting a child from religious instruction because
of the "religious misgivings" of his guardians. Although it seemed
harmless enough, the Left Liberal–Social Democratic motion actually
questioned the entire principle of religious instruction in the schools.
Exemptions because of "misgivings" were only the first step in the
process of ridding religion from the schools entirely. The Centre, which
promptly saw the motion's drift, opposed it and argued that religious
instruction was the means by which the young learned the mores of
their society. The National Liberals were neither so conservative as the
Centre, nor could they agree completely with the left, and so they
compromised. The dissidents' paragraph, as it appeared in the final
version of the school reform, provided that "children, who do not
belong to a religious congregation or who belong to a confession for
which their school . . . has no instruction" could be exempted from
religious instruction.[47] According to the compromise, the National
Liberals were not ready to relinquish the principle of religious instruction, but they were willing to concede that members of one faith need
not be forced to learn the creed of another. The compromise was very
politic in that it aimed at pleasing both those voters who constituted a
small religious minority in their own local community and the partners
of the Grand Bloc.

These small compromises over the issue of religious instruction were
minor compared to the dispute over teachers' salaries, and this dispute

46. Schofer, *Schulkämpfe*, pp. 24–29; Bachem, *Vorgeschichte*, 8 : 158; Schlemmer, "Die
Rolle der Sozialdemokratie," p. 87.

47. *Verhandlungen Baden*, 487 : May 13, 1910, p. 169. For final version of dissidents'
paragraph, ibid., 493 : Drucksache 33b, Anlage 2, p. 261.

was the issue that caused the most excitement within the National Liberal Fraktion. Although the government planned to raise the amount of their salaries, the teachers demanded a rank as middle-grade *state* officials. Classed as *community* officials in 1910, the new rating would raise their status and insure an increase in teachers' salaries every time the state raised the salaries of its officials. In the election campaign, the National Liberals had promised to do everything possible to meet the demands of the teachers, one of the major groups which supported them, and they vigorously pressed the case in the Landtag. The government countered with the threat to withdraw the whole school reform if the National Liberals remained obstinate, but they, with the help of the Social Democrats, persisted in their demands. After much handwringing and negotiation, the government agreed to include a paragraph in the school reform whereby any future revision of official salaries must include a revision of teachers' salaries even though they were not, technically, state officials. The Social Democrats had first suggested this compromise which both National Liberals and government accepted, and the new provisions were truly the work of the Grand Bloc.[48] In fact, the Grand Bloc had cooperated closely and easily in the school reform and had proved itself, in this issue at least, a viable majority.

One of the real tests of the viability of the Grand Bloc was the reform of local self-government. Baden had the most democratic local government in Germany, but its provisions dated back to 1890. The suffrage for the election of borough and city councils was a three-class one (dividing the tax-paying population into twelfths) similar to Prussia's, and the election of the mayors and executive councils was indirect in the larger towns.[49] By 1910, it was time for a change. The reform of the Landtag suffrage had generated demands for local government reform, and every party had its own platform. The Social Democrats naturally demanded an equal suffrage and the direct election of mayors. The Left Liberals also advocated the democratic, equal suffrage but declared themselves ready to compromise with any revision of the "plutocratic" system. The issue was most problematical for the National Liberals. Since a completely equal suffrage would probably deprive

48. Fraktion meetings, April 19, April 21, April 22, 1910, and *Badische nationalliberale Correspondenz,* April 21 and 22, 1910, NL Baden.

49. H. Heffter. *Die deutsche Selbstverwaltung im 19. Jahrhundert* (Stuttgart, 1950), pp. 182–184, 497, 562.

them of their dominant position on many borough and city councils, they found it difficult to relinquish the class suffrage entirely; on the other hand, they also realized it would hurt their political fortunes to appear too undemocratic in the matter of local government.

The National Liberals originally confronted this problem by making an agreement with the Left Liberals. They consented to create a more democratic suffrage by dividing the population into sixths (instead of into twelfths) in return for Left Liberal support in urban areas at election time. They would not yield, however, to the Left Liberal demand for the direct election of mayors and borough councils in the larger towns.[50] Thus the Left Liberals were able to exert some pressure for democratization within the context of the liberal Bloc, but their influence had very narrow limits.

In accordance with the liberal agreement, the government bill for local government reform, introduced in 1910, included the six-class suffrage for both boroughs and towns and foresaw no change in the indirect election of mayors and city councils. Yet this concession to the liberals did not satisfy the Social Democrats. At the beginning of the legislative session, Kolb offered to strike a bargain with the National Liberals for the complete elimination of the class suffrage, at least in villages and boroughs. Some of the members of the National Liberal Fraktion were willing to meet the Social Democrats halfway, but Rebmann and the majority decided that, since removal of the class suffrage could benefit the Social Democrats at the cost of the National Liberals, they could not arbitrarily renege on their platform.[51] They rejected Kolb's suggestion for an equal suffrage, and the class suffrage was incorporated into the final version of the bill.

Ultimately, the issue that preoccupied the liberals was not the suffrage, but the method of electing city mayors and councils. The old provision, which the government retained, called for the direct election of mayors and councils in all towns with less than *2,000* inhabitants. In 1910 the Left Liberals proposed the direct election of mayors and councils in *all* areas regardless of population. The National Liberals seriously considered voting for this proposal and even bid for Social Democratic support. But the Social Democrats, miffed by the rejection

50. "Bloc" meeting, May 7, 1907; and executive committee meeting [National Liberals], June 18, 1907, NL Baden.
51. Fraktion meeting, January 18, 1910, NL Baden.

of the equal suffrage, refused to cooperate. Eventually, the two groups of liberals failed to achieve even their own maximum demands, and in a compromise with each other and with the government, agreed to accept the indirect election of mayors in order to save the direct election of *all* town councils regardless of population.[52]

These deliberations over local government reform indicated the difficulty of achieving unity between the parties of the left or even between the liberal parties and the government in any issue concerning the extension of political democracy. The National Liberals, in particular, wanted to take only very small steps in that direction. But despite their stinginess and the bill's very limited democratic progress, the Social Democrats eventually voted for it in its final version. Their vote was one more measure of their desire to cooperate in practical politics. Kolb, in his defense of the vote before his party's state congress in 1910, admitted that the bill was not perfect but that it guaranteed "a greater influence in local government . . . for the less wealthy classes of the population."[53] Through this concession, the Social Democrats in Baden committed themselves more and more to a reformist tactic.

The third test of the Grand Bloc's feasibility was the tax reform. Since Baden's income tax law had existed for over 20 years, the legislation of 1910 was merely one more minor improvement in the existing system. The main significance of reform was the support given the government bill by the Grand Bloc in opposition to the Centre, which claimed that its own proposals guaranteed a more equable taxation for the poorer classes. In truth there was very little difference between the two proposals. Both bills called for the same taxes on upper-level incomes, but the government bill, supported by the Grand Bloc, was more rationally graduated.[54] The votes of all the members of the Grand Bloc for the tax reform indicated that the Social Democrats would vote for a money bill if it met some of their demands. In this respect, the Badenese were merely following the lead of their colleagues in the

52. Fraktion meetings March 7, April 5, June 13, June 14, 1910, NL Baden. For the various versions of reform, see *Verhandlungen Baden,* 492 : Drucksache 58b, pp. 852, 870, 875.
53. Wilhelm Kolb, *Die Tätigkeit der Sozialdemokratie im badischen Landtage, 1909–10* (Mannheim, 1910), pp. 129–131.
54. A. Rothenacker, *Die Novelle zum badischen Einkommenssteuergesetz,* Heft 11, *Badische nationalliberale Bibliothek* (Munich, 1911–12), pp. 9–10.

Reichstag who had implicitly accepted the same principle in the preceding year by voting for the inheritance tax. Indeed, as long as the liberal parties supported substantial direct taxation, they had no trouble in obtaining Social Democratic cooperation and reinforcing the idea of the Grand Bloc.

From the approval of the tax reform and the success of the Grand Bloc, it seemed but a short step to Social Democratic approval of the state budget. Yet this problem almost marred the record of liberal-socialist cooperation. Mindful of past reproaches from the national leadership and irked by slights from certain officials of the Badenese government, the Social Democrats initially decided to toe the party line and reject the budget when it came to a vote. At the last minute, they changed their minds.

There was perhaps no better example of the political differences between the German north and south than the reason for the Social Democratic reversal in 1910. The Badenese finally voted for the budget because of a speech made by the important minister of the interior, von Bodman. Baron Johann von Bodman came from an important Freiburg family of liberal persuasion. His mother was English, his wife was the American Anna Steinway-Oaks (of the New York branch of Steinway pianos), and his sister, Emma, married Heinrich von Treitschke. When he went to university, he pointedly joined a *Burschenschaft* rather than the fraternal corps usually chosen by men of his social rank. Thus he demonstrated his own national-liberal stripes. Although he originally held a medical degree, he later studied law and successfully took the civil service examination for a post in the Baden ministry of interior. After experience in the Imperial Insurance Bureau and the Bundesrat, he became a minister in 1907 during the conservative years of the Bülow Bloc. However the replacement of his predecessor, Schenkel, must only have been a symbolic concession to conservative circles since von Bodman was just as liberal and "democratic" as his forerunner. He favored progressive social legislation and he espoused the cause of the Social Democrats despite opposition from the Baden Grand Duke.[55] Throughout the legislative session of 1910, von Bodman treated the Social Democrats with more deference

---

55. W. H. Schill, "Johann Heinrich Bodman," *Deutsches Biographisches Jahrbuch* 11 (1929) : 57–62. Cf. *Neue Deutsche Biographie,* 2 : 360. I am indebted to Susan Tegel for information about von Bodman's liberal ideals and opposition to the Grand Duke.

and respect than was customary, and this courtesy was severely criticized by the Centre and the aristocratic upper chamber of the Landtag.
In retaliation against this criticism, he spoke out in defense of the
Social Democrats in a way that no other German minister had ever
dared:

> Social Democracy is a remarkable workers' movement for the
> liberation of the "fourth estate," for the uplifting of the great
> mass of workers, who want to cooperate and occupy themselves
> in the life of the state, and in this respect one must accommodate
> them. . . . It is a matter of weighing and considering the demands
> of such a movement in order to decide where one must counter
> them, and if one does not meet justified demands in time, then one
> commits a mistake which is the opposite of the maintenance of
> the state.[56]

By favoring the Social Democrats with such praise and publicity, von
Bodman placed himself in an extremely vulnerable position. To reject
the budget after such a show of confidence on the part of a minister
would have created an uproar in Baden political circles. Despite this
consideration, the decision for the Social Democrats was not an easy
one. Frank later wrote that he fought a long battle with himself in the
night before the final resolution.[57] He and his compatriots did not fool
themselves about future difficulties with the national leadership and the
party radicals. Nevertheless, in the middle of July, the Baden Social
Democratic Fraktion voted for the budget in conscious and considered
defiance of the party strictures against it.

   This action provoked a powerful storm within the national Social
Democratic party. The Badenese were threatened with exclusion from
the party, and for the first time in decades, it seemed as if the unified
German labor movement would split in two. Yet this story belongs to
the development of Social Democracy, and we shall deal with it in its
proper sequence.[58] In Baden the Social Democrats preserved the Grand
Bloc, and Frank repeatedly emphasized this point in his defense of the
Badenese Fraktion. The National Liberals, as their political partners,
also maintained a silent solidarity with the Social Democrats. They too

56. Quoted in Frank, *Aufsätze*, p. 111.
57. Frank to Leonie Meyerhof-Hildeck, July 21, 1910, in Frank, *Aufsätze*, pp. 170–171.
58. See chapter 5.

were under attack from their own national headquarters for participation in the Grand Bloc, and like the Social Democrats, they insisted on retaining their own local independence. In the weeks after the close of the legislature, the National Liberals avoided "capitalizing" on the difficulties of their socialist partners. Moreover, the state secretary learned from Kolb that a majority of the Badenese Fraktion were determined to resist the rebukes of the forthcoming Social Democratic congress, and this knowledge aroused latent hopes of a split inside the Social Democratic ranks. Rebmann wrote: "Should such a development occur, as I still quietly hope, then the beginning of a non–Social Democratic workers' party would be made in Baden, and we could also look forward to the success of our tactic in this direction."[59] These hopes shed light on the ultimate expectations of the National Liberal courtship of the Social Democrats: a workers' party divorced from its radical left wing and free to make flexible political decisions would remove the stigma, emphasized in all inimical quarters, attached to cooperation with a revolutionary, "nonnational" party and reduce the National Liberals' fear of losing favor with the government and their own voters. The Baden National Liberals had borrowed an important page from Naumann's book and adapted it to their own circumstances. But even if no split materialized, the Grand Bloc was a reality, and in Rebmann's words, it had already achieved an improvement "by honestly working together with [Social Democracy] in the hope of awaking a feeling of responsibility to the idea of the state . . . and a warmer involvement in the [state's] fate. This attempt has been made in Baden and has succeeded above all expectations."[60]

59. Thorbecke to Rebmann, July 30, 1910, NL Baden.
60. Quoted in Schofer, *Grossblock*, pp. 83–84.

5

The Parties at the Crossroads

Although the Grand Bloc succeeded in the liberal atmosphere of Baden, there was no guarantee that it could be transplanted into the harsher national climate. Before such a national bloc could exist, the three groups concerned would have to solve their internal problems, and these in turn involved their relationships with each other. Would the Left Liberals, in their efforts for unity, succeed in becoming a national, democratic party able to cooperate on an equal basis with National Liberals and Social Democrats? Would the National Liberals overcome their traditional conservatism and antipathy to Social Democracy? Would the Social Democrats resolve the conflict between reformists and radicals in favor of participation and cooperation in German parliamentary life? These were the problems that faced the parties of any projected Grand Bloc at the beginning of 1910.

THE LEFT LIBERALS

The cooperation of the Left Liberals within the framework of the Bülow Bloc accelerated the drive toward Left Liberal unity, and the crisis over the Vereinsgesetz increased, rather than decreased, the chances for unity. Local Left Liberal clubs, concerned with eliminating needless competition, began to merge with one another and hence to prove that they could overcome minor political differences. In Schleswig-Holstein, the Freisinnige Volkspartei and the Vereinigung reached a modus vivendi whereby they divided the province between them for election campaigns. In Bremen, where competition with the Social Democrats was especially strong, the two groups merged into a single club despite some important disagreements.[1] If allowed to take its

1. *Vereinigung Parteitag, 1906,* p. 22; executive committee meeting of Freisinnige Vereinigung, April 21, 1909, Gothein Papers. Also see Wilhelm Kulemann, *Zusammenschluss der*

course, unification at the local level would have overtaken the leadership and prevented it from influencing the terms of the merger.

Yet the Left Liberal leadership, and particularly the strong and conservative Freisinnige Volkspartei, wanted to supervise the merger because it was concerned about the character of the future unified party. In order to create a strong position for itself and its policies within any future group, the Volkspartei insisted on maintaining its own organizational integrity, and it pursued a petty policy of competition with and domination of the other two parties. In some instances, it went so far as attempting to oust the other two from districts where they enjoyed long-standing support.[2] These attempts to maintain and expand the Volkspartei's organization would help it to determine the future direction of a united liberal party, and this direction was sure to be more conservative than that of the Vereinigung or the South Germans. With the help of its larger organization, the Volkspartei had dictated the vote of the Fraktionsgemeinschaft for the Vereinsgesetz, and in the negotiations over unification, it repeatedly stated its desire to avoid any alliance with the Social Democrats. As late as September 1909, the *Freisinnige Zeitung* wrote:

> We . . . want to declare with all clarity that the *Freisinnige Volkspartei will not and cannot change its tactical position vis-à-vis Social Democracy* as long as the Social Democratic party has not effected a basic revision of its essential viewpoint and position vis-à-vis liberalism. . . . This difference of opinion over the position of Social Democracy can and will not remain in the background during the negotiations over a . . . fusion of the Left Liberal groups. We . . . consider it absolutely necessary that in such . . . a fusion, the compactness and fighting strength of the Freisinnige Volkspartei remains. . . .[3]

Thus one of the primary conflicts between the Left Liberal groups was the policy toward Social Democracy. This disagreement was the reason

---

Liberalen (Dresden, 1905), pp. 36, 65; Thomas Nipperdey, *Die Organisation der deutschen Parteien vor 1918* (Düsseldorf, 1961), pp. 223–224; and Hermann Kastendiek, "Der Liberalismus in Bremen" (unpublished doctoral diss., Kiel, 1952), pp. 122–131.

2. Executive committee meeting of the Freisinnige Vereinigung, April 21, 1909, Gothein Papers; Karl Schrader to Konrad Haussmann, August 26, 1909, Haussmann Papers; *Mitteilungen für die Vertrauensmänner der freisinnigen Volkspartei* (Berlin, 1909), p. 118.

3. *Freisinnige Zeitung,* August 27, 1909.

for the leadership's desire to influence the terms of any merger. With its larger and stronger organization, the Freisinnige Volkspartei hoped to insure that a new Left Liberal party would not be too conciliatory toward the left. The other two parties naturally resented the position of the Volkspartei, but they assured themselves of victory in the long run. They were dedicated to liberal unity for reasons of principle and tactics. Unless unity prevailed, the Left Liberals might cease to exist and despite the conflicts, negotiations began in the summer of 1909 and proceeded into the fall and winter. By Christmas, the program and details of leadership were completed and by the end of January 1910, all Left Liberal parties had approved a merger. At the beginning of March 1910, the newly united liberals held their first party congress.[4]

The creation of the *Fortschrittliche Volkspartei* (Progressive People's Party)—the name given to the unified organization—was a significant event in the history of liberalism. It effected the final transformation of Left Liberalism from a splintered group of liberal Weltanschauungsparteien to a democratic, national party. Through unification, the Left Liberals or Progressives increased their prestige, their strength, their bargaining power and hence their attractiveness as a partner in any projected bloc. They espoused a firm policy of cooperation with the National Liberals and thereby hoped to strengthen the entire liberal movement. At the same time, the Progressives' attitude toward Social Democracy was still unclear. Although they adopted a democratic program, there was no hint of an orientation to the left. The chairman of the newly united party, Otto Fischbeck, and over half the members of the new executive committee came from the ranks of the Freisinnige Volkspartei.[5] For the time being, the problem of future cooperation with the Social Democrats and the achievement of a Grand Bloc remained unresolved.

THE NATIONAL LIBERALS

In matters of policy toward other parties, the National Liberals experienced the same problems as the Progressives. If no right wing had

4. For the resentment, see Georg Gothein, *Lebenserinnerungen,* p. 208, Gothein Papers. On the united party congress, see *Mitteilungen . . . der freisinnigen Volkspartei,* pp. 107, 118–119. Cf. *Hilfe* 15 (1909) : 17, 35, 83.

5. *Erster Parteitag der fortschrittlichen Volkspartei* (Berlin, 1910), pp. 11, 26. Fischbeck was the chairman of the executive committee. The chairmen of the central committee and the Reichstagsfraktion, Carl Funck and Otto Wiemer respectively, also came from the old Freisinnige Volkspartei, Ludwig Elm, *Zwischen Fortschritt und Reaktion: Geschichte der*

existed within the National Liberal party, it could have easily attained a leftward direction. However a strong right wing did exist, and its power kept pace with the growing strength of the Young Liberals and the left wing. The right wing, consisting of the Prussian branch of the party and the heavy industrialists of the Centralverband, very early opposed the Young Liberals' radicalism and at the congress of 1906 had fulminated against their demands for a reform of the party's program. Those delegates who struck out most fiercely at the Young Liberals—Eugen Leidig, Wilhelm Beumer, and Paul von Krause—were all associated with the Centralverband. In the spring of 1908, representatives of heavy industry had even more reason to fear the party's radicalization. At the previous year's party congress, Bassermann had advocated support for the right of workers to organize. Stresemann, as a representative of the Saxon light industrialists and of the National Liberals, thereafter attacked the monopolistic practices of the Westphalian coal syndicate. In May 1908, representatives of both Ruhr and Saxon industry met with leading representatives of the Reichstag Fraktion. There the antilabor policies of heavy industry were attacked and the more moderate practices of collective bargaining and worker arbitration committees were advocated. The disagreement between the heavy industrialists and the other groups was so severe that one participant afterward remarked that the discussion proceeded as if the two sides had conversed in Chaldaic and Chinese. In the eyes of heavy industry, the party had deserted its former principle of freedom of enterprise and, through its advocacy of greater equality between worker and employer, had adopted a dangerous left-wing tendency toward democracy.[6]

The right wing decided to fight this tendency through the time-honored use of wealth. The rift between the heavy industrialists and the party coincided with the Prussian election campaign of 1908. In March, heavy industry threatened to withhold campaign funds from National Liberal candidates who stood too far left in the party. Shortly thereafter, Henri Axel Bueck, the director of the Centralverband, urged its members to shift their allegiance to the Free Conservatives and to send

Parteien der liberalen Bourgeoisie in Deutschland, 1893–1918 ([East] Berlin, 1968), p. 210.

6. For the attack on the Young Liberals, see *NL Vertretertag, 1906*, pp. 69, 80, 102–103. For Stresemann's attack, see Thomas Nipperdey, "Interessenverbände und Parteien in Deutschland vor dem ersten Weltkrieg," *Politische Vierteljahreschrift* 2 (1961) : 275; Dirk Stegmann, *Die Erben Bismarcks: Parteien und Verbände in der Spätphase des wilhelminischen Deutschlands* (Cologne, 1970), p. 148. For the disagreement of 1908, see Curt Köhler, *Die Industrie, die politischen Parteien und die moderne Sozialpolitik* (Leipzig, 1910), pp. 29ff.

their campaign contributions to him instead of to National Liberal party headquarters in Berlin. Presumably he intended to use the money to back candidates friendly to the Centralverband regardless of party affiliation. In the middle of April, the press reported that the Centralverband was thinking of transforming itself from an economic into a political organization similar to the Agrarian League. The motivation and purpose of such an organization was to create so much competition for the National Liberal party that it would capitulate to the wishes of the heavy industrialists.[7]

Yet the left wing had no intention of capitulating to the industrialists. During the election campaign, the Prussian Young Liberals meekly submitted their approval to the Prussian party's modest demands for suffrage reform, but they and their supporters refused to support candidates of whom they disapproved. In Berlin, they refused to support Eugen Leidig, the former executive secretary of the Centralverband, and in a Berlin suburb, they publicly opposed the compromise candidate of the National Liberals and Free Conservatives. In some areas, a struggle between Old and Young Liberals ensued over cooperation with the Left Liberals; and in Cologne, the Young Liberals defiantly favored the Social Democrats over the Centre party in the runoff election. In one northern district, two National Liberal candidates, each representing different currents in the party, ran against one another. Each current within the party struggled to dominate the other.[8]

One of the most dramatic party fights occurred in the heavily industrialized Saar, where the party had only one serious competitor—the Centre. The Young Liberals had founded a club in Saarbrücken which had helped to coalesce the progressive elements of the local party— mostly clerks and mining supervisors—against the National Liberal mine and mill owners. The origin of the fight in 1908 was the Young Liberal demand for the recognition of independent trade unions at a time when the industrialists themselves were trying to erect shop unions against the independents. This conflict on the local level directly reflected

7. On the move to withhold campaign funds, see *Berliner Tageblatt,* March 13, 1908, no. 131; Stresemann to Bassermann, April 11, 1908, Stresemann Papers. For press reports, see *Berliner Tageblatt,* April 17, 1908, no. 198. Cf. Hartmut Kaelble, *Industrielle Interessenpolitik in der wilhelminischen Gesellschaft* (Berlin, 1967), p. 198.

8. For the Young Liberals and suffrage reform see *Hilfe* 14 (1908): 338; for the Cologne runoff, *Berliner Tageblatt,* April 11, 1908, no. 188; for the northern district, see *Deutsche Volkszeitung,* June 21, 1909, Zeitgeschichtliche Sammlung, no. 103.

the disagreements over social policy occurring on the national level. The mine and mill owners wanted to nominate their own client—a mining official—but the Young Liberals wanted a more independent man who was the director of the local gymnasium. During the nominations, the Young Liberals and their supporters adamantly refused to renounce their candidate, and the leadership finally conceded to Young Liberal wishes in order to avoid a split in the local party.[9]

The drama in Saarbrücken was but a microcosm of the entire party, and the election results reflected its difficulties. While all the other parties gained, the National Liberals lost a total of eleven mandates including numerous seats in the province of Hanover, a traditional National Liberal stronghold. At least one of these seats was lost to the Social Democrats, who for the first time in Prussian history "conquered seven mandates in the Prussian Duma." A government analyst attributed the National Liberal loss in Hanover to general apathy and to the loss of support among the conservative section of the population that disagreed with the increasing leftist orientation of the provincial party and its newspaper, the *Hannoversche Courier*. Stresemann later attributed the losses to the industrialists' withdrawal of funds and to the fact that the National Liberals had no single professional or economic organization on which to rely. The losses were due either to the mood of the voters or to the lack of funds. In either case, they reflected the crisis between left and right within the National Liberal party.[10]

After the Prussian elections, the heavy industrialists also saw a diminution of their own representation in the Landtag. As a result, various suggestions for a separate party of industrialists and other employers, circulating since the previous year, gained new currency. To prevent the ultimately detrimental effects of this movement on the National Liberal party, should it succeed, Leidig and four others formed an action committee in August 1908 to canvass politicians for membership in a new "Industrial Association" of the National Liberal party.

9. Joseph Bellot, *Hundert Jahre politisches Leben an der Saar unter preussischer Herrschaft, 1815–1918* (Bonn, 1954), pp. 204ff.

10. For National Liberal losses, see Theodor Eschenburg, *Das Kaiserreich am Scheideweg* (Berlin, 1929), p. 112. Of the Social Democratic mandates won, four were later declared invalid by the Landtag's committee for the scrutiny of the polls, *Protokoll über die Verhandlung des Parteitages der sozialdemokratischen Partei Preussens* (Berlin, 1910), pp. 10, 30; see DZAP, Reichskanzlei, Landtag 2/2, I, no. 1081, report of the Regierungspräsident of Hanover on the general election to the chamber of deputies, June 5, 1908.

The committee explicitly wanted to create a "closer tie" between the party and industry to provide "expression for the needs and wishes of industry within the party." It sought to give the National Liberal Fraktion factual enlightenment, to eliminate disagreements between industry and the party through discussion and negotiation, and to contribute to a "healthy compromise between the opposing interests of the different professional groups." Leidig's plan was destined to fail; even the Centralverband rejected it in favor of an independent campaign fund. But not before it provoked a serious discussion of policy within the National Liberal leadership.[11]

In responding to Leidig's proposal, Bassermann sought the advice of both Eugen Schiffer and Gustav Stresemann. Their memoranda are worth a detailed account since they revealed some of the principal concerns of the National Liberals in the waning days of the Bülow Bloc. As their discussion also occurred in the midst of the plans for the tax reform and just before the Reichstag debates on the Daily Telegraph Affair, it may shed light on the National Liberal position during these two events.

In 1908 Schiffer, the future Democrat and justice minister, was a young delegate to the Prussian Landtag and regarded as a member of the right wing. Yet his reflections on Leidig's proposal were far from conservative. Schiffer desired two things: (1) a definite liberalization and parliamentarization of the German government, and (2) the appointment of more liberals to various posts within the government.[12] In this respect, the National Liberals shared certain goals with progressive elements within the Centre party. Both wanted more middle-class non-Conservatives in governmental positions in order to increase the power of their parties and to hasten the achievement of their aims. Such representation would also create a better balance of interests within the government and incidentally accomplish the old liberal ideal of careers open to talent—a continual demand in the years before World War I. The posts which both parties sought to fill and which Schiffer recommended were not high ministerial offices; they were, rather, assignments for "under-secretaries, ministerial directors," and for local officials who did the practical work of government. Liberal men in these

11. DZAP, Bassermann Papers, circular letter, August 20, 1908; cf. Stegmann, *Die Erben Bismarcks*, pp. 151–166.
12. Letter quoted in Eschenburg, *Das Kaiserreich*, pp. 118–119.

positions would be able to influence the formulation of policy and accomplish more liberalization through administrative procedures. Their appointments would be far better than the passage of liberal legislation which was ultimately administered by Conservatives.[13] In order to achieve these posts, the liberals must have powerful support, and an industrial association that included members of the important economic organizations would supply the necessary backing. In this respect, Schiffer's reasoning was not incorrect. Industry did influence government; its power had been proven through a series of events stretching from the protective tariffs to the Vereinsgesetz. Moreover even heavy industry did not always agree with conservative policies even though it generally allied with the Conservatives. The conflict over tax reform amply demonstrated this fact. For Schiffer, therefore, an industrial association connected with the party could be turned to liberal advantage. It could pressure the government for liberal appointments and liberal policies.

In contrast to Schiffer, whose advice ignored the democratic tendencies of prewar Germany, Stresemann stressed the use of an industrial association to increase the party's popularity. The problem of popularity confronted all liberal parties before 1914; they continually lost votes—most frequently to the Social Democrats. This loss diminished their influence in the legislature and led to the alliances which generated so much party conflict. The Badenese and the Grand Bloc merely exemplified this dilemma. Stresemann thought he could solve the problem through better organization. An industrial association connected with the party which served as an umbrella for the business interests of the nation would counteract any plans to form a special employers' party. It would thus avoid that splintering of forces that had weakened liberalism in the past, and the party could lead the new organization in the "right direction." It could distract the various industrial factions from

13. For the social background of the bureaucracy in Prussia, particularly the high percentage of conservative aristocrats in local administration, see Karl Dietrich Bracher, *Die Auflösung der Weimarer Republik,* 2nd ed. (Stuttgart and Düsseldorf, 1957), p. 180, n. 2 ; also J. C. G. Röhl, "Higher Civil Servants in Germany, 1890–1900," *Journal of Contemporary History* 2 (1967) : 116; John R. Gillis, "Aristocracy and Bureaucracy in Nineteenth-Century Prussia," *Past and Present* 44 (December, 1968) : 123. For a good idea of the worth of Schiffer's suggestion, see Arnold Brecht, *Aus nächster Nähe: Lebenserinnerungen, 1884–1927* (Stuttgart, 1966). Brecht was a railway director's son who occupied one of these "hidden" posts during the late Wilhelminian period and the Weimar Republic.

their petty quarrels by focusing on Germany's mission in the world economy. Here, Stresemann revealed the lessons learned from the 1907 election campaign. Nationalism, as well as democracy, was one of the keys to the age. By placing themselves at the head of an organization dedicated to the extension of Germany's economic prestige, the National Liberals could renew their attraction as a party of "national conscience":

> In questions of the colonies, the fleet, and a sharp foreign policy, we must absolutely assume leadership in order to win for ourselves the far-reaching circles which are organized in the Navy and Colonial Leagues and the moderate part of the Pan-German Association. In the liberal professions, there are hundreds of thousands who stand outside the economic conflicts and are not interested whether the tariff is 10 or 5 marks, [but] who yearn for a prestigious, strictly national party. . . . The maintenance of the world economic position of the German Empire is a lasting slogan, independent of the mood of the moment, which will insure us enthusiastic adherents . . . [We] must reckon with great difficulties for the future [if we remain] a middle party in the area of economic issues.[14]

Stresemann wanted to use the economic issue to reemphasize the party's traditional nationalism. This emphasis would broaden its base and increase its popularity. By this means, the party could eventually achieve that governmental influence envisioned by Schiffer.

Although the arguments of the younger men had merit for rejuvenating the party, Bassermann originally vetoed the idea of a National Liberal business organization in the interests of preserving the party's liberal character. He doubted that the party had the strength to lead and direct any economic organization containing the heavy industrialists. He had no illusions about the continued existence of the Centralverband and its reactionary policies. Closer connection between it and the party through a new economic association would lead to its greater, not lesser, domination of National Liberal policy. The new association would create its own treasury, elect its own delegates to the central committee, and push the party in its own direction. This activity would arouse great distrust among all proponents of suffrage reform and social legislation and weaken, rather than strengthen, the party's popular

14. Stresemann to Bassermann, September 5, 1908, quoted in Eschenburg, *Das Kaiserreich,* pp. 115–117.

appeal.[15] Such was Bassermann's position at the end of 1908. One year later he changed his mind due to new developments within the party.

When the National Liberals severed their links with the Agrarian League during the tax reform of 1909, they drew powerful objections from rural party conservatives represented by two Reichstag delegates from Hesse, Heyl zu Herrnsheim and the Count Waldemar Oriola. Both were expelled from the Reichstag Fraktion for voting with the Conservatives in the tax reform. but their expulsion did not silence their criticism. Heyl zu Herrnsheim, particularly, was a powerful figure in national politics and one of the leaders of the state party in Hesse, another National Liberal stronghold. When the left wing in Hesse tried to expel him from the party completely, a majority of the state party congress voted to retain his influential membership. Thereafter he became vociferous in his attack on official National Liberal policy. He and his supporters formed a right-wing clique known as the "Wormser Corner" which took its name from the city of Worms, located in the southern corner of Hesse, where Heyl dominated local politics. The Corner urged a return to the principles of the Heidelberg program and a resumption of the National Liberal alliance with the Conservatives and the Agrarian League. It rejected the increasing friendship with the Progressives. Under Heyl's auspices, the Corner published a right-wing newspaper known chiefly for its bitter attacks on Bassermann. It also reinforced the attacks of the industrialists of the Centralverband so that henceforth, there were two powerful loci of right-wing opposition within the National Liberal party.[16]

The need to combat the alliance of heavy industrialists and agrarians led to the emergence of a nucleus within the party that could properly be termed the liberal center. Drawn to Bassermann, who was supported by Saxons like Stresemann and August Weber, the party treasurer, the liberal center wanted a party that was independent of the conservative right and democratic left. It also coincidentally represented the interests of light industry within the party. In opposition to the right wing, it favored liberal suffrage reform—in contrast to democratic reform—

15. Bassermann to Stresemann, September 7, 1908, Schiffer Papers. Cf. Eschenburg, *Das Kaiserreich*, p. 126.

16. See *Hilfe* 15 (1909) : 449, for the expulsion. On the "Corner," see Günther Kriegbaum, *Die parlamentarische Tätigkeit des Freiherrn C. W. Heyl zu Herrnsheim* (Meisenheim/Glan, 1962), pp. 164–169, 194–198.

progressive social legislation, and the introduction of a national direct
tax as appropriate to a liberal "middle party." The necessity to strength-
en this middle position dictated the creation of an interest group, or
groups, that could compete with the powerful Agrarian League and the
Centralverband. During the tax reform crisis of 1909, two such groups
were finally created under National Liberal auspices: the *Deutsche
Bauernbund* (German Farmers' League) and the *Hansabund*. In the case
of the Bauernbund, the National Liberals exploited the growing resentments of the small farmers in eastern Germany against the economic
and political dominance of the larger Junker landowners. The founders
were formerly active members of the Agrarian League who contended
that the League no longer represented the smaller farmers' interests.
Their program emphasized equality for the small farmer in matters of
taxation, political representation, and economic opportunity. Since these
goals coincided with the general attitude of the liberal center, it hoped
to use the Bauernbund to bolster its own position in the rural strongholds of Conservatism. Originally, these plans seemed promising; the
new organization quickly gained new members in the east and in north-
central Germany. It was particularly successful in Franconia. Yet the
Bauernbund was never so rich nor so powerful as its counterpart in the
business world, the Hansabund. The Hansabund more nearly achieved
Stresemann's goal of linking the party to a broadly based business
organization that would supply the liberal center with important campaign funds. Although the Hansabund originally included the Centralverband, its influence was diluted by a myriad of representatives from
light industry, commerce, banking, the crafts, and from white-collar
organizations. The appointment of Jacob Riesser, director of the
Darmstädter Bank and chairman of the Central Society of Banks and
Bankers, was auspicious for the Bund's political direction. National
Liberal bankers were some of the most enthusiastic supporters of
liberal unity, and Riesser fully intended to forge strong ties with the
Progressives. His policy naturally offended the Centralverband, and it
exhibited its disdainful independence by retaining its own political fund.
Nevertheless the liberal center hoped to find sufficient sustenance for its
"middle" position from the other interests represented by the Hansabund.[17]

The liberal center's key policy was moderation. It wanted to char-

17. *Die bürgerlichen Parteien in Deutschland: Handbuch der Geschichte der bürgerlichen
Parteien und anderer bürgerlicher Interessenorganisationen vom Vormärz bis zum Jahre 1945,*

acterize the National Liberals as a "middle party" free of commitments to either right or left. Yet its campaign against the right inevitably pulled it toward the left. Indeed, the alliance with the leftist Progressives was one of the sources of conflict within the party. Many right-wing National Liberals saw the alliance as the first step toward cooperation with the Social Democrats, and the advocacy of the Grand Bloc by Progressives like Naumann only increased their fears. The liberal center publicly disavowed any association with the Social Democrats, but its struggle against the right wing necessitated its dependence on party groups that espoused such action.

The most enthusiastic advocates of cooperation with the Social Democrats were the Young Liberals, who had first considered an alliance in preparation for the Prussian elections of 1903. At that time, the radical club in Cologne, which believed it only just that the "fourth estate" be heard in the Prussian Landtag, favored local election agreements with Social Democracy if they were necessary to prevent a conservative-clerical majority. Not only the "mother party" but also the majority of the Young Liberals opposed it. The main argument against cooperation, which recurred in subsequent years, was the fear of losing voters. If it took a positive, clear-cut stand for cooperation with the Social Democrats, the party would alienate the rank and file in both Prussia and Saxony. Despite this initial rejection, the idea refused to die, and in 1908 the moderate Young Liberal from Württemberg, Robert Kauffmann, advocated a cooperation between "liberalism and democracy" in order to fight "the spirit of class and caste, the ascendency of the large landowners and large industry" which "conflicts with the well-being of the masses." Though the Young Liberals were, of course, the most vocal left-wing members of the National Liberal party, as the reformist tendency gained ground within Social Democracy, others spoke out in its favor. In 1909, the left-wing *Hannoversche Courier* admonished the National Liberals not to be deluded by the noises of Social Democratic radicalism.[18]

---

ed. Dieter Fricke, 2 vols. (Leipzig, 1970), 1: 415–417, 2: 201–208; Alfred Knoblauch, "Hansabund," *Handbuch für Politik,* ed. Paul Laband et al., 2 vols. (Berlin, 1912–13), 2: 63–67; Jürgen Bertram, *Die Wahlen zum deutschen Reichstag vom Jahre 1912* (Düsseldorf, 1964), pp. 102–107; Hans Jaeger, *Unternehmer in der deutschen Politik, 1890–1918* (Bonn, 1967), pp. 120, 153; Stegmann, *Die Erben Bismarcks,* pp. 176ff; Kaelble, *Industrielle Interessenpolitik,* pp. 182–184.

18. On the trend toward cooperation, see *Nationalliberale Jugend* 3 (1903) : 125–132, 8 (1908): 129–130; and *Hannoversche Courier,* September, 19, 1909, Zeitgeschichtliche

The possibility of rapprochement with the Social Democrats even registered within the Reichstag Fraktion. At the end of 1909, Junck, who had argued for constitutional change during the Daily Telegraph Affair, submitted a memorandum to Bassermann devoted to the entire question. He thought the Social Democratic "danger" was waning despite its growth in mandates and placed his own hopes in an eventual triumph of the reformists; he attributed more importance to the revisionistic *Sozialistische Monatshefte* than to the official *Vorwärts* and eventually expected the Social Democrats to become a radical bourgeois party. He rightly felt that their working-class supporters were more interested in industrial growth and full employment than in revolution. In view of this development, Junck urged the National Liberals to surrender their enmity toward the Social Democrats and seek an accommodation with them. The resulting cooperation could possibly win their loyalty to the national ideals so precious to the National Liberals. Junck's arguments closely resembled those of Rebmann and the Badenese, and he realized that rapprochement eventually led to the Grand Bloc. At the time, he thought the national Grand Bloc an impossibility, but he urged the National Liberals to cooperate with the Social Democrats in every way.[19] His views were supported by other, moderate elements in the party. On New Year's Day 1910, the *Kölnische Zeitung* pointed out that the previously unscalable barrier between bourgeois society and Social Democracy was slowly crumbling away, and it prophesied that Social Democrats would eventually conclude alliances with bourgeois parties. It foresaw no objections to a National Liberal election agreement with the Social Democrats if they were willing to participate in the work of the legislature.

The mounting discussion of rapprochement with the Social Democrats made the right wing increasingly nervous about the future direction of the party. Moreover, the struggle between right and left wings became sharper in 1910 due to severe differences of opinion over the Prussian suffrage movement and the Baden Grand Bloc. For the first time, right-wing attacks during the first half of 1910 endangered Bassermann's position as leader of the party. His own election district, rural Rothenburg-Hoyerswerda, delivered a vote of no-confidence in

---

Sammlung, no. 103.
  19. Eschenburg, *Das Kaiserreich*, pp. 268–269.

his position on the tax reform, and there were rumors that he would not run again for the Reichstag; the right-wing newspapers warmly greeted this news. The left wing rallied to his defense, and the election district of Saarbrücken, dominated by the left, offered him a candidacy in the next election. Bassermann tried to calm the most troubled fears of the right wing in an interview with the influential and conservative *Hamburger Nachrichten* in which he repudiated a national Grand Bloc but rejected any cooperation with the Conservatives as long as the agrarians dominated the party. In other words, Bassermann repeated the philosophy of an independent "middle party" and eschewed cooperation with either the extreme right or left. His attempts to conciliate the right wing failed; fifteen provinces sent their representatives to the party congress of 1910 with instructions to vote against his continued chairmanship of the party, and some members of the Reichstag Fraktion also supported this position.[20]

Because of these tensions, the Kassel party congress of 1910 was an important one for the party's position. The government foresaw that its chief discussion would center on political alliances and sought to steer it toward conciliation with the Conservatives. The right wing predictably propagated a conservative direction, but for the first time at a party congress, the left gave "flaming speeches" in support of the Grand Bloc. The chief spokesman for the left, Rebmann, justified the Grand Bloc in Baden by insisting that it involved no sacrifice of National Liberal principle. He was convinced that the Social Democratic vote for the budget indicated the beginning of their responsible involvement in state and national affairs and stressed the fact that it was the Social Democrats and *not* the National Liberals who first supported the idea of a national Grand Bloc. For the time being, he recognized that the Grand Bloc was applicable only to Baden, but he believed that it might eventually be a strategy possible for the nation as a whole. Others sounded the same tones. Rebmann's southern colleague, Kindermann from Stuttgart, urged the National Liberals not to isolate the Social Democrats entirely. If necessary, they should consider local, tactical arrangements with the Social Democrats in all parts of the nation. These remarks were suggestions—ideas for the future—and both men

20. Walter Koch, *Volk und Staatsführung vor dem Weltkrieg* (Stuttgart, 1935), pp. 51–54; Karola Bassermann, *Ernst Bassermann* (Mannheim, 1919), 145–147; Eschenburg, *Das Kaiserreich*, p. 272.

realized it. Yet their value for party history was the mere fact of their expression. At a congress crucial for the party's future direction, one of the options offered was a national Grand Bloc. The right wing, naturally, greeted such remarks with derision, and the congress itself officially rejected an alliance with the Social Democrats.[21]

Bassermann himself set the official tone of the congress by carving out a "middle" position for the party. As a concession to the left wing—and to his own convictions—he laid the cornerstone of National Liberal politics in an alliance with the Progressives. In order to placate the right, he explained that he considered nothing more than a tactical agreement between the National Liberals and Progressives in order to avoid any renewal of "unhealthy" animosities between them. The advantage of the Bülow Bloc had been the inclusion of the Left Liberals in constructive national politics, and for the National Liberal party as a whole, the Bülow Bloc had been an ideal arrangement. But as long as the agrarians had the upper hand in the Conservative party, it was impossible to cooperate with them. At the same time, any agreement with the Social Democrats was out of the question.[22]

Party unity demanded that Basserman pursue a moderate policy in 1910. An alliance with the Progressives was as far left as he could go. Yet the question of Bassermann's personal inclinations naturally arises. Did he privately favor a Grand Bloc policy despite his public pronouncements to the contrary? Theodor Eschenburg, the last author to cover this period, thought that Bassermann did not entirely reject the idea of the Grand Bloc. Tactical considerations against the Centre made the Social Democrats useful to the National Liberals. This pattern was, of course, followed in Baden, and there we should also seek Bassermann's views vis-à-vis the Social Democrats. He participated when the Baden executive committee first seriously discussed an alliance with the socialists. At that time, he adamantly opposed what later became the Grand Bloc policy. The meeting was private, the scope was limited; he could have expressed himself more ambiguously than he did if he had favored the policy. At the same time, his public speeches recognized

21. DZAP, Reichskanzlei, Parteien 1/3, 2, no. 1394, Hutten-Czapski to Bethmann Hollweg, September 11, 1910, and Bethmann Hollweg to Hutten-Czapski, September 15, 1910. For the right wing, see *NL Vertretertag, 1910*, pp. 51, 65–67. For right-wing preparation for the congress, see Stegmann, *Die Erben Bismarcks*, pp. 222–224. For the left wing, see *NL Vertretertag, 1910*, pp. 47–50, 52–58.

22. *NL Vertretertag, 1910*, pp. 20ff.

the gathering strength of Social Democratic revisionism, but he continued to regard the party as revolutionary and inimical to the Reich. Bassermann never completely freed himself from the Bismarckian categories of "enemies" and "friends" of the empire. A letter to von Bodman, the liberal Badenese minister of the interior, provides another clue to his personal attitudes. At the beginning of 1908, he wrote very negatively about the Badenese Grand Bloc. Liberalism, he said, seriously injured its own cause and its popularity by allying with Social Democracy. Admittedly, the words were written during the conservative period of the Bülow Bloc, but they implied an attitude stretching beyond the considerations of the Bloc. After the collapse of the Bülow Bloc, Bassermann forcefully denied all rumors of a national Grand Bloc, and there is nothing in his correspondence, not even with his protégé, Stresemann, to whom he wrote freely and frankly, to suggest a different private view. Although his judgments of the Social Democrats mellowed for a time after 1910, he still considered them the chief internal enemy of the Reich on the eve of World War I. When Bassermann opposed the Grand Bloc at the party congress of 1910, he sincerely believed his own words.[23]

In this respect, Bassermann closely resembled his Social Democratic counterpart, Bebel. Both men said they opposed the Grand Bloc for ideological reasons. Both tried to strike a moderate pose between the factions of their respective parties. Yet both were beleaguered by strong intraparty opposition: Bebel from the left, Bassermann from the right. We have already seen that Bebel was pushed by the left toward the right. Was it possible for Bassermann to be pulled in the opposite direction? The answer was both more complex and more obscure than it was for Bebel. National Liberal traditions and their role within the Reich were radically different from those of the Social Democrats. The party had helped to create, rather than to oppose, the existing German state. While it considered that state imperfect, it could never assume the radical stance of the Social Democrats. Traditionally, the National Liberals were committed to cooperation with the government. The groups that supported the party were more or less satisfied with

---

23. Eschenburg, *Das Kaiserreich*, p. 10. Bassermann expressed his opposition in executive committee meeting, October 21, 1905, NL Baden; *NL Vertretertag, 1905*, 2: 9, 31–32; Bassermann to von Bodman, January 29, 1908, von Bodman Papers; DZAP, Hutten-Czapski Papers, Bassermann to Hutten-Czapski, June 5, 1914.

existing conditions. As a middle party, the National Liberals constantly
needed to define their borders to the right and the left. Hence their room
to maneuver was somewhat limited. The same principle applied to
Bassermann. His personal background and political career were inter-
woven with National Liberal traditions and roles. He was a weaker
personality than Bebel, and his position within the party was much less
secure. This insecurity imposed limitations on his leadership. He could
support the liberal ideal of parliamentary government in the Daily Telegraph Affair. He could oppose an agrarian tax reform in favor of his
nonagrarian constituents. Yet these actions reflected the traditions of the
party. In both these issues, Bassermann occupied the same camp as
Bebel because Social Democracy grew out of liberalism, not vice versa.
He would later cooperate with Bebel in similar controversies, but this
cooperation required no radical change in the nature of his liberalism.
There were only two issues that demanded a change in traditional
liberalism: political democracy and social legislation. In these matters,
Bassermann was prepared to take some fatal steps. In 1910, he supported a quasi-democratization of the Prussian suffrage. Although he
managed to carry a majority of the party with him, his stance caused the
severe opposition of his right wing in 1910. In social policy, he was
practically alone. His really strong supporters, the light industrialists,
would not make common cause with him in all matters. Here the
organization and complexion of the party made a vital difference. Bebel
could always rely on trade unionists, southerners, and party bureaucrats in local clubs, in party congresses, and in the legislature to support him against the left. Bassermann had to conform to the interests of
"culture and property" that dominated local politics, the powerful
central committee, and nominations to the legislature. They determined
the degree to which the Grand Bloc would succeed within National
Liberalism.

In 1910, these interests opposed cooperation with the Social Democrats. Yet there were conditions that would create a majority from
Bassermann to Bebel. The alliance with the Progressives was a step in
this direction although they themselves eschewed commitment to the
"Barth-Naumann tactic." In 1910, both liberal parties intended to
pursue a course between the extremes of right and left. Both officially
insisted that Social Democracy was a dangerous revolutionary party—

the pariah of German politics. At the same time, both contained elements prepared to pursue a majority of the left.

THE SOCIAL DEMOCRATS

The plausibility of a liberal rapprochement with the Social Democrats depended on Social Democracy's willingness to cooperate with them in the work of the legislature. Before the formation of the Bülow Bloc, such willingness was rare, but a searching look at Social Democracy just prior to 1910 revealed the party's increasing reformism and its desire to play an influential role in German political life. The victory of the trade unions in 1906 and their increasing influence over party policy, Noske's speech in defense of the fatherland in 1907, the victory of the southerners at Nuremberg in 1908, and the formation and success of the Baden Grand Bloc in 1909 all pointed to increasingly responsible participation in the nation's political life. The Social Democrats, in the first decade of the twentieth century, faced the same problems as the liberals: how to gain and maintain popularity and victory at the polls. The desire for electoral victory led them to guard against any policy that exposed them to attacks on their revolutionary and "nonnational" nature and thereby endangered their popularity.

At the beginning of 1909, a small intraparty quarrel clearly showed this concern with vulnerable popularity. The party's executive committee had commissioned Kautsky to write a short pamphlet, *The Road to Power,* developing certain ideas that he had expounded two decades before in the official *Neue Zeit.* After the pamphlet was written and printed, the executive committee refused to approve its distribution because of several seemingly revolutionary passages. A long drawn-out conflict developed between Kautsky and the executive committee. Kautsky originally refused to alter the pamphlet and even appealed to the control commission, a special committee for arbitrating conflicts within the party, which decided in Kautsky's favor. The executive committee, however, refused to honor the decision of the commission, and Kautsky eventually changed the objectionable passages. Kautsky himself was disappointed and disillusioned with the executive committee and particularly with Bebel. His letters to Hugo Haase, the future leader of the party, gave an accurate reading of the leadership's increasing timidity about revolutionary rhetoric:

August's difficulty depresses me the most. . . . He also threw up
to me in the executive committee my article about Cunow's book
because [it was] too revolutionary! The word "revolution" seems to
give him naked physical discomfort. In his memorial address to
W. [ilhelm] Liebknecht, he referred to the "years of the movement" instead of the years of revolution [1848–49]. . . .

Our party is in danger of falling into the rear guard. Already at
the inter. [international] congress in Stuttgart [1907], it played a
sad role, not in the least because of August's *Angst* . . . and that
will become stronger.

August was for years the only fighter and politician in the
p[arty] e[xecutive]. Now he is exhausted. But he will not admit it,
and since he still wants to march at the fore, we should direct our
steps so that he can go along. Humanly understandable, but very
regrettable for our party.[24]

In the matter of Kautsky's pamphlet, the party executive proceeded
cautiously because it feared a trial for treason, based on the objectionable passages, which could injure the party's image with the voters.
Since Karl Liebknecht had been sent to prison only the year before
because of allegedly treasonable passages in his pamphlet, *Anti-Milita-
rism,* the leadership did not want to risk repeated unfavorable publicity
for the party's activities. Bebel himself supported this view against
Kautsky:

With regard to the contents of the pamphlet, I am of the opinion
that one can think all that and also express it in a circle of *confi-
dantes,* but it is pure folly (*Eselei*) to say it in public. . . .

If Karl [Kautsky] had the feeling for solidarity which he should
have, he would have had to declare after our first decision that he
renounced further publication. We all assured [him] that we had
not the slightest objection to the tendency of the tract, but that in
the present situation, we could not wish a trial for high treason,
against him least of all, and besides the tract was an inexhaustible
source for attacks against the party.

24. J. P. Nettl, *Rosa Luxemburg,* 2 vols. (Oxford, 1966), 1: 409. For exchange of letters
between Kautsky and Haase, Kautsky and Bebel, Kautsky and executive committee,
February 19 to March 15, 1909, Kautsky Papers. Quotes from Kautsky to Haase, February
14, 19, 1909, Kautsky Papers.

We are of the opinion that the domestic embarrassment [collapse of Bülow Bloc] compels the discovery of an outlet, and right there a virtuous socialist alarm could be welcome. Why should we then be so dumb as to serve up this feast to our enemies? Karl has no sense for such tactical questions, he looks toward the end as if hypnotized; he has no interest and no understanding for anything else.[25]

Here was a bald consideration of the interests of the party. If one wanted to get ahead, one played the political game according to the rules laid down by the existing society; if revolution were taboo and nationalism in vogue, one did not question the style. Social Democracy never was the revolutionary party thought by its enemies, but it had maintained a good fight against the self-satisfaction of existing society. Now, even this fight decreased in vigor. Bebel's statements were significant in 1909 because of the fight between reformists and radicals. Bebel and the executive committee had previously opposed the reformists and their objection had set the tone for the whole party. But by opposing the radicals from 1905 to the early part of 1909, Bebel and the executive committee tipped the scales in favor of the reformists.

The reformist drift of the party became even clearer with the Social Democratic vote for the tax reform of 1909. Although the Reichstag Fraktion merely voted for direct taxation on the first two readings and made no decision about its vote on the final reading, the party radicals claimed that its action, like that of the Badenese, violated party principle. Hence, they raised the issue at the annual party congress at Leipzig in 1909. In comparison to the previous year's drama, the discussion was tranquil. Because the inheritance tax never came to a final vote, the Fraktion was relieved of the onus of voting for the bill. The discussion therefore took place on the theoretical plane: What if we have the chance again? The arguments aired were essentially the same as the year before. The radicals wanted to oppose all money bills on principle; the reformists thought the party had a duty to relieve the burden of taxes on the working class by substituting direct for indirect taxes if the chance occurred. The reformists pointed out that the party

25. For Liebknecht, see Carl Schorske, *German Social Democracy, 1905–1917: The Development of the Great Schism* (Cambridge, Mass., 1955), pp. 78, 87. Quote from Bebel to Adler, March 6, 1909, *Briefwechsel*, p. 495.

program forbade a Social Democratic vote for indirect taxes, but it specifically demanded direct ones. Therefore a vote for direct taxes was a partial fulfillment of the party's program. The debate on tax voting ended with no resolution of the two opposing views, but it was significant that the Reichstag Fraktion defended itself with arguments similar to those used by the southerners the year before[26] and reflected the degree to which reformist thinking had penetrated the party as a whole.

Since the Social Democrats had voted with the liberals in 1909, the issue of tax voting led naturally to a discussion of cooperation with the liberal parties. Even before the congress at Leipzig convened, many influential delegates suggested the need for such cooperation. In the summer of 1909, the reformist Wolfgang Heine wrote to Vollmar requesting him to use his influence to prevent the party executive from alienating the liberals:

> As skeptically as I personally regard the hope of cooperation with bourgeois liberalism, it would, however, be the most unclever thing we could do at the present time to chop away at it and thus place ourselves on the side of the Centre and the Junkers. For the National Liberals and the Müller-Meiningens [*Freisinnige Volkspartei*], that would be an unearned feast.[27]

At the same time Molkenbuhr echoed Bernstein's view that the differences within the bourgeois camp ought to be exploited for Social Democratic purposes. Franz Mehring, in the *Neue Zeit,* thought the uncertainty of the next elections made aid to the Left Liberals a possible necessity. Nevertheless, at the party congress of 1909, the radicals introduced a motion condemning any cooperation with the liberal parties; they initially won a close majority. On the next morning, however, a group of delegates, headed by the Bavarian Erhard Auer, demanded a revote for the explicit reason of preventing "a rigid election tactic" in the future. As a result of hasty maneuvering behind the scenes, the radical motion was overturned. Convinced reformists saw the vote as another victory for themselves. Josef Bloch, the editor of the *Sozialistische Monatshefte,* wrote to Heine elaborating on this theme:

26. Schorske, *Social Democracy,* pp. 159–162.
27. Heine to Vollmar, July 10, 1909, Vollmar Papers.

We have achieved . . . a complete success in the question of cooperation with the liberals, as no one has demanded more than cooperation over parliamentary bills where both parties have the same viewpoint and . . . support in elections. . . .

In spite of all this, I'd like to request [you] not to stress this success all too much. . . . At this time it would be the most fatal mistake. . . . As you know, my opinion is that the revisionist policy which can be practiced under the present circumstances is exactly that which the party has actually practiced for years. Although they flatter themselves that they dominate the party, the radicals do not direct policy, they only determine the phraseology.[28]

The reversal of a resolution through a revote was hardly a success to celebrate, but it was advantageous insofar as it bound the party to flexibility vis-à-vis the liberals rather than inflexible isolation.

Many Left Liberals, attuned to every sound within the Social Democratic band, were jubilant over the course of the party congress of 1909 and also interpreted it as a reformist victory. This liberal jubilation may have overestimated the significance of the congress, but there were precedents for the kind of cooperation hoped for by both liberals and Social Democrats. In the six-month period before the Bülow Bloc elections, Left Liberals and Social Democrats had concurred with each other on 80 percent of the total votes taken in the Reichstag. Baden was only the best example of cooperation between liberals and Social

---

28. Molkenbuhr Diaries, July 11, 1909. For Mehring, see "Zur freisinnige Einigung," *Neue Zeit* 27 (1909) : 834. On the revote, see *SPD Parteitag, 1909*, p. 501. Cf. Schorske, *Social Democracy*, p. 169, who thinks the executive canvassed a group of "trusties" for the revote. It is much more likely that the reformists themselves reintroduced the vote since before the congress they had prepared for necessary action against the radicals. On August 24, 1909, Erhard Auer sent a circular letter to a group of reformists informing them of common reservations in the *Russischer Hof* to facilitate "quick deliberation" in case of "a squabble harmful to the party." Reservations were made for: Albert Südekum (Berlin), Robert Schmidt (Berlin), Wolfgang Heine (Berlin), Eduard David (Mainz), Karl Hildenbrand (Stuttgart), B. Böhle (Strassburg), H. Sachse (Bochum), Theodor Bömelburg (Hamburg), Carl Severing (Bielefeld), August Brey (Hanover), Gustav Noske (Chemnitz), Paul Hug (Bant), Paul Löbe (Breslau), Hugo Lindemann (Stuttgart), Ludwig Frank (Mannheim), Wilhelm Kolb (Karlsruhe), Georg Gradnauer, (Dresden), Carl Ulrich (Offenbach), Wilhelm Engler (Freiburg), Anton Geiss (Mannheim), Friedrich Profit (Ludwigshafen), Martin Segitz (Furth), Georg von Vollmar (Munich), Hermann Müller (Munich). The list included most of the dependable reformists of the prewar period as well as the leaders of the postwar party, Vollmar Papers. Quotation from DZAP, Heine Papers, Josef Bloch to Wolfgang Heine, September 20, 1909.

Democrats. In Oldenburg, in Hesse, in Hamburg, and even in Bremen, where the radicals dominated the local party, Social Democrats and Left Liberals cooperated in some instances in local elections and in the city council. During the Prussian election of 1908 the Social Democrats in several local districts had approached the Left Liberals and even the National Liberals for an election agreement. In each case, the liberals refused. Now that the Bülow Bloc had collapsed, there was a chance that the liberals would reverse their former lack of interest in cooperation. Indeed one of the first Progressive actions when the Reichstag reconvened after the collapse of the Bloc, was to solicit and receive Social Democratic support in the election for the secretary to the Reichstag. Although an alliance to fill this rather insignificant office was no great event, it tested the Social Democratic desire for cooperation.[29]

In addition to private approaches, the liberals also made public bids for cooperation with the Social Democrats. In the last part of September 1909, Conrad Haussmann published an article entitled, "An Open Letter to August Bebel," in which he chastised the Social Democrats for wasting their energies in confusing and futile demonstrations against the existing system. Instead of chasing their own impossible legislative majority, they should combine with other parties to achieve their goals. He boldly declared that past socialist obstinacy had forced the liberals to seek alliances elsewhere and hinted that this stance might change if the Social Democrats altered their tactics.[30] This plea for liberal-socialist cooperation was the most direct and public appeal yet made by liberals on the national level, and it evoked a private answer from Bebel.

Bebel began with a rejection of Haussmann's appeal: "From your open letter I experienced anew that the conceptual differences over the nature of state and society and the position which our two parties assume in political and social conflicts are unbridgeable." Bebel recalled his acquaintance with Haussmann's father, who had participated in the democratic revolution of 1848. Originally the liberalism and democracy

29. For the increasing liberal cooperation, see Koch, *Volk und Staatsführung*, pp. 28–29; *Nation* 24 (1906): 13; *Vereinigung Parteitag, 1905*, p. 27; *Hilfe* 11, no. 45 (November 12, 1905); *Die Vereinigten Liberalen in der Hamburger Bürgerschaft, 1907–1910* (Hamburg, 1910), p. 12; Kastendiek, "Der Liberalismus," p. 125; *Hilfe* 14 (1908): 301–302; *Kölnische Zeitung*, June 17, 1908, no. 646; Fraktion meeting, December 1, 1909, *SPD Fraktionsprotokolle*, 1: 220.

30. Conrad Haussmann, "Offener Brief an August Bebel," *Aus Conrad Haussmanns politischer Arbeit* (Frankfurt, 1923), pp. 46–61.

of Haussmann's father had resembled many Social Democratic goals, but in the last five decades liberalism and bourgeois democracy had abandoned their original ideals and turned more and more toward the right. He agreed that Social Democracy could renounce its purely working-class demands just as liberalism had discarded its own middle-class ones, but Social Democracy could not renounce its fight against the "exploitation and suppression of human beings by human beings. . .."; its fight was for human freedom as well as for the working class. This fight could be shared with others but never relinquished:

> What we are striving for cannot be accomplished overnight; we are marching in stages. Every progression in one direction leads us nearer the goal, therefore we must want progress in all directions.
>   . . . [W]e will also support every honest liberal demand which the representatives of the bourgeoisie make on the state. We have done that before, and we will do it again, and it will surely be a pleasure for me and all my party comrades if we find ourselves able to support the demands of the bourgeois parties right often. By doing that, we do not renounce our further . . . demands, for we would then cease to be what we are. . . .[31]

This letter answered Haussmann's appeal for a tactical change in two ways. Social Democracy would not alter its basic character; but it would cooperate with the liberals in the pursuit of its goals. Thus, Bebel's response to Haussmann combined the same ingredients of principle and tactic that he used in reconciling the two factions of his own party. Yet his conciliatory attitude did not satisfy Haussmann any more than it satisfied the factions. Haussmann wanted more:

> If you contribute to the fact that your party "marches in stages" and if this would not be pure formula but battle strategy, much progress, necessarily close to the heart of the whole left, could be achieved in time. The most important would be an education toward a constitutional regime, toward political legitimacy, which Germany needs for its own good and which is not to be accomplished [with] the present double division and confusion of political parties.[32]

31. Bebel to Haussmann, September 28, 1909, Haussmann Papers.
32. Haussmann to Bebel (concept), Haussmann Papers.

There was no reply to Haussmann's second letter, and the events of 1909 came to a close with no particular commitment to cooperation with the liberals.

In Baden, of course, the Grand Bloc was formed almost simultaneously with the correspondence between Haussmann and Bebel. We have already discussed its success and its evaluation by the participants. We also know that the existence of the Grand Bloc was one of the reasons that the Badenese Social Democrats voted for the state budget in 1910. We must now turn to the difficulties this vote caused within the party and the way in which they were resolved. Once again, the resolution of the crisis revealed more about the party's real position than did the crisis itself.

Northern Social Democrats were naturally incensed at the Badenese breach of party discipline, and the extreme radicals called for their expulsion from the party. Throughout the summer of 1910, expulsion and isolation seemed a real danger. At the most, the Badenese could hope for badly needed support from their fellow southerners, and they expected the most valuable assistance from the Bavarians. But the Bavarians were mysteriously silent. In the days following the vote, the influential Social Democratic newspaper in Bavaria, the *Münchner Post,* did not make a single comment on the situation. The silence puzzled and disturbed Ludwig Frank. On July 17, he wrote to Vollmar hoping that the Bavarians would not "abandon us in the fight to come." The Badenese intended to stand fast even in face of expulsion; they wanted the Bavarians to vote for the budget also, but the most important matter was solidarity against the rest of the party. Vollmar answered that the *Post*'s silence was due to its desire not to add fuel to the fires already raging within the party. This response failed to satisfy Frank, and he wrote three more letters to the local party leaders. By the end of July, the Badenese feared that the Bavarians would desert them, and they were not the only ones concerned by the Bavarian silence. At the end of July, David, the prominent reformist from Hesse, also wrote to Vollmar:

> This time Berlin will place the matter on a make-or-break basis. I know from a reliable source that Bebel is rashly considering the most extreme eventuality. The resolution of the Berlin . . . meetings shows that this time they want to force us to obedience without any concession whatsoever. . . . In this case, a weak,

disunified stand of the South Germans would be a . . . mistake which could never again be corrected. . . . If we do not succeed in leading the entire party into . . . a healthy development, we at least have the duty of preventing the ignorance of the majority of the North from letting this development go up in smoke for the South   the decision lies with the Bavarians. If you falter, if you let the Badenese down, then the Berliners have won. . . .

David's source was reliable; even Bebel had lost patience with the unorthodox Badenese.[33]

Shortly after the Baden vote for the budget, Bebel had written Carl Ulrich, the leader of the party in Hesse, praising a Progressive decision to support the Social Democrats in an election in Friedberg:

I am pleased at such a *Blockpolitik* for the run-off elections; there, no sacrifice of principle and intellect is demanded as is the case with our Badenese who only remember occasionally, in order to salve their consciences, that they should be Social Democrats, [but] otherwise indulge in National Liberal politics. For the National Liberals dominate, not us. In such cases it's always the left which prostitutes itself. The party has never yet been handled so foolishly and stupidly as by the "*real*-political" Badenese. . . .

Here Bebel reiterated the same principles he had written to Haussmann half a year before. Limited cooperation, yes; renunciation of principle, no. It was his fear of diluting the party's goals that provided the key to Bebel's acquiescence, for the first time in the conflict of reformists and radicals, to a party split:

A part of our people are like the National Liberals, they give up all principles and are grateful for all condescensions offered them. They have forgotten all thought, or all shame, or both. Now, I hope it will come to a clear altercation at Magdeburg [the party congress]. . . . I have had enough of this eternal discussion and needling; if we cannot fight in the same battleline anymore, then it is better we part peacefully [and] amicably. . . .[34]

33. For the clash between northerners and southerners, see Schorske, *Social Democracy,* p. 190. Frank to Vollmar, July 17, 1910, Vollmar Papers; Frank to Timm, July 21, 26, 30, 1910, Ludwig Frank, *Aufsätze, Reden, und Briefe,* ed. H. Wachenheim (Berlin 1924), pp. 171–173. For letter cited, see David to Vollmar, July 29, 1910, Vollmar Papers.

34. Bebel to Ulrich, July 23, 1910, Carl Ulrich, *Erinnerungen des ersten hessischen Staatspräsidenten* (Offenbach, 1953), pp. 207–208.

Apart from this letter of Ulrich, there was no explanation for Bebel's sudden adoption of a hard line. His position hardly meant that he favored the radical line in all instances; indeed his espousal of a limited Blockpolitik eliminated such an interpretation. He merely feared, as he said, a Social Democratic development similar to that of liberalism.

While Bebel and the radicals considered a split, the same struggle between radicals and reformists raged within the Bavarian party. Frank wanted the Bavarians to vote for their own state budget and thereby reduce the isolation of the Badenese. Yet the Bavarian budget of 1910 was unsatisfactory to many liberals; it could hardly be acceptable to the Social Democrats. If it had been a matter of local importance only, the vote on the budget in 1910 would not have been so momentous, but the need and duty to support the Baden party and the view to future action made the situation particularly tense. Bavarian silence was therefore explicable in terms of the disunity and tension within the local party. Vollmar and the circle around him wanted to approve the budget, but the Bavarian radicals, centered in Nuremberg, opposed it. As the vote on the budget grew closer, the pressure from Frank more desperate, and the need for decision more compelling, more of the Bavarian Fraktion drifted over to the side of the radicals, and in order to press on to victory, they even called a special caucus without the knowledge of the leadership. The reformists would gladly have avoided any decision at all, and they favored abstention during the vote. Despite this attempted compromise, the radicals within the party eventually conquered by a majority of one vote, and on August 5, two days before a meeting with the Badenese, the Bavarian Fraktion decided to vote actively *against* the budget.[35] This decision did not, however, mean that the Bavarians would deprive the Badenese of southern support at the party congress. Their action merely reflected the Bavarian situation of 1910 and in no way negated their belief in the independence of state parties.

Aid for the Baden party was also forthcoming from another, unexpected quarter: the party executive. Molkenbuhr remarked immediately after the Baden vote that the Nuremberg resolution had become "untenable." He observed that the resolution created grave difficulties for the party in Baden and realized that, despite all protestations of the radicals, the party congress would not expel the Badenese.

35. Auer to Vollmar, August 3, 1910, Vollmar Papers. Cf. Reinhard Jansen, *Georg von Vollmar: Eine politische Biographie* (Düsseldorf, 1958), p. 99.

Molkenbuhr's private observations were always a good indicator of the winds wafting through the party's directory. At the end of July, while the party awaited the Bavarian decision, Friedrich Ebert and Hermann Müller, respectively the future president and chancellor of the Weimar Republic and the emerging leaders of the party executive, traveled to Munich to talk with the Bavarian leadership. No one knew what Ebert and Müller accomplished in Munich, but the fact that they withheld information about their mission from Bebel and others was enough to make Bebel fear they were engaged in negotiations. Ebert had risen in the party ranks as a known reformist and trade-unionist, and he supported every policy that would hold party and trade unions together. He had once opposed making any resolution that would bind the party to an inflexible policy. At Nuremberg in 1908, he had favored a rejected compromise resolution which proposed consultation with the party executive before a state party decided to vote for the budget. Was it possible that Ebert and Müller were acting on the basis of this "consultative" resolution despite its rejection at Nuremberg? Late in August, when the Bavarian and Badenese party congresses were held, Ebert and Molkenbuhr attended and canvassed the opinions of the local organizations. As a result of these conversations, the party executive opened negotiations with the Badenese in order to prevent a needless conflict at the party congress and to consider the creation of a commission to review the whole problem of the vote for the budget. As Molkenbuhr had predicted, the executive, at least, was prepared to view the Nuremberg resolution as "untenable."[36]

Meanwhile, both sides began to develop their arguments. Kautsky, in Neue Zeit, stressed the Badenese breach of discipline; others raised the specter of party anarchy. Frank was not slow to respond. In the first issue of September's Neue Zeit, he published "The Truth about the Baden Rebellion." In this article, he made two points pertinent to the situation in Baden: (1) Former party resolutions allowed the party to

36. Molkenbuhr's views about the crisis and the account of his visits with the southerners can be found in his diary, July 15 and August 20, 1910. The degree to which Bebel was informed appears in his letter to Kautsky, July 27, 1910, Kautsky Papers, and in his letter to Ebert, August 20, 1910, Bebel Papers. For information about the executive's negotiations, see DZAP, Haenisch Papers, Zetkin to Haenisch, September 12, 1910. Cf. Zetkin to Dittmann undated photocopy, Dittmann Papers. On Ebert's role, see Georg Kotowski, Friedrich Ebert: Eine politische Biographie, vol. I: Der Aufstieg eines deutschen Arbeiterführers, 1871–1917 (Wiesbaden, 1963), pp. 207–213.

vote for the budget in case the Social Democrats were in the majority. In a number of towns, the Social Democrats had a majority on the town council and regularly voted for the budget without arousing any protest. Yet the resolutions did not provide for a case in which the Social Democrats formed a *part* of the majority as in the Badenese Grand Bloc. The Grand Bloc in Baden *was* the majority and the only one possible to counter reactionary policies. (2) The participation of the Social Democrats in the Grand Bloc was not merely a case of the Social Democratic sheep following the National Liberal wolf. The Social Democrats in Baden did not delude themselves into thinking that the liberals were interested in the ultimate goals of Social Democracy. The Social Democrats in the Grand Bloc merely compelled the liberals to endorse liberal policies: secular teachers' colleges, local government reform, an increase in teachers' wages, a reasonable income tax. These were all attainments of the cooperative majority—attainments that the radical Prussians and Saxons should carefully examine before they cut off the "rotten branch of Baden." Once again, Frank chose to defend the Badenese in terms of the Grand Bloc and its accomplishments. But in 1910, he no longer spoke of the so-called Grand Bloc. Instead he elaborated on its implications for the future of the party. Like Rebmann at the National Liberal congress, Frank intended the Grand Bloc as a serious option in Social Democratic policy.[37]

Prior to 1910, the party had never experienced a situation where it exercised considerable political power. The Badenese were the first Social Democrats to exercise real influence in a state or national legislature. Kolb, in his own defense of the Baden party, tried to describe this experience. Like Frank, he stressed the importance and the achievements of the Badenese in parliamentary participation. He even envisioned a situation in which the party had a chance to exercise ministerial responsibility without achieving its goal of republican government. "Do you really believe," he asked his fellow Social Democrats, "that the Social Democratic and the monarchical form of the state are exclusive concepts in each and every circumstance? . . . It is not a matter . . . of socialism and monarchy. . . . In both questions . . . it is a matter of something else—a matter, which in monarchies ruled by parliaments, will sooner or later become acute for

37. Schorske, *Social Democracy*. Frank, *Aufsätze*, pp. 174–183.

our party." Kolb believed the party would eventually exercise real power, and he did not think the monarchy would then disappear overnight. And he said so. Nor did he believe the Social Democrats would merely ignore the monarchy: "Such an attempt would be . . . political insanity; the consequence would be, not the disappearance of the monarchy, but the disappearance of Social Democracy."[38] Kolb's prophecies fell on deaf ears. The radicals wished a victory in 1910, and they refused to see further than the fact that the Badenese had clearly violated existing party principles.

The fight over budget voting, with Bebel and Frank as the main antagonists, lasted for two days. Frank's defense was essentially the same as his article written two weeks before: "One cannot agree to enter Parliament in order to wage a battle of obstruction against it." In contrast to his previously private bitter remarks, Bebel's public remonstrances were mild and conciliatory. For the reformists, he reiterated the necessity of adhering to party principle; for the radicals, he urged consideration of party unity. Most importantly, he linked the offensive actions of the Badenese with their participation in the Grand Bloc. Not only did the vote for the budget stem from participation in the Grand Bloc, the Grand Bloc itself violated the Dresden resolution forbidding any cooperation with bourgeois parties. The Bloc was particularly offensive because it included the most capitalistic party in the nation: the National Liberals. Yet Bebel refrained from recommending the expulsion of the Badenese even while he condemned their cooperation in the Grand Bloc. Thus his speech, like that of his liberal counterpart, Bassermann, really achieved two purposes. It maintained party unity by disavowing a majority of the left. For the Social Democrats, as for the liberals, a commitment to the Grand Bloc would be premature.[39]

The subsequent proceedings of the Social Democratic congress have been amply recorded in the annals of party history. The party executive, in order to secure party unity, introduced a motion that merely ex-

---

38. Wilhelm Kolb, *Die Taktik der badischen Sozialdemokratie und ihre Kritik* (Karisruhe, 1910), p. 32. Just after the party congress, Georg Ledebour, speaking in the Reichstag on behalf of the Social Democrats represented an almost identical viewpoint. See Rudolf Vierhaus, "Kaiser und Reichstag zur Zeit Wilhelms II," *Festschrift für Hermann Heimpel zum 70. Geburtstag am 19. September 1971*, 2 vols. (Göttingen, 1971), 1 : 273–274.

39. Frank, *Aufsätze*, pp. 195–196; *SPD Parteitag, 1910*, pp. 239–259.

pressed disapproval of the vote for the budget. It also succeeded in persuading the radicals to withdraw their motion calling for immediate expulsion if the Badenese created another budget scandal. Bebel, in order to conciliate the radicals, explained that according to existing party statutes, anyone who wished could begin expulsion proceedings within a local party organization, and he recommended their use to avoid arbitrary action that could wreck the party. Had the matter rested there, everyone could have gone home with relief that a crisis had once again been averted. But Frank, anxious to push his victory to the limit, fliply dismissed the executive's motion with the anecdote of an old beggar lady caught stealing wood who was released with the threat of a fine the *next* time. Such a threat didn't bother her a bit: "I'll steal my wood and pay my fine;" the remark exactly described Frank's position at the congress. The flippancy with which Frank chose to regard a party scandal ruffled the radicals' feathers; after the formal vote approving the executive's motion, they reintroduced their own amendments threatening expulsion proceedings should there be a subsequent vote for the budget. The South Germans left the room in a huff, and the radicals succeeded in passing the amendment easily, 228–64.[40]

After the vote, the Magdeburg congress of 1910 seemed a victory for the radicals. Although the southerners stood their ground, there was little sense of the moral victory that had followed Nuremberg. In contrast to the mood after Nuremberg, the general feeling among southerners after Magdeburg was one of caution. But, in reality, Magdeburg was the radicals' last stand. The fact that the Badenese remained in the party, that the executive negotiated with and accommodated them, that Bebel was persuaded to be conciliatory, all foreshadowed the eventual defeat of the radicals. This defeat would then remove the most formidable Social Democratic barrier to cooperation with the liberals and to the Grand Bloc.

The Progressives recognized this foreshadowing of things to come. The *Berliner Tageblatt* emphasized Bebel's mildness and toleration in dealing with the Baden party; it thought "his well-earned authority" ought to be powerful enough to determine a conciliatory position on

40. For Frank's anecdote, see Wilhelm Keil, *Erlebnisse eines Sozialdemokraten,* 2 vols. (Stuttgart, 1947–48), 1 : 220, and *SPD Parteitag, 1910,* pp. 359–367; for the amendment, pp. 376–384.

the part of the factions. Radicals and reformists would always exist, it tolerantly maintained, but reformism would have to "assert itself" in order to attain better conditions. The Left Liberal Georg Gothein wrote an article predicting that the reformists would become even stronger after Magdeburg just as they had after Dresden and Nuremberg. And the chief advocate of the Grand Bloc, Naumann, exasperatedly refused to accept the rejection of his idea by both Bassermann and Bebel at their respective party congresses. Instead he once again directed an appeal to both party leaders:

> Tell me what the left should wait for! Why do we indulge in politics? In order to dispute, or to achieve something? Is it enough for Bebel always to be the revolutionary without the revolution, and is it enough for Bassermann, . . . as the coming man, to chase after a situation which never comes? For that, too much political blood would have to flow in the veins of these two men.[41]

Naumann's exasperation reflected the halting progress of the Grand Bloc—a progress impeded by the timid hesitation of the parties involved. Yet even as Naumann wrote, political events had begun to erode this timidity.

41. See *Berliner Tageblatt,* September 21, 1910, no. 479, October 4, 1910, no. 503; *Neue Freie Presse,* September 27, 1910, clipping, Gothein Papers.

6

The German Problem and Germany

THE GERMAN PROBLEM: PRUSSIAN SUFFRAGE REFORM

In the winter of 1910, a southern visitor to Berlin described his impressions of the city in the midst of the Prussian suffrage movement:

> Everything streamed in the open air, here and there. . . . *Unter den Linden* we came up against powerful cordons of police; at the Brandenburg Gate stood police reserves and a herd of horses which bestowed upon the elegant square the appearance of a bivouac. . . . In the *Wilhelmsstrasse* a few hundred people were forced away so that they could not communicate to the . . . Chancellor their wishes for a better suffrage. . . . [W]e drove toward the palace through four or five chains of police who held back every harmless pedestrian, even women and children, a secure 500 meters in the circumference of the palace; a police lieutenant was the master of the situation here, around him a staff of ten to twelve police officers, behind each a motorised policeman as ordnance; 200 police infantry, 60 mounted stand ready; we South Germans know gendarmes only in individual or group appearances, here they form mass appearances. . . . The streetcars which run in the area of the palace park cannot stop, and the doors must be closed so that no high traitor can spring out; the Spree is watched by the river police so that no suffrage friends come to the palace by boat; the soldiers are waiting in the barracks for the eruption of revolution. . . .[1]

This "revolutionary" situation existed because the government had finally specified the terms of reform announced two years before. Now, as then, the bill was a bitter disappointment to all those who hoped for

1. *Fortschritt* 5 (1910) : 102–103.

true reform. The only important changes were the substitution of direct for indirect election and the elevation of certain educated or official persons to the next highest voting class. There was no mention of the secret vote demanded by all parties (except the Conservatives), no hint of a change in the class suffrage, no provision for a shift from the old method of districting so odious to the National Liberals. The bill contained only one feature, *Maximierung* (maximization), to reduce the plutocratic character of the suffrage: no taxes over 5,000 RM would be reckoned for the determination of voting class.[2]

This proposal clearly met neither the demands of the Progressives nor the Social Democrats, and even before deliberations began in the Landtag, these parties began cooperative and concurrent demonstrations against its limitations. As always, the Social Democrats took the lead in extraparliamentary politics. Unable to create a worthy platform within the legislature and spurred on by radical exhortations for a mass strike, they took to the streets. In February, the demonstrations gained momentum and culminated on the first Sunday in March when the *Tiergarten* suffrage march called the bluff of the Berlin police. The demonstrations assumed the character of a revolutionary movement, and the Prussian government, with its cordons of police and other prophylactic measures, reacted accordingly. The government had good reason to fear popular agitation. Although the Social Democrats led the demonstrations, for the first time in the history of the movement, they were not alone. Three years before, Naumann's Left Liberal weekly, *Hilfe*, censured the Social Democratic demonstrators. Now it wrote that although the Progressives did not expect the Social Democrats to achieve a new suffrage with their demonstrations, "there is nothing to object to if it refines this new . . . means of propaganda in order to increase, to maintain awake and alive in the consciousness of the people, the significance of the suffrage issue. . . ." These words were a clarion call for middle-class, as well as working-class, demonstrations.[3]

The Progressives, by supporting the demonstrations, had borrowed

---

2. Walter Koch, *Volk und Staatsführung vor dem Weltkrieg* (Stuttgart, 1935), p. 39.

3. On the socialists' demonstrations, see Schorske, *German Social Democracy, 1905–1917: The Development of the Great Schism* (Cambridge, Mass., 1955), pp. 177–179; *Schulthess, 1910*, p. 123. Compare *Hilfe* 12 (1907) : 466 and 16 (1910) : 99 for that magazine's tactical shift.

a page from Rosa Luxemburg. Whereas two years before, Barth had difficulty arousing even limited Left Liberal support for the socialist suffrage movement, in 1910, the Progressives themselves began to demonstrate. In at least two cities, Frankfurt and Solingen, they cooperated with the Social Democrats in staging large-scale street demonstrations. The climax of their protest came at the end of February with a large assembly of "intellectuals" in the Circus Busch in Berlin. Although the meeting was respectably middle-class, some Social Democrats attended and reinforced the idea of cooperation, and by this time the Progressives had even succeeded in drawing the National Liberals into the movement; two of their left-wing members also spoke at the Circus Busch. The meeting passed a resolution for the introduction of the Reichstag suffrage into Prussia. Afterward, the crowd of 8,000 inside the hall joined those demonstrating outside (who had come too late to be admitted), and these liberal, middle-class demonstrators thronged along the river Spree to the palace, where they shouted their disappointment with the chancellor and their pleas for the democratic suffrage. In Breslau, the local National Liberal club joined the fray by holding a public protest meeting where Bassermann himself was the main speaker, and another National Liberal group met in Altona, a neighboring city to Hamburg, to demonstrate for the secret vote.[4]

While the frustrated opposition to the Prussian suffrage vented its emotions in the streets and meeting halls of Germany, the Prussian legislature met to deliberate the specific provisions of reform. From the beginning the position of the National Liberals was particularly important for the fate of the bill. Both the Conservatives and the Centre supported the government's proposal, so it clearly had a majority. Yet the government placed great weight on the approval of the National Liberals and had privately pressured them to cooperate[5] even though the bill did not satisfy two of their important demands: the secret vote and a more equitable division of election districts. If the National Liberals compromised and approved the bill, they would retain their old position as a governmental party and insure the passage of an unpopular reform. If they held out for concessions, they ran the risk of

4. For the Frankfurt, Solingen, and Berlin demonstrations, see *Hilfe* 16 (1910) : 132–133. Cf. Koch, *Volk und Staatsführung*, p. 46; for Breslau and Altona, *Schulthess, 1910*, p. 128.

5. DZAP, Hutten-Czapski Papers, 237, penciled memorandum, no date.

alienating both government and Conservatives and endangering reform, but they also gambled on the possibility of winning a majority that could include the Centre as well as the Progressives and Social Democrats. Thus the National Liberal position was as important for the future direction of the party as it was for the fate of reform.

In this important matter, the National Liberals did not hesitate to take a direct stand; they immediately declared their opposition to the bill and maintained the direction resulting from the collapse of the Bülow Bloc. Unless the government were prepared to make important liberal concessions, the National Liberals would not cooperate.[6] But their position did not wholly stem from a decided devotion to liberal ideals. A key to their thinking was supplied by an influential member of the party, von Einem, who wrote to Schiffer during the deliberations over the bill. Like other National Liberals, von Einem realized that the most important election districts were the great industrial cities of the west, where a liberalization of the suffrage was necessary to satisfy the political aspirations of both the liberal middle classes and the Social Democrats. All of his suggestions were predicated on the maintenance of the class suffrage and the public ballot. Mainly, he wished to tinker with the suffrage in the large and growing urban areas. In these areas he wanted to introduce a system whereby the different classes voted separately instead of altogether as formerly. This change would remove some of the pressure accompanying the public ballot and allow the Social Democrats, "with justification," to capture the second class. Thereafter he would increase the number of mandates in these urban areas and institute a proportional suffrage among the classes. His plan would free "the three-class suffrage . . . from weaknesses;" indeed, by means of these last suggestions, it "would be newly fortified insofar as whole classes—*Mittelstand,* heavy industry and commerce—will have an interest in it." The proportional suffrage particularly would benefit those very classes that supported the National Liberals. It also had the additional advantage of insuring a majority for the "national" parties in urban areas, such as Upper Silesia, with a large non-German population.[7] In other words, the National Liberals, or at least a part of them, wanted to achieve a balance between their own interests, the interests of the state, and a just suffrage. In achieving such a balance, the Na-

6. Eugen Schiffer in *Verhandlungen Preussens,* Legislaturperiode 21, Session 3, 2 : 1460,
7. Von Einem to Schiffer, April 11 and c. April 13, 1910, Schiffer Papers.

tional Liberals would be able to gain the advantage over other parties and increase their own strength. They wanted to play the same game with the Prussian suffrage that their Badenese colleagues played, in the same year, with the reform of local government. They were willing to accept Social Democratic mandates—but not too many—as necessary for "peace and quiet," but they mainly wanted to insure their own survival and expansion.

An increase of National Liberal power would certainly occur at the expense of the Conservatives. This result was already implied by Basser-mann and Witting in 1908 when they both complained about Conservative political dominance. At that time, the National Liberals had hoped to make major gains in the Prussian elections since they correctly thought it would incline the government toward more liberal policies.[8] The squabbling over influence in the Prussian legislature was one cause of the collapse of the Bülow Bloc, and National Liberal jealousy of Conservative power determined their stand in the issue of suffrage reform. Their opposition was supported by industrialists who wanted to promote their own concerns rather than those of the Conservative agrarians. The farmers and residents of small towns in Hanover also favored a reform that would advance their interests at the expense of the Conservatives. In addition, any reform that diminished the power of the Conservatives would increase the stature of the parties supporting it in the eyes of all those who felt slighted or disenfranchised by the existing suffrage. Given these advantages, the National Liberals had every reason to oppose the government.

Yet every other non-Conservative party shared the desire of the National Liberals to gain at the expense of the Conservatives, and in this respect, the position of the Centre was important. In order to form a majority for any reform that was opposed by the Conservatives, the votes of the Centre were absolutely necessary. The Centre opposed an abolition of the three-class suffrage because it feared the resultant liberal and Social Democratic encroachment on the important Prussian connection between state and church. Also the Prussian Centre, like the Prussian National Liberals, was more conservative than other branches of the party. Yet it by no means agreed completely with the Prussian Conservatives. For instance, like the National Liberals, the Centre favored the introduction of both direct election and the secret vote, and

8. DZAP, Reichskanzlei, Parteien 1/3, I, no. 1393, Roell to Scheefer, August 27, 1907.

in these matters, it could have made some accommodation with the National Liberals. But apparently politics in the hotly contested areas of Rhineland-Westphalia, where Catholics had a majority and heavy industry vied for power, prevented a compromise. In his letter to Schiffer, von Einem specifically mentioned the National Liberal desire to gain at the expense of the Centre in the Rhenish west. It was impossible to gain Centre support for a reform that would diminish its power in its most important stronghold.[9]

The political avarice of the National Liberals in dealing with the Centre was most evident in the issue debated most extensively when the bill went to committee: Maximierung. In contrast to the government's plan for noncalculation of taxes over 5,000 RM, the National Liberals suggested that at least 10 percent of the voting population of larger districts constitute the first class, at least 20 percent the second class, and 70 percent the third class. When this suggestion failed to secure approval, they demanded that at least 30 voters belong to the first or second class. Both these proposals would have released the connection between voting class and taxes paid, particularly in the rural and less populous districts, and reduced the importance of wealth for the Prussian suffrage, but they would also have challenged the Centre's political strength in the Rhineland and in Silesia. Thus the Centre had no scruples about making an agreement with the Conservatives, and when the Conservatives offered a compromise maintaining indirect election but introducing the secret vote, the Centre consented.[10] Thereafter all efforts of the liberals to gain a more liberal suffrage failed in the face of the united and persistent opposition of the Centre and Conservatives, and the liberals continued to oppose the bill when it went to the upper house.

During the deliberations in the upper house, the government, accustomed to National Liberal support and dependent on the party's political weight and prestige, pressured the Conservatives to obtain a change satisfactory to the National Liberals. Under this pressure, the

9. See John Zeender, "German Catholics and the Concept of an Interconfessional Party," *Journal of Central European Affairs* 23 (1963–64): 428; Karl Bachem, *Vorgeschichte, Geschichte und Politik der deutschen Zentrumspartei,* 8 vols. (Cologne, 1927–31), 7 : 115–122.

10. For the liberals' proposals, see *Verhandlungen Preussens,* Legislaturperiode 21, Session 3, 3:3075–3083; on the Centre's response, Koch, *Volk und Staatsführung,* pp. 42–43. Cf. Bogdan, Count von Hutten-Czapski, *Sechzig Jahre Politik und Gesellschaft,* 2 vols. (Berlin, 1936), 2 : 17–18.

Conservatives in the upper house consented to introduce a more equitable method of dividing the population into thirds. In contrast to the National Liberal percentage clause, the proposal retained wealth as the determination of voting class, but it also provided for more districts with fewer inhabitants so that great variations of wealth between the classes in any given district would not exist.[11] Because of the greater homogeneity, one man's vote would carry greater weight than it previously did. Nothing shows more than these manipulations the legal and political difficulties caused by the complicated three-class suffrage. At any rate, the compromise was made with an eye on the National Liberals in Rhineland-Westphalia who had long complained that the method of districting discriminated against them and who were expected to benefit from it the most.

The compromise provoked a battle within the National Liberal party. The government, heavy industry, and the Prussian leader Friedberg all pressured the Prussian Fraktion to accept it. Within ten days in May, the Westphalian Provincial Committee, which would gain most, passed a resolution *for* the compromise, while the Hanoverian Committee, which would gain very little, passed a resolution *against* it. Indeed the compromise insured the continued dominance of the Conservatives in the rural areas of Hanover, Brandenburg, and East Prussia, and these provincial National Liberals all opposed it. Bassermann, who usually avoided interference in Prussian party affairs, warned against the compromise: "The mood of the country is completely clear; the overwhelming majority does not want the decisions of the upper chamber and if we bow before the money power of Westphalian industry, then we have lost our moral justification for existence (*sittliche Daseinsberechtigung*). . . ." Even Friedberg had to admit that the party rank and file opposed the compromise. Eventually the Prussian Fraktion resisted the pressures of government and heavy industry and refused to accept the upper chamber's proposal. Deprived of valuable National Liberal support, the government withdrew the bill, and suffrage reform in 1910 became a dead letter.[12]

11. *Verhandlungen Preussens*, Legislaturperiode 21, Session 3, 6: Drucksache no. 393, pp. 4206–4207.

12. Hutten-Czapski, *Sechzig Jahre Politik*, 2: 22ff. Heavy industry also favored the public ballot retained in the upper-house version, Stegmann, *Die Erben Bismarcks*, pp. 200–201. On the National Liberal split, see *Schulthess, 1910*, pp. 281–282. Bassermann quoted from

The National Liberals' rejection of reform once again placed them in the opposition with the other parties of the left, and this fact had implications for their future relationships with the Social Democrats. As in the tax reform, the National Liberals did not consciously ally with the Social Democrats; it was rather the Social Democrats who sought to find some common ground with them. After noting with disappointment the National Liberal hesitation over the upper chamber's compromise, the Social Democrats outlined a future strategy for the left:

> My dear gentlemen from the National Liberal party, . . . I demand nothing impossible from you, I do not expect that you support the equal suffrage, [but] I hope that you will now hold fast to National Liberal principles. . . . How will the parties constitute the next bill? . . . [C]are must be taken that it is formed by the entire left. . . . If you get to work more energetically, if you enlighten the people through the press and through assemblies, and if the Progressives do their part, then the Centre will also find it necessary to attach themselves . . . to the left and not to the Conservatives . . . [I]f the reform is made by the left, it will be [a] different [reform]. I take that for granted from the National Liberals; and the Centre will not allow itself to be overshadowed in a democratic way by the National Liberals.[13]

This hope for reform from the left implied the future cooperation of the Social Democrats, but since the structure of the Prussian suffrage precluded any large Social Democratic contingent in the Landtag, their future support would only be nominal. The significance of the Social Democratic statement was to be found in its change of tone and policy. Instead of pronounced resistance to any reform that fell short of their total democratic demands, the Social Democrats in Prussia, like their colleagues in Baden, agreed to approve even the limited reform favored by the National Liberals. There could be no more positive evidence of the reformist character of Social Democracy and its willingness to cooperate with other parties if only it were met halfway.

Bassermann to Schiffer, May 24, 1910, Bassermann remnant 303/17. Friedburg's admission in DZAP, Reichskanzlei, Landtag 2/1, III, no. 1071, Hutten-Czapski to Bethmann Hollweg, April 29, 1910.

13. Heinrich Ströbel in *Verhandlungen Preussens,* Legislaturperiode 21, Session 3, 5: 6026–6028.

POLITICAL DEMOCRACY

The issue of Prussian suffrage reform involved the further liberalization or democratization of German politics, and this issue united all the parties left of the Conservatives since all stood to increase their own power as a result of such reform. Despite its alliance with the Conservatives, the Centre, as well as the liberals, desired to augment its influence, and its participation in the Black and Blue Bloc was the same kind of bid for power as the liberal participation in the Bülow Bloc. Moreover the Centre's democratic elements sometimes placed it at the head of reforming movements. In Baden its concentrated agitation, in cooperation with Progressives and Social Democrats, had finally forced the National Liberals to approve a thoroughly democratic reform. Naturally the reform benefited the Centre. On the other hand, in Prussia, the National Liberals stood to gain at the Centrist expense, and this eventuality accounted for the Centrist lack of cooperation and the failure of Prussian suffrage reform. In both instances, the stand of the middle parties, National Liberals and Centre, was important because they possessed the most influence with the government and hence decided the fate of the reform. Also they usually acted as leaders of the other two parties. After the Centre won the suffrage battle in Baden, the National Liberals led in the formation and functioning of the Grand Bloc. At the time of the Bülow Bloc, the Centre had helped to lead the opposition to the Vereinsgesetz; the National Liberals led the campaign against the tax reform. Both middle parties competed with one another for leadership over the parties of the left, and the idea of the Grand Bloc was the result not only of Naumann's political schemes but of this competition; the Grand Bloc formed the infantry for the National Liberal generals. Because Baden had an insignificant Conservative movement, the Grand Bloc functioned purely against the Centre. Because of the heavy Conservative weight in Prussia, the Grand Bloc formed a nucleus that could develop a magnetic attraction for the Centre. In the Reichstag, the Grand Bloc could function in much the same way, and its attraction for the Centre was very strong in the matter of political democracy. Since the national Centre party was much more liberal than its Prussian appendage, the magnetic quality of the Grand Bloc was particularly apparent in the 1911 debates over the constitution for Alsace-Lorraine.

Alsace-Lorraine became part of the German empire after the Franco-Prussian War, but it was not incorporated with the same autonomous rights and privileges as the other German states. Instead, it was given the status of a territory (*Reichsland*) under the theoretical administration of the Reichstag. In practice, the kaiser administered the territory and appointed a governor and a military commander. The territory sent fifteen delegates to the Reichstag and three delegates to the Bundesrat, but the latter three exercised a mere advisory function and had no right to vote. The territory's representative assembly of notables, elected by an indirect class suffrage, could be overruled by the Bundesrat or the Reichstag at any time. This inferior political status had long irritated the inhabitants of the territory, and in 1908 the governor of Alsace-Lorraine, Count Karl von Wedel, suggested a constitution granting Alsace-Lorraine the same autonomy as other states in order "to free [its inhabitants] from the humiliating feeling, coming more and more sharply to the fore, of being second-class Germans."[14] The imperial government finally heeded his admonitions and at the end of 1910 produced a constitution. Yet even this constitution did not completely eliminate the second-class status of Alsace-Lorraine since it provided for a governor appointed by the kaiser and denied it any vote in the Bundesrat. Both the government and Conservatives feared that Alsatian votes would ally with those of the other southern states to threaten Prussia's dominance in the Reich. Hence important aspects of second-class status were retained, and the only significant change was the transformation of the assembly of notables into a bona fide legislature of two houses with the lower house elected by a plural suffrage.

When the government introduced the constitution to the Reichstag at the end of January 1911, none of the parties reacted favorably. The Conservatives thought too many concessions had been made, the other parties thought not enough, and virtually all the parties left of the Conservatives wanted to grant Alsace-Lorraine three votes in the Bundesrat. In the matter of the suffrage for the lower house, the National Liberals, Progressives, and Social Democrats wanted to set aside the plural suffrage proposed by the government in favor of a more equitable proportional suffrage.

14. Quoted in Hans-Günter Zmarzlik, *Bethmann Hollweg als Reichskanzler, 1909–1914* (Düsseldorf, 1957). p. 86. Subsequent background information from the same source, pp. 92ff. Also Dan P. Silverman, *Reluctant Union: Alsace-Lorraine and Imperial Germany,*

The Reichstag committee that deliberated the constitution tackled
the issue of the votes in the Bundesrat first, and its initial decision was
to grant Alsace-Lorraine three votes in the Bundesrat against the wishes
of the Conservatives. In this matter, Centre, National Liberals, Progressives, and Social Democrats acted concertedly. Each genuinely
believed that this reform was necessary and just, and each could benefit
from it politically in Alsace-Lorraine. This insistence confronted the
government with a dilemma. As long as the kaiser continued to appoint
the Alsatian governor and administration, Prussia would determine the
votes of the three members in the Bundesrat. As a result, the South
German states could demand compensation for the de facto increase
in Prussian power. Once such compensation were made, a new problem
would arise. If Alsace-Lorraine ever became a German state similar to
the others, with its own princely house and government, it would probably ally with the other southern states against Prussia. In both the short
and the long term, the three Alsatian votes threatened Prussian supremacy in Germany. Bethmann Hollweg, as Prussian minister-president,
found the problem disagreeable. Faced, however, with the determination
of all the non-Conservative parties, he decided to compromise. The
compromise stipulated that the three votes would not be counted if they
were the only three votes needed to pass a measure supported by Prussia.
In this way, he avoided the need to compensate the South German
states and preserved Prussia's role in the Bundesrat.

The matter of the suffrage proved more difficult. As in the Prussian
reform, the chief conflict resulted from the competition between Centre
and National Liberals. If the existing suffrage were changed, one of
these two parties ran the risk of losing mandates. In Alsace-Lorraine,
the Centre feared losses if proportional suffrage, advocated by the
liberals, were introduced. Instead the Centre wanted the Reichstag
suffrage, which provided for the representation of districts rather than
parties and granted it an electoral advantage. At the same time, the
difficulty of introducing the Reichstag suffrage into Alsace-Lorraine
was the implied connection between it and suffrage reform in Prussia.
A reform of the Alsatian suffrage presaged reform in Prussia and
thus generated Conservative opposition. Because it divided the
Conservatives from the other parties and caused conflict between the
middle parties, suffrage reform in Alsace-Lorraine was problematical.

1871–1918 (University Park, Pa., 1972).

Yet this problem would decide the fate of the constitution for Alsace-Lorraine. Finally at the beginning of May 1911, a series of informal meetings began which dragged on for two weeks while Centre and National Liberals hectically haggled over their respective political positions in Alsace-Lorraine. Agreements between the two were made and broken repeatedly, and the outlook for a genuine constitution for Alsace-Lorraine looked grim. But just as negotiations seemed about to break down, a change occurred within Social Democracy. On May 17, at the height of the disagreement, *Vorwärts* printed an article that promised Social Democratic support for the constitution if the plural suffrage proposed by the government were changed. On the very next day, Clemens von Delbrück, the secretary of the interior who had hitherto ignored the Social Democrats, invited them for the first time to the informal negotiations, and on the basis of an agreement reached on May 18, the Reichstag suffrage was approved for Alsace-Lorraine. This settlement meant that the constitution for Alsace-Lorraine would be passed in a form that altered the government's proposal considerably. It would also be passed against the wishes of the Conservatives by a majority of the Centre combined with the Grand Bloc.[15]

In fact there were several remarkable maneuvers connected with the Alsatian constitution. It was the first time in decades that the government consented to the passage of a major bill that did not have the approval of the Conservatives. In contrast to its previous insistence on cooperation between Conservatives and National Liberals in the Prussian suffrage reform, the government, in the case of the Alsatian constitution, counted more on the support of the Centre and National Liberals backed by the left than it did on the Conservatives. Secondly, it was willing to accept Social Democratic pressure for a successful compromise measure. When the Social Democrats, the Centre, and the Progressives declared their vote for the Reichstag suffrage, they clearly composed a majority. Thereafter the National Liberals were persuaded to join them, and their cooperation assured the passage of the Reichstag suffrage. Under pressure from the same combination of parties, the National Liberals had accepted the Reichstag suffrage in every other southern state. Why not in Alsace-Lorraine? Yet their decision was

15. *Hilfe* 16 (1910) : 425. On the Conservative opposition, see von Payer to Haussmann, May 15, 1911, Haussmann Papers. Cf. Albert Südekum, "Die Elsass-Lothringische Verfassung und die Sozialdemokratie," *Sozialistische Monatshefte* 15 (1911) : 817. For the Social Democratic action, see *Vorwärts*, May 9 to 20, 1911.

probably influenced by the knowledge that a Grand Bloc policy was already being formulated in Alsace-Lorraine that would even their political score with the Centre.[16] Thus the Social Democrats played a double role in Alsatian constitutional reform. Their weight in the Reich obtained the Reichstag suffrage for the Centre; their cooperation in Alsace-Lorraine promised Grand Bloc leadership for the National Liberals.

The Social Democratic double role was, however, exceeded by the significance of its maneuver for the direction of the party. In the tax reform of 1909, the party had played a passive, if positive, role in supporting direct taxation. Now, for the first time in the Reichstag, they *offered* to play an *active* and positive role in an important political issue. Once again, their position indicated the truly reformist nature of the party. As was the case whenever reformism reared its ugly head, the radicals needled the Fraktion to maintain its "pure" opposition, but even the Fraktion was divided; in caucus, fourteen members (out of forty-four present) voted against accepting the Alsatian constitution. Some requested and were granted the right to absent themselves from the voting as long as nonparticipation had "no demonstrative character," and this strategy would be used again as reformism grew stronger and factional differences increased. Ludwig Frank, who handled the negotiations with the government and the other parties, explained why Social Democracy played its remarkable role:

> The Social Democratic Fraktion regrets profusely that it has not succeeded in obtaining for Alsace-Lorraine a democratic constitution corresponding to its demands. The transferral of the state's power to the Kaiser and the institution of an upper house are in contradiction to the wishes of the majority of the [people of] Alsace-Lorraine whose interests we have represented. . . . However we trust that the universal, equal, secret and direct suffrage . . . will have the strength to carry through the will of the people of Alsace-Lorraine . . . against the first chamber and the power of the Kaiser, and we are convinced, that the repercussion of the introduction of this suffrage on the other states [which are] backward in this respect, can also not be detained.

16. *Die Parteien: Urkunden und Bibliographie der Parteikunde*, vol.1: *Beihefte zur Zeitschrift für Politik* (Berlin, 1912–1913), p. 230.

Political concessions were acceptable to the Social Democrats even if they were not the demanded total democracy. Thus in the Reich, as in Baden and Prussia, the Social Democrats would constructively participate in parliament if the chances for political democracy were increased.[17]

The actions of the non-Conservative parties in the negotiations over the Alsatian suffrage had important implications for the theory of the Grand Bloc. It meant that such a bloc could include the Centre as well as the liberals and socialists. In Prussia, the Social Democrats admonished the National Liberals to strive for a reform that the Centre could support. In the Reichstag negotiations over the Alsatian suffrage, they effected a compromise between Centre and National Liberals. In both cases, the government indicated it would yield to an anti-Conservative reform only if *both* Centre and liberals supported it. In Prussia and in the Reich, the situation differed from the one in Baden. There, no important Conservative party existed, and politics naturally divided the Centre from the liberals and Social Democrats. In the north, the enormous power of the Conservatives, lodged in the Prussian administration and the Landtag, required the heavy counterweight of the combined non-Conservative parties in order to achieve stable and permanent reforms. The government could not risk offending the Conservatives unless it had the support of the two middle parties. Therefore any bloc desiring to wring liberal or democratic concessions from the government *had* to consist of the Centre, the National Liberals, and the parties of the left.

Although the Centre frequently allied with the Conservatives, it also shared many common interests with the liberals and Social Democrats. In effect, the Centrists were fence straddlers like the National Liberals, and their party divided between similar left and right wings. When the right wing dominated, as it did in the tax bill and the Prussian suffrage reform, no cooperation with liberals or socialists was possible. When the left wing succeeded, a national Grand Bloc was formed. Henceforth, the various parties would continue to discuss the Grand Bloc as if it

17. For the vote, see Fraktion meeting, May 26, 1911, *SPD Fraktionsprotokolle*, 1 : 248. Karl Albrecht, Joseph Emmel, Ernst Geck, and Georg Ledebour were absent during the vote in the Reichstag. Heine was also absent, but as a reformist, he could hardly have protested the vote, *Verhandlungen des Reichstages*, 267 : 7158–7160. Frank's speech appears in 267 : 7127.

included only liberals and Social Democrats. In actual practice, however, this narrow bloc could not succeed without the Centre's support. In reality, a successful national Grand Bloc was a majority of all the non-Conservative parties.

SOCIAL LEGISLATION

Even though the Grand Bloc could function in political reforms, there was one issue where cooperation was extremely difficult: social legislation. The difficulty was already apparent in the debate and passage of the Vereinsgesetz where paragraph 7 had been inserted with an eye toward curbing trade-union activities. A similar issue arose and preoccupied the parties simultaneously with the negotiations over the Alsatian constitution.

In January 1909, the government proposed a bill to institute a system of *Arbeitskammern* (literally, chambers of labor) as the workers' counterpart to the existing Chambers of Commerce, Chambers of Agriculture, and Chambers of Handicrafts. Similar bodies existed in France with much benefit to the workers, and although most of the parties agreed on the necessity for such chambers, there was an important disagreement over the role these chambers should play. Should they be labor arbitration committees, made up of both workers and employers, concerned with keeping the "economic peace," or should they consist purely of workers concerned with protecting their own interests? The government's bill provided for committees primarily concerned with keeping the "economic peace." Their duties would consist of conducting studies of the industrial and economic circumstances of their districts, of stimulating measures for improving the economic position and well-being of the workers, of acting as employment bureaus, of cooperating in collective dargaining, and of arbitrating industrial disputes. In order to appease the opposition of many industrialists, who feared the committees would fall under trade-union influence, the government, during the formulation of the bill, had consulted industrial pressure groups such as the Centralverband and the Association of Saxon Industrialists. Their influence was successful insofar as the bill included employers as well as workers on the committees and excluded trade-union officials.[18]

18. Karl Erich Born, *Staat und Sozialpolitik seit Bismarcks Sturz* (Wiesbaden, 1957), pp. 178, 225–230, says the bill contained little evidence of industrial influence. *Hilfe* 14

Although there were a host of other objections to the government bill, it was the exclusion of trade-union officials from the committees that became the central issue, particularly since officials of employers' organizations were not excluded. As representatives of industrial interests, the National Liberals supported the provision. As representatives of the trade unions, the Social Democrats opposed it, and in committee, they banded together with the Centre and the Progressives, whose parties also included trade unionists, and amended the bill to allow for trade-union representation. This proposed change henceforth evoked much bitterness between National Liberals and Social Democrats. The National Liberals accused the Social Democrats of wanting to include trade-union officials for "purely political purposes." In their view, the officials could not

> possibly withdraw themselves from the influence of the trade unions, and it is to be assumed with . . . compelling necessity that the [Social Democratic] trade unions will exploit the labor committees . . . through the medium of their officials. . . . Such a lively opposition will arise on the side of the employer that the labor committees [will] not become instruments of peace, instead they will further conflict.

The National Liberals opposed trade-union representation because they feared that the unions would eventually control the committees in a way detrimental to industrial interests. For their part, the Social Democrats objected to the inclusion of employers on the committees because they would not grant the workers the "same power" that other economic groups possessed. The inclusion of the trade-union officials would achieve a certain independence of the worker from his employer and at the same time give official recognition and power to the trade unions. The National Liberals and industry naturally objected to this official independence; they favored labor committees only if they were so constructed that the employers could control them. In the vote over including trade-union officials, the National Liberals and the Conservatives voted against, while the Centre, Left Liberals, and Social Democrats voted for, inclusion. Although the parties for in-

---

(1908) : 100, noted that these organizations had all protested against the bill out of fear of the trade unions. For text of bill see *Verhandlungen des Reichstages,* 276; Drucksache no. 523.

clusion constituted a majority, even without the Social Democrats, the government, once again deprived of National Liberal support, withdrew the bill.[19]

In the proposal for the Arbeitskammern, the economic interests of the National Liberals confronted those of Social Democracy directly. Because each party felt it could not benefit from a compromise in the economic sphere, a Grand Bloc failed to develop; hence there was no reform. In this case, the National Liberals considered it more advantageous to side with the Conservatives just as the Centre had previously joined them in the issue of direct taxation. The National Liberal stance revealed one of their basic attitudes. Although they shared with Social Democracy a desire for political reform, they were not willing to recognize Social Democratic power in the socioeconomic sphere of German life.

The best example of this socioeconomic antagonism to Social Democracy occurred during the debates on the National Insurance Reform. Since the 1880s, Germany had a full-scale program of national workers' insurance. The reform of 1911 proposed to consolidate the separate programs—sickness, accident, and old-age insurance—and place them more directly under the control of the central government. It also intended to introduce a survivors' insurance and to extend all insurance coverage to rural and domestic workers, who had not previously been fully protected.[20] In principle, all parties from the Conservatives to the Social Democrats agreed with these aims, and the government was sure to find a majority for the bill.

The most serious issue that divided the parties was the personnel of the administrating agencies for sickness insurance and the method of making decisions within these agencies. Under the existing law, the workers administered their own sickness insurance since they paid two-thirds of the premiums, and the law therefore entitled them to two-thirds membership on the administrating agencies; employers, who paid only one-third of the premiums, received only one-third representation. In the course of time, the Social Democratic trade unions had captured

19. For Social Democratic opposition, see Heyl zu Herrnsheim and Karl Legien in *Verhandlungen des Reichstages*, 234 : 6295–6307; for the amendment, see Born, *Staat und Sozialpolitik*, p. 232. National Liberals' reaction expressed by Max Horn in *Verhandlungen des Reichstages*, 262 : 3481–3482. For the bill's final disposition, see *Hilfe* 15 (1910) : 818.

20. *Akten zur staatlichen Sozialpolitik in Deutschland, 1890–1914,* ed. Peter Rassow and Karl Erich Born (Wiesbaden, 1959), p. 412. Cf. Adelbert Wahl, *Deutsche Geschichte, 1871–1914,* 4 vols. (Stuttgart, 1926–1936), 4 : 86–89.

the workers' representation on the administrating agencies, and the employers began to complain about the Social Democrats' administrative abuses. In formulating the bill, the government heeded the employers' complaints and changed the proportional payment of premiums and the representation on the administrating agencies. Henceforth, employers and employees would share the cost of the sickness insurance premiums equally and each would receive half the representation on the administrative committees. This provision increased the influence of employers in the administrating agencies and deprived the workers and the trade unions of their previous advantageous position in the appointment of insurance officials and in the decisions over the amount of payment to sick workers. Once again the economic interests of Social Democrats and National Liberals clashed. The National Liberals, together with the Conservatives, agreed with the government's measure to redress the balance of representation in the administrating agencies; Social Democrats, Progressives, and Centre opposed it, and when the bill went to committee, these three parties voted to reinstate the previous system of representation. The National Liberals accepted this change because representation was not the only issue.[21]

The control of administration was also at stake, and here the National Liberals won a victory. Although the Centre agreed with the Progressives and the Social Democrats on the issue of representation, it was not willing to grant full administrative powers to the workers or to the Social Democrats. Accordingly, the Centre voted together with the Conservatives and the National Liberals for a provision that the chairman of the administrating agencies had to be agreeable to the majority of the employers' representatives on the one hand and to the majority of the employees' representatives on the other hand. Each group would vote separately for the chairman of the entire agency. This provision would have almost the same effect as the government's representation provision; it would deprive workers, trade unions, and Social Democrats from enjoying the power they had previously exercised. Yet because of the weight of the workers as a group, it could give them more

21. On the employers' complaints, see *Politisches Handbuch der nationalliberalen Partei* (Berlin, 1908), pp. 104–105; for the government's response, *Akten zur . . . Sozialpolitik,* p. 412. Cf. Wahl, *Deutsche Geschichte,* 4: 86–89. The National Liberal, Max Horn, supported the government's bill and Franz Behrens reported the position of the other non-Conservative parties in *Verhandlungen des Reichstages,* 261 : 2469; 266 : 6621.

bargaining power than the employers. For their part, the Social Democrats thought this provision gave the upper hand to the employers and would cause bitterness among the workers, and they wanted to reinstate the old method of electing the chairman by a simple majority of all members of the agencies voting together. When they introduced a motion to this effect in the Reichstag, the debate which followed was laden with emotional resentment. Once again, the National Liberals used the occasion for an attack on the previous system and on the Social Democratic abuses in the administrating agencies:

> . . . A natural opposition exists between employer and employee and . . . the purpose of the state's . . . social legislation . . . is to reconcile these differences . . . in the interest of the state. . . .
>
> The present legal situation in the local sickness insurance agencies is now demonstrably one in which the employees have the upper hand . . . in every case . . . . [This] has had consequences which we must condemn under all circumstances. If the political battle spills over into social legislation in the way it does in Germany, then there is the chance that it also reverberates in the sickness insurance agencies and that Social Democracy as such tries to win influence over the . . . agencies through the workers and through the law. . . .
>
> . . . [W]e ought never to relinquish to one political party those institutions which we have erected to the furtherance of social welfare in the interest of social peace . . . and least of all to a party which endeavors to disturb the social peace in the way that the Social Democratic party does.[22]

Because they feared Social Democratic power in the socioeconomic sphere, the National Liberals wanted to rid the public insurance agencies of its officials just as they had wanted to bar trade-union officials from the Arbeitskammern. Since one of the underlying principles of German sickness insurance was self-administration, and since the National Liberals were willing to fight for such self-administration in rural areas where Social Democracy was weak,[23] this battle against

22. For the controversy over the chairman, see *Verhandlungen des Reichstages,* 280: Drucksache no. 946, Teil 7, pp. 124–25; no. 951, 5148. For quotation, see Max Horn. 266 : 6615–6621.

23. Horn in ibid., 261 : 2468.

the Social Democrats in the administrating agencies was social and economic discrimination insofar as the National Liberals wanted to deny the Social Democrats, as representatives of the workers, responsibility and control over their own economic affairs. The National Liberals, as representatives of important industrial interests, did not want to pass any legislation that would limit the "freedom" of the industrialists and lead to their estrangement from the party.

In contrast to the position of the National Liberals, the Progressives supported the Social Democrats. They particularly felt that the provision for election of the agencies' chairmen was unjust. They feared that the new measure would only increase bitterness between employer and employee and would lead to abuses on the part of the employer. As a solution to the problem, the Progressives suggested a proportional election of chairmen which would prevent both employees and employers from gaining the upper hand and allow for possible coalitions between the two groups.[24] Only the Progressives and the Social Democrats voted for this suggestion, so the provision for the separate election of the agency chairman was passed into law. Here the party constellation was hopelessly splintered. The Centre, which first suggested the separate election, occupied a mediating position between the left and the National Liberals, but the spirit of the law favored the antiworker attitudes of the National Liberals and was a reactionary rather than a reformist measure.

There was one other provision of the National Insurance Reform that showed how hard it was for the National Liberals to endorse any kind of social or economic reform. Under the old insurance provisions, a worker was eligible for an old-age pension only after the age of seventy, but the Social Democrats introduced a motion to reduce the age of eligibility to sixty-five. The government argued that such a provision would cost too much money, but both Progressives and National Liberals originally supported the Social Democrats and stated that the extra nine million marks needed for reducing the age limit could easily be raised. The motion was only defeated by the votes of the Conservatives and the Centre. The Centre said it favored child-care payments first. In an attempt to put the measure on the books, the Progressives then introduced a motion whereby sixty-five would become the eligible age in 1917. The Social Democrats supported this motion, but the

24. Cuno in ibid., 266: 6637–6640.

National Liberals completely reversed themselves. Whereas the National Liberals originally supported the lower eligibility age, the majority now voted against the compromise Progressive motion. Only two South Germans—Ernst Blankenhorn (Baden) and Friedrich Thoma (Bavaria) —voted for it, and five National Liberals, among them Bassermann, abstained.[25]

This discrepancy in the National Liberal vote did not reflect ambivalence over social legislation as much as uneasiness over the orientation of the party in general. The principal debates and decisions of the National Insurance Reform were made in committee during the summer of 1910. At that time practically the only Reichstag members in Berlin were those working on the proposed reform, and after a long day's work in committee, they found themselves dependent on one another for entertainment in the evening. The National Liberal delegates met in a Berlin night spot called the *Dessauer Garten:*

> There one entered into deep conversations, particularly about whether a leftist departure had occurred in the party, or whether it was imminent, or even whether the way for a Grand Bloc policy was being paved. One felt it necessary to stress more strongly the differences between liberalism and democracy and talked himself into many kinds of bad temper which had no foundation.[26]

Those delegates who worked on the insurance committee were not the most liberal party members, and they were bombarded every day with Social Democratic motions for extensions of social welfare and workers' representation. They were also subject to pressure from the government. Bassermann himself complained that the committee delegates had too much contact with and had been too much influenced by the government. The leader of the Fraktion during the committee deliberations on the insurance bill was the archconservative Saxon jurist, Rudolf Heinze, who, according to Bassermann, became very anxious about democracy or parliamentary government and opposed a policy of the Grand Bloc unconditionally. In addition to pressure from the government, the

25. For the parties' positions on the lower age limit, see Otto Mugdan, FVP: Emil Faben, SPD; Johannes Becker, Z; and Gustav Stresemann, NL in ibid. 267: 6916ff; for the revote, see 267: 7332–7335. For the Left Liberal motion, see 281: Drucksache no. 1057, paragraph 3.

26. Bassermann notations, no date, Bassermann remnant 303/17.

National Liberals also had to deal with pressure from the Centralverband. After the second reading of the insurance bill in the Reichstag, when the National Liberals had voted for the lower pension age, the Centralverband met in Berlin and passed a resolution against the "increase of the burden of insurance" which endangered the "position of German industry." Although this act was a rejection of the entire insurance reform, it was also an implicit censure of the Fraktion's stand on old-age pensions. The Centralverband's chairman explicitly opposed the Progressive agreement with the Social Democrats on many points of the insurance bill,[27] and he thereby implicitly objected to the National Liberal "friendship" with the Progressives. The awareness of the Centralverband's displeasure with the bill and its importance for the party must have influenced many National Liberal representatives in the Reichstag. Thus the majority of the Fraktion voted against the extension of old-age pensions in the third reading. Although Bassermann urged the party's support for progressive social legislation, the National Liberals were unwilling to oppose the government or important industrial interests, and above all they wanted to avoid the appearance of being a leftist party on socioeconomic matters.

When the final vote on the insurance bill occurred, the Social Democrats were the only party that voted en bloc against it as a reactionary law directed against themselves. The National Liberals, the Conservatives, and the Centre voted for the bill. These were predictable votes. The Progressives, however, found themselves in a dilemma. Should they vote with the National Liberals and preserve liberal unity? Or should they vote with the Social Democrats as a demonstration of their democratic liberalism? Eventually they split; twenty-five voted for the bill, ten voted against it and one abstained. The only strong supporter of the bill was Naumann, and even his support was equivocal. He felt the Progressives ought to vote for the bill to show their support for such social legislation as sickness insurance for agricultural workers and survivors' insurance. On the other hand, his criticisms of the bill resembled those made by the Social Democrats: the representation of workers in the administrating agencies was worse than before.[28]

In general, the Progressives and the Centre straddled the fence between the National Liberals and the Social Democrats in social legisla-

27. *Vorwärts*, April 29, 1911, no. 100.
28. For the Progressive position, see *Die Parteien*, pp. 63–64; *Hilfe* 17 (1911): 354–355.

tion. Both represented a middle position between the two extremes since both had to resolve the conflicting interests of business and labor within their own parties. Yet neither could find a compromise palatable to both National Liberals and Social Democrats. In the proposal for the Arbeitskammern, their stand favored the trade unions and hence the Social Democrats, but it offended the business interests of the National Liberals. In the National Insurance Bill, they supported a compromise designed to balance the interests of business and labor. Their compromise failed to win Social Democratic support. In truth, the conflicting interests of National Liberal business and Social Democratic labor were almost unbridgeable. Thus a Grand Bloc policy in socioeconomic legislation was almost impossible.

IMPERIALISM

If political democracy and the social question were two important issues of prewar Germany, imperialism and its relationship to nationalism and foreign affairs was a third. In 1911, the Moroccan crisis brought this problem to the attention of the Reichstag. The Moroccan crisis is much too familiar to bear much retelling. Briefly, Morocco was an area where French and German imperialist ambitions clashed, and it had already sparked a previous crisis in 1905 and a diplomatic defeat for Germany at the Algeciras Conference of 1906. In 1909, the two states signed a treaty that gave the French "political dominance" and the Germans "commercial equality" in Morocco. But when the French exercised their treaty rights and established a protectorate over Morocco in 1911, the German government decided to use it as a ploy for some sort of imperialist compensation. In a threatening gesture, they sent the warship, the *Panther*, to the Moroccan port of Agadir to force the French to negotiate. This action generated a crisis that kept all Europe on tenterhooks during the summer of 1911 but finally led to a treaty between France and Germany granting equal trading rights to Germans in Morocco and the cession of the northern slice of the French Congo to the German Cameroons. As an adjustment, the Germans gave a small piece of the Cameroons to French Equatorial Africa.

This peaceful settlement, while pleasing to some, dissatisfied the many Germans who linked national prestige and imperial policy. The National Liberals, with their strong commitment to German imperialism, were particularly disappointed with the compensation granted by

France. From the beginning of Germany's tentative imperialistic ventures, they unquestioningly believed in her right to expand and protect her economic interests throughout the world. In order to create and uphold the position (Weltstellung) she deserved, she had the same right to colonies and spheres of influence as every other European power. Insofar as the *Panther* upheld Germany's Weltstellung in Morocco and in Africa, its presence in Agadir in 1911 aroused the "highest satisfaction" within the party. Its mood was "nervous, restless . . . and thirsty for deeds . . .," and it expected the crisis either to save Morocco from the French or to wrest as compensation an equally valuable prize from the French colonial empire. In September, Bassermann called for increased German armaments as if the implied threat of war could force more consideration from the French. The party even entertained the notion of a "great middle African empire." Throughout the crisis, the National Liberal business interests supported the party's demands, and in some cases, egged it on. The nationalist-imperialist tone of the National Liberal press was so intense that the secretary of the foreign office, Alfred von Kiderlen-Wächter, had an interview with Schiffer in the middle of August where he "sharply and clearly" explained the limited aims of the government and requested a milder tone in the future. The interview had little effect. Instead, the government's willingness to accept moderate compensation aroused a storm of protest. All over the land, local National Liberal clubs met to censure the government. The resolutions of greater Berlin and the province of Brandenburg aptly expressed their mood:

> We expect . . . that the rest of the powers grant the German Reich and people that measure of economic possibility of expansion and political influence that we can and must claim by virtue of our strength and our quickly growing population. . . . The alleged offer of France to transfer to us parts of the French Congo for concessions in Morocco must be rejected as fully insufficient.

The final settlement, which took shape during the fall of 1911, hardly satisfied this imperialist hunger. Bassermann later labeled the grants from the Congo the "two old bones (*Entenbeine*)" which could not "be compared to the advantages that France derived from the treaty."[29]

29. On the National Liberal response to the Moroccan crisis, see Bassermann notations, no date, Bassermann remnant 303/17; DZAP, Hutten-Czapski Papers, Schiffer to Hutten-

As it became apparent that the government intended to ignore their "thirsty" desires for more compensation, the National Liberals pounced upon a scheme to embarrass its negotiations with the French through a forced public debate. In the middle of October, the Reichstag convened, and all parties immediately interpellated the chancellor about the Moroccan question. At that time, the treaties were not yet signed, and the government wanted no political disturbance to abort the final settlement. Thus Bethmann Hollweg refused to answer any interpellations. His silence made all parties, including the National Liberals, fear that the opinion of the Reichstag would be ignored in this very important issue.[30] Constitutionally, the Reichstag was helpless to do anything about treaties with foreign countries. Treaties that directly affected the budgetary or taxing powers of the Reichstag definitely needed its approval, but in other areas, the constitution was quite vague. The constitutional gap causing the most concern to the National Liberals in 1911 was the powerlessness of the Reichstag to control acquisitions or cessions of national territory. One constitutional clause ambiguously hinted at parliamentary jurisdiction in these matters, but the government had no intention of interpreting it in favor of the Reichstag. In 1911, such an interpretation would have involved the approval or disapproval of the treaties with the French and amounted to parliamentary control over foreign affairs. In this respect, the constitution was quite clear: the kaiser was sovereign in foreign relations.

This was the situation that the National Liberals set out to change in the fall of 1911. Angered, disappointed, and thwarted over the loss of their "middle African empire," they formulated, for parliamentary action, a motion whereby the chancellor could not sign the treaties with the French "*before* the Reichstag, as the designated representatives of the German people, has been heard on the matter." Although the motion did not go so far as to specify the approval or disapproval of treaties with foreign countries, it was a definite bid to extend the powers

---

Czapski, August 17, 1911; *Die Parteien,* pp. 26, 217; Ernst Bassermann in *Verhandlung des Reichstages,* 268 : 7734–7736; Georg W. F. Hallgarten, *Imperialismus vor 1914 : Die soziologischen Grundlagen der Aussenpolitik europäischer Grossmächte vor dem ersten Weltkrieg,* 2 vols., 2nd ed. (Munich, 1968), 2 : 238ff. Also Klaus Wernecke, *Der Wille zur Weltgeltung: Aussenpolitik und Oeffentlichkeit am Vorabend des ersten Weltkrieges* (Düsseldorf, 1970), pp. 42, 75–79, 110ff.

30. *Vorwärts,* October 18, 1911.

of the Reichstag into the realm of foreign affairs. If the National Liberals could force the government for the first time to hear the opinions of the Reichstag *before* it signed a treaty instead of afterward, they hoped to influence the government's approval of the treaty and thereby set a precedent for the future. Also, by adding a second part to the motion, they hoped to force the chancellor to solicit the approval of the Reichstag for the cession or acquisition of German protectorates or colonial territories.[31] In essence, the National Liberals wanted to clarify the constitution in favor of the Reichstag. The sense of the addition was to force the government to obtain the consent of the Reichstag to the Moroccan treaties and to all future imperialist acquisitions. Once the Reichstag's right to approve acquisitions had been established, there remained the possibility of finding some way to extend that right into other areas of foreign affairs.

As in the Daily Telegraph Affair and the various suffrage reforms, an increase in the power of the Reichstag would promote a liberalization of German politics. It was thus a rallying point for the non-Conservative parties. If they supported the National Liberal motion, they would challenge the authority of the government and provoke a new constitutional crisis. In its timing, the measure was so delicate that it caused a controversy in the powerful senior committee (*Seniorenkonvent*) which determined the Reichstag's agenda. There the representatives of the various parties—the Centre, Progressives, Social Democrats—had to decide whether or not to admit the motion to the floor of the Reichstag, where a debate could possibly undermine the position of the German government vis-à-vis the French.

The motion placed the Progressives in a quandary. They favored its reformist trend but disliked the motives behind it. The virus of Weltstellung had never completely infected them, and they did not regard the Moroccan crisis as a test of national honor. Like the National Liberals, they urged the government to use the French occupation of Morocco to Germany's best advantage, but they had no expectations of a middle African empire. They merely wanted the protection of German commercial interests and some worthwhile compensation. In accordance with their moderate calculations, they quietly and reasonably supported the government's negotiations with the French and refused to share the bitter condemnation expressed by the National Liberals. This

31. *Die Parteien*, p. 217.

refusal stemmed from their concern over the exaggerated nationalism that the Moroccan crisis aroused. *Hilfe* condemned the "chauvinistic super-patriots" who envisioned a conflict with France in order to protect German interests, and the *Frankfurter Zeitung* tried to pour rational water over nationalistic fires:

> There has seldom been such an abuse of the concept of nationalism as in the various phases of the Moroccan affair. A wild chauvinism . . . accepted as honest coin every sensational report of the foreign press . . . and . . . hoisted a ceremonious noise of war as if Germany's prestige had been shaken at the core and could only be repaired through a declaration of war! . . . The matter, however, does not stand so. The really national feeling has nothing to do with these chauvinistic circles. It presumes a degree of self-reliance which must exclude . . . such an easy gamble with peace.

The Progressives were also disappointed with the meager compensations, but they felt that nothing should endanger the relaxation of international tensions that would result from agreement with the French. Thus they could not support the National Liberal motion and voted against it in the senior committee.[32]

The Centre found itself in the same dilemma as the Progressives. It too desired some compensation for the French occupation of Morocco and an energetic defense of German interests. It also thought the Reichstag should discuss and vote on the treaties. Later the Centrist delegate Adolf Gröber advanced the daring view that the agreements with the French were little more than trade treaties. Hence the Reichstag already possessed the right to approve them. He even doubted the kaiser's sovereignty in national territories and his right to determine their fate. In this case, the Reichstag should definitely vote on the acquisition of the Congo. On the other hand, the nationalism aroused by the crisis also alarmed the Centre. At the beginning of August, it called for a calming of tempers in much the same way that the Progressives chastised the "super-patriots." Speaking later in the Reichstag, Georg von Hertling called for moderation and objectivity in judging the treaties. The Centre also suspected the motives behind the National

32. For the Progressives' response, see *Die Parteien*, pp. 68, 252. Cf. Wernecke, *Der Wille*, pp. 47–49, 86, 117; and *Hilfe* 17 (1911) : 273, 466–467. *Frankfurter Zeitung*, August 9, 1911, no. 219.

Liberal motion, and it too voted against placing it on the Reichstag's agenda. Its votes, combined with those of Progressives and Conservatives, who opposed any increase of the Reichstag's powers anyway, were enough to defeat the motion in the senior committee and thwart the National Liberals. No debate occurred before the treaties were signed, and the government averted a serious domestic crisis.[33]

Ultimately, only one minor change resulted from the Moroccan crisis. When the treaties were finally signed in November, and no danger of embarrassment existed, the government at last submitted the treaties to the Reichstag. Now, all parties introduced motions for a change in existing procedures. The National Liberals moved for an outright constitutional change permitting the Reichstag to approve acquisitions or cessions of national territory. The Centre and Progressives merely wanted to alter the law concerning protectorates. The government was willing to grant this last demand, and the Reichstag eventually passed a measure providing for its cooperation when the Reich lost or gained territory. This provision did nothing to alter the constitution or to increase the powers of the Reichstag in foreign affairs. The Moroccan crisis ended with no significant domestic reform.[34]

Yet the thrust toward and the failure of domestic reform did not constitute the full importance of the Moroccan crisis. For the discussion of the Grand Bloc, the party positions were just as significant. All the non-Conservative parties played decisive roles during October and November, 1911. The National Liberals with their motion tried to link domestic reform to German imperialism. In rejecting that motion, the Centre and Progressives, though they traditionally demanded increased powers for the Reichstag, chose to support the government and reject reform rather than submit to a wave of dangerous nationalism. Even though both had given increasing allegiance and sympathy to imperialist programs in the two decades before 1911, the threat of war and the signs of German chauvinism repelled them into moderation. Ironically, party roles were reversed in the process. Whereas the

33. *Die Parteien*, pp. 42–43. Cf. Wernecke, *Der Wille*, pp. 83–85, 105–106. Adolf Gröber in *Verhandlungen des Reichstages*, 268 : 7769–7770; also Georg von Hertling, 268 : 7713–7714. On the vote, see *Vorwärts*, October 19, 1911.

34. *Verhandlungen des Reichstages*, 282: 5945, 5951. Cf. Brigitte Haberland Barth, *Die Innenpolitik des Reiches unter der Kanzlerschaft Bethmann Hollwegs, 1909–1914* (doctoral diss., Kiel, 1950), p. 104.

National Liberals had once shelved domestic reform for the satisfaction of nationalist aims, they now sought reform in order to further nationalist ends. The Centre and Progressives now dampened their reformist demands because of their relative antinationalism. Both refused to harness domestic reform to the nationalistic engine.

In this reversal of roles, the Social Democrats played the strangest part of all. We have seen how the party, in various ways, accommodated the forces of nationalism after the election of 1907. Thereafter they also displayed more sympathy toward imperialistic ventures. That this change stemmed from concern for the party's popularity was manifest in the summer of 1911. When Social Democratic radicals demonstrated against the government for sending the *Panther* to Agadir, the party's executive almost ignored them, and only under pressure did it issue an official protest. When the secretary of the Socialist International Bureau in Brussels asked the executive if it considered the time ripe for a meeting of the bureau, Molkenbuhr replied negatively, "If we should prematurely engage ourselves and even give precedence to the Moroccan question . . . so that an effective electoral slogan could be developed against us, then the consequences will be unforeseeable. . . ." Although official party theory still dictated its duty of doing everything in its power to prevent war, party practice considered the survival of the party more important than the prevention of war. Later, when the other parties of the Reichstag criticized the radicals' demonstrations as preparations for a mass strike in case of war, Bebel rose to his feet in denial and carefully explained that German Social Democracy at International Congresses from 1892 to 1907 had rejected this use of the mass strike. His explanations and denials revealed no more than what already stood in the official protocols of the International Congress, but the context in which he spoke in 1911 was important. Attacked by the other parties and by his own colleagues, pressed by the coming elections which threatened the strength of the party, Bebel opted to deny the actions of his own radical colleagues rather than suffer the condemnation of his bourgeois opponents.[35]

A similar ambivalence arose with respect to the National Liberal

35. Hallgarten, *Imperialismus,* 2 : 77, 257. Cf. Hans-Christoph Schröder, *Sozialismus und Imperialismus* (Hanover, 1968), pp. 188ff. Molkenbuhr is quoted in Schorske, *Social Democracy,* p. 199; Bebel's denial in *Verhandlungen des Reichstages,* 268 : 7805.

motion presented in October before the signing of the treaties. Like the Centre and the Progressives, the Social Democrats abhorred the extreme nationalism accompanying the Moroccan crisis. They too supported the final settlement with France as necessary for international peace. At the end of October, therefore, they rejected a debate *before* the signing of the treaties since "under certain circumstances" it "could assume a character, which was not at all intended." Yet the Social Democrats also saw the opportunity of using the Moroccan crisis to increase the powers of the Reichstag. After rejecting the original National Liberal motion in the senior committee, Bebel had two conversations with Bassermann where he proposed a "common motion of the minority parties"—National Liberals, Progressives, Social Democrats—for the "preservation in principle of the rights of the Reichstag in the matter of the Moroccan agreement."[36] Since the Reichstag had no clearly defined rights, Bebel really meant their extension in the sense of the National Liberal motion. When the radicals in the Social Democratic Fraktion criticized Bebel and urged an independent motion, he objected on the grounds that the field already belonged to the National Liberals. In suggesting a common motion, he tried to initiate a Grand Bloc which would bring the National Liberals under the more moderate influence of the Progressives and Social Democrats and thereby control their nationalism. His act was important since it imitated the Badenese Grand Bloc on two counts. Bebel and the Social Democrats made the first explicit move toward cooperation, and they expected the National Liberals to lead the action. Once again the Social Democrats indicated that they would actively follow and aid any reformist move of the bourgeois parties. In October 1911, Bebel's attempts at a common motion failed. Both National Liberals and Progressives preferred to go their separate ways, and the Social Democrats finally formulated an independent motion.

Their motion went further than all the others by advocating the Reichstag's right to vote on all foreign treaties. This proposal had absolutely no chance of success, and the Social Democrats knew it. However, its defense in the Reichstag was important as an index of the party's willingness to compromise democracy with nationalism. Bebel himself developed the argument:

36. Fraktion meetings, October 23, 25, 1911, *SPD Fraktionsprotokolle,* 1 : 251.

We cannot further put up with the fact that the Reichstag is treated as a *quantité négligeable*. This summer the whole bourgeois camp resounded: the Reichstag, the German people were pushed into the background in this affair . . . !

. . . The case could occur, that [the government] gives a colony away to another state. According to the present version [of the constitution] we have nothing to say about that. According to the . . . treaty over the Congo, a piece of colony which has . . . caused Germany great sacrifice, will be ceded. You [the other parties] are complaining about that. Quite correctly. However if you want to prevent that in the future, you must have the right, not only to speak here [in the Reichstag], but also to be able to vote; otherwise it is impossible that you can enforce your viewpoint.[37]

Since Bebel was pleading for support for his own motion, he implicitly agreed to support the policy of imperialism provided the Social Democrats received some concession to their demands for a liberalization of the existing system. *Vorwärts* made this stand clear in an even more cynical fashion:

Social Democracy knows that the National Liberal party as the ruling party would only mean a strengthening of militarism and the projects of the fleet and colonies, that the imperial policy would then first embark on a course of imperial (*weltpolitischen*) adventure. . . . This knowledge does not need to hinder us from exploiting the present situation. . . . If the National Liberals, in league with other bourgeois parties, should finally see themselves forced to go about a change in the constitution, for reasons with which we have nothing in common, . . . they can be certain of our support.[38]

This explanation was no longer a defense of the Social Democratic motion but another guarantee of cooperation in a Grand Bloc reformist policy. The Social Democrats avoided any explicit approval of German imperialism, but they implied a willingness to accommodate it if it led to liberalization at home. In effect, they agreed to support imperialism if they received some concessions to their own demands. With this startling change in Social Democracy's policy, the Moroccan crisis and 1911 came to a close.

37. *Verhandlungen des Reichstages*, 268 : 7724.
38. *Vorwärts*, November 9, 1911.

What was the balance among the non-Conservative parties after the Reichstag session of 1911? Was there any inclination toward a national Grand Bloc? Had any pattern emerged that would be useful as a prognosis for the future? In matters involving political democracy or liberalization, there was little question that the parties could cooperate. In the Prussian suffrage reform, in the Alsatian constitution, and in the extension of the Reichstag's powers, all non-Conservative parties, although they differed about degree and self-interest, agreed in principle that some reform was necessary. In these instances, the idea of the Grand Bloc functioned to bring liberals and Social Democrats together and to attract the support of the Centre for their policies. In issues such as imperialism, National Liberal nationalism estranged them from the other parties but did not totally preclude cooperation. The Progressives, the Social Democrats, and the Centre all thought a moderate national pride and patriotism served the best interests of Germany. They preferred a more tempered National Liberal attitude, and until that moderation occurred, cooperation between the Grand Bloc or between Grand Bloc and Centre was unlikely in national issues. It was also difficult for the parties to cooperate to in social democratic reforms. During the debates on the Arbeitskammern and the National Insurance Bill, the parties divided ambiguously. Here the opposition between National Liberals and Social Democrats was irreconcilable. Where the Social Democrats demanded the full recognition of the workers as equal partners in socioeconomic matters, the National Liberals opposed such recognition unconditionally. In this issue, the Progressives and the Centre occupied a middle position that favored the independence of the trade unions and their right to economic and social representation *but* also wanted reconciliation between the bitterly opposing interests. In the issue of social democracy, the Progressives and the Centre were closer in spirit to the Social Democrats than to the National Liberals, but full cooperation between the parties in any social issue would be difficult. Yet despite all obstacles, the idea of the Grand Bloc persisted throughout the Reichstag of 1911, and this persistence strengthened the belief that it was a possibility under the proper circumstances.

7

The National Grand Bloc: To Be or Not to Be?

THE ELECTIONS OF 1912

The possibility of bridging political differences and creating a Grand Bloc for the Reich assumed immediate importance as the parties girded themselves for the elections of 1912. The mood of the voters, for a variety of reasons, definitely inclined toward the left. In the fourteen by-elections held after the collapse of the Bülow Bloc, the Social Democrats retained one existing seat and won seven new ones. This radical atmosphere contributed to speculations about a Grand Bloc election policy, and the aid given by the Progressives to the Social Democrats in two by-elections increased its prospects. As the campaign began, a pattern also emerged that recalled the tactics used in the previous two Baden elections. The Social Democrats announced their intention of supporting the Progressives in the runoff elections, and the Progressives and National Liberals concluded a series of agreements throughout the Reich similar to the liberal bloc formed in Baden in 1905. During these preliminary arrangements, the Progressives made no move to return Social Democracy's generosity, and no one dared to mention cooperation between National Liberals and Social Democrats. Yet all parties realized that certain decisions about a Grand Bloc policy were only deferred until after the general election.[1]

The complex situation of the National Liberals in the Reich made such deferral necessary. A glance at their agreements with the Progressives revealed the pressures operating upon them. The agreements naturally enough included the four southern states of Baden, Bavaria,

---

1. *SPD Parteitag, 1910*, p. 29; *Elbwart*, 1 : 172; *Die Parteien*, p. 249. On the lack of reciprocity, see Jürgen Bertram, *Die Wahlen zum deutschen Reichstag vom Jahre 1912: Parteien und Verbände in der Innenpolitik des wilhelminischen Reiches* (Düsseldorf, 1964), pp. 50ff.

Württemberg, and Alsace-Lorraine, where the moderate and left-wing National Liberals were fairly strong and cooperation well-established. In the northern states of Saxony, Thuringia, Mecklenburg, Bremen, and Lübeck and in the Prussian provinces of Brandenburg, East Prussia, Silesia, Pomerania, Hanover, and Saxony, the will to defeat the Conservatives welded the two parties into a united front. But this united liberal front failed in those areas where the right-wing National Liberals were strong: in Hesse and Schleswig-Holstein, where the National Liberals had strong traditional ties with the Agrarian League and where competition with the Progressives was keen; in Hamburg, where the right-wing National Liberals resented and feared the close relationship between Progressives and Social Democrats; and in Westphalia, where the Centralverband dominated National Liberal politics. The intense interest of the Centralverband in a conservative strategy was most clearly manifested in the middle of 1911, when it broke its connections with the Hansabund because of the latter's active financial support of left-wing National Liberals and Progressives.[2] Thus right-wing National Liberals threatened even the relatively acceptable liberal bloc. In its stead, the right wing preferred the government's Sammlungspolitik (collective policy), which advocated a concerted campaign of all the bourgeois parties against the Social Democrats. The official National Liberal campaign, waged against Conservatives and Social Democrats, disturbed this sanctioned policy, and the government itself pressured the party to change its strategy. In the summer of 1911, when all Germany and the National Liberal leadership were on vacation, the government contacted the impressionable right-wing business secretary, Paul Fuhrmann, and lured him into beginning negotiations for a Sammlungspolitik. These negotiations ended abruptly when

2. Bertram, *Die Wahlen,* pp. 60–61, 79; DZAP, Reichskanzlei, Parteien 1/3, II, no. 1394, newspaper clipping from the *Hamburger Nachrichten,* October 16, 1910. Cf. *Die Parteien,* pp. 65–66. On the National Liberals and the Centralverband, see DZAP, Reichskanzlei, Parteien 1/12, I, no. 1422/4, series of clippings and memos from June 12–22, 1911; Cf. *Frankfurter Zeitung,* June 22, 1911, no. 171 and June 24, 1911, no. 173. Cf. Dirk Stegmann, *Die Erben Bismarcks: Parteien und Verbände in der Spätphase des wilhelminischen Deutschlands* (Cologne, 1970), pp. 237–243. At the same time, the president of the Hansabund called for a "conditional cooperation" between liberals and Social Democrats in the next election, a tactic that horrified the Centralverband, *Die bürgerlichen Parteien in Deutschland, 1830–1945: Handbuch der Geschichte der bürgerlichen Parteien und anderer bürgerlicher Interessenorganisationen vom Vormärz bis zum Jahre 1945,* 2 vols. (Leipzig, 1970), 2 : 204–205.

Bassermann intervened and demanded a Prussian suffrage reform and a direct imperial tax as the price for an agreement with the Conservatives. Despite their antisocialist enthusiasm, neither government nor Conservatives could commit themselves to significant liberal concessions, and Bassermann's intervention spelled the end of any significant Sammlungspolitik.[3] Right-wing National Liberals thereafter acquiesced in their party's alliance with the Progressives.

The Centre continued to play the anomalous role it assumed in 1909 when it helped to shatter the Bülow Bloc. Though it rather consistently voted with the left in the Reichstag of 1911, the public associated it with the Conservatives in the Black and Blue Bloc of the tax reform and the unsuccessful Prussian suffrage bill. At the end of December, the Centre denied the existence of the Black and Blue Bloc, though its election agreements hardly supported this contention. It committed its voters to conservative parties in 98 districts, and received a promise of support from them in 33. In several districts, it offered to support the National Liberals, but this assistance hardly matched the scope of its aid to Conservatives. The Centre decided to follow the government's line in the elections of 1912, and its contribution to a Grand Bloc policy was nil.[4] Throughout the campaign, the real hub of cooperation lay with the liberal bloc and the possibility of its expansion to a Grand Bloc of liberals and Social Democrats.

But loyalty to the liberal bloc helped neither contracting party during the first round of voting on January 12. The National Liberals won only four seats, and the Progressives, without a single mandate, suffered a great defeat.[5] For both parties, further gains depended on the runoff elections, and the situation closely resembled the last two elections in Baden, where the temptation toward a Grand Bloc tactic was very strong.

The defeat of the Progressives posed an embarrassing dilemma. Quite early in the campaign, they realized that Social Democracy was not only an ally, it was also their main competitor. Even before the election, Naumann had written that

> . . . Social Democracy will take away from us a whole series of districts and will also drive us out of the runoff elections in many

3. Bassermann notations, no date, Bassermann remnant 303/17.
4. On the Centre, see *Die Parteien*, p. 161; Bertram, *Die Wahlen*, pp. 46–47.
5. *kürschners, 1912*, p. 19.

cases, so that after January 12, the greatest majority of the liberals will be far more dependent on the right than on the left. In this situation the most embarrassing surprises inside the party are almost unavoidable. The slogan "Front against the right" will simply not be able to be applied. . . .

Naumann explicitly aired the Progressive problem of remaining true to liberal principle in the face of electoral defeat. As a direct solution, he suggested an agreement with Social Democracy for the general election, but neither Progressives nor Social Democrats warmed to his plan. A projected agreement for the runoff election caused "internal friction" since there were large groups of voters in the city and in the countryside who refused to consider an alliance with Social Democracy because of its competition or because of its program.[6]

The resistance of the rank and file to any discussion of alliance led the Progressives to ignore the tactics of the runoff elections until pressed by the results of January 12. These results were the chief consideration of the business committee when it met on January 14 to consider a variety of remedies. Some members wanted to leave the local districts free to make their own decisions. This freedom would leave the door open to cooperation with either the Conservatives or the Social Democrats dedending on the character of the district. Yet this action meshed neither with Progressive principles nor with their previous strategy, and it was ultimately rejected. The only other alternative was some kind of agreement with the Social Democrats. One member, Rothschild, courageously suggested a comprehensive Grand Bloc agreement in order to prevent a Conservative-Centre majority. He pointed out that although such an agreement would lead to the deliberate failure of some Progressive candidates, the results—a strong majority of the left in the Reichstag—would be well worth it. Although this plan was already operative in the Baden city of Freiburg due to the efforts of local party leaders, not even Naumann thought the Grand Bloc could be instituted on such a national scale. The choice narrowed down to a limited Progressive agreement with the Social Democrats, and the committee decided to sound them out confidentially before making a decision. When it met again on January 16, two mem-

6. Quoted passage from DZAP, Naumann Papers, Naumann to Dernburg, December 23, 1911. For attempts at agreement, see DZAP, Naumann Papers, Heuss to Naumann, October 27, 1910.

bers reported that the Social Democrats were ready to begin negotiations, and the die was cast for the first national election contract between Progressives and Social Democrats.[7]

The terms of the agreement, after much hard bargaining, clearly benefited the Progressives. In 16 districts where Progressives stood against Social Democrats, the latter promised to "dampen" their campaign to give the Progressives an edge. In 25 districts, the Social Democrats pledged outright support for Progressives against the Conservatives or the Centre. For their part, the Progressives agreed to vote for Social Democrats in 31 districts. In the runoff elections, the agreement had a moderate success. There was little evidence that the Social Democrats ever really "dampened" their campaign as promised. Yet the Social Democrats delivered their votes in other districts with much more discipline than the Progressives. They helped to elect 20 to 25 Progressives, whereas Progressives only aided 11 to 15 Social Democrats to victory. Considering the general lack of previous Progressive discipline, the score was quite good, but the Social Democrats certainly sacrificed more for the agreement than their partners.[8]

In contrast to the Progressives, the National Liberals could not consider a formal agreement with the Social Democrats, and they were not nearly so scrupulous about agreement with the right. The government continued to propagate a Sammlungspolitik for the runoff elec-

7. DZAP, FVP, executive committee meeting, January 14, 16, 1912; Friedrich Meinecke, *Erlebtes, 1862–1919* (Stuttgart, 1964), p. 239; cf. Bertram, *Die Wahlen,* pp. 142–143. For a different interpretation, not based on the Progressive documents, see Bertram, *Die Wahlen,* p. 226. Bertram's conclusion that Progressives bargained for an advantageous deal with the right cannot be correct in light of the discussions in the executive committee meeting.

8. Bertram, *Die Wahlen,* p. 227 and Carl Schorske, *German Social Democracy,* p. 229, report that the Social Democrats would "dampen" in 16 districts. Only ten districts were named in DZAP, FVP, executive committee meeting, January 17, 1912. The Left Liberals agreed to support the Social Democrats in: (1) Danzig, (2) Westpriegnitz, (3) Ruppin-Templin, (4) Potsdam-Osthavelland, (5) Zeuch-Belzig, (6) Landsberg-Soldin, (7) Königsberg-Neumark, (8) Kotbus-Spremberg, (9) Kalau-Luckau, (10) Uckermünde-Usedom, (11) Striegau-Schweidnitz, (12) Grünberg-Freistadt, (13) Sagan-Sprottau, (14) Landeshut-Jauer, (15) Rothenberg-Hoyerswerda, (16) Jerichow, (17) Bitterfeld, (18) Marsfeld, (19) Mühlhausen-Langensalza, (20) Bielefeld-Wiedebrück, (21) Eschwege-Schmalkalden, (22) Stadt Köln, (23) Elberfeld-Barmen, (24) Düsseldorf, (25) Heilbronn, (26) Giessen-Nidda, (27) Hagenow, (28) Güstrow, (29) Jena, (30) Altenburg, (31) Strassburg-Land. This information is not found in the Progressive documents but in a communication of the Social Democratic executive committee about the runoff election, 1912, Kautsky Papers. For the Progressives' vote delivery, see Bertram, *Die Wahlen,* pp. 229–232, 238–239; cf. Schorske, *Social Democracy,* pp. 232–233.

tion, and the National Liberals found themselves in quandary. Whereas the Progressives immediately declined a governmental invitation to an interparty conference scheduled for January 17, the National Liberals were reluctant to renounce any support from the right which might result from it. After a discussion with the leaders of the provincial organizations who wanted to make individual local decisions, Bassermann and Friedberg originally rejected the government's invitation, and even though governmental persistence finally succeeded in getting them to the conference, it failed to gain their acquiescence in a Sammlungspolitik.[9] However this episode demonstrated National Liberal ambivalence about liberal principles and election tactics.

Even though official National Liberal policy trod a moderate middle way, the party could do nothing about local agreements with either right or left. Many National Liberals cooperated with Conservatives and Centre in time-honored fashion, but in some districts an informal Grand Bloc policy prevailed. Social Democrats helped to elect 13 National Liberal delegates to the Reichstag, including Bassermann. In fact, his victory was a bargaining point in at least one tacit agreement that occurred between Saarbrücken, where he was a candidate, and Cologne, which had a strong liberal left wing. Without any previous negotiations, the National Liberals in Cologne received word from Saarbrücken socialists two days before the runoff election that Bassermann's election was assured. The National Liberals reciprocated by electing a Social Democrat in Cologne. And Cologne was not the only district where National Liberals broke the prejudice of generations. In Hanover and in Düsseldorf, they helped the Social Democrats to victory. Although cooperation happened only in isolated instances, its very occurrence signaled a relaxation of the animosity between National Liberals and Social Democrats and boded well for future agreements.[10]

9. DZAP, Reichskanzlei, Reichstag 2/3, I, no. 1808, Wahnschaffe to Bethmann Hollweg, January 16, 1912; *Schulthess, 1912*, p. 5.

10. For National Liberal cooperation with right, see Bertram, *Die Wahlen*, pp. 223–224, 236, 238–240. Social Democrats helped the following National Liberals; Felix Schwabach, Willi Stöve, Georg Schulenberg, Hermann Hepp, Hermann Paasche, Karl Lützel, Fritz van Calker, Friedrich Thoma, Ernst Blankenhorn, Leopold Kölsch, Friedrich Heck, and Ludwig Roland-Lücke. Schwabach also received help from the parties of the right, see *Kürschners, 1912*. One or both of the Blue-Black parties helped to elect 21 National Liberals or approximately 50 percent of the Fraktion. For National Liberal assistance to

In truth, the results of the election were such that a Grand Bloc policy was feasible in the Reichstag. The Social Democrats with their 110 mandates emerged as the largest party. If they cooperated with the 43 National Liberals and 42 Progressives, there would be a Grand Bloc majority of 195 which outnumbered the combined votes of 59 Conservatives and 92 Centrists.[11] These results had a force separate from any concerted action of the Grand Bloc. There were now certain issues in which the government would have to appeal to the Grand Bloc in order to get a majority, and the Grand Bloc parties certainly realized their newly won power to wring liberal concessions from the government. Moreover the possibility still existed that the Centre would join the Grand Bloc if its interests were involved. In order to assess the future Centrist role, we must shift our focus from north to south for a different view of the German political scene.

BAVARIA

The impact of the Baden Grand Bloc on national political thought and action has already demonstrated the influence of local politics on German affairs, and events in Baden influenced parties in other states as well as the parties in the Reichstag. At the time of the first budget crisis, the Württemberg Social Democrats ordered their actions with a view toward cooperation with the liberals, and the fight over the Alsatian suffrage was partially resolved because a Grand Bloc policy had already been planned for local elections. In Bavaria, the largest of the southern states, a local Grand Bloc election coincided with the national elections of 1912. The Bavarian election would not merit any further attention except that it represented the culmination of a long and tenuous process and netted results which, like the Grand Bloc policy itself, had implications for further developments within the Reich.

The process that culminated in the election of 1912 was a product of Bavaria's social and political history. Like all southern states, Bavaria,

the left, see Bertram, *Die Wahlen*, p. 287; cf. Josef Bellot, *Hundert Jahre politisches Leben an der Saar unter preussischen Herrschaft, 1815–1918* (Bonn, 1954), pp. 233–234, who maintains that the Young Liberals were instrumental in bringing about the agreement both in Saarbrücken and in Cologne. For verification of figures in Cologne, Hanover, and Düsseldorf, see *Kürschners, 1912*, pp. 160, 201, 210.

11. Arthur Dix, *Die deutschen Reichstagswahlen 1871–1930 und die Wandlungen der Volksgliederung* (Tübingen, 1930), p. 21.

with its Catholic majority, opposed and resented the Protestant Prussian unification of Germany, and particularist sentiments were always very strong. The liberals were the one force behind unification in Bavaria, and they supported the predominantly liberal ministers appointed by the king and later the regent. The union of government and liberals throughout the period after 1870 affronted the Catholic Centre, and it determined to gain political influence through one means or another. Its first weapon was suffrage reform, and during the 1890s it allied with the Social Democrats in this cause and made the first formal election agreement with them in 1899. This agreement was renewed in 1905. The Centrist–Social Democratic alliance and its agitation for reform eroded the liberal vote, and finally produced a majority which won a sweeping reform in 1906. Bavaria received the most liberal suffrage in the Reich; henceforth a simple relative majority in each district would decide the outcome of the general election without a need for a runoff.[12]

The loss of their vote and approximately half their seats in the Landtag was a serious blow to the liberals. In order to prevent any further inroads on their position by either Centre or Social Democrats, a major regeneration was necessary, and in Bavaria, as elsewhere, the Young Liberals took the lead in rejuvenating the movement. The Bavarian Young Liberals were undoubtedly the most radical in the Reich; they had been bitten by Naumann's national-democratic ideals more than any other group, and it would not be unfair to say that they were more "Naumannian" than Naumann himself. Like him, they believed it necessary to unite all liberals into one strong popular party. To this end, they first launched a campaign to democratize the various liberal parties, and this effort resulted in a joint program that later served as a model for the Frankfurt Minimal Program of the Progressives. Secondly, they drew up an elaborate scheme to unify, deepen, and broaden the liberal party organization. To some extent, they succeeded in uniting all those of a Left Liberal persuasion, but they failed to receive the whole-hearted cooperation of the National Liberals. Since the National Liberals were the largest liberal party in Bavaria,

12. On the Centrist–Social Democratic alliance in Bavaria, see Benno Hubensteiner, *Bayersiche Geschichte* (Munich, 1951), pp. 372ff; Reinhard Jansen, *Georg von Vollmar Eine politische Biographie* (Düsseldorf, 1958), pp. 67–70; and *Hilfe* 13 (1907) : 242.

their lack of commitment to liberal unity meant that the movement as a whole remained weak.[13]

Organizational weakness also contributed to a diminution of liberal political influence. The loss of power was especially evident when the Centre began to curry favor with the government just after reform, and the liberals found themselves pushed into opposition. For instance, a state tax reform bill coincided with the national tax bill of 1909. The Bavarian bill planned to introduce the progressive state income tax, but at the same time it retained the outmoded "produce" tax, which fell more heavily on urban than on rural "products" and lent itself to inequities in assessment and administration. In its stead, the Bavarian liberals wanted the same tax on property supported by their colleagues in the Reichstag because it distributed the tax burden more equally between town and country. The Centre, with its electoral strongholds in the countryside, naturally opposed it. After two years of threatening to withhold their votes for the entire bill, the liberals finally received a governmental promise to introduce a tax on property in seven years. The real significance of the compromise was not the terms forced upon the government but the seldom-used threat to obtain them: wholesale withdrawal of support for a governmental measure.[14]

The tax bill was not the only issue vexing the liberals after the Bavarian suffrage reform. There was also the plight of the teachers, an interest group that strongly supported them. In 1908, a small movement for a salary increase began among Bavarian teachers and was vigorously supported by a choleric young Progressive teacher named Jacob Beyhl, who was an admirer of Naumann and the editor of the *Freie Bayerische Schulzeitung.* After a particularly bitter speech against the Bavarian government and society for refusing its teachers the pay they deserved, Beyhl was reprimanded for inflammatory language by the government.

13. For the liberal losses, see H. Kalkhoff, *Nationalliberale Parlamentarier 1867–1917 des Reichstages und der Einzellandtage* (Berlin, 1917), p. 272. For a short summary of the Bavarian Young Liberal organization, see *Hilfe* 15 (1909) : 612–613. It eventually joined the Progressives in 1910, ibid. 16 (1910) : 280. For National Liberal difficulties with Bavarian Young Liberals, see DZAP, Bassermann Papers, memorandum of executive committee, no date. The Young Liberals founded a weekly magazine, *Fortschritt,* in 1906 to further their cause. Though somewhat biased in its emphasis, it is a gold mine of information on the liberal organizations in Bavaria. For similarity to Frankfurt Program, see Wilhelm Kulemann, *Zusammenschluss der Liberalen* (Dresden, 1905), pp. 87–89. On Young Liberals' reorganization plan, see *Hilfe* 14 (1908) : 434. Cf. *Fortschritt* 3 (1908) : 230–231, 377.

14. *Fortschritt* 3 (1908): 265, 390, 397; 5 (1910) : 263–264.

The Centre vigorously supported the action. The liberals vainly protested this treatment in the Landtag as a violation of Beyhl's freedom of speech. Shortly thereafter, the budget of 1908 was passed with the votes of Centre, and it contained no substantial salary increase for teachers. Yet these incidents were only a prelude to further irritation. In 1910, the liberals complained that teachers were hired more for their religious affiliation than for their professional qualifications. In 1911 several articles in the *Bayerische Lehrerzeitung* caused a serious controversy between individual liberal teachers on the one hand and bishops, school administrators, and government on the other hand. Eventually the government instructed teachers not to belong to any organization opposed to the "interest of the state and the profession." The liberals viewed this regulation as a discriminatory measure directed against the Bavarian Teachers' Association, which supported the offensive *Bayerische Schulzeitung* and protected the financial and legal interests of the teachers. They also thought the heavy clerical hand of the Catholic Centre lay behind the government's action. Regardless of the merits of the liberals' complaints (and there was certainly bad judgment on both sides), the charge of discrimination rang true when considered in the light of events occurring later in the year.[15]

In Bavaria, as in other areas, the Social Democratic or 'free" trade unions existed side by side with the so-called Christian trade unions sponsored by the German Catholics to counteract the "atheist" influence of the Social Democrats. The free trade unions were much stronger, and in 1911, the Bavarian Centre decided to challenge this strength by attacking their alleged willingness to strike against their employer, the state. As a target, the Centre singled out the South German Railway Workers' Union, to which many employees of the state-owned railways belonged. There is evidence that the Bavarian government provoked this attack by pardoning a group of Social Democratic railway workers and reprimanding the Catholic workers, both of whom had picketed the station, in the small town of Weiden. The difference in treatment possibly stemmed from a desire to win the support of the Social Democrats in the legislature against the power of the Centre. As the Centre's attack on the Railway Union developed in 1911, it was clear that the union was merely a pawn in a political struggle

15. Ibid. 3 (1908) : 178–179, 185, 233. Cf. *Hilfe* 14 (1908) : 429–430, 446; 16 (1910) : 408; 17 (1911) : 33–34, 66, 113, 145–146, 290–291.

between the Centre and the liberal government. During the committee deliberations on the state budget, the Centre demanded that the government suppress the South German Railway Workers' Union since it was associated with the Social Democrats and since its striking propensities were detrimental to the welfare of the state. The Centrist press even faulted the transportation minister, Heinrich von Frauendorfer, for not furthering the growth of the Christian railway workers' organizations. Frauendorfer defended himself by citing the lack of proof for Social Democracy's link with the South German Railway Union and refused to suppress it. The Baron Klemens von Podewils, the liberal prime minister, supported his stand. This position so incensed the Centre that it finally refused to cooperate with the government entirely and walked out of the finance committee and the budget deliberations at the beginning of November. Since the Centre's majority in the Landtag was absolute, the government could not pass the budget without it, but rather than yield to the Centre's challenge, the government chose to dissolve the Landtag in the hope that new elections would bring a more cooperative majority.[16]

At the time of dissolution, the Centre's domination of the Bavarian legislature had drawn the other parties together to oppose it just as fear of such dominance had created the Grand Bloc in Baden. In Bavaria, however, it was more difficult to bring liberals and Social Democrats together because of the previous socialist–Centrist alliance. In addition, the pitifully weak Left Liberals were hardly a worthy partner, and the National Liberals were simply not interested in courting the Social Democrats. Hence no Bavarian Grand Bloc tactic occurred before 1911. Then, the accumulation of National Liberal grievances, the pressure of the Young Liberals, the example in Baden, and the more general liberalization of the party pushed the liberals toward the Social Democrats. On the other side, the Centre's attack on the Railway Union forced Social Democracy into the arms of the liberals. Their election agreement, which included all the Bavarian parties except Centre and Conservatives, covered every district in the state. Thus, at the same time that the national parties maneuvered and negotiated their way through a national election to the Reichstag, the liberals and Social Democrats in Bavaria entered into a more sweeping contract than any thus far

16. For the Weiden incident, see DZAP, Reichsamt des Innern, Politische Parteien 1/5, Prussian Legate Schozer to Bethmann Hollweg, October 24, 1910. For the government's reaction, see *Schulthess, 1911*, pp. 154–155, 174–175, 188–189, 264–265.

conceived in the Reich. The generosity of the contract testified to the formidability of the opponent. But in the elections of February 5, 1912, held about a month after the Reichstag election, the Bavarian Grand Bloc policy hardly made a dent in the Centre majority. Although the liberals obtained 33 and the Social Democrats 30 seats in the Landtag, they were not enough to counteract the 87 Centrists. The Centre's power remained the same before and after the elections.[17]

Yet neither the ineffective Grand Bloc agreement nor the election results were the most significant aspect of the Bavarian election. The changes made after the election said more about the future direction of German politics than did the election itself. On February 8, three days after the Bavarian election, the prince regent asked the prominent leader of the Centre, Count Georg von Hertling, to replace the liberal Baron von Podewils as prime minister of Bavaria. To be sure, von Hertling disavowed all party connections after becoming prime minister, but the lesson of his appointment was not lost on those with political instincts.[18] After four decades of liberal ministers, maintained in the face of a mounting Centrist majority, the regent appointed a minister consonant with that majority after it refused to cooperate with unrepresentative ministers any longer. Through the appointment of Count von Hertling, Bavaria began to introduce responsible parliamentary government. No written constitutional change occurred; the prince regent simply thought it prudent to concede to the wishes of the majority. This important change in Bavaria, though noted at the time, was almost imperceptible in its implications. Count von Hertling was politically conservative and did not intend any radical reforms; nor was he a Bavarian particularist, and this fact interested Berlin more than the circumstances of his appointment. However, these circumstances pointed the way toward reform; more than anything else, they acted as a guide for the Grand Bloc in the Reichstag. A Grand Bloc majority only needed to refuse its cooperation in important issues, as demonstrated by the Bavarian Centre in the matter of the budget, and it could force the government to make concessions. Concerted action, and not formal written amendments, has usually determined the course of political events.

17. On the election agreement, see Jansen, *Georg von Vollmar*, pp. 101–102; for results, *Schulthess, 1912*, p. 18.
18. *Schulthess, 1912*, pp. 65, 67–68. Cf. *Hilfe* 18 (1912) : 100.

THE REICHSTAG PRAESIDIUM

National politics were not as advanced as those in Bavaria, and the kaiser was not the Bavarian prince regent. No liberal chancellor would be appointed to match the Grand Bloc majority in the Reichstag. Moreover, no one was certain that the National Liberals, as the leaders of the Grand Bloc, would exercise a determination similar to that of the Bavarian Centre. For this reason, the Reichstag praesidium elections assumed a prophetic character; they registered the willingness of the National Liberals to pursue a Grand Bloc policy. Their support for a "leftist" praesidium would radically alter the dominant constellation of the Reichstag, one which had not changed appreciably for three decades. It would commit them to progressive liberal policies in cooperation with the Social Democrats. Such action would also represent the first step in pressuring the government for some urgent liberal reforms. Therefore the election of the praesidium scheduled for February 9 generated an atmosphere of provocative tension.

The crux of the praesidium election was the inclusion of the Social Democrats. The question of their participation dated back to the elections of 1903 and the Dresden resolution. Significantly, those who opposed participation in 1903 argued that the praesidium was a measure of political influence as well as a register of numerical strength within the Reichstag. At that time, the Social Democrats had no hope of exercising any influence over events or legislation, and thus they renounced a seat in the praesidium. In the short decade since Dresden, the political scene had altered. The Baden Bloc, the limited cooperation of liberals and Social Democrats in a number of other states, the cautious rapprochement between liberals and Social Democrats after the collapse of the Bülow Bloc, the fact and moderate success of the election agreement of 1912—all indicated the possibility of limited Social Democratic influence within the Reichstag. Within the party, the reformists assembled their forces in favor of cooperation.

Shortly before the Reichstag convened, Heine wrote to Vollmar urgently requesting him to be in Berlin for the first meeting of the Fraktion in order to counteract the "forces at work . . . to disturb the success" of the election agreement and to exercise his reformist influence over Bebel. Yet Vollmar's presence in Berlin was almost unnecessary. The Fraktion decided almost immediately to participate in the praesidium as first vice-president and to solicit the support of the liberals to gain this post. The Social Democrats would then support the liberals, and a Grand Bloc praesidium would result. It was significant that the Social Democrats themselves initially approached the liberals; they did not wait for the liberals to come to them. There could be no better proof that they were far more willing and anxious than the liberals to create a leftist majority in the Reichstag. Concurrently however, they were still reluctant to relinquish all traces of their former ideology. Once again, the difficulties of a Social Democratic appearance at court obstructed the path toward parliamentary cooperation. The Fraktion, knowing this question would sooner or later arise during its negotiations with the liberals, discussed the problem thoroughly. By a very narrow vote, which divided the Fraktion into two equal halves, it decided to accept only those duties explicitly mentioned in the written parliamentary procedure of the Reichstag. Parliamentary procedure demanded only that the president present the credentials of the newly convened Reichstag to the kaiser; the customary appearance of *all* members of the praesidium was merely custom, and one of the reasons why the Social Democrats bid only for the vice-presidency was to enable them "legally" to avoid the presentation at court. Through this decision, they hoped to persuade the liberals to admit them to the club of respectable politicians and to overlook the revolutionary crustaceans they found so hard to shed.[19]

The Social Democratic bid for the vice-presidency partially depended on the Progressives, who were more inclined toward cooperation than the other parties. In February 1912, they showed the most understanding of the Social Democrats by immediately recognizing their right to sit in the praesidium and by tactfully ignoring their refusal to appear at court.[20] Throughout the subsequent negotiations, the Progressives actively worked to include the Social Democrats and to prevent the National Liberals from veering toward the right. They became the self-appointed arbiters between Social Democrats and National Liberals in a wholehearted attempt to create a Grand Bloc praesidium.

19. Heine to Vollmar, February 3, 1912, Vollmar Papers. On the decision to seek a post in the praesidium, see *SPD Parteitag, 1912,* pp. 100–101; Bassermann notations, no date, Bassermann remnant, 303/10; Fraktion meeting, February 6, 1912, *SPD Fraktionsprotokolle,* 1 : 257; Friedrich W. von Rauchhaupt, *Handbuch der deutschen Wahlgesetze und Geschäftsordnungen* (Munich, 1916), p. 23.

20. Fraktion meeting, February 7, 1912, *SPD Fraktionsprotokolle,* 1 : 258.

Inevitably, the most important partners in the negotiations with the Social Democrats were the National Liberals. If they committed their votes to a Social Democratic vice-president, they would openly recognize Social Democracy's right to full integration in German politics and reinforce the concept of the Grand Bloc and its intimations of reform. It was therefore significant that the National Liberal Fraktion tended to use the results of the election as guides to the composition of the praesidium. Thus they rejected a Conservative-Centre or Black and Blue combination since it no longer enjoyed a parliamentary majority. Instead, they wanted a post for themselves and for the Social Democrats regardless of whether or not they appeared at court. These decisions, made immediately after the Reichstag convened, were important concessions to a Grand Bloc policy. Yet for tactical reasons, they could not totally assent to a Grand Bloc praesidium. First of all, the Fraktion's right wing objected to such a blatant leftist course, and secondly no one was sure that such a praesidium would be stable enough to resist the first "check" of the Centre. Bassermann later told Bebel that since right and left "approximately hold the balance between each other," he considered "the inclusion of the right necessary in the formation of the praesidium."[21]

In this case, the right was the Centre, and Bassermann told Bebel to contact it before continuing negotiations with the liberals. From the viewpoint of numbers alone, the suggestion was natural and sensible. It was also good politics. Once again, it demonstrated the need for the Centre's inclusion in any national Grand Bloc. In accepting the offer of partnership with the Social Democrats, the National Liberals wanted and needed the support of a powerful ally. The Centre's cooperation would help to silence all the voices of dissent, from Conservatives, the government, and others as well, to a "revolutionary" vice-president of the Reichstag. With its reputation as a governmental middle party, the Centre would lend additional sanction to the political integration of the Social Democrats. As in the Alsatian suffrage reform, the achievement of democracy or the extension of political recognition required a solid front of non-Conservatives.

The Centre, however, rejected the National Liberal scheme. It re-

21. Bassermann notations, no date, Bassermann remnant, 303/10; *SPD Parteitag, 1912*, pp. 100–101. Also see Fraktion meetings, February 8 and 9, 1912, NL Akten, R 45 1/10.

fused to blink discreetly at the Social Democratic refusal to appear at court, and it offered its own model praesidium, originally advocated by the government, which excluded the socialists entirely. It consisted of four, rather than three, men: two from the right and two from the liberals.[22] Since it would be the largest party in such a praesidium, the Centre had everything to gain from the plan. Through conciliating the government, it could hope to influence policy. The tactics differed from those in Bavaria, but the aim was the same: more parliamentary power and more attention from the government. In 1912, the gain of the Social Democrats made the Centre the second, rather than the first, largest party in the Reichstag. In any praesidium shared with the Social Democrats, the Centre's weight would be diluted by the presence of the larger party. The Centre could not help but suffer a twinge of jealous resentment against its competitor. In the light of Centrist policy both before and after the elections, this seems the only plausible reason for its actions in February 1912. Their response certainly did not stem from a conservative ideological aversion to Social Democracy as such. When such an alliance served its purpose, the Centre cooperated readily with the Social Democrats—more readily than the National Liberals. Tactical considerations determined its desire to exclude the Social Democrats from the praesidium, and the Centre's negotiations with Bebel were doomed before they began.

In response to the Centre's tactics, the National Liberals began to waver. At one point, they approached the Conservatives for a revival of the old Bülow Bloc praesidium. The Conservatives, for their part, supported the four-man praesidium and insisted on the inclusion of the Centre. Here, the Progressives drew the line. They refused to enter into any agreement that excluded the Social Democrats. The National Liberals were then faced with the choice of continuing cooperation with the Progressives or concluding their own agreement with the right. To their liberal credit, they chose to maintain the liberal Bloc. The implication of this decision, imperfectly perceived by the National Liberals, was a Grand Bloc praesidium, particularly since they now wanted and needed Social Democratic support for their own bid for the presidency. Yet necessity itself could not induce them to consent completely to Social Democratic demands. When the Fraktion vote was taken for

22. Fraktion meeting, February 9, 1912, *SPD Fraktionsprotokolle*, 1 : 260–261; Bassermann notations, no date, Bassermann remnant, 303/10.

supporting a Social Democrat for *first* vice-president, it failed, 21–20. Subsequently, they decided to vote only for a Social Democratic *second* vice-president. Once again, these decisions demonstrated the ambivalent National Liberal position vis-à-vis the Social Democrats and vis-à-vis their own liberal role within the Reich. Although they progressed far enough to grant the Social Democrats a seat in the praesidium, tradition, the right wing, and a feeling of inadequacy prevented them from elevating the Social Democrats to a symbolically important place.[23]

For their part, the Social Democrats, affronted by these decisions, declined to strike a bargain on National Liberal terms. They refused to support a National Liberal for president and thus relinquished support for the vice-presidency. Both sides entered the praesidium election free from prior commitments. Only the Progressives pledged their votes: to the National Liberals for the presidency, to the Social Democrats for the first vice-presidency.[24]

The intensity and uncertainty of the negotiations before the election pervaded the atmosphere of the Reichstag during the praesidium balloting. The chief contenders for the presidency were Spahn for the Centre, Schoenaich-Carolath for the National Liberals, and Bebel for the Social Democrats; three rounds of balloting were required before Spahn received a majority of 196 against Bebel's 175 votes. This number of votes for Bebel was significant. The Social Democrats with 110, and the Left Liberals with 43 mandates both voted for him; together that made 153 votes, but the source of the extra 22 votes proved a thorny problem for the future of the National Liberal party. In the excitement afterward, a number of National Liberals openly confessed to casting their ballots for Bebel, and this action was only a prelude to National Liberal radicalism. After Spahn had been elected president, Schiffer unexpectedly reported to Bassermann that since Spahn's election excluded a Grand Bloc praesidium, a majority of the Fraktion were now willing to vote for Scheidemann as the Social Democratic candidate for first vice-president. Bassermann gave his consent despite misgivings, and Scheidemann was elected first vice-president with the help of the

23. On National Liberal contacts with the conservatives, see Bassermann notations, no date, Bassermann remnant, 303/10; for voting and communication to the Social Democrats by Bassermann after the Fraktion meeting, see February 9, 1912, NL Akten, R 45 1/10.

24. Fraktion meeting, February 9, 1912, *SPD Fraktionsprotokolle,* 1: 260–261; cf. *Der zweite Parteitag der fortschrittlichen Volkspartei* (Berlin, 1912), p. 42.

National Liberals. The Social Democrats reciprocated by helping to elect the National Liberal, Paasche, as second vice-president. In this inadvertent way, the National Liberals finally achieved their goal of a "balanced" praesidium, and the Social Democrats, for the first time, filled a Reichstag vice-presidency.[25]

This latter fact now created an especially difficult obligation for the Social Democrats. Although they had refused court attendance during the negotiations, the issue was reopened immediately after the election. On February 10 Vollmar wrote a strong letter to Scheidemann urging his appearance:

> It is quite possible that His Majesty is not so eager to see a Social Democrat and therefore will be satisfied with a written "notification." . . . Should it then come to a personal visit, I hold it for desirable, . . . that you participate in this simple formality. If W[ilhelm] behaves decently, as gentleman to gentleman, then the matter is settled with a few exchanged greetings; should he turn against you, then you would not remain at a loss for an answer. At any rate, such a dangling thread ought not to obstruct further political development in this [session of the] Reichstag.[26]

Vollmar hoped to solve the problem regarding recognition of the monarchy in the same easy manner as the Badenese. For him, the important issue was not the theoretical question of form and principle but the pragmatic question of achieving the most benefits for Social Democracy in the course of parliamentary work. But Vollmar's experience was mainly southern and in dealing with affairs in Berlin, he miscalculated the cloudier political climate.

Vollmar's advice to Scheidemann was typical for a southern reformist, but it was Bebel who played the strangest role in the drama of court duties. Members of the bourgeois parties—Centre, National Liberal, and Progressive—later claimed that during the preelection negotiations, Bebel, under pressure from the Centre, agreed that the Social Democratic vice-president would go to court, as called for by parliamentary custom, should the president himself be prevented from doing so. They claimed that to give himself protective political cover, he refused to

25. For the praesidium vote, see *Schulthess, 1912,* pp. 22–23; Bassermann notations, no date, Bassermann remnant, 303/10.
26. Vollmar to Scheidemann, February 10, 1912, Vollmar Papers.

guarantee that the vice-president would not suddenly become indisposed on such an occasion. Although Bebel heatedly denied this claim when it was made, there was additional evidence that he entertained a compromise with the traditional obligation. Bassermann reported a conversation held during the balloting for president. Half in jest, he asked Bebel what he would do in case of his election. Laughingly, Bebel retorted that he would willingly visit the kaiser but without the other two presidents since the parliamentary rules did not include them, and he remarked that he would find a conversation with the kaiser very interesting. Both Bassermann and Bebel knew that Bebel's chances of victory were slim, and there was little danger—or possibility—of his visiting the kaiser. The accusation of the bourgeois parties and the bantering conversation with Bassermann were only important in that they once again reflected the tragic flaw in the connection between Social Democratic theory and practice. In theory, they refused to recognize the monarch and his system; in practice, if the monarch and his system, i.e., the other parties, recognized Social Democracy to the extent of electing one of its representatives to the highest post in the Reichstag praesidium, Social Democracy might compromise of its own accord. *Vorwärts,* in its jubilation over Scheidemann's election, aptly expressed the Social Democratic attitude:

> . . . It was a question of achieving the recognition of the full equality of the party [at least] by the liberals. Therefore our Fraktion could not allow any conditions to be dictated by the other parties. That would have transformed the recognition into a humiliation.

It was important that any compromise be chosen freely and not imposed.[27]

While the Social Democrats celebrated their election to the praesidium, trouble brewed in other quarters. The Centre, true to its previous tactics, did not relish a partnership with Social Democracy, and they forced Spahn to resign from the presidency. His resignation reverberated in the ranks of the National Liberals, where right-wing local organizations were protesting the votes cast both for Bebel and for Scheidemann.

27. On Bassermann's alleged agreement, *Nationalliberale Jugend*, 12 (1912) : 34; *SPD Parteitag, 1912,* p. 104; on his jesting remark, Bassermann notations, no date, Bassermann remnant, 303/10. Quotation is from *Vorwärts,* February 10, 1912.

As the complaints thundered into Berlin, the National Liberal Fraktion found it hard to ignore its own rank and file. In one last effort, it tried to persuade the Centre to remain in the presidency, and when this attempt failed, they forced their own second vice-president, Paasche, to resign in order to avoid the lonely stigma of associating with the Social Democrats. After the resignations of Spahn and Paasche, two Progressives, Johannes Kaempf and Heinrich Dove, were elected to the two vacant seats. Yet even this new combination was short-lived. The kaiser, on Bethmann Hollweg's advice, refused to receive the praesidium without Scheidemann for fear of setting a precedent in the future. When the Reichstag elected a permanent praesidium four weeks later, Scheidemann was not reelected; instead two Progressives and a National Liberal were the final choices. Within one short month, the recognition so eagerly sought by the Social Democrats gave way to the humiliation they sought to avoid.[28]

Events eliminated the presence of the Social Democrats in the praesidium of 1912. The Centre's tactics and monarchical principles played into the hands of the government and its desire to exclude the Social Democrats. Its position also deprived the National Liberals of the support needed to justify their toleration of the Social Democrats to their own local organizations. However, the final praesidium was a new combination with reformist implications for the Reich. It represented the liberal bloc that Bassermann demanded five years before when arranging the abortive Bülow Bloc. At that time, it was too radical for the Conservatives and even for many National Liberals; in 1912, the liberal praesidium was further left than any previous one. Even if a bona fide Grand Bloc praesidium could not be elected, the exclusion of the right implied a partial shift of power from right to left within the Reichstag.

PARLIAMENTARY CHANGES

This shift within the Reichstag had immediate political effects. The liberal parties harbored one traditional and some recent liberal demands

28. For the resignation of Spahn, see *SPD Parteitag, 1912*, pp. 103–104; for Paasche, Fraktion meeting, February 12, 1912, NL Akten, R 45 1/10; also DZAP, Hutten-Czapski Papers, Schönaich-Carolath to Hutten-Czapski, February 12, 1912. Cf. Fraktion meeting February 13, 1912, *SPD Fraktionsprotokolle*, 1 : 261. On their replacements, see election of Reichstag president, 1912, Gothein Papers. On the permanent praesidium, see *Schulthess, 1912*, p. 45; *Hilfe* 18 (1912) : 161.

which they wanted to implement now that they had some political strength. This strength of course depended on Social Democratic support, and even though the Social Democrats had failed to gain a seat in the praesidium, there were other ways of giving them parliamentary power. The praesidium was not the only measure of a Grand Bloc policy, nor was it the only sign of the Centre's attitude toward the "leftist" parties.

Shortly after the Reichstag convened, the Social Democrats let it be known that they, as the largest party in the Reichstag, had a right to certain committee posts and that they intended to exercise this right. Thus they demanded the chairmanship of the budget committee and responsibility for various items in the budget. Once again, the Social Democrats followed the same pattern as the Badenese. Contrary to the situation in Baden, however, they had to depend not on the grace of a single party, the National Liberals, but on the collective leaders of all the parties in the Reichstag's senior committee. The senior committee, in which the liberals and the Centre had an influential majority, responded in much the same way as the Baden National Liberals. It appointed as chairman of the budget committee a member of the strongest bourgeois party, the Centre, and made the Social Democrat, Albert Südekum, his deputy.[29] The senior committee thereby recognized the Social Democratic right to certain parliamentary responsibilities, but it refused to grant the Social Democrats a position of leadership. Later, when the Social Democrats demanded the responsibility for the army budget, they received co-responsibility for the less traditional naval budget. Since the members of the Reichstag enjoyed great initiative vis-à-vis the government in the committee deliberations, the Social Democrats could hope to win more influence over legislation through their committee posts. The appointment to these posts was an important step toward the political integration of the Social Democrats.

Having recognized the Social Democratic right to increased political influence, the Grand Bloc turned to the power of the Reichstag itself. Since 1908, all the non-Conservative parties explicitly supported an expansion of parliamentary power, and their strength in the Reichstag of 1912 made it an unavoidable issue. Still smarting from their defeat in the Moroccan crisis, the National Liberals were the first to expend their efforts in this direction. Even before the praesidium elections, Bassermann discussed with Bethmann Hollweg the possibility of

---

29. Fraktion meeting, February 14, 1912, *SPD Fraktionsprotokolle*, 1 : 263.

giving the "Reichstag a greater measure of influence," and he reported back to the party that he had "found a hearing."[30] In the light of later developments, it is difficult to know exactly what the chancellor said to Bassermann. Governmental attempts to influence the praesidium elections may indicate that it was willing to grant more influence to a Reichstag controlled by a moderate majority. The praesidium elections, however, definitely revealed a more radical majority than desired by the government. In any case, neither the National Liberals nor the other non-Conservative parties intended to let the matter drift.

Striking in February in the radical aftermath of the first praesidium elections, all the non-Conservative parties submitted motions for changing the Reichstag's rules to allow for approval or disapproval of the chancellor's answers to interpellations.[31] In effect, this meant the institution of a vote of no-confidence which could, in time, lead to ministerial responsibility. This goal was more explicitly expressed by the National Liberals, who demanded a law making the chancellor responsible for all governmental acts of the kaiser and liable to prosecution before a high court for abuse of his powers. Significantly, the National Liberals did not ask for constitutional change. Yet the law they demanded would have a constitutional effect. It would allow the Reichstag to control the chancellor and, through him, the kaiser. In essence, it was designed to put teeth into the vote of no-confidence and challenge the authority of the monarchy.

Ultimately, of course, the motions of 1912 were the same as those introduced in the Daily Telegraph Affair when concern with the kaiser's powers first became acute. In 1908, both proposed changes were buried in committee. In 1912, however, at least one of the motions got immediate action. Within two weeks after they went to the Rules Committee, a Grand Bloc majority, including the Centre, decided to allow the Reichstag to approve or disapprove the acts of the chancellor.[32]

The best comment on the significance of the change was the reaction of the government itself. Bethmann Hollweg had sworn to fight "a parliamentary system . . . to the bitter end," and the change in the Reichstag's rules certainly steered in that direction. Consequently, the lawyers in the chancellor's office drew up a report on its constitutional and political aspects. Basing their arguments on Laband, Germany's

30. Fraktion meeting, January 31, 1912, NL Baden.
31. *Verhandlungen des Reichstages,* 298: Drucksachen no. 12, no. 47, no. 93, no. 152.
32. *Hilfe* 18 (1912) : 161.

foremost constitutional jurist, they concluded that though it might be very important politically, the proposed vote of no-confidence was constitutionally without effect. Its ineffectiveness could only lead to conflicts between chancellor and Reichstag whereby the Reichstag, and not the chancellor, would lose influence and prestige. The kaiser would be obliged to retain the chancellor and would eventually have to dissolve a Reichstag that was in continual conflict with the chancellor. But even a mild form of the vote of no-confidence, whereby the Reichstag expressed its agreement or disagreement in contrast to approval or disapproval with the chancellor, was not "free from misgivings, because, through such a resolution, the appearance is awakened that the assent of the Reichstag is necessary in cases other than those foreseen by the constitution. . . ." The government foresaw a series of conflicts growing out of the change, and although it confidently predicted the victory of the monarchy, the tone was dubious. The government never raised the question of just how long a political conflict between kaiser and Reichstag could continue without a major upheaval. In a democratic age, how long could the kaiser continue to resist democracy?[33]

The unstated questions of the government's memorandum themselves revealed an alteration in the relative positions of government and Reichstag. In 1908, the non-Conservative forces were still weak enough for the government to divide them and prevent any liberalizing measures from coming to a vote. In 1912, the government could still prevent a law on the chancellor's responsibility, since the Bundesrat, as the final authority, was unlikely to approve such legislation. But it could no longer control the internal affairs of the Reichstag itself. In May, all the non-Conservative parties supported the incorporation of a vote of no-confidence in the Reichstag's rules,[34] and the government itself realized that this vote had political significance. The government's fear of conflict would force it to pay more attention to the Reichstag's present and future majority. And since that majority was bound to be heavily weighted toward the left, some liberal concessions might be expected. Twelve years after publication, the reformist goals of *Demokratie und Kaisertum* appeared to be within the grasp of the Reichstag.

33. For Bethmann Hollweg's resolve, see DZAP, Reichskanzlei, Parteien 1, I, no. 1391, Bethmann Hollweg to Schwerin-Löwitz, July 1, 1911. Quoted passage from DZAP, Reichskanzlei, Reichstag 4/1, I, no. 1832, memorandum, March 19, 1912.

34. *Verhandlungen des Reichstages,* 285 : 1676–1687, 1773–1776.

Part III: Reform or Revolution?

8

The National Liberals: National or Liberal?

The full realization of Naumann's schemes depended on the firm and unwavering determination of a strong National Liberal party. Yet the praesidium election of February 1912, which reflected the electoral victory of the Grand Bloc and its reforming possibilities, caused a crisis that threatened the party's unity and undermined its will. All of the divisive tensions—between north and south, young and old, heavy and light industry—suddenly burst into a full-scale struggle for control of the party and its policies. All previous differences were suddenly reduced to the one conflict between right and left, and tempers raged on both sides. The right wing saw the praesidium election as a significant battle won by the left which, if it remained unchallenged, would determine the course of the war for the party's soul. In this crusade, the right attacked and the left defended; compromising peacemakers were unwanted obstacles to total victory.

Right-wing headquarters were lodged in Berlin, where two influential members of the party's secretariat, Rudolf Breithaupt and Paul Fuhrmann, helped bring the crisis to maturity. Due to their constant contact with Friedberg and the conservative members of the Prussian party, to their dependence on the generous contributions of the right wing, and to their daily exposure to radical Social Democracy, these two men had deep sympathies with the conservative opinions in the party, and their experience in organization and agitation gave them valuable knowledge for catalyzing the right-wing attack. Their location in Berlin also allowed them to sense the pulse of events and organize a unified front faster than the scattered local organizations. As soon as they ascertained that the National Liberals had cast their votes for Bebel as Reichstag president, Breithaupt and Fuhrmann telephoned the information to the local organizations and requested them to draft resolutions against the Reichstag Fraktion.[1]

Reaction was swift. Some organizations immediately telegraphed their displeasure: the Dresden party directed the Fraktion to cast no more votes for Bebel or a Grand Bloc praesidium; Magdeburg found the election had done "great damage to the national and monarchical concept." On February 11, two days after the praesidium election, a meeting of local leaders from all over the Reich assembled in Berlin to express their dissatisfaction with the election and to urge their supporters to remain "by the old flag." They drafted a resolution which stated their battle cry in no uncertain terms: "Only if all the true champions of the unconditional national, glorious traditions of our party unanimously persevere . . . can we weather the present crisis [and] also attain a recovery of temperateness in the Reichstag." These protests were not only directed against the Fraktion but against Bassermann as well. The *Rheinisch-Westfälische Zeitung,* the press organ of the heavy industrialists, blamed him for the votes cast for Bebel and Scheidemann and predicted a growing confusion in the party due to his contradictory policies. The local party in Magdeburg (which had elected Schiffer) criticized the lack of an "aware and well-advised leadership of the Fraktion" and made Bassermann "responsible for its 'nonnational' position." In Bielefeld (Westphalia), the local club demanded that the "leadership of the party be placed in hands which [would] not allow the undermining of the secure basis of patriotic dependability and bourgeois solidarity" vis-à-vis Social Democracy. Unequivocal support for both the Fraktion and Bassermann came only from the Baden party and the Young Liberals, and their voices were almost muffled by the cannonades from the right.[2]

At the beginning of the crisis, both sides demanded a meeting of the powerful central committee in order to clarify the situation. The meeting was set for March 24, and many viewed the certain clashes of opinion with apprehension. Observers inside and outside the party feared and

1. Hopf to Thorbecke, March 26, 1912, NL Baden.
2. For National Liberal reactions, see *Die Parteien, Urkunden und Bibliographie der Parteikunde,* vol. I, *Beihefte zur Zeitschrift für Politik* (Berlin, 1912–1913), pp. 177–178. Magdeburg's attack on Bassermann is quoted in the *Hannoversche Landeszeitung,* February 17, 1912, Zeitgeschichtliche Sammlung, no. 103; Bielefeld, in *Die Parteien,* p. 180. For left-wing support of vote, see pp. 178–183.

expected the industrialists to secede from the party if the left pushed too hard and too far. As the industrialists continued to attack Bassermann, many right-wing members considered electing Schiffer as chairman of the party, and when the Badenese protested that the executive committee allotted it too few seats on the central committee, Breithaupt bruskly ignored its complaint and demanded new elections to choose the Baden delegates. Since one of the best ways to insure a right-wing orientation of the party was to pack the central committee with conservative members, the secretariat in Berlin probably hoped the new elections would get rid of those Baden delegates who stood on the extreme left. But it was not only necessary to insure conservative membership on the central committee, the right-wing had also to secure a firm hold on the executive committee. In the past, the central committee elected the executive committee by voting for a slate submitted en bloc by the previous executives. In this way membership on the executive committee was almost self-perpetuating, but in 1912, Friedberg, the Prussian leader and co-chairman of the party, determined to replace the moderate and somewhat leftist executives by electing each member individually, thus permitting right-wing nominations and clear-cut votes.[3]

Another way of insuring right-wing domination of the party was to deprive the left of its organization. In the middle of March, the right circulated a motion for disbanding the national association of Young Liberals and requiring the integration of its members into the regular local clubs. This attack on the Young Liberals was the most extreme measure in a series dating back to the party congress of 1906. The right wing persistently saw the Young Liberals as the rallying point for all the abhorrent democratic tendencies in the party and thought that by eradicating the organization, it could suppress the ideas. By the end of March, its preparations assured its success in the meeting of the central committee, and after a short strategy session the night before March 24, the right wing retired confident of victory on the morrow.[4]

3. For the industrialists, see *Hilfe* 18 (1912): 115. On the election of Schiffer, see Stresemann to Bassermann, March 2, 1912, Stresemann Papers. On the Badenese response, see exchange of letters between Breithaupt and the Baden party secretary Thorbecke, February 14 to 17, 1912, NL Baden. On Friedberg's plan for electing the executive committee, see Bassermann to Stresemann, March 8, 1912, Schiffer Papers.
4. Circular letter of the National Association of National Liberal Youth, March 21,

While the right wing was busy consolidating its position, its opponents were not idle. The influential Prussian, von Einem, wrote to Schiffer that he, together with many other "good liberals," would regard an alliance with the Centre and Conservatives "with great concern," and he recommended that the party continue to ally itself firmly with the Progressives. He "desperately" requested Schiffer to take up the cause of the left within the party in order to avoid conservative damage. The Young Liberals, stressing that they had only worked for the good of the party, distributed a letter informing members of the impending motion against them and requesting support in the coming fray. In addition, the leaders of the Pomeranian party and some left-wing members from Berlin sent invitations, presumably to sympathizers of the liberal center and the left, to a confidential meeting to be held on the eve of the central committee meeting. In an effort to counter every right-wing measure, their agenda concerned the reelection of Bassermann as chairman of the party, the composition of the executive committee, and a formula for a solution to the crisis. Yet these plans fell short of the mark because the opponents of the right were hopelessly divided. On the eve of the central committee's meeting, the convocation of the "left" could reach no agreement. The lack of agreement occurred because the "left" included both genuine left-wing democrats, like the southern Young Liberals, and moderate liberals like Bassermann and Stresemann who wanted change but not radicalism. Moreover, everyone wanted to avoid a party split. The moderate Bahr from Baden succinctly posed the problem confronting all those who opposed the right:

> Can it come to a split? The Babbitts (*Spiesser*) in north and middle Germany, some in the smaller cities, don't know which way to turn. Therefore it seems to me [that] a quiet treatment of this apparently abnormal occurrence is correct; we left-minded people must defend our viewpoint but also take care not to overstrain the bow. I would hold a new secession for an unspeakable misfortune for the whole of liberalism in Germany; we will not help anybody, not even the Progressive People's party.

1912, Stresemann Papers. The motion was supposedly signed by 70 National Liberals from Westphalia, 14 from Schleswig-Holstein, 9 from Magdeburg, and 5 from Bavaria, *Nationalliberale Jugend* 12 (March 30, 1912). On the preparations for March 24 meeting, see *Frankfurter Zeitung,* April 11, 1912, no. 102.

In hopes of avoiding an enervating party split, progressive National Liberals could only build temporary dikes against the right-wing flood.[5]

The central committee meeting of March 24 had three tasks: the election of the chairman of the party, the election of the executive committee, and a decision about the Young Liberals. In the course of executing each task, the right-wing pitted its forces against the left, the liberal center, and against Bassermann as a personal symbol of these unhealthy elements. Knowing that the meeting was packed against him, Bassermann initially tried to prevent the seating of three delegates from Hesse because of an "irregular election" and suffered his first defeat. His subsequent losses occurred during the elections for party chairman. As the left moved to reelect him by acclamation, the right protested with catcalls. Thereafter the election of both Bassermann and Friedberg, for the position of co-chairman, took place by ballot. In the case of Bassermann, 30 abstained; in the case of Friedberg, 28 abstained. The conservative Heinze later claimed that the abstentions for Bassermann were only meant as a warning against his progressive policies; the abstentions for Friedberg were presumably protests against his conservatism. Both men acted as symbols for the fight between right and left. Furthermore, the elections to the executive committee also reflected this fight, but the results were less obvious. Of the fifteen previous members, twelve were reelected, including Schiffer and Breithaupt. Rudolf Heinze, the extreme conservative from Saxony, and Hermann Fischer, a leader of the Young Liberals, failed to regain their seats. Stresemann, handicapped by the loss of his Reichstag seat in the election of 1912, was also removed from the executive committee because of his outspoken opposition to heavy industry. Yet the central committee did not elect blatant right-wingers to the vacancies. Anton Beck, from Heidelberg, belonged to the right wing of the Baden party but could be reckoned as a moderate in the national context. Fritz Hausmann owned a textile factory near Hanover and could be counted as a spokesman for

5. For von Einem to Schiffer letter, see March 8, 1912, Schiffer Papers. Circular letter of the National Association of National Liberal Youth, March 21, 1912, is in Stresemann Papers. Circular invitations of Ludewig and Ossent, no date, and circular invitation of Marwitz, March 19, 1912, appear in NL Baden. For the moderates' meeting, see *Frankfurter Zeitung,* April 11, 1912, no. 102. Quotation is Bahr to Thorbecke, February 19, 1912, NL Baden.

industry though not necessarily heavy industry. Felix Schwabach was a moderate member of the left wing who owed his mandate in the Reichstag to both Conservatives and Social Democrats. It was impossible to know which group voted for whom; what seemed certain was that the moderates had dominated the elections to the executive committee and had taken care to create a balance between the two extremes. Stresemann and Fischer were sacrificed to the right wing; Heinze was sacrificed to the left wing. As a result, the right wing won only a slight edge in the executive committee.[6]

In the case of the Young Liberals, right-wing victory was total. Heinze, the spokesman for the right, accused them of driving the party down an antimonarchical and prodemocratic path, of striving for a true "parliamentarism," and severing the party's ties with the government. In his eyes, the Young Liberals were responsible for all those policies inimical to the right. As if to confirm this direct connection between Young Liberals and party policy, the central committee voted 63–43 that only those organizations connected with the provincial or state parties could have special recognition in the national party. In effect, this vote meant the dissolution of the Young Liberal organization and the loss of its former separate representation at central committee meetings and party congresses. Such action would also deprive the progressive liberal center of the Young Liberals' corporate support and facilitate right-wing influence within the party.[7]

The dam thus erected against the disruptive, radical forces within the party permitted the central committee to conclude the meeting of March 24 by condemning the cause of the entire crisis. It passed a resolution pledging the party to cooperation with the other bourgeois parties and disapproved the policy of the Grand Bloc. In this way, it ruled out any cooperation with the Social Democrats such as occurred during the

6. On the balloting for Bassermann, see report of the central committee meeting, March 24, 1912, Stresemann Papers; Fraktion meeting, March 25, 1912, NL Baden. For Heinze's sentiments, see speech made to National Liberal club at Dresden, April 17, 1912, Stresemann Papers. For executive committee members before 1912, see the annual report of the executive committee, March 19, 1911, NL Baden. For results of 1912 election, see the notations of Paul Breithaupt, Stresemann Papers. Cf. *Von Bassermann zu Stresemann: Die Sitzungen des nationalliberalen Zentralvorstandes, 1912–1917,* ed. Klaus-Peter Reiss (Düsseldorf, 1967), p. 92. Dirk Stegmann, *Die Erben Bismarcks: Parteien und Verbände in der Spätphase des wilhelminischen Deutschlands* (Cologne, 1970), p. 306, oversimplifies in designating two of the newly elected members as right-wing National Liberals.

7. Fraktion meeting, March 26, 1912, NL Baden. For the vote, see *Hilfe* 18 (1912) : 231.

praesidium elections. It also implied a prohibition against any sweeping policy of reform. As Hutten-Czapski wrote to Bethmann Hollweg: "The danger of a swing to the left seem[ed] . . . eliminated for the foreseeable future." All that remained was the ratification of the committee's action by the party congress scheduled for the beginning of May.[8]

The prevention of a swing to the left was only one effect of the central committee's meeting. A more serious consequence for the party was the alienation of Bassermann, the liberal center, and the entire left wing. Immediately after the meeting, Bassermann, together with some of his supporters, declined to attend the banquet that traditionally followed central committee meetings and served as a symbol of party unity. More seriously, the left wing now determined to mass its own forces for the forthcoming party congress. On March 27, three days after the meeting of the central committee, Robert Kauffmann, the chairman of the Young Liberals, wrote to Stresemann with plans to drum up a narrow majority for the maintenance of the Young Liberal organization. He believed that the disbanding of the Young Liberals would lead to a much more damaging split than a right-wing secession, which would have "no dangerous extent." Furthermore, he wanted to bring a series of motions before the party congress that would show a "clear division of the spirits." These motions included additional delegates to the executive committee and the maintenance of the Young Liberals' formal representation in the party. These plans, if successful, would effectively reverse the most important decisions of the central committee.[9]

The difficulty with Kauffmann's plan, as the party treasurer Weber pointed out, was the broad support enjoyed by the right wing. He estimated that at least 100 delegates to the party congress would support the central committee's motion against the Young Liberals and that the danger of a right-wing secession was therefore a much greater gamble than Kauffmann believed. Secession also would have grave financial consequences; the right-wing clubs, such as existed in Westphalia, simply contributed more money to the party than the "financially less powerful" clubs of the liberal center, the left wing, and the Young

8. *Von Bassermann zu Stresemann,* p. 188; DZAP, Hutten-Czapski Papers, Hutten-Czapski to Bethmann Hollweg, March 25, 1912.

9. DZAP, Hutten-Czapski Papers, Hutten-Czapski to Bethmann Hollweg, March 25, 1912; Kauffmann to Stresemann, March 27, 1912, Stresemann Papers.

Liberals. The party had already experienced the loss of votes accompanying the withdrawal of right-wing funds in the Prussian and national elections, and Weber implicitly recalled those humiliating events. In addition, he pointed out that opposition to the right was neither so extensive nor so dependable as the left believed. Only four provincial or state organizations—the Rhine province, Württemberg, Baden, and Bavaria—absolutely supported the left wing. Silesia, Saxony, and Pomerania supported Bassermann and the more moderate liberal center, while Hesse, Oldenburg, Westphalia, and Braunschweig absolutely opposed the liberal center and the left wing. Split and uncertain opposition to the right occurred in Thuringia and the Prussian provinces of Saxony, Posen, and East and West Prussia. And although Weber did not mention them in his analysis, there were two other powerful state organizations whose influence could not be denied: Hanover was proleft; Schleswig-Holstein was pro-right. In terms of pure numbers, there were seven provincial or state organizations that unequivocally opposed the right; five definitely supported it, and five were uncertain. Although they had no absolute majority within the party, the progressive elements were stronger than their opponents, and their vote-gathering ability exceeded that of any other group. In the elections of 1912, the organizations that supported the liberal center and the left wing amassed 22 mandates as opposed to 9 of the pro-right and 6 of the uncertain organizations. Measured both in organization and in mandates, a right-wing secession would decimate the party to approximately two-thirds of its former strength. This numerical loss would not be so devastating, but in the last analysis the financial power of the right wing was probably the strongest argument against a split. Weber wrote to Stresemann urging him to restrain his fighting spirit. Without the right wing, he said, "We cannot continue to exist financially, and a good portion of the Saxon industry will not follow you . . . [or] me since the advance of Social Democracy has unleashed currents which I see growing day by day in [my] business dealings." What Weber noticed was a change in the attitudes of those light industrialists who had previously been inclined to progressivism and thus to deal less harshly with the Social Democrats. Social Democracy's increase in mandates (43 to 110 or over 150 percent) had produced a scare, a hysteria perhaps, within the ranks of the large and small businessmen upon whom the party depended for its financial and political support. Given this current, the Young Liberals and the left wing could hardly count on a majority favorable to its cause within the party.[10]

But even if it were impossible to reverse the decisions of the central committee entirely, they could be modified and stripped of their more conservative implications. In particular, Stresemann thought that 1912 was the last chance to establish an enlightened liberalism within the party and preserve the party's unity. If this opportunity were lost, the right wing, backed by the Centralverband, would control the National Liberal treasury, the press, and eventually the leadership. They would find a more conservative successor to Bassermann and would push the left wing into the Progressive Party. A part of the Reichstag Fraktion had already threatened to join the Progressives if the "dictatorship" of the central committee did not cease after the party congress. If the left seceded, the Progressives would inherit the mantle of liberalism, and its spirit would cease to exist within the National Liberal party. Together with Stresemann, there were many who wanted to preserve the party's liberal traditions, and they felt their survival depended on Bassermann's leadership and the continued existence of the Young Liberals. Stresemann's supporters wanted to pack the party congress— just as the right wing had packed the central committee—with delegates who subscrided to their own progressive views. By the beginning of April, Bassermann himself had assumed a fighting spirit:

> It is not necessary for me to develop a program. . . . [M]y political activity is a program and exactly that is disputed . . . . [On the right] the powerful press, on the left the metropolitan press, and we, almost without a press. I will continue to conduct the fight according to my honest conviction . . . ; I stand and fall on the basis of my opinions (*Anschauungen*). The party congress may decide on that.

Bassermann saw himself and his friends as the enlightened middle way between the two extremes of the party. He too desired a unified, *liberal* party, and if he intended to pursue that course, the party congress would

10. Weber's analysis from his letter to the business office of the Württemberg National Liberal party, and to Stresemann, March 28, 1912, Stresemann Papers; compare with *Kürschners, 1912*.

have to overrule the central committee and reestablish the previous balance between right and left.[11]

The National Liberal party congress met in Berlin on May 12, 1912. This was the last party congress before the war, and all the divisive issues were verbally molded into the rock of party history. The historian who pauses in his analysis can look backward and forward in National Liberal development and see its difficulties written permanently large in the records of the 1912 congress. On the one hand was the conservative, financially powerful right wing, defender of the status quo because its own selfish interests were served best by this defense. Against it were ranged the progressives, including moderates like Bassermann and Stresemann, and radicals like the Young Liberals. These groups had their own interests at stake, but they saw that adaptability to liberal and sometimes democratic change could benefit both the party and the state. The debates at the congress of 1912 gave specific form and substance to the hopes and fears of both sides.

In the eyes of the right wing, the preservation of the status quo meant preserving the party's link with the Conservatives. It was Friedberg, the head of the Prussian party, who developed the main reasons for preserving this link. According to him, the party's troubles began with the alliance with the Progressives and their unhealthy cooperation with the Social Democrats. The pursuit of Prussian suffrage reform and democracy by both these parties was a disruptive force within the nation. Moreover, Social Democracy's methods—mass demonstrations, economic boycotts, parliamentary obstruction—proved that the aim of integrating them into the nation's political life was idle folly.[12] Political ill-health, disturbance, negativism were used by Friedberg to discredit any National Liberal association with the left. Yet while there was some substance to all these charges, Friedberg's arguments lacked logical conviction. In each case, evidence could be cited to prove that Social Democracy would cooperate peacefully with the bourgeois parties if encouraged to do so. In reality, Friedberg was saying that the right-wing National Liberals refused to cooperate with the Social Democrats, but he gave no rational justification for this course.

11. Stresemann to Weber, March 29, 1912, Stresemann Papers; Bassermann to Stresemann, April 6, 1912, Schiffer Papers.
12. *NL Vertretertag, 1912*, pp. 59–68.

The real reason for avoiding Social Democracy was given by another right-wing speaker, Leidig, who emphasized social legislation as the principal point of difference within the party. Leidig was a former official of the Centralverband, and his arguments stressed the cost of social legislation. Every social measure must be viewed in light of the burden borne by the businessman:

> We must . . . consider and weigh whether that which the individual certainly can give with full and open hands ought to be inflicted upon our German industry through the force of the state and whether we are not destroying the basis of the favorable development which has brought prosperity . . . to our German fatherland. . . . The small [businessman] suffers first and most under too extensive and impractical social [legislation].

Leidig cleverly mixed laissez-faire with German patriotism and the interests of the small businessman in order to appeal to the emotions of the majority of the party's supporters and to obscure the fact that it was the heavy industrial interests that opposed social legislation and the party's progressive policy most bitterly. Another representative of Westphalian industry, Walter Lohmann, chastised the Fraktion's position on the National Insurance Bill for clearly violating the limits of economic common sense. The whole range of social legislation symbolized in the National Insurance Bill was unprofitable because it had never achieved its original goal: the diminution of Social Democratic influence in the state. Unwittingly, Lohmann provided the real reasons for Friedberg's attack on the left. Social Democracy was indissolubly linked with the social legislation so costly to National Liberal business interests. If the National Liberals helped to strengthen Social Democracy, they would also increase unprofitable social measures. Social Democratic reformism, which advocated independent workers' organizations and better working conditions, would never appeal to these men because it hampered their unchallenged pursuit of mammon. Even the Social Democrats' goal of political democracy, shared by progressive National Liberals, threatened to cost money in the long run: the power to vote was the power to tax; the power to tax was the power to ruin. No right-wing speaker ever justified his political convictions in such crass terms, and no doubt many sincerely believed in the health, stability, and positivism mentioned by Friedberg. But ultimately the cash nexus determined their politics.[13]

In his diatribe against the left, Friedberg accused the Young Liberals of furthering the evils of democracy that were so costly to the right wing. And the drive to prevent a right-wing capture of the party focused on the survival of the Young Liberals and the maintenance of their ideals within the party. The decision to defend the Young Liberals involved a double phalanx against the right; and each of the two flanks concentrated on *one* important task. The maneuver to save the Young Liberals originated with Stresemann and his National Liberal club in Dresden and was supported by the parties of the Rhineland, Hanover, Württemberg, and of course, Baden. These groups successfully suggested the formation of an "unbiased committee" to negotiate a compromise which would make the continued existence of the Young Liberal organization palatable to the rest of the party. The committee, once formed, was truly "unbiased"—consisting of Friedberg and three members of the executive committee, three members from the Rhineland, and three Young Liberals—and its compromise considered the feelings of all National Liberal groups. In order to assuage the left wing, it decided that the Young Liberals and "any other group" had the right to organize independently. As a sop to the right wing, it ruled that such independent organizations henceforth had no right to privileged representation on the party's governing bodies. Although the Young Liberals could still exist and give corporate support to progressive liberalism, their direct influence within the party would be diminished through the loss of their corporate voting power. In the future, the Young Liberals could receive representation only through voting in regular National Liberal clubs. The right wing expected the contact with older members to quench the Young Liberal fire, but the mingling between old and young could also have the opposite effect of radicalizing the elders and winning converts to progressive policies.[14]

An example of the tactic of conversion occurred at the party congress itself. On the day before the congress, two different progressive groups met to plan their retorts to the right wing and forestall its domination. Rebmann and the Badenese invited all the leaders of the state organiza-

13. For quoted passage, see ibid., p. 80; for Lohmann, pp. 46–53.

14. *Die Parteien*, pp. 186–190, 192; *Kölnische Zeitung*, May 12, 1912, no. 540; *NL Vertretertag, 1912*, p. 4.

tions to a meeting in the morning in an attempt to rally prestigious, popular support against the right. In the evening, Stresemann met with a group of reliable individuals from the state parties, from the Reichstag Fraktion, and from the Young Liberals. It was perhaps a symptom of the National Liberals' disease that these two groups never got together even after their cooperation was suggested. Now, as before, a unified opposition to the right was lacking. Nevertheless, the unity of purpose sufficed to prevent a disaster similar to the central committee meeting. When the right wing finished its speeches at the meeting of the congress, it tried to silence all left-wing debate by moving for adjournment, but this caused such a violent disturbance that it was impossible to dismiss the congress before the left aired its convictions.[15]

The left attacked the right on three counts: liberal tradition, social legislation, and Social Democracy. In many ways, its arguments closely resembled the themes of *Demokratie und Kaisertum*. Kauffmann, the Young Liberal chairman, reminded the party of its early liberal ideals of responsible government and of loyal opposition. He argued that the desertion of liberal ideals had weakened the party's popularity, long a National Liberal sore point, and that an enlightened social policy had to be fitted into the framework of liberal tradition in order to win working-class support for liberalism and increase the party's popular appeal. In answer to Leidig's fear that social legislation would disadvantageously burden German industry in the international market, he pointed to similar legislation and similar burdens in other countries. The equation of democracy and social welfare with a decrease in

15. Motions of the Baden party for the National Liberal party congress, April 30, 1912 and Frey to Rebmann, April 30, 1912, NL Baden. On the lack of cooperation, see Helle to Thorbecke, May 4, 1912; Thorbecke to Beck, May 6, 1912; Paul Liepmann to Rebmann, May 5 and 7, 1912, NL Baden. Liepmann wanted Rebmann to invite the following individuals to his meeting of state leaders: Gustav Stresemann, Bruno Marwitz, Oskar Poensgen, Ludewig, C. Ossent, Fritz Mittelmann, Franz Moldenhauer, Prof. Otto Hebel, Kommerzienrat Georg Rosensweig (Kassel), Bernhard Falk (Köln), Bernhard Mettenheimer (Frankfurt), Leopold Kölsch, Heinrich, Prinz zu Schoenaich-Carolath, Julius Sieg, Ernst Blankenhorn, Anton Beck, Johannes Junck, Hermann Fischer, Robert Künne (Elberfeld), Ernst Brües, Vogel (Saarbrücken), Friedrich Wachhorst de Wente, Carl Andres (Gutlechthof-Kreuznach), Prof. Erich Brandenburg (Leipzig), Rechtsanwalt Hermann Freigang (Chemnitz), Stadtrat Franz Kübel (Cannstadt), Theodor Bickes (Feuerbach), Otto Keinath (Stuttgart), Friedrich List (Reutlingen), Ernst Frey (Karlsruhe), Carl Heimann-Kreuser (Mülheim), Helbeck (Elberfeld), Robert Kauffmann (Stuttgart), Fritz van Calker, Ludwig Roland-Lücke, Gerhart Bollert, Hartmann von Richthofen. On the outburst against the railroading tactics of the right, see *NL Vertretertag, 1912*, p. 70.

industrial strength and national power was false; true national greatness went hand in hand with internal freedom and social progress. Thus
it was only logical that national greatness also depended on integrating
the Social Democrats into the nation's politics.[16]

Rebmann was the party's most eloquent defender of the Social Democratic Party, and the task of justifying closer relations between National
Liberals and Social Democrats fell squarely on his shoulders throughout
the crisis and during the party congress. He naturally resorted to his
experience with the Grand Bloc in Baden and termed it a partnership
that was viable for the Reich as well. He realized that conditions were
not yet ripe for a national Grand Bloc but insisted that the National
Liberals must strive in this direction and not lapse into a backward
conservative policy. A National Liberal commitment to a Grand Bloc
would encourage Social Democratic cooperation and prevent their
relapse into a radical "mire." He argued fervently for an understanding
of Social Democracy and its problems:

> Social Democrat and Social Democrat are two different things.
> And if you see that we in the south are dependent on cooperation
> with them, in the north however the opposite, then you also see the
> two souls which live in the breast of Social Democracy itself: one
> which holds fast to the dogma of the past; the other which looks to
> the future . . . . [O]ne must look the possibility of future develop-
> ment in the eye, and if one believes in these . . . possibilities,
> [one] has the patience to wait for that development. One must
> consider that what . . . the misery of life and an unbelievable
> assiduous, embittering, and exasperating work has hammered into
> these heads will change only slowly. . . .[17]

Drawing on his experience with the Grand Bloc in Baden, Rebmann
summarily countered all the right-wing fears about Social Democracy.
In one breath, he diagnosed the most serious problem of his party.
Neither the past nor the present were adequate guides to the future,
and only a courageous new course could insure the progress of National
Liberalism.

Despite the exhortations of right and left, when the party congress
ended, both factions still existed. They would continue to conflict each

---

16. *NL Vertretertag, 1912*, pp. 53–59.
17. Ibid., pp. 72–78.

time a serious issue or a new election occurred. Yet the results of the congress revealed that despite the massive right-wing attack, the National Liberal progressives had managed to hold their own. The compromise over the Young Liberals and the reelection of Bassermann as chairman of the party manifested a progressive victory. Although Bassermann was not a member of the left, he symbolized its ideas, and his congress speech repeated his convictions in one of the strongest statements of political belief he ever made. He praised the Young Liberals for infusing a new idealism into the party. He stressed the liberal virtues of alliance with the Progressives. He justified the need for social legislation and suffrage reform. Above all, he called for a party that was independent of all nonliberal forces, from Conservatives and government as well as from Social Democracy.[18] Each point mentioned clashed with the strong conservative views of the right wing. Yet it had to accept him and his beliefs because he unified the party; no other chairman was as acceptable to so many groups as Bassermann.

This unifying personality was unable, however, to solve all the splintering problems confronting the party. Although the National Liberals did not split in 1912, they were beginning to crumble at the edges. The Bavarian Young Liberals had already left the party to join the Progressives. As a result of the Bavarian liberal "partnership" and its inclination to Social Democracy, some right-wing members withdrew and joined the Conservatives, and the same right-wing unrest existed in Baden. In Hesse, a left-wing secession protested against the continued membership and influence of Heyl and Becker in the state party. Throughout the various state organizations, dissatisfaction with one direction or the other forced the dissidents to withdraw and seek a new political nest.[19]

At the same time, a larger split developed on the national scene. The right wing had threatened during the crisis of March and April to found their own organization if the Young Liberals were not disbanded, and indeed the compromise resolution accepted by the party congress in May explicitly sanctioned such an organization. Dissatisfied with the compromise, the right wing met on the eve of the party congress, at

18. Ibid., pp. 21–42.
19. On the secession of left and right, see *Hilfe* 16 (1910) : 280; Annual Report of National Liberal Party, 1912, NL Akten, R 45 1/4; Günther Kriegbaum, *Die parlamentarische Tätigkeit des Freiherrn C. W. Heyl zu Herrnsheim* (Meisenheim/Glan, 1962), pp. 194–200.

the same time that the left wing was planning strategy, and decided to form an organizational counterweight to the Young Liberals. This new organization was called the Imperial Association of Old National Liberals or, in abbreviated form, "Old Liberals." The term Old Liberal dated back to the liberal conflict in Prussia during the constitutional struggle, and its use was revived shortly after the turn of the century. For more than a year before the congress of 1912, an informal organization existed that called itself the Old Liberals. The Westphalians and the "Wormser Corner" formed the nucleus of this group, and it included the parties in Schleswig-Holstein, Braunschweig, Hamburg, and Prussian Saxony. These groups corresponded with one another from time to time and held infrequent meetings to discuss problems. The Imperial Association was an effort to formalize these contacts, to expand them, and to attract new members and organizations throughout the nation. The leadership of the new organization was divided between prominent representatives of Westphalian industry and members of the Prussian legislative Fraktion, and its general secretary was Fuhrmann, who helped to precipitate the crisis over the praesidium election. The organization's money also came from Westphalian industry. At the beginning of June 1912, the Old Liberals began to publish a new weekly, the *Old National Liberal Correspondence,* which propagated all those principles reiterated over the years by the right wing at meetings and party congresses: no German democracy and no interference with free enterprise. The tone of the paper was always bitter and sometimes slanderous toward its opponents within the party. Its publication did nothing to conciliate the left wing or to heal the split in the party, and there was a real danger that the party would shatter into a kaleidescope of independent organizations.[20]

Soon after the formal organization of the Old Liberals, a group of moderate National Liberals, primarily those associated with the Bauernbund and Hansabund, publicly protested the weakening effects of such separatist groups. Bassermann and Stresemann, determined to prevent

20. On the old Liberals, see *Kölnische Zeitung,* May 7, no. 514; May 15, no. 554; and May 20, no. 573, 1912; meeting of the state committee, September 27, 1903, NL Baden; *Frankfurter Zeitung,* April 11, 1912, no. 102. On their finance, see Hartwig Thieme, *Nationaler Liberalismus in der Krise: Die nationalliberale Fraktion des preussischen Abgeordnetenhauses, 1914–1918* (Boppard/Rhine, 1963), pp. 47–49; also Stegmann, *Die Erben Bismarcks,* pp. 311–313. On the faction's organ, see *Altnationalliberale Reichskorrespondenz* 1 (June 11, 1912), Stresemann Papers.

domination by heavy industry and the swing to the right desired by the Old Liberals, bound the party more closely to the commercial and light industrial interests represented by the Hansabund and the League of Industrialists. Stresemann particularly wanted to combat "the policy of resignation" embodied by the Old Liberals and those who refused to fight them:

> The gentlemen Friedberg, Schiffer, Heinze, Schmieding are the party of resignation. For them it is enough if the National Liberals are seen as a corps of the second class and if the sun of the government's grace shines on them to some extent at least. They embody the saturated bourgeoisie. Unfortunately we have no conscious gentry which is . . . "self-assured" . . . ; we have only a newly arrived bourgeoisie which is blessed if it can marry into the so-called upper class. All these people have no understanding of the fight for the equality of liberalism. Power politics means to lead the fight for this equality through the exploitation of the given circumstances and the maintenance of influence in city, state, and nation. The fight in Baden must also be regarded from this viewpoint . . . ; it is simply a question of the National Liberal party remaining in power and not relinquishing control to the Centre by recoiling from an agreement with Social Democracy.[21]

Stresemann's denunciation of the "saturated" National Liberal bourgeoisie reflected his Young Liberal background, but it also reflected the struggles of Bassermann and even Rebmann to gain a greater influence for liberalism with the government and with the people. It would never attain such influence by conceding to conservative policies at every turn. It could gain popular strength and stature only if it pressured the government for recognition of liberal interests, liberal demands, liberal policies. If liberalism dedicated itself wholeheartedly to political reform, it could unite the entire left from Bassermann to Bebel and wrest power and influence from all groups that supported the status quo. Its fight for more power for the Reichstag must also be seen in this light. Yet the main battleground was Prussia; it was the Prussian Conservatives supported by right-wing National Liberals who were under attack. The Old Liberals were therefore a defensive organization formed to deny

21. On the swing to the right, see Stegmann, *Die Erben Bismarcks,* pp. 313–314. Quotation from Stresemann to Rebmann, May 17, 1912, NL Baden.

the development of the basic feature of liberal government everywhere: a government responsive to the will of the people. When Stresemann talked of the saturated bourgeoisie, he meant those National Liberals who were no longer liberal.

Although the right wing never succeeded in dominating the party before the war, it did prevent any further left-wing inroads on the influence it retained. The defensive measures of the right were exemplified in the last important skirmish before the war. At the central committee meeting of February 9, 1913, the left wing moved to reorganize the party's office in Berlin "in the direction of closer contact with party members throughout the country." This motion was a bid to provide better communication between the rank and file and the leadership and to liberalize the party's organization. The left wing hoped to increase the influence of the grass roots and break the stranglehold of the executive and central committees over the party's policies. The proposal reflected the desire of the Young Liberals first expressed at the congress of 1906 and, as such, was certainly unpalatable to the executive committee, which wanted to "regulate" and "discipline" the rank and file. The left wing argued against this "discipline," but it found little support. The majority of the central committee agreed that "discipline" should be "maintained," and the left-wing motion was defeated. There was no party congress to reverse or modify the conservative decisions of the central committee.[22]

In part, the failure of this challenge to authority reflected certain reversals in the economic trends important to National Liberal interests. At the beginning of 1913, an economic recession occurred which led to a modest rapprochement between heavy and light industry.[23] The two groups were now inclined to work with rather than against one another in both the economic and the political spheres. As a result political alliances within the central committee shifted and contributed to its decision. The liberal center, supported by the light industrialists, no longer explicitly sympathized with the Young Liberals and their radical supporters. The party's pendulum had swung once more toward the right.

22. Meeting of the executive committee, February 6, 1912, The motion was signed by the prominent former Young Liberals Bruno Marwitz, Oskar Poensgen, Paul Liepmann, and Oskar Blank, central committee meeting February 9, 1913, NL Akten, R 45 1/1.

23. Roswitha Leckebush, *Entstehung und Wandlungen der Zielsetzungen, der Struktur und der Wirkungen von Arbeitgeberverbände* ([East] Berlin, 1966), p. 61; Hartmut Kaelble, *Industrielle Interessenpolitik in der wilhelminischen Gesellschaft* (Berlin, 1967), p. 173.

In the last year before the war, the National Liberals became more conservative, but there was no diminution of differences within the party. It continued to lose financial contributions, and Bassermann attributed this to the Reichstag election of 1912. The largest donors disliked the party's allegedly leftist orientation, and attacks on Bassermann in the right-wing press continued. In 1913, the Reichstag Fraktion decided to readmit the conservative Becker from Hesse against the votes of the left wing and a part of the liberal center. The right wing dominated the Prussian Landtag election of 1913 and attacked the leftist orientation of the Reichstag Fraktion. In an effort to recreate party unity, the central committee resolved to dissolve both Old and Young Liberals in the spring of 1914. Both refused to disband, and the Young Liberals even defended the special organizations as substitutes for the specter of secession. The constant bickering in the press, the knowledge of the conflict between the extremes, the back-biting which occurred in private letters, all tended to disillusion even the most loyal members of the party. One local party leader closed a letter to Schiffer on a note of doubt, "One gradually beholds his membership in that which one still has the courage to call a party. . . . Brrr!"[24]

24. DZAP, Bassermann Papers, financial report, 1912–1913. For Becker, see *Altnationalliberale Reichskorrespondenz* 2 (February 28, 1913), Stresemann Papers. For refusal to disband, see *Fortschritt* 9 (1913) : 192; *Nationalliberale Jugend* 8 (1913) : 103–104; Thieme, *Nationaler Liberalismus*, p. 187. For quotation, see Rudolf von Campe to Schiffer, June 27, 1914, Schiffer Papers.

9

The National Grand Bloc: A Short-lived Experiment

The crisis within the National Liberal party erupted because of the alliance with Social Democracy. As we have seen, the sociopolitical implications of that alliance endangered the interests of the financially powerful right wing. So much was evident in the right-wing speeches of the party congress. More than anything, right-wing National Liberals feared any maneuver or policy committing them to compromise with the Social Democrats. The intransigeance of the right wing also explains why Bassermann attempted to win the Centre for a Grand Bloc praesidium in 1912. This alliance would have provided a bulwark, not only against the Conservatives, but against the dissenters within his own party. Alliance, commitment, and compromise with the Centre, because of its more similar interests, did not arouse the same qualms and objections as did cooperation with Social Democracy. This fact provided yet another reason why the Centre, in practical terms, had to belong to any viable national Grand Bloc. Yet the theory of the Bloc included the Social Democrats, and paradoxically, the National Liberals accepted their cooperation when it served their interests. They hardly hesitated to elect a National Liberal to the praesidium with the help of Social Democratic votes. The Social Democrats also contributed to the majority that changed the Reichstag's rules for a vote of no-confidence. Both measures represented National Liberal goals; thus they welcomed Social Democratic aid if it were granted on their terms. This circumstance was particularly evident where tax reform was concerned. Since 1909, the National Liberals had sought to rectify the imbalance between the tax on agricultural and industrial capital. The degree to which they were willing or unwilling to cooperate with Social Democracy in this venture was instructive for any future Grand Bloc policy.

TAX REFORM

The opportunity for tax reform arose almost immediately in the Reichstag of 1912 in connection with the funding of a naval bill. The government itself realized that the bill raised the specter of tax reform, and at first both Bethmann Hollweg and his secretary of the treasury sincerely hoped to introduce the national property tax demanded by the liberals since the collapse of the Bülow Bloc. However, government circles, the Bundesrat, and the Conservatives all opposed a property tax, and Bethmann Hollweg finally succumbed to their pressure and resorted to the government's usual method of indirect taxes on liquor and other consumer goods. As soon as this tax bill reached the Reichstag, the National Liberals notified the government that they were dissatisfied with its feeble provisions. Realizing that they now had a majority for tax reform if they chose to activate the Grand Bloc, they scorned Bethmann Hollweg's pleas for the indirect taxes. Bassermann clearly stated that the party did not intend to approve any bill that did not include the direct national tax demanded by the National Liberal program:

> The . . . Chancellor turns . . . to those who are supporters of the inheritance tax and implores them, in the interest of peace among the bourgeois parties, not to suggest the inheritance tax to finance the military bill. . . . Why doesn't he seek to convert the right to the insight that . . . the introduction of a direct tax . . . is a necessity? Why doesn't he say to the right: approve the inheritance tax . . . in order to achieve peace among the bourgeois parties? . . .

The National Liberals intended to maintain their opposition to the government in matters of taxation, and they were also willing to cooperate with Social Democracy to attain their ends.[1]

Bassermann supported his strong statements by moving to create a

---

1. Hans-Günter Zmarzlik, *Bethmann Hollweg als Reichskanzler, 1909–1914* (Düsseldorf, 1957), pp. 51–57. Cf. Peter-Christian Witt, *Die Finanzpolitik des deutschen Reiches von 1903 bis 1913: Eine Studie zur Innenpolitik des wilhelminischen Deutschlands,* vol. 415 of *Historische Studien,* ed. W. Berges et al. (Lübeck and Hamburg, 1970), pp. 337–353; and Hans Teschemacher, *Reichsfinanzreform und innere Reichspolitik* (Berlin, 1915), p. 73. Ernst Bassermann's is found in *Verhandlungen des Reichstages,* 284 : 1329.

special committee for debating the liquor tax. This special committee would evade the powerful Reichstag budget committee and could devote full time to a discussion of the tax bill. Moreover, any committee debating the liquor tax would eventually have to deal with the infamous Liebesgabe, the subsidy to the "agrarian" distillers of liquor, which had exploded the Bülow Bloc in 1909 and was opposed by both liberals and Social Democrats. Through his motion, Bassermann hoped to outflank the Conservatives and the Centre, and with the help of the Progressives and Social Democrats, he succeeded. The Reichstag voted 160 to 158 to create the special committee.[2] The vote initiated a Grand Bloc policy for tax reform. The National Liberals assumed the leadership, and the parties of the left fell in behind them.

When the committee began its deliberations at the beginning of May 1912, the Social Democrats furthered the cause that Bassermann began by declaring their willingness "to vote for a . . . direct tax, if [it] could achieve, as in the present situation, a . . . substitution for an indirect tax." This statement was no contemplative hedging on the matter of tax reform as in 1909 but a firm declaration of an ultimate Social Democratic vote for a direct tax. The occasion for the Social Democratic declaration was their motion, in the special committee, to reduce the indirect tax on liquor; if their motion were accepted, they intended to introduce a motion for an inheritance tax to cover the deficit caused by the reduction. In other words, the Social Democrats created a situation in which they could substitute a direct for an indirect tax and kill two birds with one stone. They would satisfy a part of their own program and also indicate their willingness to cooperate with the other parties in the Reichstag. Their desire for cooperation led to negotiations with the Progressives in which the Social Democrats promised to support a Progressive motion for an inheritance tax. This was not the first time that the Social Democrats had successfully negotiated with the Progressives, but it was the first large issue in which the two agreed to cooperate in the Reichstag. As such, it represented the culmination of all the past overtures and agreements between the two. The leftist parties were finally sharing responsibility for an important reform which both had demanded for a long time.[3]

2. *Verhandlungen des Reichstages,* 284: 1328–1329. Cf. Fraktion meeting, April 18, 1912, *SPD Fraktionsprotokolle,* 1: 272. Also *Hilfe* 18 (1912): 273.
    3. For Social Democratic motion, see *Hilfe* 18 (1912): 289–290; for motivation and

The Progressive–Social Democratic plans acted as a spur to the National Liberal leadership. It also created a dilemma. Although the Progressive–Social Democratic inheritance tax would fulfill National Liberal demands, support for their motion would immediately create a Grand Bloc and alienate the National Liberal right wing. Having activated the Grand Bloc for creating the special tax committee, the National Liberals now shied away from it. Once more, intraparty problems impeded a clear-cut policy. Since the deliberations on the tax bill coincided with the preparations for the National Liberal party congress of 1912—the crisis congress—the action of the Reichstag Fraktion would bear directly on the threat of right-wing secession. It was therefore important to avoid the *appearance* of a Grand Bloc, although it was already functioning, in order to preserve party unity. The National Liberals had thus to find some way of introducing direct taxes without relying completely on the Progressives and Social Democrats. As a remedy, the National Liberals agreed to the famous Erzberger-Bassermann compromise of 1912, which combined the National Liberals and the Centre in the cause of tax reform.

The Erzberger-Bassermann compromise originated with the Centre. During the opening debates on the tax bill, the Centre declared its willingness to give up the Liebesgabe, since the recent introduction of a less costly medium-quality liquor and a price-regulating agency made it unnecessary. This announcement was the first indication that the Centre might cooperate with the National Liberals in some kind of tax reform, and in the special committee, it voted with National Liberals and Conservatives to reduce the Liebesgabe. This reduction then prompted the Social Democratic declaration in support of direct taxation, but the Centre, at that time, did not yet favor direct taxes. In order to cover the deficit created by the reduction of the Liebesgabe, it wanted to extend the existing indirect tax on sugar which the government wanted to decrease. When the Centre originally moved to extend the sugar tax, the National Liberals opposed it. But their continued opposition could have resulted in a reintroduction of the previous Liebesgabe—a measure which was highly unpopular with National Liberal voters. Caught in the crush between a blatant Grand Bloc policy and the unpopular reintroduction of the Liebesgabe, a com-

---

subsequent cooperation, Fraktion meeting, April 24, May 14, 1912, *SPD Fraktionsprotokolle* 1 : 272, 275–276.

promise with the Centre was the only feasible National Liberal course. According to the compromise, the sugar tax would continue only until it was replaced by a direct property tax; such a tax must also be presented to the Reichstag no later than April 30, 1913. The preparation of a new tax bill partially satisfied National Liberal demands. But because the Centre itself made no commitment to direct taxation, its compromise merely deferred the issue of reform until the following year.[4]

I have not found any evidence giving the details of the negotiations for the Erzberger-Bassermann compromise, but since it bore their names, these two men were probably chiefly responsible for it. Erzberger's role in the compromise is obscure. Although he belonged to the left wing of the party and was a great advocate of Centrist democracy, his speeches in the Reichstag at the time of the tax reform firmly rejected a national property tax.[5] On the other hand, he shared the desire of all Centrist leaders for increased political influence, and he may have persuaded his party to accept the compromise on these grounds. In other words, the Centre used a different gambit in the tax reform than in the praesidium elections. Rather than excluding itself from the Grand Bloc for reasons of influence, it decided to join the Bloc to protect its interests. In negotiating the compromise, Bassermann may have threatened to use the Grand Bloc to pass the tax reform. If he employed this tactic, it was a bluff directed at the Centre; Bassermann used the weight, and not the votes, of a Grand Bloc to attract the Centre's compromise for tax reform. Yet regardless of the tactics, the Grand Bloc again cooperated with the Centre to force the acceptance of a measure which neither the government nor the Conservatives originally desired.

Eventually, all parties in the Reichstag, including the Conservatives, voted for the Erzberger-Bassermann compromise. The government could not ignore this unanimous majority, and it began work on a new tax bill immediately. The task was particularly difficult because there was no general agreement about the kind of direct taxation. The Progressives and Social Democrats put forth their motion for an inheritance

4. Martin Spahn in *Verhandlungen des Reichstages*, 284: 1321–1322; 285: 2131. On the sugar tax, see Fraktion meetings, May 10 and 15 (1 and 2), 1912, NL Akten, R 45 1/10; *Schulthess, 1912*, p. 177.
5. *Verhandlungen des Reichstages*, 284 : 1383.

tax as a corollary to the Erzberger-Bassermann compromise, and the National Liberals supported them. This action created a Grand Bloc majority for the inheritance tax, but the Conservatives and Centre opposed it.[6]

Because of the Black and Blue opposition, the government was loath to introduce an inheritance tax. Bethmann Hollweg particularly objected to cooperating with the Grand Bloc which favored it:

> The parties of the left are so confused, in their Progressive ele-
> ments dependent in such a measure on Social Democracy, that
> they, even when they represent a greater numerical majority,
> which they really are, cannot possibly be treated as a party bloc
> upon which the government could base its property tax as a matter
> of course. If it did so anyway, then it would sanction the Grand
> Bloc . . . and thereby point the way to a tactic which would be
> incompatible with the prerequisites of the life of the empire. The
> consequences of such a policy would be as dangerous for the several
> states as well as for the nation.[7]

These remarks clearly alluded to the government's dilemma. It did not fail to grasp the implications of all the important developments since the elections of 1912. The Grand Bloc threatened the constitutional integrity of the Reich. If the government deigned to recognize its strength and to depend on it for major legislation, the Grand Bloc and later the Reichstag would determine governmental policy. In this process, the roles of government and Reichstag would be reversed: the government would become the agent and not the leader of the Reichstag and parliamentary government would prevail. Once this condition prevailed in the Reich, its eventual accomplishment in the several states would be but a matter of time. Essentially of course, this development had already begun in Baden and Bavaria, but Bethmann Hollweg wanted to prevent its further dissemination into the Reich and eventually to Prussia. Any chancellor appointed by the kaiser would find himself in the same dilemma vis-à-vis the growing power of the Reichstag. Even if he thought that greater parliamentary power would benefit the state in the long run, his duty to preserve the royal prerogative would

6. *Schulthess, 1912*, p. 177. Cf. *Hilfe*, 18 (1912) : 491.
7. Quoted in Zmarzlik, *Bethmann Hollweg*, p. 62.

prevent any hasty concessions to parliamentary government. Thus the form of direct taxation had a significance far beyond its ability to fund a naval bill and to stem popular dissatisfaction.

In 1913, the confluence of two events eased the task of introducing a direct tax. First of all, the nation celebrated the centennial of the Battle of Nations and the silver anniversary of Wilhelm II's reign with all the nationalistic effusions usually attendant on such occasions. Secondly, the first Balkan war and the introduction of the three-year service period in France produced sufficient uneasiness in government and military circles to warrant the introduction of a military bill increasing the manpower and technical efficiency of the German army. The combination of a national celebration with a national threat guaranteed the passage of the military bill. It also insured the approval of the mammoth expenditure that the military bill required. The threat to the nation and the concomitant needs of the military were deemed so great that the government conceived the idea of a single military contribution (*Wehrbeitrag*) to be raised by a tax on incomes and corporations.[8] This contribution was supposed to be a temporary feature of the taxation program, but its proposal facilitated the deliberations of the permanent direct tax. The government knew that all the bourgeois parties, particularly the Conservatives and the Centre, would vote for the contribution, and it was expected that they would not flinch at voting the extra permanent property tax introduced at the same time.

It was this permanent tax that fulfilled the stipulations of the Erzberger-Bassermann compromise and had the most significance for German domestic politics in 1913. In order to avoid dependence on the Grand Bloc, it was necessary to gain the votes of Centre and Conservatives, and to this end the government constructed a tax bill likely to attract their support as well as that of the liberals. In the future, the individual states were to pay an additional, stipulated sum per person, in effect an extra Matrikularbeitrag, and this sum would be raised through a direct tax on property. The states themselves would determine the type of tax, but if a state failed to introduce a direct tax by 1916, then the Bundesrat would levy a capital gains tax to be collected by the central government.[9] This measure satisfied the Conservatives and the Bundesrat by

8. Hans Herzfeld, *Die deutsche Rüstungspolitik vor dem Weltkrieg* (Bonn, 1923), pp. 14–46, 111.

9. *Verhandlungen des Reichstages*, 302: Drucksache no. 1111, 2201.

preserving states' rights in matters of taxation and by avoiding the inheritance tax; it satisfied the liberals by introducing the direct taxation of property. By providing for a secondary or state tax instead of a primary or national tax, the government believed it had found the golden mean in the issue of direct taxation.

In constructing a tax bill that appealed to all the bourgeois parties, the government intended to exclude the Social Democrats. Yet they refused to be excluded, and in the Reichstag they promised to participate actively in shaping the final legislation. The liberals also rejected the government's attempt to ignore the Social Democrats and once again created a nebulous Grand Bloc. Speaking for the Progressives, von Payer frankly said that the bid for a bourgeois majority for the tax reform stemmed from a "false superiority" and led to "ridiculous consequences." The National Liberals, though they carefully avoided identifying themselves with the Social Democrats, publicly credited them with inspiring the direct tax. Solidarity with the Social Democrats stemmed from the liberals' unanimous dissatisfaction with the government's bill. First and foremost, they opposed the state tax in favor of the immediate introduction of an imperial or national tax. Secondly, none of the Grand Bloc parties favored the capital gains tax. The National Liberals once again demanded a tax on property in general, and although the Progressives and Social Democrats preferred an inheritance tax, they agreed to support the National Liberals. Despite the government's efforts to the contrary, the Grand Bloc had combined to reject the proposed bill.[10]

For several reasons, this opposition attracted the Centre into the Grand Bloc's orbit. First of all, the Centre itself opposed certain parts of the government's bill. Despite the attempt to appease it with a secondary or state tax, the Centre objected to the imperial government's proposed interference in the taxing programs of the various states. It also disliked the inclusion of an inheritance tax in the capital gains tax, and it criticized some inequities included in the bill. Moreover, the Centre decided to honor the Erzberger-Bassermann compromise by supporting some kind of direct imperial taxation. Thus in the very first plenary reading of the tax bill, it hinted its willingness to compromise with the Grand Bloc parties in the budget committee. The Centre's

10. See Paasche for the National Liberals, von Payer for the Progressives, Südekum for the Social Democrats in ibid., 289 : 4622, 4635, 4639, 4660, 4663–4664; 290 : 5835.

amenability to compromise stemmed from two causes. The right wing of the party, which opposed direct taxation, was steadily losing influence within the Reichstag Fraktion. By 1913, the left wing, which favored a more equitable taxing system, had more strength than it had the year before. As a result, the Centre could now explicitly espouse direct taxation. Secondly, the Centre still wanted to regain its former influence in the Reichstag. At the beginning of 1913, when plans for the military bill and the tax reform were first published, the Centre raised so many objections that many feared it would filibuster both bills until the government was forced to dissolve the Reichstag. Through this means, the Centre hoped to displace the Social Democrats as the largest party in the Reichstag. This displacement would shift the balance of power away from the Social Democrats and the Grand Bloc toward the Centre, which would then become the decisive voice in major legislation just as it had been before the elections of 1912. Yet the government could ill afford to use the weapon of dissolution. Both foreign and domestic policy advised against it. The alleged urgency of the military bill did not allow for a time-consuming new election campaign. Moreover, there was no guarantee that the Centre could recoup its losses of 1912. The government feared that new elections would only bring greater gains for the left and enhance the chances and the efficacy of a Grand Bloc policy. The Centre certainly knew the risks involved and acted accordingly. If a filibuster would not force a dissolution of the Reichstag, the threat of obstruction could cajole the government and the liberal parties into cooperation with the Centre. The chances for cooperation between Centre and liberals were increased by the Social Democrats' virulent and impolitic opposition to the military bill, which offended many voters. Neither National Liberals nor Progressives desired to depend wholly on Social Democracy for a tax reform majority since this alliance could deprive them of much grass-roots support.[11]

This difficulty rendered the tax reform a very complex issue. The liberals wished to activate the Grand Bloc to force compromises from the government and the Centre, but they did not intend to use it to

11. For the Centre's role, see Karl Speck in ibid., 289 : 4634–4638; Rudolf Morsey, *Die deutsche Zentrumspartei, 1917–1923* (Düsseldorf, 1966), pp. 38–39; Bebel to Adler, February 28, 1913, *Briefwechsel,* pp. 562–563. Cf. Zmarzlik, *Bethmann Hollweg,* pp. 72–73. For the hesitancy to rely on the Social Democrats, see Ernst Bassermann, "Die politische Bedeutung der Deckung der Heeresvorlage," Stresemann Papers.

achieve the final reform. In this case, as in the Erzberger-Bassermann compromise, agreement with the Centre was essential. Yet this course was fairly easy once the liberals determined to insist on direct taxation. The best example of their determination was their refusal to discuss any facet of the military bill until after the passage of tax reform. Since they, with the votes of the Social Democrats, had a majority on the senior committee which determined the Reichstag's agenda, nothing could be done about the all-important matter of defense until both Centre and government yielded. Here the liberals borrowed the tactics of the Bavarian Centrists before the elections of 1912. They refused to discuss the government's important concerns until their own demands were met. This stubbornness bolstered the left-wing currents within the Centre and drove it to the side of the liberals. In a series of conversations at the end of May 1913, the liberals and the Centre united over a primary general property tax, and together, this non-Conservative majority confronted the government with a measure it wanted to avoid.[12]

At this point, enter the Bundesrat. It had originally favored an inheritance tax because it involved the least loss in state revenues and because it fit into the existing system of secondary, or state, taxation. However, Bethmann Hollweg, with an eye on the Centre's opposition, had persuaded it to accept a secondary capital gains tax. After the Reichstag's committee deliberations, the Bundesrat was faced with a serious threat to federalism and severe demands on local revenues, and it firmly rejected the primary general property tax. Its rejection, then, renewed the discussion about the inheritance tax. Yet no one could seriously entertain it. The Centre, after fighting an inheritance tax since 1909, could hardly vote for it. Without the Centre, the inheritance tax would be a creature of the Grand Bloc, and the National Liberals would have difficulty justifying it to their right wing. The chancellor, who feared the political implications of a Grand Bloc policy and was determined to exclude the Social Democrats from the tax reform majority, could not consent to it. All had to find some way out of the dilemma.

12. For the Centre's move left, see *Verhandlungen des Reichstages,* 302 : Drucksache no. 1111, 2165–2169. Bassermann, "Die politische Bedeutung der Deckung . . . ," Stresemann Papers. Also, Fraktion meetings, April 4, 1913, May 27 and 28, 1913, NL Akten, R 45 1/10. Cf. Georg Gothein in the *Berliner Tageblatt,* July 7, 1913, no. 339. For the property tax, see Zmarzlik, *Bethmann Hollweg,* p. 71. Also Fischbeck to Gothein, May 23, 1913, Gothein Papers.

Furious negotiations began on June 12, the very day that the Bundesrat rejected the primary general property tax. By June 18, the Centre, the liberals, and the chancellor had arranged another compromise. A primary, or imperial, tax would be immediately introduced in the form of a capital gains tax. The states would lose some control over direct taxation, but they would retain important revenues. In committee, only the Social Democrats voted against this solution. Their vote gave Bethmann Hollweg his weapon with the Bundesrat. He persuaded it to accept the primary capital gains tax as the tortuous compromise of the bourgeois parties—a majority which excluded the Social Democrats. Federalism must be sacrificed to avert the threat from the left.[13]

However, the last act of tax reform displayed its own political irony. In the plenum of the Reichstag, the Social Democrats voted for the compromise, the Conservatives against. And so we come once more to the problem of the Grand Bloc and tax reform. There can be little doubt that without the sustained opposition of the Grand Bloc, the government's original proposal for a state tax would have passed. The Centre supported it publicly, until the last hour before compromise. The National Liberals would have consented since they could hardly hold up the military bill, for which the taxes were destined, indefinitely. They achieved a direct imperial tax only because they could use the *threat* of alliance with the Social Democrats. Even if they did not finally intend to vote with the Social Democrats, the threat itself inclined both Centre and government toward compromise.[14]

It is idle to speculate about events had compromise failed. A recent writer, in referring to the direct property tax, suggests that the government would have been forced to concede to the Grand Bloc and the Reichstag had the liberals and the Centre not accepted the capital gains tax. Then, he says, "an inner transformation" would have occurred. This assertion expects too much from the political process. No development is so mechanical that a twitch on the switch will set a whole series

13. On the Bundesrat action, see Zmarzlik, *Bethmann Hollweg*, pp. 63ff. Also Fritz Fischer, *Krieg der Illusionen: Die deutsche Politik von 1911 bis 1914* (Düsseldorf, 1969), pp. 257–266; Fraktion meetings, June 12, 26, 1913, NL Akten R 45 1/10. For the compromise, see Brigitte Haberland Barth, *Die Innenpolitik des Reiches unter der Kanzlerschaft Bethmann Hollwegs, 1909–1914* (doctoral diss., Kiel, 1950), p. 158. Cf. Zmarzlik, *Bethmann Hollweg*, pp. 71ff.

14. On the vote, see *Verhandlungen des Reichstages*, 290: 5939. For the bitter fight of the Conservatives against the final compromise, see Witt, *Die Finanzpolitik*, pp. 369–373. On the Centre's stand, see Barth, *Die Innenpolitik*, p. 158.

of new parts in motion. In Germany, a "transformation" had only begun to occur. The government accepted legislation opposed by the Conservatives. It agreed to a liberal praesidium and made liberal concessions for the first time in three decades. The fact that the government had to pressure the Bundesrat in its favor reveals the power attained by the Reichstag. Even if it could not cooperate with a genuine Grand Bloc, the government could and did create better communications with the Social Democrats. The presence of 110 socialist Reichstag delegates forced it to draw them more and more into governmental business. At the end of November 1912, it gave them information about the imperial petroleum monopoly and invited them to a discussion on foreign policy. In December, Bernstein and Südekum attended a briefing about the gold reserves in the Reichsbank, and the Social Democratic Fraktion agreed to hold secret any information the government wished. This was the first time that the government included them in business of this nature, and their reaction revealed how flattered they were. Never before had Social Democrats withheld important information from their membership and their voters. Reciprocal changes occurred on both sides. Liberal resolve resulted in governmental concessions, and both evoked increasing moderation in Social Democracy. These were not momentous events, but they did represent an alteration of previous practices and attitudes.[15]

THE SOCIAL DEMOCRATS

The most genuine sign of increasing moderation inside Social Democracy was its vote for the tax reform of 1913. Even after a bourgeois majority was certain, the Fraktion decided to cast its vote in favor of funds clearly designed to cover military expenses. The vote, however, did not occur without opposition. In the caucus of the Fraktion, there was deep division. The final vote, 52 for the taxes, 41 against,[16] reflected the opposition of many members to the purpose of the taxes, and their objections were placed on the agenda of the party congress at Jena in October. Unexpectedly, the course and conclusion of the debate stem-

15. On the "transformation," see Zmarzlik, *Bethmann Hollweg*, pp. 72–73; on the Social Democratic cooperation, Fraktion meetings, November 29 and December 18, 1912, *SPD Fraktionsprotokolle*, 1 : 280–281, 284.

16. Carl Schorske, *German Social Democracy, 1905–1917: The Development of the Great Schism* (Cambridge, Mass., 1955), p. 266, records a vote of 52–37. This was the vote taken on June 25. The final vote was taken on June 27, 1913, *SPD Fraktionsprotokolle*, 1: 300, 301.

ming from this opposition merely reinforced the significance of the vote itself.

Essentially, the radicals and others who objected to the Fraktion's vote used the old orthodox arguments against the military, the state, and the budget. A vote for the budget was a vote for the existing order and all its paraphernalia. Yet in 1913, this argument had a new twist. In recent years, Social Democrats had systematically explored the phenomenon of imperialism and concluded that it was a necessary phase of capitalism. Furthermore, the pernicious effects of imperialism became even more evident after 1911, when the Moroccan crisis almost brought Europe to the brink of war. The fears generated by the Moroccan crisis led to a resolution committing the party "to leave nothing undone in order to extenuate the effects" of imperialism. In this way, imperialism became another hallowed devil of the Social Democrats, linked to nationalism, militarism, and the existing order. The radicals could not understand how the Fraktion could vote for funds destined to further the military which permitted the pursuit of capitalistic imperialism so detrimental to the working classes. They wanted to censure the Fraktion and reject all future taxes designed to finance militarism. Thus they attempted once again to steer the party on a strictly "anti-national" course.[17]

In 1913, the radicals still believed in the operation of Social Democratic theory. They failed to realize that theory determined only the rhetoric and not the practice of the party. Practical opposition to national issues had ceased after the "national" election of 1907. Signs of this development had been posted all along the way: Bebel's "Fatherland" speech in 1907, Molkenbuhr's fumbling of the Moroccan crisis in 1911, the party's support of the Franco-German "imperialistic" treaty. Still, the party had not yet indulged in so blatant a gesture as a vote for military funds, and it was necessary in 1913 to find an explanation that would square theory and practice in the vote for the tax reform.

As usual, the party executive led the way toward compromise. If the radicals chose to emphasize traditional theory in the realm of "national" issues, the executive could utilize traditional views on finances. The

17. *SPD Parteitag, 1912,* p. 529. Also J. P. Nettl, *Rosa Luxemburg,* 2 vols. (Oxford, 1966), 2 : 530–531, and Abraham Ascher, " 'Radical' Imperialists within German Social Democracy, 1912–1918, " *Political Science Quarterly* 76 (1961) : 557–564. For the radicals' stand, see *SPD Parteitag, 1913,* pp. 198, 476.

tradition, as laid down in the resolutions of Frankfurt, Lübeck, Nuremberg, and Magdeburg, called for the rejection of the budget, or the rejection of taxes, except when a worse budget or worse taxation would result for the working class. The executive's motion in 1913 added one small change to this formula:

> Every . . . tax is also to be rejected . . . in case its application contradicts the interests of the working class, *except when the rejection of the direct taxes . . . does not prevent the acceptance of the combatted measure* and would have, as a consequence, a less favorable taxation for the working class.[18]

The executive admitted to the radicals that the purpose of taxation was just as important as the kind of taxation; a military purpose offended the interest of the working class. On the other hand, the executive argued that the party could not prevent the passage of the military bill, but it could prevent some indirect taxation and ease the burden on the workers. Thus it was bound to vote for direct taxation despite its application. Although this motion *seemed* to satisfy the radicals' emphasis on continuing opposition, it *really* undermined their whole theoretical system. It severed the interconnecting links in the established order. Issues should no longer be judged in terms of their service to the reactionary state and their hindrance to revolution. Instead they were to be judged in the light of their immediate effect on working-class interests. The theory of intransigent opposition was replaced by the theory of reformism.

This change of Social Democratic theory was all the more significant because it was unnecessary. In 1913, the Social Democratic vote was not vital to the tax reform. The liberals and the Centre already had a majority for the direct tax. Therefore, the Fraktion and the executive had to find an additional defense of their vote. In arguing the case for the Fraktion, the reformist Südekum stressed the duty of positive cooperation in the Reichstag and the chance to fulfill a long-standing demand of the Social Democratic program. The very size and weight of the Fraktion in the Reichstag demanded its active participation in legislation in order to justify the support of the voters. Inactivity in the old style might result in the loss of electoral support. Moreover, the

18. Italics are the author's, *SPD Parteitag, 1913*, p. 187.

great size of the Fraktion had resulted in the first tactical cooperation, in a "grand style," between Social Democracy and "parts of the liberal bourgeoisie . . . with the aim of a new orientation in domestic politics." Südekum admitted that a majority for reform existed without the votes of the Social Democrats. But he argued that Social Democratic participation had acted as a prod on the liberals to stiffen their resolve for tax reform and ensure a majority for it once the government agreed to concessions. Südekum's remarks included references to a "cooperation from Bebel to Bassermann," a "tax bloc," and the "three leftist parties." For him, Social Democratic participation in a bloc was just as important as insuring the passage of tax reform. His argument for the "tax bloc" closely resembled the arguments of the southerners at previous debates on the budget. They too had argued for positive participation in parliament and cooperation with the bourgeois parties. When they voted for the budget, their votes were also not necessary for a majority. They did so to induce further cooperation in achieving reform. The vote for tax reform in the Reichstag did not help to form a majority, but it did make a bid for an extension of the Grand Bloc to other issues. The defense of the Fraktion at the party congress thus signaled the razing of one of the last barriers between Social Democracy as an opposition party and Social Democracy as a "governmental" party.[19]

The majority of the party congress in 1913 accepted the Fraktion's defense and adopted the executive's motion by a large majority. This majority was probably influenced by Bebel's recent death and the knowledge that he also intended to vote for reform and defend his actions. Two days before his death, he wrote to Molkenbuhr:

> I am of the opinion that we wring the neck of the debate about the Fraktion. We can best do that if we get together . . . excerpts from our speeches to the military bills since the year 1893, our income tax motions to the fleet bill and to the recent tax laws of 1906, 1909. . . . Further, the suitable excerpts from the common proclamations which we negotiated with the French. . . . I am willing . . . to put [the material] together and pour a critical sauce over it in which the various attacks receive their due. I would render the "jewel" in the form of a speech and we [can] let it be

19. On reformism, see ibid., pp. 456, 460.

printed and distributed at the party congress. I am unfortunately incapable of speaking.[20]

This was the combative old man's last battle; and he believed he was firmly adhering to principle in fighting it. Of course, we have no way of knowing what the defense of the Fraktion would have been had Bebel lived. It is only ironic that his radical spirit should have aided the triumph of reformism within the party. It was an index of the times that the man who began his career as a herald of the Paris Commune should have ended it by supporting a very limited direct tax as a fulfillment of the Social Democratic program.

When Bebel began his career, the party had two men in the Reichstag and little chance of influencing legislation. In 1913, it had 110 men and entertained notions of forming a "bloc." The composition of the Reichstag Fraktion itself reflected the change in the party and the change of circumstances. Of the 110 men, the great majority were either trade-union men with a bent toward reformism or party bureaucrats who had a stake in the continued life and success of the party. In addition, most of them had entered politics after the repeal of the antisocialist laws and had not experienced severe repression. Many had served in state and local legislatures where participation in the legislative process was more frequent and more rewarding than in the Reichstag. It was more natural for the Fraktion of 1913 to expect to contribute to legislation than for any of its predecessors. Südekum noted in his diary that even Bebel admitted an increase in parliamentary influence during his lifetime. Reformists like Südekum believed that a certain democratization had gradually occurred in German public life and that it would continue as a matter of course. Naturally, not all Social Democrats shared his beliefs, and the party still had its radical elements which caused division and "acrimony" in the ranks. But the congress of 1913 demonstrated their waning influence better than any other event.[21]

Decreasing radicalism and increasing moderation also had repercussions on the attitudes of the other parties and the government toward Social Democracy. Both liberal parties refrained from officially at-

20. Bebel to Molkenbuhr, August 11, 1913, carbon copy, Bebel Papers.

21. On the change in Social Democracy, John Snell, "German Socialists in the last Imperial Reichstag, 1912–1918," *International Review of Social History* 7 (1952) : 196–205; Südekum Diaries, stenographic notes, I, 32, 111 (typewritten transliteration, 101, I, 39–40, 136–137), Südekum Papers.

tacking it as a nonnational and revolutionary party; only the Conservatives attempted to capitalize on this tradition. In 1913, Bassermann devoted an entire section of his speech on the military bill to the attitudinal changes toward imperialism and war apparent in Social Democratic practice. Shortly after the passage of the tax reform, he wrote Bülow that a Social Democracy which had just approved such enormous sums for military purposes, even though that was not its intent, was quite a different party from the one that existed ten years before. He even predicted that its further development "toward . . . a moderate policy" would be "correspondingly significant." Men like Rebmann continued to use Naumann's argument that the Social Democrats could be won for the national cause. It is hard to determine how successful these men were within the National Liberal party; the Old Liberal *Correspondenz* certainly maintained a permanent campaign against Social Democracy. A good deal of doubt also existed in the minds of the National Liberal rank and file as to Social Democracy's reliability in a national emergency. In his memoirs, Friedrich Meinecke related how surprised and relieved he was when the Social Democrats voted the war credits in 1914. In contrast, the Progressives were more enlightened and more willing to give the Social Democrats the benefit of the doubt in matters concerning the national welfare and the stability of the state. The liberal parties at least were groping toward the acceptance of Social Democracy as an integral force in German politics.[22]

This political integration did not, however, signify the end of the social discrimination which was half the reason for Social Democracy's existence. At the time of the tax reform, a Progressive deputy from Baden, Gerhard von Schulze-Gaevernitz, wrote that "the social discrimination against Social Democrats, as . . . practiced in Berlin, . . . in its political context, [was] extraordinarily harmful." A good example of the harm that could be done occurred in 1914, when the secretary of the treasury held a private meeting of the leaders of all the important Fraktionen. The secretary told Bassermann to invite one of the Social Democrats, and Scheidemann attended the meeting. Afterward, the Conservative leader, Count von Westarp, drew Bassermann

22. On the change in attitude toward Social Democrats, *Verhandlungen des Reichstages,* 289: 4532, 4544, 4547; Bassermann to Bülow, July 18, 1913, Bülow Papers; Friedrich Meinecke, *Erlebtes, 1862–1919* (Stuttgart, 1964), p. 246.

aside and told him that the Conservatives opposed in principle all private discussions with the Social Democrats and would not have appeared had they known Scheidemann would be present. In the same year, the reformist Gustav Noske, who sat on the budget committee, was invited to tour the docks in connection with new government expenditures for the navy. As he made his rounds, not one officer shook his hand, and he later heard that they had been ordered not to do so. Many political maneuvers, decisions, and compromises occur not in the halls of parliament but at private teas, dinners, or gatherings such as the ones mentioned above. If the Social Democrats were ever to complete their political integration, they would have to crash that social barrier which labeled them not "*salonsfähig,*" unfit to be present at the social gatherings that determined policy in the second Reich.[23]

THE PRUSSIAN ELECTIONS OF 1913

It was the sociopolitical snobbery of Berlin and Prussia that impeded the further integration of Social Democracy. In Prussia even its political integration had hardly begun because of the Conservative domination of Prussian politics. Although a reform of the three-class suffrage was necessary for a significant breach of Conservative domination, there were measures the other parties could take to diminish Conservative strength in the Landtag. In pursuing this goal, the formation of election agreements and blocs in other states and in the Reich provided a guide. Such agreements were not foreign to Prussia, but prior to 1913, neither liberals nor Social Democrats had used them as a weapon against the Conservatives. In the state elections of 1908, the Bülow Bloc demanded the cooperation of liberals with the Conservatives and not against them. Since then, political circumstances and considerations had changed, and the liberals were free to consider anti-Conservative alliances for the Prussian elections of 1913.

By this time, the liberal bloc was a pillar of liberal policy, and both liberal parties had little difficulty in reaching agreements. As in the Reichstag elections, alliances were made in those areas where the Conservatives were strongest and the National Liberal right wing was weak: in East and West Prussia, Brandenburg, Silesia, the province of

23. On discrimination, see *Hilfe* 19 (1913) : 341; Bassermann notations, no date, Bassermann remnant, 303/17; Gustav Noske, *Erlebtes aus Aufstieg und Niedergang einer Demokratie* (Offenbach, 1947), pp. 40ff.

Saxony, and the province of Hesse. Most of these agreements were made locally, with guidance from the central offices in Berlin, and they significantly failed to cover Rhineland-Westphalia and Schleswig-Holstein. The gaps in the arrangements made both parties fearful of extra-liberal alliances,[24] but neither could prevent the National Liberals from collusion with the Conservatives nor the Progressives from accommodation with the Social Democrats.

Liberal cooperation with the Conservatives was not unusual, and everyone expected it. Liberal cooperation with the Social Democrats had never occurred in Prussia. Yet the precedents established in other elections facilitated an innovation in Prussian politics, and both Progressives and Social Democrats realized the opportunity provided by the election. Significantly, the Social Democrats were the first to break tradition and announce their intention of supporting Progressives if they received reciprocation. The Progressives could not publicly accept this offer for fear of offending the National Liberals and their own rank and file, but privately, they decided to pursue local agreements in the runoff elections. To be sure, these decisions did not foresee any comprehensive arrangements such as those which occurred in Baden, Bavaria, and the Reich. They were tailored to the limitations of Prussian conditions, but they did represent the first application of the Barth-Naumann tactic to Prussian politics.[25]

The general election took place on May 16, 1913. Twenty-five Progressives and seven Social Democrats received absolute majorities, and thirteen Progressives and nineteen Social Democrats qualified for the runoff elections. Although their scope was limited, negotiations between the two parties began immediately. The hinge upon which these negotiations hung was the election district of Ober-und-Niederbarnim, with a total of three mandates, just outside Berlin. Berlin and its environs were a hotly contested area between Progressives and Social Democrats and, in this particular suburb, the Social Democrats had won a relative majority. For the Progressives, the choice lay between an absolute Social Democratic majority or an agreement with the

---

24. *Mitteilungen für die Vertrauensmänner der fortschrittlichen Volkspartei* (Berlin, 1913), p. 24; *Hilfe* 19 (1913) : 126, 174. Cf. Hartwig Thieme, *Nationaler Liberalismus in der Krise: Die nationalliberale Fraktion des preussischen Abgeordnetenhauses, 1914–1918* (Boppard/Rhine, 1963), p. 17.

25. *Hilfe* 19 (1913) : 64 (iv); DZAP, FVP, discussion between leaders of Progressives and National Liberals, June 11, 1912.

Conservatives whereby the liberals would receive at least one of the three mandates. The choice was a difficult one; the local club wanted to reject the Conservative offer, but it also desired a seat for itself. Thus the local club offered to concede *one* mandate to the Social Democrats in return for aid to its own candidate. On the other hand, the leadership in Berlin wanted to sacrifice all three mandates in Niederbarnim for the sake of Social Democratic help in other districts, and it viewed the desires of the local with "consternation." In a letter to the local, the leadership "desperately" begged it "not to undertake any measures which could have an uncalculated influence on the whole party. Please consider that the fate of not less than nine mandates in other areas depends on Ober-und-Niederbarnim." Ultimately, the leadership's pressure was successful, the Progressive candidate in Niederbarnim withdrew, and his supporters abstained to assure a Social Democratic majority. In return, the Social Democrats helped to win twelve Progressive mandates in other districts. Once again, the liberals benefited excessively from the agreement. For them, it was a cheap investment; by giving three mandates for twelve, they won a 300 percent profit without casting one stigmatizing vote for a Social Democrat.[26]

One historian of Social Democracy has claimed that the limited nature of this agreement and other simultaneous developments indicated a deterioration of the Progressive–Social Democratic relationship.[27] This view can muster a certain amount of support. The Prussian agreement was hardly as extensive as the previous year's commitment for the Reichstag election. Concurrently with the Prussian elections, the Progressives demurred to cooperate with the Social Democrats in the delicate issue of tax reform. On the other hand, the events of 1913 must be seen in the light of the nonexistent cooperation in previous Prussian elections. The Progressives had never before consented to withdraw their candidates in order to aid Social Democracy. The abstention in Ober-und-Niederbarnim was a lesser commitment than voting outright for

26. *Vorwärts,* May 20, June 4, 1913; DZAP, FVP, Neumann to executive committee, May 18, 1913; letter from election committee of the United Conservatives, Free Conservatives . . . of Oberbarnim—Eberswalde—Niederbarnim and Lichtenberg to the election committee of united liberals of the district . . . , May 19, 1913; Neumann to executive committee, May 24, 1913; executive committee to Neumann, May 27, 1913; Erdmanndorfer to Fischbeck, May 30, 1913; Goldschmidt to Issberner, May 30, 1913. Molkenbuhr Diaries, June 2, 1912.
27. Schorske, *Social Democracy,* p. 268.

the Social Democrats, but in the Prussian context, where the public ballot still prevailed, it was necessary to protect the voters from political, social, and economic retaliation. Moreover, the Social Democrats' antinational stance on the military bill made cooperation even more precarious. Given this situation, the Progressives could simply have refused to compromise themselves by associating with Social Democracy. The fact that agreement occurred at all, not its meagerness, is the true reflection of Progressive–Social Democratic relationships. The agreement of 1913 maintained and extended to Prussia their cooperation built up over a period of years in other states and in the Reichstag. Furthermore, it followed the agreement of the Prussian liberal bloc. The pattern established elsewhere, liberal bloc to Grand Bloc, began to invade Prussia. This reasoning does not imply that the process was as well-developed as in Baden, Bavaria, or the Reich; in Prussia, cooperation was in an embryonic stage. The presence of the Old Liberals, who increased their strength in the Landtag in 1913, militated against a radical change in Prussian politics. But it is not inconceivable that, with persistence, patience, time, and an unclouded political atmosphere, a rapprochement between all Prussian liberals and Social Democrats would take root and grow.

Einheit vs. Freiheit

The relative domestic peace that accompanied the tax reform and the Prussian elections was finally broken by the last great issue to confront the German Reichstag before the outbreak of war: the famous Zabern Affair. Zabern was a small town in Alsace-Lorraine where the constitution of 1911 had not yet resolved the conflict between French nationalism and Germanization. The cause of the affair was a young lieutenant, von Forstner, who, during an instruction period for recruits at the end of October 1913, promised ten marks for each knifed Alsatian "Wackes," a derogatory term. This statement and other provocations by the military so aggravated the townspeople of Zabern that they began to heckle the military with catcalls and street demonstrations until the commander of the Zabern regiment, Colonel von Reuter, declared martial law at the end of November and arrested twenty-seven persons. The incident aroused the whole of Alsace-Lorraine, and protest meetings occurred throughout the month of November. After the declaration of martial law, the Zabern town council sent a telegram to the governor, to the chancellor, to the minister of war, and to the Reichstag requesting protection against the military.[28]

The cry of outrage in Zabern and in Alsace-Lorraine was caused by the fact that the military had taken matters into its own hands; there was a complete breakdown of communication and trust between the military and the civilian authorities. This collapse of confidence, which resulted in the military's proclamation of martial law, merely revealed a deeper problem characteristic of the constitution of Prussia and the German Empire. There was no clear-cut definition of the relationship between civilian and military authorities. Reuter based the declaration of martial law on a Prussian military order dating back to 1899 which sanctioned the precedence of the military authority where the civilians failed to maintain order. Both the civilian governor and the army commander in Alsace-Lorraine had direct responsibility to the kaiser, but there was no prescribed legal link between them. In the event of conflict between the two, the kaiser had to resolve the dispute. Yet the chancellor was constitutionally "responsible" for the kaiser's decisions. In the Zabern Affair, the kaiser approved Reuter's declaration of martial law on the basis of the military report and refused to talk to the civilian governor, von Wedel, who asked for a personal interview. Wedel's reports convinced Bethmann Hollweg that the military had overstepped its authority, and he demanded Reuter's recall. The kaiser disagreed with him. The Zabern incident therefore produced a crisis between civilian and military authority that fitted easily into the previous chain of crises over the chancellor's responsibility.

The parties of the Reichstag followed the incident in Zabern with alarm. At the end of November, the Alsatians, the Progressives, and the Social Democrats all introduced interpellations demanding an explanation of the events in Alsace-Lorraine. When Bethmann Hollweg answered these interpellations at the beginning of December, his speech was more or less a defense of the military; the government had begun an investigation which was not yet concluded, and meanwhile, the honor and physical safety of the army must be protected and good

28. For this and subsequent material, see Erwin Schenk, *Der Fall Zabern* (Stuttgart, 1927), pp. 3–43; and Hans-Ulrich Wehler, "Der Fall Zabern," *Die Welt als Geschichte* 23 (1963) : 27–46. Cf. Zmarzlik, *Bethmann Hollweg*, pp. 114–123. The best account of the "affair" in English is Martin Kitchen, *The German Officer Corps, 1890–1914* (Oxford, 1968), pp. 187–221.

relations reestablished between it and the civilian authorities. He said nothing about the correct relationship between military and civilian authorities, and this aspect of the problem was the most urgent for the majority of parties in the Reichstag. The speaker of each non-Conservative party, from the Centre to the Social Democrats, emphasized the "unbelievable" interference of the military "in the rights of the civilian police authorities." They denounced the "lack of legality and the series of offenses against fundamental principles of . . . freedom." In answer to the chancellor's defense, the Progressives and the Social Democrats introduced almost identical motions for a vote of no-confidence which the Reichstag accepted, 293 to 54, on December 4; only the Conservatives voted against it. Once again, the national Grand Bloc acted to uphold a liberal principle against the actions of the government.[29]

It was a foregone conclusion that the vote of no-confidence would have very little influence on the wheels of government. Bethmann Hollweg did what he could. Although the kaiser, who was on a hunting trip in the south, could only be reached after a sixteen-hour train trip, the chancellor finally succeeded in arranging a personal interview between him, the military commander, and the civilian governor. Wedel was assured of the removal of the Zabern regiment from the town and the limitation of the military in the future. The chancellor also sent a high civilian official to Zabern to consult with the municipal authorities and to give evidence of the government's good faith.

Meanwhile, two important courts-martial had grown out of the Zabern Affair: Lieutenant von Forstner was prosecuted for assault and battery and Colonel von Reuter for illegal exercise of power and for illegal limitation of personal freedom (*Freiheitsberaubung*). At the beginning of January 1914, both officers were acquitted by the military courts. The decision in the Reuter case was the most disturbing. The court based its decision on a previous ruling of a civilian court whereby military officers were government officials, and a government official who overstepped the limits of his authority was not punishable. Insofar as every court decision set a precedent for the future, the decision in the Reuter case only confirmed the constitutional ambiguity of the relationship between military and civilian authority. It therefore reignited the

29. See the National Liberal Fritz van Calker, *Verhandlungen des Reichstages,* 291 : 6170; the Progressive Ludwig Haas, p. 6188. The vote, pp. 6196–6200.

passions aroused by the initial incident at Zabern. The newspapers of all the major parties to the left of the Conservatives strongly disapproved the decision, and the Alsatian Landtag, stung by the implications of the decision, appealed to the Reichstag for the legal limitation of the military.[30]

This appeal involved far more than a legally ineffective vote of no-confidence. Theoretically, any action limiting the powers of the military involved a constitutional change altering the monarch's exercise of military power. A constitutional change would obligate the kaiser to listen to his civilian advisers first and weigh their considerations more heavily in any conflict between the civilian and the military authorities. He would no longer have freedom of choice in the matter. For instance, in the case of the Zabern Affair, when Bethmann Hollweg called for Colonel von Reuter's dismissal, the kaiser would have been bound to follow the chancellor's advice. The monarchy would be stripped of its traditional military aspect and would be "pacified." If it so chose, the Reichstag could then exert more power vis-à-vis the monarchy since the kaiser's civilian advisers acted as the mediators between the Reichstag and the monarchy.[31] Logically, the kaiser would no longer be able to use the military against the civil government. In all the previous constitutional crises, this issue had not been raised. In the Daily Telegraph Affair and in the Moroccan crisis, the Reichstag had tried to control only the civilian aspect of the monarchy; it had not attempted to rob the monarchy of the military means to control the civil government. If the Reichstag raised the constitutional issue in the Zabern Affair, it would be a serious challenge to the monarchy itself.

It was a measure of their monarchism that none of the German parties suggested a constitutional change during the Zabern Affair. There is no evidence to suggest that they even thought of this aspect of

30. Schenk, *Der Fall Zabern,* pp. 34–70. Even the ministry of justice considered the army's actions in Zabern illegal and addressed a complaint to the war ministry, to no avail, Kitchen, *German Officer Corps,* p. 214.

31. This problem had already arisen in 1883 when the Prussian War Minister Kameke was forced to resign because of his conciliatory attitude to the Reichstag. Thereafter, care was taken to keep the military independent, Eberhard Kessel, "Die Entlassung von Kameke und Stosch im Jahre 1883," *Forschungen zu Staat und Verfassung,* ed. R. Dietrich and G. Oestrich (Berlin, 1958), pp. 445–450. For military independence under Bethmann Hollweg, see H. O. Meisner, "Die monarchische Regierungsform in Brandenburg—Preussen," ibid., pp. 240, 245. Cf. Gordon Craig, *The Politics of the Prussian Army, 1640–1945* (New York, Galaxy Book, 1964), pp. 217–232.

the problem. The Social Democrats drew the logical conclusion from the vote of no-confidence and demanded the chancellor's resignation, but they did not suggest a formal constitutional change. Furthermore, the other non-Conservative parties immediately denounced this demand and dissociated themselves from it and the Social Democrats.[32] No one wanted to exploit the Zabern Affair to increase the explicit powers of the Reichstag. Instead, they wanted a resolution or a law, not a constitutional amendment, that would clearly establish the supremacy of the civilian over the military authority.

Initially, this suggestion came from an alliance between the Centre and the Progressives, both of whom then solicited National Liberal support. The Centrist-Progressive goal was a non-Conservative bourgeois majority to support a common resolution calling for the "independence of the civilian administration." It was an attempt to repeat the majority that had previously satisfied the government in the combined issues of the military bill and the tax reform. The desire to avoid the leftist majority feared by the government was so great that the Progressives temporarily severed their connection with the Social Democrats. It was certain that the Social Democrats would support the resolution, but National Liberal votes were necessary for negotiation with the government. However, the National Liberals refused to join the alliance,[33] and no united bourgeois proposal ever went before the Reichstag or the government.

The National Liberals failed to support the Centre and the Progressives because of the "mood of the voters."[34] The Zabern Affair had not only raised a serious constitutional issue, it had also stirred the "national consciousness" of the German populace and evoked the nationalistic traditions of the National Liberals. One of the best examples of the nationalism aroused by the Zabern Affair was given in the Prussian Landtag by Karl Röchling, a member of the famous industrial family of the Saarland, where the economy was closely linked to Alsace-Lorraine. Röchling also sat on the party's executive committee. He began by calling Alsace-Lorraine a "borderland, which is a possession of the entire German states." There was no recognition on his part of the new Alsatian constitution that attempted to integrate the area into the Reich

32. Schenk, *Der Fall Zabern,* pp. 51–52.
33. Bassermann notations, no date, Bassermann remnant, 303/17.
34. Ibid.

on a semiequal footing with the other German states. Rather it was "owned" like a colony which was an exposed and vulnerable possession. This interpretation placed the Zabern Affair in a category with the former uprisings in Africa and Asia. The people in this possession had the cheek to hurl derogatory phrases at the occupying Prussian army "as a kind of sport," and no action was taken against them by the civilian authorities. In the Zabern Affair the military, "aroused by these continual pinpricks," had protected itself by taking "jurisdiction over public security and order into its own hands." Thus the "possession" was secured and defended for the German Reich. This was the light in which Röchling viewed the declaration of martial law. In this case, it was not the freedom of the individual that counted but the "fate of the nation as a whole," which depended "in the last analysis on the constitution of the army" and "its spirit of initiative, of independent responsibility and the highly tensed feeling of honor" of the "Prussian officer corps." Since the defense of the Reich and its possessions was only guaranteed by the independence of the military, Bethmann Hollweg's insistence that civilian authority be restored and the military removed was an "indigestible circumstance with regard to the prestige of our Fatherland." Röchling thought that Bethmann Hollweg's concern for justice in the Zabern Affair was "regrettable" since "a leading statesman, in such matters, ought not and cannot treat according to the viewpoint of justice. Here, the reason of state must intervene. . . ."[35] Needless to say, if Bethmann Hollweg's action was nationally remiss, the vote of no-confidence supported by the National Liberal Reichstag Fraktion was nearly treasonable. Röchling linked "the fate of the nation" with the preponderance of the military in its "possessions." No other consideration took precedence over raison d'état. The reference to the very ambiguous status of Alsace-Lorraine hinted that National Liberals of Röchling's stripe would not blink at applying his formula to the other German states should reason of state demand it. Blatant nationalism conquered every other political ideal.

Not all National Liberals agreed with this statement, and many, including Bassermann, were embarrassed by its extremism. In the Prussian Landtag itself, Schiffer hastily contradicted Röchling's views by reiterating the "inadequacy of [the] entire legal situation. . . ." But no one could ignore the existence of such ideas within the party's

35. *Verhandlungen Preussens,* Legislaturperiode 22, Session 1, 1 : 111–118.

leadership and its rank and file. Given this "mood," common action with the Centre and the Progressives to limit the independence of the military would have alienated many National Liberal voters. No one could say whether the party could survive a crisis evoked by wounded national feelings. Bassermann and the left tried to salvage some liberal honor by introducing an independent motion in the Reichstag:

> The Reichstag acknowledges that an investigation over the regulation of . . . 1899 concerning the use of weapons by the military has been ordered after the recent events in Zabern have produced doubts whether the jurisdiction of the civil and military officials is correctly delineated.
>
> The Reichstag requests the . . . Chancellor to make known . . . the results of this investigation as soon as possible.

This inquiry was no bold demand for change, no outraged indignation over the lack of respect for the rights and freedoms of citizens. It was a plea to the chancellor to find his own way toward legality. It reflected the paralysis inflicted upon the party by the conflict between the right and left wings, between the Prussian party and the national party, between the opponents of a more responsible government and its advocates. The paralysis had advanced so far that even a minimal liberalism collapsed when confronted by national crisis.[36]

When the National Liberals decided to act independently, they also dissolved the temporary unity between Centre and Progressives. From the beginning the Progressives wanted a more radical motion than the Centre. Whereas the Centre formulated a vague resolution requesting the chancellor to "regulate" the military, the Progressives favored clear-cut legislation declaring that only the civil authorities could proclaim martial law. When no majority could be found for the Centre's milder formula, the Progressives returned to cooperation with the Social Democrats because they also desired some definitive legal settlement of the problem. These two parties introduced almost identical motions for the supremacy of the civilian authorities at the same time that the Centre and the National Liberals introduced their independent resolutions.[37]

Thus the conflicts and emotions engendered by the Zabern Affair

36. Ibid., pp. 297–390. *Verhandlungen des Reichstages,* 303 : Drucksache no. 1303.
37. *Verhandlungen des Reichstages,* 303: Drucksache no. 1304, no. 1281, no. 1302, no. 1309.

shattered the tenuous unity of the national Grand Bloc. Only a half-hearted cooperation existed when Centre, Progressives, and Social Democrats voted for the Centre's resolution for the "independence of the civilian authority" and for the transferral of the other motions to a committee. The National Liberals did not join this alliance since they foresaw "no practical benefit from the deliberation of the motions in a committee." Eventually, Bethmann Hollweg succeeded in changing the previous military orders so that definite objective circumstances had to exist before the army could interfere in civil disorders. In this way, he fulfilled the requirements of the National Liberal resolution but did not establish the precedence of the civilian over military authority. By failing to create a united front, the non-Conservative parties missed the opportunity to regulate, at least partially, a constitutional problem that bothered a majority of the Reichstag. For had the National Liberals not catered to the prejudices of their right wing, a majority was probably available for the Centre's resolution. In the Alsatian reform, in the vote of no-confidence, in the tax reform, the national Grand Bloc from Centre to Social Democrats forced the government to make concessions. In the Zabern Affair, this Bloc collapsed because it could not weather the onslaught of nationalism.[38]

THE DISSOLUTION OF THE BADEN GRAND BLOC

Nationalism not only destroyed the Grand Bloc in the Reichstag, it also disturbed the Grand Bloc policy in Baden. The Baden budget of 1912 included an item of 15,000 marks for nonpolitical and nonconfessional clubs that furthered "gymnastics, games, hikes" and other bodily exercise contributing to the physical fitness and health of German youth. The proposal was accompanied by a list of organizations designated to receive the monies, and it included the *Jungdeutschlandbund,* whose aim was the physical development of youth for military purposes and whose tone was antagonistic to Social Democracy. The list excluded the workers' *Turnvereine.* Because it favored an organization devoted to military purposes and discriminated against the workers, the Social Democrats had a double reason for rejecting the projected distribution of the public funds and they tried to persuade the National Liberals to reject the item also.[39]

In making this request, the Social Democrats posed a severe problem

38. Ibid., 292 : 6787-6788, 6791; Zmarzlik, *Bethmann Hollweg,* p. 124.
39. *Volksfreund,* June 24, July 16 and 17, 1912.

for the National Liberals. If they rejected the item for the Turnvereine, they risked a political explosion since gymnastics was a traditional "national" sport and symbolically linked with national honor. Yet they wanted to avoid giving money to semipolitical organizations like the Jungdeutschlandbund precisely because all the workers' Turnvereine, associated with Social Democracy, would theoretically have a claim on the monies also. Therefore they eventually succumbed to Social Democratic pressure and voted against the 15,000 marks. This vote against a budget item strongly identified with national purpose aroused a storm of protest within the state party. To make matters worse, the vote occurred simultaneously with the critical national party crisis of 1912. Rebmann, however, chose to ignore the storm in favor of his previous policy:

> The National Liberals based their vote on the fact that they could not wish to increase the existent point of friction. . . . One does not fight Social Democrats by giving them a reason to complain that they are treated as second-class citizens; one [thereby] only gives them an additional, poisonous . . . means for agitation.

For the time being, the National Liberals in Baden intended to preserve the Grand Bloc despite the irritation to national loyalties and party traditions.[40]

Although the National Liberals compromised their national principles and irritated their northern colleagues in order to preserve the Bloc, the Badenese government pursued the same antisocialist policies as the government in Berlin. In 1912, it not only discriminated against Social Democracy in the budget, it also publicly declared that it did not recognize the "civil equality" of party members, and it pointedly refused to employ them as civil servants.[41] In retaliation, the Social Democrats refused to vote for the budget of 1912. This was the first time since the inception of the Grand Bloc that the Social Democrats rejected the budget, and their action provoked varying reactions from their political partners.

Of the two parties, the Progressives were more sympathetic toward

40. For the National Liberals' resistance to the club provision, see Fraktion meeting, June 26, 1912, NL Baden. For the vote, see July 4, 1912, NL Baden. Rebmann is quoted from the *Berliner Tageblatt,* August 2, 1912.

41. Wilhelm Kolb, *Die Tätigkeit der Sozialdemokratie im badischen Landtage, 1911/12* (Mannheim, 1912), pp. 14, 158.

the Social Democrats. They regretted the rejection, but they agreed perfectly with Social Democracy's reasons. The government was responsible for the rejection of the budget because of its unjust treatment of Social Democracy. In this way, the Progressives maintained their active alliance with the Social Democrats. The National Liberals, because of their more complex composition, displayed a mixed reaction to the rejection. Thinking prudence the better part of virtue, the Landtag Fraktion remained silent, but the press reacted vigorously. Most liberal newspapers saw the rejection as a partial consequence of the government's attitude, but they were far more critical of the Social Democrats than were the Progressives. The official National Liberal newspaper complained that the Social Democrats had not cooperated as much as possible in the last session of the legislature and that their tone, both in the legislature and in the press, had grown sharper. Furthermore it found the rejection of the budget "inastute" inasmuch as it endangered the survival of the Bloc. Other more conservative papers were shocked that their own National Liberal Fraktion had not supported the government against a party which lacked the proper respect for the "national idea." Once again the latent National Liberal prejudices against Social Democracy were churned up by the budget rejection, and these emotions endangered the policy of the Baden Grand Bloc.[42]

The danger was all the more acute since, in tune with the crisis in the National Liberal party, there was a strong current toward the right within the Baden party itself. In August, Thorbecke, the party secretary in Baden, told Bassermann that this current existed because many supporters thought Rebmann had transformed the Grand Bloc from a "tactical" into a "programmatical" cooperation. In November 1912, Obkircher, the former chairman of the Baden party, explained that the dangers of the Grand Bloc lay in its tendency to blur the significant differences between the parties. He thought "that a National Liberal party ought not to bind itself for better or worse with the left and the Social Democrats" but should maintain its position as a middle party. Obkircher published his thoughts just as the National Liberals began to contemplate their tactics for the next Baden election, and he reminded them of their freedom of choice; they could either choose the Grand

42. Ibid., p. 154. For the National Liberal press reaction, see *Badische Landeszeitung*, July 16 and July 20, 1912, clippings in NL Baden; *Konstanzer Zeitung*, July 20, 1912, clipping in NL Baden.

Bloc or they could stand alone. He favored an independent stance, and Bassermann supported him. At the end of November, Bassermann wrote to Rebmann:

> I am compelled to write you a note about Baden politics. I do not know how the party thinks about election tactics, but I have . . . steadily growing misgivings against the Grand Bloc. I fear that we are experiencing a storm within the party such as never before and that our friends will not follow on the same wave length. The times are serious[?]; when the Balkan war is over, then the Triple Entente will threaten us as never before. . . . The sharper the national idea remains in the foreground, the stronger the disinclination in [our] circles against Social Democracy. I can only desperately advise against the Grand Bloc. Prince Max told me . . . he feared that we were in danger of losing many supporters with the policy of the Grand Bloc.

There certainly were signs that many National Liberals in Baden were dissatisfied. In Karlsruhe, some renounced their party membership and founded a local Free Conservative party, and southern industrial circles openly disapproved of the Grand Bloc. On the other hand, industrial circles in the north, particularly in the area of Mannheim, approved the policy as did the Baden Young Liberals. This divergence of opinion had to be taken into consideration when the National Liberals considered future policy.[43]

Rebmann therefore, in outlining a feasible election tactic, defended the Grand Bloc in very strong terms throughout the end of 1912 and the beginning of 1913. He stressed that the partnership with the Social Democrats had not limited the National Liberals' independence in the legislature. Sometimes they voted with the left and sometimes with the Centre. The common interests of National Liberals and Social Democrats involved cultural affairs and "progressive liberal tasks," and they occasionally parted ways even in cultural affairs. In economic issues,

43. Bassermann to Stresemann, August 18, 1912, Stresemann Papers. Rudolf Obkircher, "Die nationalliberale Partei Badens in Vergangenheit und Gegenwart," *Der Panther* 1, no. 9 (November 15, 1912): 261–270, clipping in NL Baden. Quotation from Bassermann to Rebmann, November 22, 1912, NL Baden. For the Free Conservatives in Baden, see *Volksfreund,* June 13, 1912. On some National Liberal support for Grand Bloc, see Thorbecke to Rebmann, August 24, 1912; circular letter of E. Frey, chairman of the State Association of Young Liberal Clubs in Baden, December 12, 1912, NL Baden.

particularly when they concerned the middle-class businessman, the parties definitely did not see eye to eye. Rebmann tried to reconcile the policy of the Grand Bloc with that of a middle party; in Baden, the National Liberals played the game both ways. Even in national issues it was possible to pursue a double role:

> The feeling runs through the whole National Liberal party that we have the sharpest condemnation for the behavior of Social Democracy in the question of war . . . [W]e find it very painful that in the moment in which our German empire in certain circumstances is placed before the question, war or peace, Social Democracy . . . attacks from the rear . . . [But] it is not true . . . that this party has the power to enforce the peace of the world. . . . In every single case it has been proven that the entire International has quickly collapsed under self-interest and the enthusiasm of the people. . . . My firm conviction is that the German Social Democratic worker, if worst comes to worst, will fight for our Fatherland in the rank and file with his bourgeois comrades, and if need be will also die [with them]. . . .

Rebmann condemned the Social Democratic attitude toward war, but he also tried to expose the myth of Social Democratic internationalism. He tried to scale the "national" barrier between National Liberals and Social Democrats and to overcome the national hysteria so worrisome to Bassermann. Instead he elevated the liberal over the national ideal. He appealed to the National Liberals' pride in the policies and influence of the party:

> In the years up until 1905, we had the majority in the legislature, . . . [T]he entire legislature and the government received its direction from [us], and in Baden, there was a liberal government. The agreements of the left in 1905 and 1909 and the subsequent cooperation made it possible that the whole character of the government . . . could be maintained. If the new elections create a situation . . . whereby the Social Democrats come into the legislature rejected and isolated, whereby the National Liberal party is forced down into an insignificant minority, that would mean the collapse of the party. The government will change, and we will have to deal with a basically different situation. . . .

In order to maintain liberal government in Baden, the policy of the Grand Bloc must be continued. Therefore, it was imperative for the National Liberals once again to conclude election agreements with the Progressives and Social Democrats.[44]

These arguments finally won the day, and the Fraktion and the executive committee agreed to maintain the Grand Bloc. During the summer of 1913, the liberal parties negotiated an agreement for the general election and worked out preliminary arrangements with the Social Democrats for the runoff election. The misgivings and differences of opinion in the National Liberal party caused little disarray. There were only two election districts where the local clubs complained about an agreement with the Progressives because of their radical policies, and only one district, Heidelberg, bolted the party line and made a deal with the Centre. The National Liberals could afford to feel confident; the political tide was turning in their favor.[45]

The turn of the tide was evident in the election results of October 1913. The National Liberals gained three mandates, the Progressives lost two, and the Social Democrats lost seven; the right gained six seats at the expense of the left. Whereas the previous Baden elections represented a pull toward the left, the elections of 1913 represented a pull toward the right. In a postelection article, Ludwig Frank attributed this result to the peculiar circumstances surrounding the elections. The Social Democratic gains of the last Baden election had been due to the failure of the national tax reform and to the fear of unemployment. Since these matters were no longer political issues, the voters swung back to the Centre. Many railroad employees had deserted Social Democracy because of the scare caused by events in Bavaria, where the Centrist government forbade railway workers to join in the Social Democratic trade union. Other voters deserted because of the nationalist political climate created by the centennial of 1913. In 1913, the voters inclined toward

44. For the economic differences and Rebmann's quote, see *Badische nationalliberale Correspondenz,* Politische Nachrichten, Landesversammlung . . . [1912], Blatt 5 and 11; protocol of the executive committee meeting of the National Liberal Party of the Grand Duchy of Baden held in the Krokodil on February 23, 1913, NL Baden.

45. The vote was 9–7, February 23, 1913, NL Baden. For complaints, see meeting of election district representatives, April 20, 1913. Also Rebmann to Hopf, June 23, 1913; and Schweier to Zwiebelhofer, August 2, 1913, NL Baden. For Heidelberg, see Alfred Rapp, *Die Parteibewegung in Baden, 1905–1928* (Karlsruhe, 1929), p. 50.

the right because there was no political issue working against it; indeed there was a political climate favoring the right.[46]

This conservative climate further infected the National Liberals. When the Landtag convened after the elections, the nation was in the midst of the Zabern Affair and its accompanying emotions. Moreover the National Liberal electoral success had returned many conservatives to the Fraktion, and they interfered with Rebmann's liberal policies. Thus it was very difficult for him to persuade the Fraktion to elect a Grand Bloc praesidium. In the Fraktion's first meeting of the session, various members objected that a Grand Bloc praesidium could not be elected without "further ado" since the mood of the voters was against such a policy. These objections quickly forced a review of the Grand Bloc policy. Most of the members of the Fraktion wanted to forego a purely Grand Bloc tactic and include the Centre in the praesidium in some capacity—either as president or as first vice-president. There were even a few arch-conservatives who wanted to exclude the Social Democrats entirely. Although Rebmann argued long and hard for a Grand Bloc praesidium, the Fraktion overruled him in favor of the Centre in the first vice-presidency. The Centre naturally rejected the post and the former praesidium was finally elected. The incident, however, revealed the deepening conservative mood of the National Liberals, and this mood boded ill for the future of the Grand Bloc.[47]

It was only a matter of time before the fatal breach, and in May 1914, the final crisis of the Baden Grand Bloc occurred. Ironically, it was a cultural issue—the relationship between church and state—that caused the disagreement. Without previously informing the National Liberals, the Progressives introduced a motion, supported by the Social Democrats, to allow any teacher to refuse to teach religion "because [it] contradict[ed] his personal conviction." The National Liberals saw this motion in the same light as they had seen the 1910 motion on dissidents; it was a step toward the elimination of religious instruction in the schools. This was a cause that the National Liberals could not

---

46. Alfred Rapp, *Die badischen Landtagsabgeordneten, 1905–1929* (Karlsruhe, 1929), p. 105. Ludwig Frank, *Aufsätze, Reden und Briefe,* ed. H. Wachenheim (Berlin, 1924), pp. 293–297.

47. The record of the first caucus of the session was not dated. Fraktion meetings, November 26, 27, and 28, 1913, NL Baden. Cf. *Hilfe* 18 (1913) : 769.

afford to espouse. These were already signs that Protestant circles in Baden, from which the National Liberals drew heavy support, feared a radicalization in the issue of church and state and that they were prepared to desert the National Liberals should such a radicalization occur. Therefore the National Liberal delegate Neck promptly declared the Fraktion's unwillingness to vote for the motion:

> The consolidation of the religio-ethical attitude is a chief activity of our schools. . . . [The school] must help . . . in the fight against radicalism and materialism. . . . Obligatory religious instruction must be maintained in the elementary school.

This speech, with its veiled references to Social Democratic radicalism and unaccompanied by any milder National Liberal tones, offended both Progressives and Social Democrats. In response, one Progressive called the National Liberals "undependable," and Kolb questioned the continued existence of the Grand Bloc:

> . . . The trouble with the National Liberals is that the most varied opinions stand side by side, and consequently no beneficial political activity can come about. The Grand Bloc . . . has been forged together for tactical reasons, but you will not contradict, Mr. Rebmann, if I say: the tactic only makes sense if a certain political purpose is pursued. . . . A political purpose would be understood . . . if it should become fact that the National Liberals are suitable partners for the Centre in cultural issues; then there would be no more cooperation for us; then we will go our way alone and we will not lose anything thereby. . . .

Since one of the principal purposes of the Grand Bloc was cooperation in cultural issues, Kolb's remarks were apropos. If the National Liberals really considered cooperating with the Centre in these matters, then Kolb served notice that the Grand Bloc's days were numbered.[48]

On the day after Kolb's speech, the National Liberal Fraktion met to discuss policy in the light of his remarks. In the course of the discussion,

48. For the Progressives' motion, see *Verhandlungen Baden,* 509: Drucksache no. 37c, 387. On Protestants, see Thorbecke to Rebmann, August 9, 1910, and for the "undependable," see "Die Lage in Baden und die Nationalliberale Partei," *Badische nationalliberale Correspondenz,* May 10, 1913, NL Baden. Neck and Kolb quoted from the *Volksfreund,* May 2, 8, 1914.

they agreed that the political situation had changed considerably since the beginning of the legislative session and concluded that the Grand Bloc no longer benefited them. This decision finally severed the bond between National Liberals and Social Democrats in Baden. At the same time, the Progressives declared that they would no longer cooperate with the National Liberals, and this declaration destroyed the long-standing policy of liberal unity. During the remaining two months of the legislature, the National Liberals became further estranged from their former partners. Increasingly, they claimed to uphold the "Old Liberal" tradition of their founders and accused the Progressives and Social Democrats of democratic radicalism. For their part, the Progressives and Social Democrats tended to cooperate more and more with one another against the National Liberals. The Grand Bloc had outlived its tactical usefulness and had dissolved.[49]

The dissolution of the Grand Bloc in Baden occurred only three months after the National Liberals dissociated themselves from the Centre and the left in the Reichstag during the Zabern Affair. Although the issues involved in these two events were seemingly unrelated, the National Liberal withdrawal from the Baden Grand Bloc and disengagement in the Reichstag had the same basic causes. The mood of the voters in the national issue had prevented the National Liberals from cooperation in the Zabern Affair. It also opposed the Grand Bloc in Baden. National conservatism in the Reichstag and religious conservatism in the Baden Landtag were two sides of the same conservative coin. Primarily, the voters objected to cooperation with unpatriotic Social Democrats in a period of an increasing threat to the nation's defense.

National insecurity was both an accompaniment to and a facade for deepening social cleavage. Since the Reichstag elections of 1912, when the National Liberals rejected the Sammlungspolitik, the Conservative agrarians and heavy industrialists had faced increasing political isolation. Their plight grew more severe when the Centre also turned its back on the "collective policy" during the tax reform of 1913. These spurnings of former Conservative tactics were then complemented by the limited

49. Fraktion meetings, May 8, 11, 1914. "Nochmals: Die Lage in Baden und die national-alliberale Partei," *Badische nationalliberale Correspondenz,* May 14, 1914. For the cooperation between Progressives and Social Democrats see Fraktion meeting, July 1, 1914, NL Baden.

cooperation with the Social Democrats in the tax reform. Both agrarians and industrialists began to despair of ever protecting their interests through the established party system. As this despair mounted, the economic recession of 1913 sparked a wave of strikes protesting unemployment and the downward trend in wages. Labor unrest was always unsettling for the heavy industrialists, and they now demanded the curtailment of trade-union activities by the Reichstag. All the non-Conservative parties, including the National Liberals, refused to support such action. Feeling more isolated than ever before, the Centralverband joined together in August 1913 with the Landlords' League and the Imperial German Mittelstands Association, a pressure group of the "old" middle class, to form an extraparliamentary *Kartell der schaffenden Stände* (Cartel of Productive Estates). The very use of the word Kartell symbolized the movement's goals. It recalled the old alliance between agrarians and heavy industry which was utilized by Bismarck to maintain his authoritarian system. And authoritarianism definitely marked the Kartell's program. It wanted antisocialist and antitrade-union legislation. It agitated for the once-rejected Bismarckian idea of an economic or "corporate" parliament. It entertained hopes for a coup d'état against the Reichstag, a reactionary revision of the Reichstag suffrage, and a military dictatorship to reverse the perceived trend toward democratic reform.[50]

Not surprisingly, many right-wing National Liberals joined with Conservatives and former army officers in founding the Kartell.[51] Their revival of the old alliance with the Conservatives through participation in this extraparliamentary movement aggravated the crisis within National Liberalism. The party was now confronted with both a conservative splinter organization within its midst—the Old Liberals—and a more dangerous, external movement which could prompt a new secession feared by all the party leaders. To its credit, the party withstood the blatant reactionary demands. But it became increasingly difficult to explain cooperation in the Grand Bloc as an agreement among the bourgeois parties. Every time the Social Democrats joined this majority, they created the impression of movement toward the leftist bloc so offensive to the right-wing National Liberals.

A further complication arose with the disclosure in 1913 that Russia

50. Schorske, *Social Democracy*, pp. 260–261; Stegmann, *Die Erben Bismarcks*, pp. 360ff.; and Fischer, *Krieg der Illusionen*, pp. 388–390.

51. Stegmann, *Die Erben Bismarcks*, pp. 365, 395–400.

and other countries intended to raise their tariffs and exclude German industrial and agricultural products. All the causes of the former Kartell between agrarians and heavy industrialists had now recurred: economic decline, tight markets abroad, social unrest at home, and increasing Social Democratic power. In previous decades, high German tariffs and repressive legislation had remedied these vexing problems. Neither was any longer feasible. As an antidote, the Kartell allied itself with the most reactionary elements in the Pan-German League to urge the pursuit of an aggressive foreign policy and war to maintain and extend Germany's economic power abroad. At the same time, these partners hoped an expansionist war would deflect attention away from domestic reform and shore up their declining influence at home. The dissolution of the Grand Bloc in both the Reich and Baden must be seen against the backdrop of this agitation. As the party most responsible for the unification of Germany, the National Liberals were obliged to support the maintenance and extension of German power. In their bid for party unity, National Liberal leaders, including Bassermann, increased their nationalist rhetoric after 1912. At the same time, they had to approach any cooperation with the other Grand Bloc parties cautiously. The latter were, after all, the traditional, nonnationalist parties, and the National Liberals could not risk a heavy right-wing attack on their supposed lack of patriotism. These calculations preserved party unity, but they also contributed to the growing estrangement between National Liberals on the one hand and Centre, Progressives, and Socialists on the other.[52]

The cleft was deepest between National Liberals and Social Democrats. The latter were the primary targets of the Kartell. Shortly after the Zabern Affair, an event occurred that created even greater antagonism between the two groups. The government, which either ignored or rejected most of the Kartell's reactionary schemes, finally recognized one demand of this self-serving organization. Prompted by the argument that social legislation sapped Germany's industrial strength by making its workers soft, the government announced its opposition to any additional social legislation at the beginning of 1914. This decision crushed all the hopes for the national unemployment insurance being considered at the time. Trade-union and social reformist circles correctly viewed the announcement as a capitulation to the heavy industrialists. On May 10, the Society for Social Reform, the Christian trade

52. Ibid., pp. 328ff., 434ff.; Fischer, *Krieg der Illusionen*, pp. 328, 359–360, 398–401, 434ff.

unions, and the Hirsch-Duncker Gewerkvereine held a large protest meeting in Berlin. However, the Social Democrats, as the chief representatives of the working class, felt the sting most acutely. Although there is no direct evidence that one event led to the other, the Social Democratic Reichstag Fraktion, in a meeting dominated by the radicals on February 4, voted to demonstrate their displeasure by ostentatiously remaining in their seats during the traditional Hoch to the kaiser at the end of the Reichstag session. This decision was a radical departure from the previous practice of discreetly leaving the hall, and it was kept secret for three long months.[53]

The Reichstag session ended on May 20, just one week after the collapse of the Baden Grand Bloc, and the Social Democrats did refuse the Hoch to the kaiser, causing great consternation and outrage among the parties of the Reichstag and in German society as a whole.[54] Once again, the "radical" Social Democrats assumed their outcast role in German politics. Yet they had ample provocation for their act. Millions were being spent for a new military bill, but not one penny for new social legislation. The government catered to the wishes of industrialists who refused the equal vote to the majority of the Prussian people. Just as the Hoch to the kaiser was a symbol of regard for the nation as well as the monarchy, the refusal to give it was a symbol of disrespect for a regime that ignored the interests and the wishes of the nation's largest bloc of voters. The action of May 20 thus represented the resumption of Social Democratic isolation from German politics. It symbolized, in a wider sense, the isolation from power that occurred when the National Liberals returned to their former conservatism by refusing cooperation in state legislatures and in the Reichstag. Their help was needed for the achievement of certain Social Democratic goals; their refusal to help meant the exclusion of the Social Democratic influence from legislation. When the Social Democrats refused to honor the kaiser, they merely dramatized the fact of their isolation. In this way, nationalist and social policies interacted to divide, rather than unite the parties. Thus, in the spring of 1914, the schemes of *Demokratie und Kaisertum,* so promising a short time before, seemed no closer to achievement than when Naumann had first proposed them.

53. Stegmann, *Die Erben Bismarcks,* pp. 388–397, 412. Also Karl Erich Born, *Staat und Sozialpolitik seit Bismarcks Sturz* (Wiesbaden, 1957), pp. 247–248. Fraktion meeting, February 4, 1914, *SPD Fraktionsprotokolle,* 1 : 310.
    54. *Verhandlungen des Reichstages,* 295 : 9170–9171.

10

The Failure of the Grand Bloc

When the Grand Bloc dissolved in both Baden and the Reich in May 1914, Germany was poised on the brink of World War I. Four years later, the war ended in a shattering national defeat and revolution. The effects of that cataclysmic double event contributed to the eclipse of the democratic empire envisioned by Naumann when he first conceived the bloc from Bassermann to Bebel. This context must provide the framework for an assessment of the Grand Bloc. The Grand Bloc was an instrument for the evolution of the Kaisserreich toward parliamentary democracy; its blunted edge was a substitute for the trauma of revolution. When Meinecke proclaimed it the "missed opportunity" in German history, he viewed it as a more palatable alternative to the actual course of events after 1914. Therefore the question posed at the beginning of this book persists. Was the strategy of *Demokratie und Kaisertum* possible? Was it feasible for the Grand Bloc to achieve a democratic, parliamentary regime within the second empire?

By 1914, the Grand Bloc had already established a firm course toward reform. Drawn together by their desire to modernize Germany politically, its members could force the government to make concessions whenever they chose to cooperate. When the Grand Bloc parties skillfully gained a compromise giving Alsace-Lorraine three votes in the Bundesrat and universal, equal suffrage, they won an important concession to both democracy and parliamentary power. In 1912, the change in the Reichstag's rules set the stage for a more effective influence over the German chancellor: the vote of no-confidence. During the next two years, the Grand Bloc's espousal of tax reform signaled to both government and Conservatives the desire of a German majority for a tax structure more suitable to an industrial society. The economic privileges enjoyed by the Prussian agrarians would no longer be secure.

With every victory, the Grand Bloc increased the powers of the Reichstag and the potential for a democratic regime.

This trend could continue as long as the Grand Bloc from Centre to Social Democrats cooperated. Only an "extended" Bloc possessed the momentum and strength necessary to force the government to yield to liberal democratic demands. If the Centre and the "left" (Progressives and Social Democrats) formed the majority as they did in the Arbeitskammergesetz, the government, reluctant to dispense with the support of the National Liberals, withdrew the bill. If the liberals and Social Democrats formed the majority, as in the praesidium election of 1912, the government refused to recognize it. Only when all worked together, as in the Alsatian constitutional reform and the tax reform of 1913, did the government acquiesce in a measure which offended the Conservatives, increased the power of the Reichstag, and contributed to the democratization of German politics. In all these cases, the government's goal was a majority of bourgeois parties, a desire to avoid reliance on the Social Democrats. Yet this bourgeois majority was insufficient to accomplish the reforms necessary for instituting parliamentary democracy. This study has shown that a "majority of the middle" did not form without an impetus from the Social Democrats. Sometimes they played an initiating role. In 1913, Bassermann openly credited them with the stimulation of tax reform. As the most numerous party and as the potential source of instability in German politics, they forced the others to attend to their democratic demands. In some instances, they helped to bridge the gap between the middle parties themselves. Both Centre and liberals could bury their differences in a common reformist policy because they feared to lose either votes or influence to the Social Democrats. Once the Social Democrats succeeded in prodding the others into action, they then supported reform, though it might be limited, with their own votes. Because of the interdependence between the bourgeois parties and the Social Democrats in striving for and achieving change, a "majority of the middle"[1] was synonymous with the Grand Bloc.

For this reason, the Grand Bloc was as much a creature of Social

1. Gustav Schmidt, "Innenpolitische Blockbildungen am Vorabend des ersten Weltkrieges," *Aus Politik und Zeitgeschichte,* Beilage zur Wochenzeitung *Das Parlament,* B20/72 (May 13, 1972), pp. 3–32, uses this phrase in a variety of ways: to describe the Grand Bloc, excluding the left-wing Social Democrats; and to denote an alliance of Centre and National Liberals which he thinks was an "immanent coalition" on the eve of war.

Democratic practice as of Naumann's imagination. By 1914, the Social Democrats were no longer a revolutionary, nonnational party. They accepted the idea of a powerful Reich and were willing to cooperate within the existing system. After the isolating shock of the "national elections" of 1907, they never strongly opposed an actively nationalistic policy. During the Zabern Affair, their failure to demand constitutional change implied the acceptance of the kaiser's military authority and its representation of German power. The monarchy had become a fact of life to which the majority of Social Democrats had adjusted. At the same time, the Social Democrats actively worked to integrate themselves into the existing legislative process and to win influence through a willingness to compromise. Their participation in election agreements, their tentative offer to vote for a Prussian suffrage that fell short of their democratic demands, all evidenced an almost desperate desire for acceptance by the other elements in German society. As Naumann had once predicted, reformism had triumphed as the policy of the party; it had also won democratic concessions through cooperation in the Grand Bloc. But the reformists could only remain successful, could only justify their practical work in the legislative process, if the other parties continued to extend the olive branch toward them. If the Centre and the liberals—the "majority of the middle"—ceased to cooperate in the work of liberalizing and democratizing German government, the party was forced back into its former negative stance. Such was the meaning of the sensational refusal to give the Hoch to the kaiser at the end of the Reichstag's session of 1914. The short-sighted social policies of the government, encouraged by the disarray within the Grand Bloc, evoked the old "revolutionary" protests. Without the cooperation of the Grand Bloc, the Social Democrats were isolated, their democratic demands unheeded and evolution toward reform impeded.

As prewar events demonstrated, disunity among the members of the Grand Bloc hindered the trend toward reform. Their disagreements were more threatening to the achievement of a parliamentary, democratic regime than the desperate, reactionary demands of the Kartell der schaffenden Stände. Although it is valuable to investigate such "counterrevolutionary" groups as the Kartell because of their ultimate triumph, it is equally important to remember that in 1914, "revolutionary" currents contested the "counterrevolutionary" ones; it was difficult to assess which, in the long run, would prove to be the stronger. In that year, many signs pointed toward a victory for the forces of reform. The majority of Germans greeted the Kartell's plans with a distinct lack of enthusiasm, and both the Reichstag and the government rejected any attempt to destroy the already existing degree of democracy in German life.[2] Many responsible members of the government, Bethmann Hollweg above all, realized the impossibility of resisting the long-term democratic trend. Within the army, by no means a monolithic institution, a few realistic men had already gracefully lost the battle with democracy.[3] At the same time, the long-standing power of the Conservatives in the Prussian Landtag, in the Prussian and national bureaucracies, and in the army made the government reluctant to offend Conservative interests and sensibilities by actively pursuing reform. To the extent that these Conservative forces contributed to the work of the Kartell, the Kartell could temporarily check reform. But in 1914, it could not reverse the reformist trend. The Kartell's existence merely posed an increased challenge to democratic forces. In order to push forward the cause of reform and to avoid political stagnation, an anti-Conservative front, such as the Grand Bloc, had to exhibit a greater unity and determination than the Kartell.

An evolutionary development of the monarchy therefore depended on the translation of the intermittent, limited Grand Bloc agreements of the years between 1911 and 1914 into a cohesive, integrated and permanent majority. Only through permanence could the Grand Bloc secure the established trend, displace the Conservative influence, and acquire the experience necessary for gradually assuming full control of the government. Recently, scholars have blamed the failure of parliamentarization on the parties' inability and unwillingness to assume governmental responsibility.[4] This inadequacy was serious, particularly

2. Dirk Stegmann, *Die Erben Bismarcks: Parteien und Verbände in der Spätphase des wilhelminischen Deutschlands* (Cologne, 1970), pp. 397ff. For an approach to "counter-revolutionary studies," see Arno J. Mayer, *Dynamics of Counterrevolution in Europe, 1870–1956: An Analytic Framework* (New York, 1971). The same author has also tentatively developed a theme similar to this conclusion in "Domestic Causes of the First World War," in *The Responsibility of Power,* ed. L. Krieger and F. Stein (New York, Anchor edition, 1969), pp. 308–324.

3. Martin Kitchen, *The German Officer Corps, 1890–1914* (Oxford, 1968), pp. 167, 181.

4. Udo Bermbach, *Vorformen parlamentarischer Kabinettsbildung in Deutschland: Der Interfraktionelle Ausschuss 1917–18 und die Parlamentarisierung der Reichsregierung* (Cologne, 1967), pp. 61ff., and Dieter Grosser, *Vom monarchischen Konstitutionalismus zur*

when we seek to explain the weaknesses of Weimar by examining the prerevolutionary positions of the German parties. On the other hand, it is necessary to understand the prewar atmosphere. For a variety of reasons, not the least of which was German popular sentiment, an immediate assumption of power by parliamentarians, itself a revolutionary act, was impossible. All the Grand Bloc parties, including the Social Democrats, expected reform to advance through a series of stages that would insure continuity, stability, and the consolidation of previous gains. Successful evolution required the kaiser's government to lend its authority to a democratic policy determined by the Grand Bloc long before parliament itself assumed total control. Only a transitional cooperation between the Grand Bloc and the monarchy could persuade the Conservatives and their allies to accept democracy and to desist in their reactionary threats. As commitment to reform progressed, it could be expected to awaken the need to introduce parliamentary leaders into the imperial government—as indeed occurred during the crisis of 1917–18. But before it could adopt such radical measures, the government had to be forced to do so by a consistent, reliable majority. The ultimate success of the Grand Bloc therefore depended on its functioning as a governmental coalition even *before* it achieved that status.

Any governmental coalition survives only through compromise. The final assessment of the Grand Bloc's capabilities therefore rests with the propensities of its members to transcend their isolated "sociocultural milieux," to sacrifice the identity associated with party principle,[5] and to overcome the disagreements engendered by conflicting socioeconomic interests. These faults were common to all the parties, but in 1914, they were already beginning to overcome them. The Grand Bloc, as either idea or fact, would not have become so important a force in German prewar politics had social and political isolation persisted. As for party identity, any multiparty system encounters this problem. Coalitions are possible because the participants are willing to compromise over the important issues of the day. In Germany before 1914, these important issues numbered three: social legislation, Prussian suffrage reform, and the "national question." All created conflicts

parlamentarischen Demokratie: Die Verfassungspolitik der deutschen Parteien im letzten Jahrzehnt des Kaiserreiches (The Hague, 1970), pp. 33ff.
    5. Schmidt, "Innenpolitische Blockbildungen," p. 22.

among the Grand Bloc parties as well as between its various members
and the Conservatives. Could the members of the Grand Bloc resolve
their internal differences over these issues in order to create that permanent "coalition" necessary for a reform of the monarchy?

One of the most severe conflicts impeding the formation of a Reichstag Grand Bloc in the years before the war involved social legislation.
As demonstrated by Reichstag debates, the extension of social insurance
and the official recognition of trade unions aroused the most vicious
political emotions—so vicious it is difficult to imagine conditions under
which the parties might have resolved their differences. The crux of the
problem was the patent conflict of interest between National Liberals
and Social Democrats; Centrists and Progressives tried to play a
mediating role and failed. Yet if the Grand Bloc were to become
permanent, social legislation was one issue on which the parties must
compromise. Were there any areas in which agreement among them
might be found? The debates and votes of 1911 partially answer that
question. In the Reichstag, both Centrists and National Liberals opposed the extension of pensions to those between sixty-five and seventy
years of age while Progressives and Social Democrats supported it. The
Centre was not opposed in principle to the expenditure; it merely ranked
child care as the higher priority. Even the National Liberals were not
totally opposed to an extension of social insurance. Their negative votes
in the third reading were prompted by the objections of the Centralverband and the concomitant consideration of party unity. The stated
argument against the extension was cost, and insofar as the tax reform
of 1913 later diminished reliance on indirect taxes, so onerous to the
National Liberals, and contributed a solution to the problem of financing, the objections to increased costs might ultimately have ceased. In
1913 National Liberal industrialists further opposed the introduction of
unemployment insurance by arguing that its cost would decrease
German industry's effectiveness in international competition. Yet
Bassermann, as a member of the Society for Social Reform, strongly
protested the government's rejection of new social legislation. His
stance represented the national party's leadership and the more leftist
orientation of the Reichstag Fraktion. It is possible that once the
economic recession of 1913–14 had waned and prosperity returned, the
fears of the industrialists might have diminished, and the leadership
could have won the support of the party for increased social insurance.

The National Liberals had, after all, supported social insurance for three decades; its extension could have been viewed as merely another stone in the structure of the already existing paternalistic insurance programs. Had National Liberal support for social insurance been achieved, it could have brought the Grand Bloc parties closer together and contributed to the achievement of permanent cooperation.

Before a total rapprochement in social issues could occur, however, one additional problem had to be solved: the official recognition of trade unions in governmental and quasi-governmental agencies. This issue was a major point of division between the National Liberals and the other Grand Bloc parties. As the debates of 1911 revealed, the National Liberals in their majority resisted the social and economic equality implied in such official acceptance. Recognition of organized labor was a change that could directly affect profits, management techniques, and the mental sets of businessmen. Even those National Liberals who sought reform in other areas were equivocal about union recognition. Nevertheless, National Liberals were not completely antiunion any more than they were totally opposed to an extension of social insurance. Attitudes within the party and even within the Centralverband ranged from the rabid antiunionists, usually the heavy industrialists, to those willing to entertain some accommodation with trade unions. The presence of a potential prounion group within the party made possible some future agreement between National Liberals and the other parties of the Grand Bloc. If National Liberal business interests could have been convinced that some larger goal—political stability or national security —required it, compromise could have occurred. The experience of the war years demonstrated this premise clearly. In 1916, the National Liberals did ally with the other Grand Bloc parties, against the wishes of the government and their own right wing, to achieve the "triumph of labor" in the *Hilfdienstgesetz*. Most of the demands of the Social Democrats were written into law. Unions became equal participants in socioeconomic affairs; workers' committees were established in factories; arbitration was instituted for industrial disputes. This victory did not occur without Social Democratic concessions: they agreed to limit labor's mobility at a time when it was extremely advantageous for workers to pursue higher wages by changing jobs. Moreover it was significant that the Reichstag was responsible for the passage of this law. In contrast to the Prussian Landtag, the Reichstag contained a preponderance of the National Liberal left wing and liberal center who could be persuaded to ignore the strictures of the party conservatives against socioeconomic equality if a German victory depended on the recognition of union interests. Certainly, General Groener's insistence, as chief of the war office, on the need for unqualified union cooperation in increasing the production of war matériel convinced the National Liberals to support labor's triumph.[6] Thus the achievement of union recognition was due primarily to a concern for the larger goal of national security. In the vote on the Hilfdienstgesetz, Naumann's principles were most perfectly realized. To make Germany strong, National Liberals could espouse equality, and Social Democrats could support the state. Together they could gain the support of the monarchy for democracy.

In any "normal" peacetime situation, the Social Democratic trade unions could not have expected to gain equality so easily nor could they have depended on an alliance with the army. It is more likely that some pressure, similar to the demonstrations and other tactics employed in the suffrage fight, might have been necessary. Already before the war, the industrial strike was a powerful weapon capable of a massive use in behalf of union recognition, but its efficacy depended on careful timing and orchestration in order to avoid wholesale lockouts and intervention by the army. In the absence of such countermeasures, it is doubtful that such a concentrated attack in peacetime could have forced the National Liberals to compromise. Because union recognition involved the objectionable increment of socioeconomic equality, it could probably not have occurred before the suffrage issue had been settled. A more liberal suffrage would probably have decreased the numbers of right-wing National Liberals in the Prussian Landtag and deprived that group of important power. After a diminution of right-wing strength, the National Liberals might have been less concerned about threats to party unity and more inclined to seek a rapprochement with Social Democracy. Rapprochement could have included the recognition of trade unions. Because the suffrage was closely related to the social question, it was probably wise for the Social Democrats to reserve their semiviolent tactics for the suffrage battle. In this matter, they could count on a community of interest among the Grand Bloc parties in the

6. Gerald Feldman, *Army, Industry and Labor in Germany, 1914–1918* (Princeton, 1966), pp. 197ff.

Reichstag and on the support which could have led to significant reform.

Because the parliamentarization of Germany depended on Prussian suffrage reform, it was the primary problem for the Grand Bloc. Not until reform had created a degree of consistency between representation in the Reichstag and representation in the Landtag, could it have been possible to cease reliance on conservative Prussian bureaucrats and ministers who helped to determine policy in the Reich and who exerted a powerful brake on the forces of reform and parliamentarization. Yet the reform of the Prussian suffrage was particularly difficult, not only because the Conservatives in the Landtag desperately resisted democracy, but because many Prussian Centrists and National Liberals, on whose votes reform depended, also opposed it despite mounting pressure from their non-Prussian colleagues. For the Grand Bloc, the attitudes of the Prussians posed a double problem. Because the Prussian suffrage was important for the future development of Germany, the non-Prussian parties had to agree on a viable reform. Yet once the majority of non-Prussians concurred, they could not assure acceptance by their Prussian counterparts since the latter jealously guarded the Landtag's independence from the "democratic" Reichstag. Accordingly, if the Grand Bloc were to succeed in reforming the suffrage, both Centrists and National Liberals in Prussia would have to be convinced of its necessity. Moreover, a majority for reform required the votes of *all* Centrists and National Liberals. Serious division within the Fraktionen could not exist. At the same time, any change had to be acceptable to the Social Democrats. These stringent conditions made reform seem almost impossible.

Yet the events of 1910, the last significant prewar attempt at reform, provided a clue to the possible solution of the problem. Three years before, the liberals in Prussia and in the Reichstag had insisted on an alteration of the Prussian suffrage as a quid pro quo for their participation in the Bülow Bloc. The government, itself perceiving the need for reform, finally responded by introducing a bill. Despite this reponse, spokesmen for both liberal parties in the Landtag opposed the government's bill because it was insufficiently "democratic." In committee and in plenum, they made additional, concrete proposals for liberalizing the three-class suffrage. When the rest of the Landtag rejected their suggestions, they retaliated by voting en bloc against the bill. In this instance, at least, the National Liberals proved they could muster the discipline necessary to combat the Conservatives. Their action evoked an important response from the Social Democrats. Although the liberal position fell far short of their total democratic demands, the Social Democrats surprisingly hinted their willingness to accept it. This seeming capitulation to the liberals could occur, however, only if certain terms were met. In expressing their desire to cooperate, the Social Democrats openly advocated that the "left" or Grand Bloc, and not the right, construct the final version of reform. Like their colleagues in Baden, the Social Democrats in Prussia were as eager to influence as to achieve reform, and for this reason they could accept a less than equal suffrage. In 1910, of course, the Social Democrats did not influence reform; there was no "majority of the left"; there was not even a "majority of the middle." Instead the Centre allied with the Conservatives to produce a bill that dissatisfied liberals as well as Social Democrats. The government withdrew the measure for lack of adequate support, and there was no further attempt at significant reform until the crisis of World War I demanded it. If the war and its effects had not occurred however, the failure of 1910 could not be viewed as the final act in the peacetime drama of reform. The problem would have continued to exist, and the Grand Bloc would have been the only group capable of achieving its solution.

In any evolutionary process, several rehearsals for the decisive act usually occur. Lines are changed, players rearranged, cues clarified. In 1910, liberal and Social Democratic positions converged. For the future remained the task, as the Social Democrats noted, of solidifying the National Liberal stance in order to attract the votes of the Centre. Neither conservative National Liberals nor conservative Centrists could countenance a totally democratic suffrage at any time between 1910 and 1918.[7] Yet the Social Democratic willingness to accept less might have conciliated both parties sufficiently to encourage them to support some other significant reform. Two years before, the Prussian National Liberals had endorsed a plural suffrage which, if passed, would have demolished the three-class suffrage and paved the way for further progress. As for the Centre, that party had long espoused an equal

7. For the story of Prussian suffrage reform during the war, Reinhard Patemann, *Der Kampf um die preussische Wahlreform im ersten Weltkrieg* (Düsseldorf, 1964); and Hartwig Thieme, *Nationaler Liberalismus in der Krise: Die nationalliberale Fraktion des preussischen Abgeordnetenhauses, 1914–1918* (Boppard / Rhine, 1963), pp. 106ff.

suffrage in principle and was inhibited in its cooperation with the "left" not only by its right wing, but also by its desire, similar to that of the Social Democrats themselves, to exercise parliamentary influence. In 1910, the intention of regaining the influence lost during the period of the Bülow Bloc certainly played a role in the Centre's compromise with the Conservatives. In order to woo the Centre away from the Conservatives, it would have to be assured of the maintenance of its power under any reform. At the same time, a similar assurance to the National Liberals could have encouraged their continued support. During the deliberations on the Alsatian constitution, the Social Democrats had promised to aid the National Liberals in a local Grand Bloc in return for the latter's agreement to the equal suffrage. It is conceivable that a Prussian variant of Social Democracy's tactic in Alsace-Lorraine, whereby both Centre and National Liberals were guaranteed support, could have led both to participate in a Grand Bloc dedicated to reform. This alignment would not have occurred immediately. Most probably, it would have been preceded by election agreements and tentative parliamentary alliances similar to those in other states and in the Reich. The limited cooperation between Progressives and Social Democrats in the Prussian elections of 1913 was already a step in this direction. Had this tentative arrangement developed into a Prussian Grand Bloc, as it had in other states and in the Reichstag, the final breakthrough to reform could have occurred.

In providing the thrust toward reform, the Prussian parties would not have been thrown back upon themselves. The interest of the Reichstag parties in changing the suffrage was itself a source of pressure on the Landtag. In 1910, Bassermann, though not a Prussian, had interfered in Prussian affairs by insisting on a National Liberal vote against the truncated bill created by the Prussian Herrenhaus. Unintentionally, he heralded a possible future solution to the German problem. In the absence of decisive action by the Landtag, the Reichstag itself would eventually have to initiate reform. During the war, the national parliament actually took this step. At the beginning of 1917, the Reichstag's constitutional committee, established through a concerted action of the Grand Bloc, explicitly supported the equal suffrage for Prussia as a corollary to its demands for parliamentarization. In the crisis engendered by growing discontent with wartime hardships and hopes occasioned by the first Russian Revolution, the leaders of the Grand Bloc

were convinced that only reform would preserve the integrity of the
state and the monarchy. This pressure from a wide Reichstag majority
then convinced Bethmann Hollweg, on the eve of his resignation, to
wring from the kaiser the promise to introduce a bill for the equal
suffrage into Prussia.[8] Although the wartime crisis enabled the chancellor to extract this commitment from the kaiser, it is possible that events
in more "normal" times would have led to the same conclusion.
Elites and governments in other countries have usually responded to
requests for reform only when they were accompanied by force or the
threat of force and/or when the governmental leadership has insisted
that such reform was necessary for the preservation of the state. The
history of Prussia was not so very different. Prussia's constitution and her
universal, though unequal, suffrage had been created only because the
revolution of 1848 had convinced the king and his advisers that political stability required it. When the equal, universal suffrage was established for the Reich at the time of German unification, Bismarck argued
that it was essential to strengthen the new state from within. He thereby
demonstrated that governments at peace, as well as at war, desire to
maintain stability through moral, as well as armed, authority. It is
therefore possible that an escalation of Social Democratic and liberal
agitation—suffrage demonstrations, legislative resolutions, threats to
cease cooperation in the Reichstag—could have created sufficient instability to induce the passage of reform. Before the war, there was no
evidence that the Social Democrats intended to cease their agitation on
behalf of the suffrage; even the party reformists believed in carrying the
fight for reform into the streets of Berlin and other cities. After 1910,
when the liberals participated in demonstrations, the Social Democrats
knew they could count on increasing liberal support. Given the southern
Centre's previous battle for the equal suffrage and the community of
interest between Social Democratic and Centrist labor, it was not
unreasonable for the Social Democrats to have expected the Centre
eventually to join in the general agitation. According to the Social
Democrats' own utterances, a reform that resulted from this peacetime
agitation could have been more limited than the equal suffrage demanded during the war and could therefore have satisfied the broad spectrum

8. *Der Interfraktionelle Ausschuss,* ed. E. Matthias and R. Morsey, 2 parts (Düsseldorf,
1959), 1: xxviii; and Konrad Jarausch, *The Enigmatic Chancellor: Bethmann Hollweg and
the Hubris of Imperial Germany* (New Haven, 1973), pp. 342–347.

of interests represented by the Grand Bloc parties. After the outbreak of war with its attendant sacrifices, it was no longer feasible for the Social Democrats to accept less than the equal suffrage. The Grand Bloc parties in the Reichstag understood this problem and exerted massive pressure on their colleagues in the Landtag. Despite their urgings, the Prussian Centrists and National Liberals refused to relinquish their long-standing opposition to democracy. During the war, the positions of all sides had hardened to such an extent that even the extreme circumstance of political instability, Reichstag intervention, and the commitment of the government failed to accomplish the reform necessary for the survival of the Kaisertum.

In addition to preventing compromise among the members of the Grand Bloc, the war had another effect detrimental to the achievement of reform. Had the Grand Bloc parties, the chancellor, and the kaiser all accepted significant change in peacetime, they would still have experienced the truculence of the Prussian Conservatives and their allies in the army. After unification, Bismarck had set the precedent of using real or imagined threats to national security to thwart, rather than to further, reform. Conservatives had learned this lesson well. In the immediate prewar period, there was a demonstrable relationship between the delay of reform and increasing international tensions. So long as perceived threats to national security existed, Conservatives could use them as excuses to inhibit reform indefinitely. To the extent that the international tensions themselves were due to conservative German chauvinism, the Conservatives created the conditions for impeding reform. It was not until war broke out, however, that the Conservatives were able to ally actively with military leaders to block the evolution of the monarchy. Had the civilian government initiated reform in a time of peace, the army would certainly have provided a stumbling block, but it is hard to imagine that it would have meddled in political affairs so blatantly as it did during World War I. There is no evidence that the General Staff or the various military commanders directly interfered, as they did during the war, in the various prewar attempts to change the Prussian suffrage. Nor is there any evidence that military leaders conspired, as in 1917, to remove the chancellor for his domestic and foreign policy decisions. During the Zabern Affair, the military defended its actions and sought to influence the kaiser, but it did not try to overthrow Bethmann Hollweg for his efforts to avoid a

similar future occurrence. At all times before the war, the kaiser's
authority in military, as well as in civilian matters, remained intact and
inhibited the army from clashing openly with the civilian government.
Only the war, which increased the reliance on the military both at home
and abroad, enabled the army, through the Supreme Command, to
usurp the authority of the kaiser in both military and civilian affairs
and impede both suffrage reform and parliamentarization. Moreover,
in the absence of war, it is difficult to imagine a constitutional crisis so
severe as to facilitate the army's counterrevolutionary role. In 1917, the
separate problems of internal reform and national defense became so
intimately related that the army possessed an "unnatural" power in
domestic matters. During July of that year, the army was able to
exploit the popular demands for an unqualified victory to topple Bethmann Hollweg's government and defeat his plans for peace and reform.
Later, when Bethmann Hollweg's successors wanted to use the threat of
the Landtag's dissolution to force a positive vote on suffrage reform,
the Supreme Command protested on the grounds of the disruption of
the war effort and the unfairness to the men at the front.[9] Through its
own extravagant claims, the Supreme Command fostered the conviction among Prussian Conservatives and their allies that if only reform
could be put off until victory was won, it would no longer be necessary.
Prior to World War I, the German military had certainly exercised
political influence, but the war and the possibility of territorial expansion permitted it to acquire almost unlimited power in civilian
affairs and to inhibit reform indefinitely. Ironically the war evoked not
only increased demands for reform but also the means by which those
demands were fought.

After the war, Bethmann Hollweg wrote that in 1917, he had not
"refused the establishment of a parliamentary majority;" rather it had
"refused" him.[10] By implication, he was referring to the famous meeting,
arranged by the Supreme Command in July, between the crown prince
and the parliamentary leaders, where the latter professed their lack of
confidence in the chancellor. That meeting included the leaders of the
Reichstag Grand Bloc. Just days before, the Grand Bloc had organized

9. For specific references, see Patemann, *Der Kampf,* and Thieme, *Nationaler Liberalismus;* also *Militär und Innenpolitik im Weltkrieg, 1914–1918,* 2 parts (Düsseldorf, 1970),
pt. 2.
10. Quoted in Jarausch, *Enigmatic Chancellor,* p. 379.

itself into an Interparty Caucus (*Interfraktioneller Ausschuss*) designed
to function as a majority to achieve reform and a negotiated peace.
Bethmann Hollweg had indicated his willingness to cooperate with
that majority. Why did it then desert him? Why did it allow itself to be
manipulated by the Supreme Command against a chancellor who would
institute the domestic changes explicitly requested for over a decade?
The explanation can be found by examining the conflicts among the
Grand Bloc members over the "national question." For more than six
months, the National Liberals, together with the Conservatives, had
contributed to the crisis of confidence in the government by fulmi-
nating against Bethmann Hollweg's lack of imperialistic fervor in the
prosecution of the war. The National Liberals seized upon the events of
July 1917 as a means of achieving their own ends in foreign policy and
led the others to express that lack of confidence in the chancellor which
ultimately persuaded the kaiser to accept Bethmann Hollweg's resignation.[11] While the National Liberals were fully prepared to support
the reformist demands of the Interparty Caucus, they would not endorse
the group's demands for a negotiated peace. Although they originally
cooperated with the Interparty Caucus, they notified it a few days
after Bethmann Hollweg's resignation that they would no longer
participate because of the wording of the Peace Resolution. By achieving Bethmann Hollweg's removal from office and by withdrawing from
the Caucus for nationalistic reasons, they destroyed the unity of the
Grand Bloc, the hope for meaningful cooperation between government
and parliamentary majority, and the hope for a reform of the Kaiserreich.

The nationalism of the National Liberals during the decisive crisis of
the monarchy explains why a permanent Grand Bloc, and hence an
evolution toward parliamentary democracy, was almost impossible in
peace or in war. While the parties could accommodate one another on
matters of social legislation and Prussian suffrage reform, there was
little prospect for unity on the "national question." Any parliamentary
coalition must agree on foreign policy; it must also establish control

11. A comparison of the accounts given in Klaus Epstein, *Matthias Erzberger and the
Dilemma of German Democracy* (Princeton, 1959), pp. 195ff.; and John Williamson, *Karl
Helfferich, 1872–1924: Economist, Financier, Politician* (Princeton, 1971), p. 227, clearly
demonstrates that the National Liberals played the crucial role among the parties in achieving Bethmann Hollweg's downfall.

over the army. If the Grand Bloc were to obtain the ultimate goal of parliamentary power, a common approach to both was necessary. Yet it was unlikely that such community could develop until the extreme nationalism of the National Liberals had abated. As evidenced during the Moroccan crisis, they could not formulate a unified approach to foreign policy because they could not temper their expansionist demands to conform to the more moderate stance of the other Grand Bloc parties. In the Zabern Affair, the Grand Bloc's initial vote of no-confidence at least encouraged Bethmann Hollweg's attempt to restrain the military. At the same time, the Grand Bloc missed the opportunity to establish civilian control of the army, a necessary step toward a parliamentary regime, because the National Liberals declined to support firm civilian authority. Later, as the Grand Bloc groped toward a bona fide parliamentary regime in the crisis of 1917, the disagreement over foreign policy and the subsequent lack of control over the military's annexationist policies scuttled effective action.

Despite its occurrence during an "abnormal" period of war, the crisis of 1917, by forcing the prewar positions of the Grand Bloc parties to their logical extremes, illuminates the difficulty of ultimately forming a permanent Grand Bloc capable of instituting a parliamentary regime. Bethmann Hollweg essentially agreed both with the reform proposals and the moderate foreign policy of the Peace Resolution majority. As he divined, support for his policies by a parliamentary majority and the resulting cooperation between the government and the Reichstag could have provided the transitional cooperation necessary for a successful evolution toward a parliamentary regime. Yet, contrary to the chancellor's assumptions, that majority had to include the National Liberals. Without them, no chancellor possessed a base popular and prestigious enough from which successfully to oppose both Prussian Conservatives and the German military. In the crisis of 1917, the National Liberals deprived the Reichstag majority and the chancellor of their vital support because they disagreed with the latter's stance on the "national question." Thereafter, they periodically returned to the Interparty Caucus to work for domestic reform, but they steered an independent course whenever the other Grand Bloc parties resumed the basic foreign policies of the Peace Resolution. By failing to renounce their extreme nationalism in the interests of compromise with the other three parties, the National Liberals defeated the Grand Bloc from

within its own ranks and thereby destroyed the hopes for an evolution
of the monarchy. The crisis of 1917, by reflecting certain basic prewar
trends, therefore provides an accurate insight into the fate of the
Grand Bloc had war not occurred. Disagreement between the National
Liberals and the other parties on the "national question" would have
indefinitely prevented the formation of a permanent "coalition" capable
of achieving a breakthrough to parliamentary democracy.

The disastrous defection from the Grand Bloc by the National
Liberals because of their stance on the "national question" cannot be
viewed in isolation from the issues of social legislation and suffrage
reform. Ironically, it was the approaching Grand Bloc compromise on
political and social reform that contributed to the disagreement over the
"national question." As reform seriously threatened the political and
economic interests of the Prussian heavy industrialists, they stridently
demanded attention to their needs. They represented the flaw in Naumann's scheme. He had believed that the "industrial aristocracy"
could espouse democracy in the interests of a strong, industrialized
Germany. Instead, the industrialists succumbed to the same defensive
hysteria as the agrarian Conservatives. Their continual complaints
against the reformist trend and their participation in the reactionary
Kartell harassed the National Liberal leadership and strained the
party's unity. In order to paper over the party's internal differences, the
leaders carried one of Naumann's axioms to the extreme. They increasingly stressed the party's "national mission." Although they never
capitulated to the right wing's antidemocratic demands, they com-
pensated by appealing to the right-wing enthusiasm for aggressive
imperialism and war. Since the nationalistic, imperialistic motif had a
party-wide appeal, this tactic guaranteed party unity. The Young
Liberals were fervent imperialists as well as democrats. The Hansabund,
the most reliable support of the moderate liberal center, desired an
aggressive foreign policy in order to strengthen Germany's position in
the international marketplace.[12] The majority of National Liberals
thus favored expansion as well as reform, and the need to placate the
reactionary right wing increased the imperialistic current.

It is possible that had suffrage reform and improved social legislation
been achieved before war broke out, the "national question" would no

12. Fritz Fischer, *Krieg der Illusionen: Die deutsche Politik vom 1911 bis 1914* (Düsseldorf,
1969), p. 649.

longer have loomed as a barrier to a permanent cooperation among all parties of the Grand Bloc. The achievement of domestic reform under the aegis of the monarchy might have alleviated the worst resentments of the National Liberal right wing against democracy and lessened the need of the leadership to stress the party's "national mission." This change could have facilitated the formation of a permanent Grand Bloc. Already before the war, there was more agreement on the "national question" between National Liberals on the one hand and Centrists and Progressives on the other hand than between National Liberals and Social Democrats. This greater agreement was due as much to their ability to compromise over domestic issues as to the espousal of nationalism by both Centre and Progressives. As awareness of the Social Democrats' national loyalty and pride grew within the National Liberal party, it might have been possible for the leadership to persuade the right wing to espouse reforms gradually. Conciliation between National Liberals and Social Democrats over social legislation and suffrage reform could in turn have furthered rapprochement on the "national question." This rapprochement would almost certainly have involved a moderation of National Liberal nationalistic fervor to provide more consonance with the views of the other parties. As accord on the "national question" developed among the Grand Bloc parties, they could have devised a strategy successful for gaining control over foreign policy and the military. Yet this process of accommodation and adjustment would have required both time and "normalcy." Economic depression and/or war could only have exacerbated existing conflicts and prevented cooperation. After the beginning of World War I, the strains of the war effort increased the demands of the reformists and intensified the reaction of the expansionists. These diverging positions prevented conciliatory postures, hindered the operation of the Grand Bloc, and destroyed the possibility of peaceful evolution.

Because of this relationship between World War I and the failure of the Grand Bloc, the causes of the war are particularly important. Paradoxically, the failure itself might have been one factor contributing to the outbreak of war. Recent scholars have argued that the National Liberals' extreme nationalism, combined with that of the Conservatives, pressured the government into the aggressive foreign policy and the "calculated risk" that precipitated war. Had the National Liberals been able or willing to compromise with the other parties of the Grand Bloc on the "national question," the diminution of their chauvinistic attacks on the government might have led it to adopt a more cautious tack in the crisis of July 1914, and to have avoided the war itself.[13] Thus, the inability of the National Liberals to join in the formation of a permanent Grand Bloc, espousing a moderate foreign policy, contributed to the disaster which befell the Germans in 1918. This failure also proves the soundness of Naumann's prediction. Parliamentary democracy was truly necessary for the maintenance of German power in the twentieth century. Its absence led to war, humiliating defeat, and revolution. As the prime obstacles to democratic unity, the National Liberals must shoulder the responsibility for this destruction. It is a sober irony of German history that their nationalism, so instrumental in the creation of the Kaiserreich, also contributed to its collapse.

13. For a summary and analysis of the massive literature on the outbreak of war, see Konrad Jarausch, "World Power or Tragic Fate? The *Kriegsschuldfrage* as Historical Neurosis," *Central European History* 5 (1972) : 72–92. Recently, Wolfgang J. Mommsen, "Domestic Factors in German Foreign Policy before 1914," *Central European History* 6 (1973) : 3–43, has explored the pressures placed on Bethmann Hollweg's government by conservative forces and has reached a conclusion similar, though not identical, to that of the author's.

Appendix 1

Annual Congresses of the Social Democratic Party

1903	September 13–20 Dresden
1904	September 18–24 Bremen
1905	September 17–23 Jena
1906	September 23–29 Mannheim
1907	September 15–21 Essen
1908	September 13–19 Nuremberg
1909	September 12–18 Leipzig
1910	September 18–24 Magdeburg
1911	September 10–16 Jena
1912	September 15–21 Chemnitz
1913	September 14–20 Jena

Appendix 2

Congresses of the National Liberal Party

1902	October 10–13	Eisenach (no. 6)
1903	May 3	Berlin (no. 7)
1905	May 19–21	Dresden (no. 8)
1906	October 5–6	Goslar (no. 9)
1907	October 5–6	Wiesbaden (no. 10)
1909	July 3–4	Berlin (no. 11)
1910	October 1–2	Kassel (no. 12)
1911	November 1	Berlin (no. 13)
1912	May 12	Berlin (no. 14)

Appendix 3

Congresses of the Left Liberal Parties

Freisinnige Vereinigung

1905	February 11–12	Berlin (General Meeting)
1906	February 17–18	Berlin (no. 1)
1907	April 6–7	Berlin (no. 2)
1908	April 21–22	Frankfurt/Main (no. 3)
1909	July 3–4	Berlin (no. 4)
1910	March 5	Berlin (no. 5)

Freisinnige Volkspartei

1902	September 27–29	Hamburg (no. 5)
1905	September 23–25	Wiesbaden (no. 6)
1907	September 12–16	Berlin (no. 7)

Fortschrittliche Volkspartei

1910	March 6	Berlin (no. 1)
1912	October 5–7	Mannheim (no. 2)

Bibliographical Essay

This bibliography, especially where secondary materials are concerned, makes no claim to comprehensiveness. The author has cited those books which were most helpful for specific or background information. At appropriate places, she has indicated sources of additional bibliography. The footnotes of the text also provide a guide to helpful articles and books.

ARCHIVAL AND BIBLIOGRAPHICAL GUIDES

The two basic guides to unpublished sources in German history and politics list the holdings (as of the date of publication) in the central archives in East and West Germany. For East Germany, the initial catalogue is the *Uebersicht über die Bestände des deutschen Zentralarchivs Potsdam* ([East] Berlin, 1957). In addition, an updated and thorough introduction to all the East German archives, some of which will be helpful for future municipal and regional party histories, has been prepared by Gordon R. Mork, "The Archives of the German Democratic Republic," *Central European History* 2 (1969): pp. 273–284. For West Germany, the standard work is *Das Bundesarchiv und seine Bestände,* ed. F. Facius et al. (Boppard/Rhine, 1961). A recently published guide to private papers lodged in German archives and libraries is *Verzeichnis der schriftlichen Nachlässe in deutschen Archiven und Bibliotheken,* vol. 1, part 1: *Einleitung und Verzeichnis: Die Nachlässe in der deutschen-Archiven (mit Ergänzung aus anderen Bestände),* ed. W. A. Mommsen (Boppard/Rhine, 1971). Until the second part of this guide appears, researchers can refer to the director of the *Bundesarchiv* in Kolbenz, who maintains a file of the location of private papers available in libraries and in private collections. Additional materials concerning the relationships of the parties to the German Foreign Office can be found in a *Catalogue of Files and Microfilms of the German Foreign Ministry Archives, 1867–1920* (1959).

An excellent introduction to party newspapers, pamphlets, and histories is Thomas Nipperdey, *Die Organisation der deutschen Parteien vor 1918* (Düsseldorf, 1961). Nipperdey's book contains the most thorough list of party newspapers in print. The location of these papers in Germany and Europe may be ascertained by writing to the newspaper service at the Staatsbibliothek in Bremen. Other newspapers and pamphlets came to light through an arduous search in Kayser's *Deutsches Bücherverzeichnis* for the years 1900 to 1914. The best guide to recent secondary materials is James J. Sheehan, "Germany, 1890–1918: A Survey of Recent Research," *Central European History* I (1968) : 345–372.

Much more research could be devoted to the history of and the relationships among the parties on the local level. For Baden, most of the printed sources utilized by this author were found in Friedrich Lautenschlager, *Bibliographie der badischen Geschichte,* 2 pts. (Karlsruhe, 1929–30 and 1933–38). For party history in Württemberg, Wilhelm Heyd, *Bibliographie der württembergische Geschichte* (Stuttgart, 1895–1929) is a multi-volume and lucrative guide. Anyone beginning a study of political parties in Hamburg should consult Kurt Detlev Mollor and A. Tecke, eds., *Bücherkunde zur hamburgischen Geschichte* (Hamburg, 1939). More studies of the parties in Saxony would not only increase our knowledge of this important German state but would also deepen our insight into political and socioeconomic relationships for all of Germany. Rudolf Bermman, *Bibliographie der sächsischen Geschichte,* 5 pts. (Leipzig, 1918–32) gives a detailed list of sources. Unfortunately, many of them are unavailable in West German libraries.

Archival Materials

One of the most important German archives, the Deutsche Zentralarchiv Potsdam houses a great many valuable materials. The Akten des Reichsministerium des Innern und der Reichskanzlei are important for understanding the relationship between the parties and the government during the crucial periods of elections and election campaigns. The Akten der fortschrittlichen Volkspartei are necessary for anyone writing a history of the Left Liberals; these documents contain much material from the secretariats of the two Freisinnige parties as well as material from the secretariat of the Progressive People's Party formed in 1910. In addition to these governmental and party documents, there are many useful collections of private papers. The most valuable collections for this particular history were those belonging to Bogdan, Graf von

Hutten-Czapski, the self-appointed liaison between the government and the National Liberals after 1909, and the papers of Wolfgang Heine, Ernst Bassermann, and Friedrich Naumann. The two latter sets of papers are not complete and must be supplemented with other materials found in West Germany. The papers of the Left Liberals Theodor Barth and Max Broemel and of the Social Democrats Wilhelm Blos, Edmund Fisher, Konrad Haenisch, Karl Legien, Karl Liebknecht, and Paul Löbe were of lesser value but useful for illuminating some limited aspects of party history.

Another source of productive materials is the Bundesarchiv Koblenz. The Akten der nationalliberalen Partei are important both for the actions of the National Liberal Fraktion in the Reichstag and for a partial record of the developing split within the party. A remnant of the Bassermann papers designated as Kleiner Erwerb 303/17 and some notes on the praesidium elections, probably made by Bassermann, contained in Kleiner Erwerb 303/10 supplement the documents pertaining to the National Liberals. Also helpful were the papers of Bernhard, Prince von Bülow. Two other sources for the history of the National Liberals are the papers of August Weber, Kleiner Erwerb 384, and Robert Friedberg, Kleiner Erwerb 303/9. Letters and materials pertaining to the history of the Left Liberals can be found in the papers of Lujo Brentano, Georg Gothein, and Friedrich von Payer. The diaries of Albert Südekum illuminate the attitudes of reformist Social Democrats just prior to 1914. The Zeitgeschichtliche Sammlung 103 contains the *Mitteilungen für die Vertrauensmänner der freisinnigen Volkspartei* (1909) and the *Mitteilungen für die Vertrauensmänner der fortschrittlichen Volkspartei* (1910–14), as well as pamphlets and valuable newspaper clippings relating to the history of all the parties.

Two archives exclusively devoted to Social Democratic papers and other materials are particularly important for historians of the party. The Archiv der Sozialdemokratischen Partei Deutschlands in Bonn lodges the Molkenbuhr papers, and anyone wishing to understand the Social Democratic executive committee in the period before the war should consult the mixture of objective political consideration and Social Democratic homily exhibited in Molkenbuhr's diaries. The party archives also contain the papers of the trade unionist Carl Severing consisting mostly of newspaper clippings, and the papers of Wilhelm Dittmann and Alfred Henke. The latter papers did not contain much that was helpful to me, but they may be valuable for someone investigating a different aspect of party history. In addition, the foresight and courage of one of its former directors have made the International Institute for Social History in Amsterdam an indispensable archive for historians of German Social Democracy. The voluminous papers of August Bebel, Eduard Bernstein, Karl Kautsky, and Georg von Vollmar were particularly pertinent to this study.

There are two lesser, but equally important, archives in South Germany. The Badische Generallandesarchiv in Karlsruhe houses the Akten der nationalliberalen Partei Badens, valuable for the party as a whole as well as for the state party. Part of the von Bodman papers are also in the archive at Karlsruhe and contain letters from Bassermann explaining his attitude to the Grand Bloc in Baden and the nation as a whole. The Staatshauptarchiv in Stuttgart contains the papers of Conrad Haussmann, which are valuable chiefly for the light they shed on the relationships between Left Liberals and Social Democrats in 1909. In North Germany, the Geheime Staatsarchiv in Berlin-Dahlem holds the papers of Eugen Schiffer, which this author found to be of limited value. The records of the Berlin City Council, valuable for any local history, are also in the archives in Dahlem.

Last, but not least, anyone writing about the National Liberals must consult the Stresemann papers. The papers themselves are in the Politische Abteilung of the Auswärtiges Amt in Bonn, but this author used the microfilm owned by the archive at Koblenz. The film is also available at the National Archives in Washington, D.C. Anyone desiring to use specific portions of the film will find a useful guide in Hans W. Gatzke, "The Stresemann Papers," *The Journal of Modern History* 26 (1954): 49–59.

STENOGRAPHIC REPORTS

The *Stenographische Berichte über die Verhandlungen des deutschen Reichstages* contain the debates and the committee reports so important for determining the relative stands of the parties on important national issues. For Prussia, the relevant materials are the *Stenographische Berichte über die Verhandlungen des preussischen Hauses der Abgeordneten*. In Baden, the *Verhandlungen der zweiten Kammer der Stände-Versammlung des Grossherzogtums Baden* report only the bills introduced by the government, the various motions made by the parties, and the decisions finally taken. For the protocols of the Baden legislature, one must consult the *Amtliche Berichte über die Verhandlungen der badischen Ständeversammlung, Beilagen zu der Karlsruher Zeitung*.

The debates of the party congresses are necessary, not only for tracing the various party conflicts, but also for determining the political attitudes of the parties. For the National Liberals, the student should consult the *Allgemeine Delegiertentage (Vertretertage) der nationalliberalen Partei* (Berlin, 1905–12) and the *Preussische Vertretertage der nationalliberalen Partei* (Berlin: 1908, 1913). A new and important source for the proceedings of the party's central committee is *Von Bassermann zu Stresemann: Die Sitzungen des nationalliberalen Zentralvorstandes, 1912–1917,* ed. Klaus-Peter Reiss (Düsseldorf, 1967).

For the Left Liberals, the relevant materials are the protocols of the *Parteitage der freisinnigen Volkspartei* (Berlin, 1905, 1907), which this author found in printed form at the archives of the Federal Republic in Koblenz. The debates of the party congresses of the Freisinnige Vereinigung are recorded in the *Delegiertentage des Wahlvereins der Liberalen* (Berlin, 1906–10). After the Left Liberals merged in 1910, there were two congresses held: *Parteitage der fortschrittlichen Volkspartei* (Berlin, 1910, 1912).

This writer also used the voluminous *Protokolle über die Verhandlungen des Parteitages der sozialdemokratischen Partei Deutschlands* (Berlin, 1903–1913), which, like the party newspapers and periodicals, will continue to yield information on many varied aspects of party history. The party in Württemberg also published thorough reports in the *Berichte des Landesvorstandes, der Landtagsfraktion und Protokoll der Landesversammlung* (Stuttgart, 1907–1914), which illuminate the position of the reformists within the party and the growing split between reformists and radicals. One source that gives a great deal of insight into the actions of the party in the Reichstag is *Die Reichstagsfraktion der deutschen Sozialdemokratie, 1898 bis 1918,* eds. Erich Matthias und Eberhard Pikart, 2 pts. (Düsseldorf, 1966). By exposing the tactics of the Reichstag Fraktion, this source indicates, perhaps better than any other, the growing inclination of the Social Democrats to cooperate both with the government and the liberals.

PERIODICALS

Two sources of a general nature that apply to all the parties are

Heinrich Schulthess, ed., *Europäischer Geschichtskalender* (Nördlingen, 1900–1914) and *Die Parteien, Urkunden und Bibliographie der Partei-kunde,* vol. 1, *Beihefte zur Zeitschrift für Politik* (Berlin, 1912–13). The latter contains quotes relating to the issues of the day from important party newspapers and is particularly helpful for the period from the Moroccan crisis of 1911 to the tax reform of 1913.

The historian of the German liberal parties is particularly dependent on periodical materials. The *National Zeitung* would be an important source for the National Liberals, but since it is available only at the British Museum, this author did not make use of it. Instead, the moderate *Kölnische Zeitung* proved to be a valuable substitute, particularly since it made a habit of constantly reviewing events and crises within the party. For a long time, the organ of the right-wing National Liberals was the *Rheinisch-Westfälische Zeitung*. This was supplemented in May 1912 by the *Altnationalliberale Reichskorrespondenz*, which I found in the Stresemann papers. Another National Liberal magazine with a conservative cast was the *Elbwart: Nationalliberale Halbmonatschrift* (Hamburg, 1910–1914). A counterweight to these conservative organs was the *Hannoversche Courier*, which was generally seen as an organ of the left wing of the party. The Young Liberal organ was a weekly, the *National-liberale Jugend* (Cologne, 1901–1914), which, because of its bias, must be used in conjunction with some other periodical when dealing with the affairs of the party as a whole. Spanning the distance between the National Liberals and the Left Liberals was a southern weekly, *Fort-schritt: Liberales Wochenblatt* (Munich, 1906–14), which was originally the organ of the Bavarian Young Liberals dedicated to the cause of liberal unity. When the Bavarian Young Liberals merged with the Progressives in 1910, the magazine became the Bavarian Left Liberal organ. Because of its orientation, the weekly was particularly helpful in following the ins and outs of liberal unity. The most valuable weekly for this purpose, however, was Friedrich Naumann's *Hilfe*. Naumann's periodical both molded and reflected the attitudes of the Left Liberals, and particularly the Freisinnige Vereinigung, toward the important issues of the day. Two other newspapers helpful for Left Liberal attitudes and actions were the *Frankfurter Zeitung* and the *Freisinnige Zeitung*. The *Berliner Tageblatt* was not a party newspaper, but it had connections with the Left Liberals and reported their activities regularly. Naturally, any periodical bibliography must include Theodor Barth's

Die Nation (Berlin, 1884–1908), which is especially important for the period of the nineties but is supplanted in value by *Hilfe* after 1903. The South German weekly, *März* (Munich, 1907–13) is good for supplementary information about the Left Liberals.

The periodical literature of the Social Democrats is, by this time, very familiar to the student of German politics. The official party newspaper, *Vorwärts,* and the official weekly, *Die Neue Zeit,* can be mined for information again and again. The revisionist magazine, *Sozialistische Monatshefte,* was also important for this study because it urged an alliance with the liberals. This author did not consult any of the organs of the radicals since they opposed the idea of the Grand Bloc.

PROGRAMS

The most complete compilation of German party programs is Wilhelm Mommsen, ed., *Deutsche Parteiprogramme: Eine Auswahl vom Vormärz bis zur Gegenwart* (Munich, 1952). A helpful reference to the National Liberal viewpoint on numerous issues of the period just prior to 1914 is the *Politisches Handbuch der Nationalliberalen Partei* (Berlin, 1908). An insight into the problems involved in the unification of the Progressives was provided by *Die Freisinnige Volkspartei, ihr Programm und ihre Organization* (Berlin, 1909). After Left Liberal unification the arguments used in resolving programmatical differences, as well as an explanation of the various program points, were presented, under contract from the party, in Conrad Haussmann, *Das Arbeitsprogramm der fortschrittlichen Volkspartei* (Berlin, 1911). On a different level, Wilhelm Kolb, *Die Tätigkeit der Sozialdemokratie im badischen Landtage, 1909–10 and 1911–22* (Mannheim, 1910, 1912) demonstrated the attitudes and the activities of the Badenese Socialists.

PAMPHLETS AND ESSAYS

In the years after 1900, many pamphleteers treated the subject of liberal unification and of cooperation between liberals and Social Democrats. The original systematic statement naturally was Friedrich Naumann, *Demokratie und Kaisertum: Ein Handbuch für innere Politik* (Berlin-Schöneberg, 1900). The second edition (1900) was used for this work. The book, with explanations of the subsequent editions, is also reprinted in Friedrich Naumann, *Politische Schriften,* ed. Theodor Schieder, vol. 4 in *Werke,* 4 vols. (Cologne, 1964). Five years later, the same theme occurred in Ludwig Haas, *Die Einigung des Liberalismus und der Demokratie* (Frankfurt/Main, 1905). Haas belonged to the South German Volkspartei and was a deputy to the Baden Landtag. Much more work could be done on the attempt and failure of liberal unification in the Kaiserreich. Wilhelm Kulemann, *Der Zusammenschluss der Liberalen* (Dresden, 1905) presented the most cogent argument for unification. In a different vein, but very much related to the history of the Grand Bloc, was Curt Köhler, *Die Industrie, die politischen Parteien und die moderne Sozialpolitik* (Leipzig, 1910). Köhler was a Young Liberal journalist who also wrote *Der Jungliberalismus* (Cologne, 1912), which is a good introduction to the organization, its history, and its goals. From the Social Democratic side, Wilhelm Kolb, *Die Taktik der badischen Sozialdemokratie und ihre Kritik* (Karlsruhe, 1910) is a defense of the Baden Grand Bloc. For another view of the Baden Grand Bloc, a highly entertaining and informative account is Josef Schofer, *Grossblock-Bilanz: Zeitgemässe politische Erinnerungen* (Freiburg/Breisgau, 1913). Schofer was one of the leaders of the Baden Centre party and was very much concerned with the Grand Bloc's cultural policies in *Zehn Jahre badischer Schulkämpfe,* 4th ed. (Freiburg / Breisgau, 1911).

Memoirs and Letters

For the period treated in this book, the memoirs of the two chancellors most concerned with the Grand Bloc are very important. Bernhard, Prince von Bülow, *Memoirs,* trans. G. Dunlop, 4 vols. (Boston, 1931–32), is particularly good for an insight into the attitudes of the court and the government toward the parties of the Reichstag. Theobald von Bethmann Hollweg, *Betrachtungen zum Weltkriege,* 2 vols. (Berlin, 1919–21) is valuable mostly for its portrait of the German mood before the war.

For the Social Democrats, Viktor Adler, *Briefwechsel mit August Bebel und Karl Kautsky,* ed. Friedrich Adler (Vienna, 1954) is one of the best published sets of letters because it shows three sides of the same story. Another valuable source of letters is Ludwig Frank, *Aufsätze, Reden und Briefe,* ed. Hedwig Wachenheim (Berlin, 1924). Excellent both for developments in Württemberg and in the national party is Wilhelm Keil, *Erlebnisse eines Sozialdemokraten,* 2 vols. (Stuttgart, 1947–48). For Hesse and for letters to other party leaders, Carl Ulrich.

Erinnerungen des ersten hessischen Staatspräsidenten, ed. Ludwig Bergsträsser (Offenbach / Main, 1953) is particularly valuable. For this period, Carl Severing, *Mein Lebensweg,* 2 vols. (Cologne, 1950) is very informative about trade-union activities and municipal politics in Bielefeld. Gustav Noske, *Erlebtes aus Aufstieg und Niedergang einer Demokratie* (Offenbach, 1947) vividly presents the petty infighting between reformists and radicals. Also good for the intraparty conflict is Philip Scheidemann, *Memoiren eines Sozialdemokraten* (Dresden, 1930). Of limited utility are the two works by Friedrich Stampfer, *Die ersten vierzehn Jahren der deutschen Republik* (Offenbach/Main, 1947) and *Erfahrungen und Erkenntnisse: Aufzeichnungen aus meinem Leben* (Cologne, 1957).

As the self-appointed National Liberal liaison with Bethmann Hollweg, Bogdan, Graf von Hutten-Czapski, in *Sechzig Jahre Politik und Gesellschaft,* 2 vols. (Berlin, 1936) provides valuable material for the party crisis of 1909–10. As a left-winger with "national-social" sympathies, Wilhelm Kulemann, *Erinnerungen* (Berlin, 1911), describes the dissonance within the party even before the advent of the Young Liberals. Good sources for the "mood" of the National Liberals in both north and south after 1909 are Eugen Schiffer, *Ein Leben für den Liberalismus* (Berlin-Grünewald, 1951) and Friedrich Meinecke, *Erlebtes, 1862–1919* (Stuttgart, 1964). Another description of mood, from a Baden Centrist, is Heinrich Köhler, *Lebenserinnerungen des Politikers und Staatsmannes, 1878–1949* (Stuttgart, 1964).

On the Left Liberal side, *Aus Conrad Haussmanns politischer Arbeit,* edited by his friends (Frankfurt / Main, 1923) is most informative for the South German viewpoint. Related to this work but useful exclusively for wartime interparty relationships are Haussmann's *Schlaglichter, Reichstagsbriefe und Aufzeichnungen* (Frankfurt / Main, 1924). Because of the author's attempts to bring the Left Liberals together on both a local and national level and because of his moderation toward Social Democracy, Carl Funck, *Lebenserinnerungen* (Frankfurt / Main, 1921) provides good information about spurs and impediments to liberal unity. Ernst Müller-Meiningen, *Parlamentarismus: Betrachtungen, Lehren und Erinnerungen aus deutschen Parlamenten* (Berlin, 1926) supplies little information about inter- and intraparty relationships, but his book is good for verbal portraits of political personalities.

Statistical Guides and References

For statistics relating to Reichstag elections, the most helpful works are F. Spect and P. Schwabe, *Die Reichstagswahlen von 1867–1903* (Berlin, 1904) and *Kürschners deutscher Reichstag: Biographisch-statistisches Handbuch* (Berlin, 1893–1912). The last is particularly valuable for statistics concerning individual election districts as well as for individual delegates. For Prussia, *Zeitschrift des königlichen preussischen statistischen Landesamtes,* Ergänzungshefte 23, 30, 43: *Die preussischen Landtagswahlen* (Berlin, 1905, 1909, 1916) give exhaustive materials on taxes, class-voting, and results in precinct and district elections. For Baden, a superficial guide to election results, Alfred Rapp, *Die Parteibewegung in Baden, 1905/1928* (Karlsruhe, 1929) provides information for each district.

Invaluable for work on a national and local basis are Friedrick W. von Rauchhaupt, *Handbuch der deutschen Wahlgesetze und Geschäftsordnungen* (Munich, 1916) and Felix Storck, *Handbuch der deutschen Verfassungen,* ed. F. W. von Rauchhaupt, 2nd ed. (Munich, 1913). In addition, short descriptions and explanations of political currents, terms, and organizations can be found in the *Handbuch für Politik,* ed. Paul Laband et al., 2 vols. (Berlin and Leipzig, 1912–13).

Biographies

Various biographical handbooks exist for this period. *Kürschners Deutscher Reichstag,* mentioned above, is a good source for biographical information. The *Neue Deutsche Biographie* (Berlin, 1953–), though not yet complete, contains excellent, comprehensive accounts as well as bibliographies for important political figures. Less well known, but equally helpful, the *Deutsches Biographisches Jahrbuch* (Stuttgart, 1914–) contains articles about men who died in the decade after the revolution of 1918. Unfortunately, no comprehensive index exists for the several volumes. A straight-forward guide containing the most important information is Max Schwarz, *MdR: Biographisches Handbuch der Reichstage* (Hanover, 1965). Hermann Kalkhoff, *National-liberale Parlamentarier 1867–1917 des Reichstages und der Einzellandtage* (Berlin, 1917) is invaluable for a study of the National Liberals. For Baden, Alfred Rapp, *Die badischen Landtagsabgeordneten, 1905–1929* (Karlsruhe, 1929) presents both biographical and statistical materials as well as helpful bibliography. A more recent source for the Social Democrats is Franz Osterroth, *Biographisches Lexikon des Sozialismus,* vol. 1 : *Verstorbene Persönlichkeiten* (Hanover, 1960).

There are two worthwhile biographies of Bethmann Hollweg, the chancellor who watched the birthpangs of the Grand Bloc coalition. The first is an impressionistic work that relies heavily on letters written by Bethmann to one of his closest friends and gives a private view of his attitude toward politics: Eberhard von Vietsch, *Bethmann Hollweg: Staatsmann zwischen Macht und Ethos* (Boppard / Rhine, 1969). Konrad Jarausch, *The Enigmatic Chancellor: Bethmann Hollweg and the Hubris of Imperial Germany* (New Haven, 1973) concentrates on his activities during the war but also supports the theory that he shared views similar to Naumann's, though not as democratic, even before the war. Hans-Günter Zmarzlik, *Bethmann Hollweg als Reichskanzler, 1909–1914* (Düsseldorf, 1957) is still the best introduction to his prewar direction of the government.

Three Left Liberals have left us with biographical portraits of their contemporaries. Theodor Barth, *Politische Porträts* (Berlin, 1923) was published posthumously. Richard Eickhoff, *Politische Profile: Erinnerungen aus vier Jahrzehnten* (Dresden, 1927) and Hermann Pachnicke, *Führende Männer im alten und im neuen Reich* (Berlin, 1930) describe men both in and outside the Left Liberal camp. The latter is good for internal affairs of the Freisinnige Vereinigung.

There are several good biographies of individual Social Democrats. However, there is not yet a definitive biography of Bebel. A short, concise introduction to the life of this very complex individual is Ernst Schraepler, *August Bebel* (Göttingen, 1966). Reinhard Jansen, *Georg von Vollmar* (Düsseldorf, 1958) is valuable for the development of reformism and for liberal-socialist relations in Bavaria. Another good source for reformism, particularly the activity in Bremen before 1905, is Georg Kotowski, *Friedrich Ebert,* vol. 1 : *Der Aufstieg eines deutschen Arbeiterführers* (Wiesbaden, 1963). A classic work on revisionism is, of course, Peter Gay, *The Dilemma of Democratic Socialism* (First Collier Books edition, New York, 1962). Sally Grünebaum, *Ludwig Frank: Ein Beitrag zur Entwicklung der deutschen Sozialdemokratie* (Heidelberg, 1924) is a sympathetic, relatively superficial account of his life in Baden and in the party. For the radicals, the most thorough and highly entertaining story is J. P. Nettl, *Rosa Luxemburg,* 2 vols. (Oxford, 1966).

More local in detail, but valuable nonetheless for understanding the party, is Günther Haselier, "Adolf Geck als Politiker und Mensch im Spiegel seines schriftlichen Nachlasses," *Zeitschrift für die Geschichte des Oberrheins* 115 (1967) : 331–430.

On the Left Liberal side, there is a wealth of material on Naumann. For this author, the most helpful were Theodor Heuss, *Friedrich Naumann* (Stuttgart, 1937) and Werner Conze, "Friedrich Naumann: Grundlagen und Ansatz seiner Politik in der nationalsozialen Zeit (1895 bis 1903)," *Schicksalswege deutscher Vergangenheit,* ed. W. Hubatsch (Düsseldorf, 1950), pp. 355–386. Heuss, of course, was a younger friend of Naumann's and substantially influenced in his own thinking by the older man. For Weber's influence on Naumann and Weber's illumination of the Zeitgeist and the liberal movement before 1914, Wolfgang Mommsen, *Max Weber und die deutsche Politik* (Tübingen, 1959) is indispensable. A eulogistic biography is E. Feder, *Theodor Barth und der demokratische Gedanke* (Gotha, 1919). More recent and more objective, Konstanze Wegner, *Theodor Barth und die Freisinnige Vereinigung: Studie zur Geschichte des Linksliberalismus in wilhelminsichen Deutschland 1893–1910* (Tübingen, 1968) contains valuable sociological information on both northern Left Liberal parties.

For the National Liberals, Karola Bassermann, *Ernst Bassermann: Das Lebensbild eines Parlamentariers aus Deutschlands glücklicher Zeit* (Mannheim, 1919) is an extremely informative account of his family and political life by his daughter. More superficial, as its name implies, is Elisabeth von Roon, *Ernst Bassermann: Eine Politische Skizze* (Berlin, 1925). Another excellent biography, for its story of the man and of local and right-wing politics, is Günther Kriegbaum, *Die Parlamentarische Tätigkeit des Freiherrn C. W. Heyl zu Herrnsheim* (Meisenheim/ Glan, 1962).

The literature on Stresemann continues to grow, but there is still no authoritative work that covers his whole life. A useful guide to the literature is Hans Gatzke, "Gustav Stresemann: A Bibliographical Article," *Journal of Modern History* 36 (1964) : 1–13. An earlier guide, Gustav Zwoch, *Gustav-Stresemann Bibliographie* (Düsseldorf, 1953) lists the articles and speeches of Stresemann for the period before the war. The most recent guide to the Stresemann literature is Martin Waldorff, *Bibliographie Gustav Stresemann* (Düsseldorf, 1972). Rochus, Freiherr von Rheinbaben, *Stresemann, Der Mensch und der*

Staatsmann (Dresden, 1930) is not helpful for this earlier period. A short introduction to the study of his life is Felix Hirsch, *Gustav Stresemann: Patriot und Europäer* (Göttingen, 1964). For the period studied here, Donald Warren, Jr., *The Red Kingdom of Saxony: Lobbying Grounds for Gustav Stresemann, 1901–1909* (The Hague, 1964) is particularly valuable for the relationships between business interests and politics. It also contains a comprehensive bibliography for the study of Saxony. Stresemann's role in the Weimar Republic is covered best by Henry Ashby Turner, Jr., *Stresemann and the Politics of the Weimar Republic* (Princeton, 1963).

Last, but not least, the best biography for the development of Centrist democracy is Klaus Epstein, *Matthias Erzberger and the Dilemma of German Democracy* (Princeton, 1959). Until recently, the student of the Centre party was dependent on this work for a modern account of the years between 1910 and 1920.

Party Histories

The standard history of the German parties is Ludwig Bergsträsser, *Geschichte der politischen Parteien in Deutschland,* 10th ed. (Munich, 1960), and 11th ed. (Munich, 1965). The tenth edition contains a more detailed text, while the eleventh edition includes more bibliographical aids. Thomas Nipperdey, *Die Organisation der deutschen Parteien vor 1918* (Düsseldorf, 1961) is more than the history of party organization; it also provides a brief party history and is useful for establishing fundamental facts and concepts. An older work, good for the developments of programs and attitudes before 1910, is Oscar Stillich, *Die politischen Parteien in Deutschland,* 2 vols. (Leipzig, 1908–11). An excellent reference both for the parties and the organizations which supported them is *Die bürgerlichen Parteien in Deutschland, 1830–1945: Handbuch der Geschichte der bürgerlichen Parteien und anderer bürgerliche Interessenorganisationen vom Vormärz bis zum Jahre 1945,* ed. Dieter Fricke, 2 vols. (Leipzig, 1970).

For the development of German liberalism, there are two books describing background and development. F. C. Sell, *Die Tragödie des deutschen Liberalismus* (Stuttgart, 1953) provides a generally superficial account. Leonard Krieger, *The German Idea of Freedom* (Boston, 1957) brilliantly describes the intellectual origins of the split between the liberals, so problemmatical for the period studied in this work. Histories of the National Liberals are few and far between. Erich Brandenburg, *Fünfzig Jahre Nationalliberaler Politik* (Berlin, 1917) is an official party pamphlet history and virtually useless. The older basic study of one aspect of National Liberal development in the monarchy, Theodor Eschenburg, *Das Kaiserreich am Scheideweg: Bassermann, Bülow und der Block* (Berlin, 1929) is still valuable because Eschenburg used the then extant private papers of Bassermann. Excellent for sociological information and providing a short introduction to the Prussian party on the eve of World War I is Hartwig Thieme, *Nationaler Liberalismus in der Krise: Die nationalliberale Fraktion des preussischen Abgeordnetenhauses, 1914–18* (Boppard / Rhine, 1963). Historians of the last few decades have also paid little attention to the Left Liberals. Now two books have been published that increase our information and our understanding of this neglected group. The first is Konstanze Wegner's history, mentioned above, which combines a biography of Theodor Barth with a history of the Freisinnige Vereinigung. The second is a more extensive study which also explores the relationships between Left Liberals and Social Democrats: Ludwig Elm, *Zwischen Fortschritt und Reaktion: Geschichte der liberalen Bourgeoisie in Deutschland, 1893–1918* ([East] Berlin, 1968). There is one short, old-fashioned monograph on the South Germans: Klaus Heger, *Die deutsche demokratische Partei in Württemberg und ihre Organisation* (Leipzig, 1927). A new history of the South German Volkspartei would be an excellent contribution to regional history. An older history of Naumann's first political venture, written by an original member of the group, Martin Wenck, *Die Geschichte der Nationalsozialen von 1895 bis 1903* (Berlin-Schöneberg, 1905), describes very well the party's ambivalence toward Social Democracy. Wenck's work has now been superseded by Dieter Düding, *Der Nationalsoziale Verein, 1896–1903* (Munich, 1972), which uses valuable correspondence among club members available in the Potsdam archives and affords a good glimpse of their important differences of opinion.

The Social Democrats have increasingly occupied the center of the historians' stage in the last few years. The classic work for their development in the period studied here is Carl Schorske, *German Social Democracy, 1905–1917: The Development of the Great Schism* (Cambridge, 1955). Although the use of archival materials has altered some facts and shifted some interpretations, his work is so thorough and so accurate that it is difficult to supersede it in any way. His bibliography is still the best basic introduction to German Social Democracy, and I will limit my list to important and useful works which appeared after his publication. Histories that deal with the period just prior to this one and which helped considerably in my orientation to Social Democratic reformism and parliamentarism are Gerhard A. Ritter, *Die Arbeiterbewegung im wilhelminischen Reich* (Berlin-Dahlem, 1959) and Vernon E. Lidtke, *The Outlawed Party: Social Democracy in Germany, 1878–1890* (Princeton, 1966). Both have become as well-known and as well-used as Schorske's book. Two thought-provoking sociological interpretations of Social Democracy, useful also to historians, have appeared in the last decade. The first is Gunther Roth, *The Social Democrats in Imperial Germany: A Study in Working-Class Isolation and National Integration* (Totowa, 1963). Roth's argument about Social Democratic isolation and "negative" integration is more than supported by even a superficial reading of Eduard David's war diaries. The second, J. P. Nettl, "The German Social Democratic Party, 1890–1914, as a Political Model," *Past and Present* 30 (April 1965) refers back to Roth's thesis but argues that their isolation was self-imposed. This view is reinforced by Erich Matthias, "Kautsky und der Kautskyanismus: Die Funktion der Ideologie in der deutschen Sozialdemokratie vor dem ersten Weltkrieg," *Schriften der evangelischen Studiengemeinschaft* (Tübingen, 1957), 5 : 151–197, and by Walter Holzheuer, *Karl Kautskys Werk als Weltanschauung: Beitrag zur Ideologie der Sozialdemokratie vor dem ersten Weltkrieg* (Munich, 1972). In addition, there are two books that examine Social Democratic attitudes critically. Susanne Miller, *Das Problem der Freiheit in Sozialismus* (Frankfurt / Main, 1964) is quite good for a careful definition of how terms were used by the Social Democrats. Peter Lösche, *Der Bolschewismus im Urteil der deutschen Sozialdemokratie, 1903–1920* (Berlin, 1967) merely shows how remote was the possibility of a German Bolshevik revolution. Articles of special help on imperialism are Abraham Ascher, "Imperialists within German Social Democracy prior to 1914," *Journal of Central European Affairs* 20 (1960–61) : 397–422, and " 'Radical' Imperialists within German Social Democracy, 1912–1918," *Political Science Quarterly* 76 (1961) : 555–575. Another thorough insight into Social Democracy's attitudes toward imperialism, particularly before 1890, is Hans-Christoph Schroeder, *Sozialismus und Imperialismus,* pt. 1 : *Die Auseindersetzung der deutschen Sozialdemokratie mit dem Imperialismusproblem und der "Weltpolitik" vor 1914* (Hanover, 1968). More tangential, but nevertheless related to the problem of imperialism, is Hans-Ulrich Wehler, *Sozialdemokratie und Nationalstaat* (Würzburg, 1962). John Snell, "German Socialists in the last Imperial Reichstag, 1912–1918," *International Review of Social History* 7 (1952) : 196–205, presents a helpful sociological study of the Reichstag Fraktion that voted for the war credits. A study which became available to the author only as this book went to press is Dieter Groh, *Negative Integration und revolutionären Attentismus. Die deutsche Sozialdemokratie am Vorabend des 1. Weltkrieges 1909–1914* (Berlin, 1973).

The German Centre party desperately needs a new historian. The mammoth work of Karl Bachem, *Vorgeschichte, Geschichte und Politik der deutschen Zentrumspartei,* 8 vols. (Cologne, 1927–31), is good for a factual and descriptive account, but its lack of social and economic analysis as well as its lack of attention to internal difficulties are major gaps for a modern historian. For a good introduction to the Centre in this period as well as for information about the difficulties of writing a party history, see Rudolf Morsey, *Die deutsche Zentrumspartei, 1917–1923* (Düsseldorf, 1966). A good summary of the fights within the party is John K. Zeender, "German Catholics and the Concept of an Interconfessional Party, 1900–1922," *Journal of Central European Affairs* 23 (1963–64) : 424–439.

LOCAL HISTORIES

The best introduction to Baden in this period is *Das Grossherzogtum Baden,* ed. E. Rebmann et al. (Karlsruhe, 1912). It contains political, legal, and economic information which is detailed and helpful. A small history, Hans Herzfeld, *Das Land Baden* (1948) was not available to this author. A microcosmic approach to elections, based on the district surrounding Heidelberg, is Bernhard Vogel and Peter Haungs, *Wahlkampf und Wählertradition: Eine Studie zur Bundestagswahl von 1961* (Cologne, 1961). The two authors give background information which includes the monarchy and the Weimar republic and thereby apply a method suggested more than sixty years ago by Max Weber. For Bavaria, Martin Doeberl, *Entwicklungsgeschichte Bayerns,* 3 vols. (Munich, 1928–31) gives the necessary background information on Bavarian politics. A better summary is Karl Bosl, "Gesellschaft und

Politik in Bayern vor dem Ende der Monarchie," *Zeitschrift für bayerische Landesgeschichte* 28 (1965) : 1–31. Wolfgang Zorn, *Kleine Wirtschafts-und-Sozialgeschichte Bayerns, 1806–1933* (Munich, 1962) provides a good introduction to the subject. At present, there is a great need for a history of Bavaria during the period of the Kaiserreich. Better attention has perhaps been paid to Württemberg than to either Baden or Bavaria. Walter Grube, *Der Stuttgarter Landtag, 1457–1957* judiciously selects the most pertinent material for each period and presents it in an interesting way.

Moving northward into Prussia, one of the best regional studies to date is Josef Bellot, *Hundert Jahre politisches Leben an der Saar unter preussischer Herrschaft, 1815–1918* (Bonn, 1954). A good story of social change in an industrial city is Wolfgang Hofmann, *Die Bielefelder Stadtverordneten: Ein Beitrag zu bürgerlicher Selbstverwaltung und sozialer Wandel, 1850 bis 1914* (Lübeck and Hamburg, 1964), while political attitudes in a rural area are presented in a fascinating way by Rudolf Heberle, *Landbevölkerung und Nationalsozialismus: Eine soziologische Untersuchung der politischen Willensbildung in Schleswg-Holstein, 1918–1932* (Stuttgart, 1963). This is a German edition of an earlier work published in English; it can be supplemented with Gerhard Stoltenberg, *Politische Strömungen im schleswig-holsteinischen Landvolk, 1918–1933* (Düsseldorf, 1962).

One of the best regional party histories is Hermann Kastendiek, "Der Liberalismus in Bremen" (unpublished doctoral diss., Kiel, 1952). The conflicts in Bremen shed much light on difficulties within the liberal movement as a whole. When one considers simultaneous difficulties within Bremen Social Democracy, the city's politics become an attractive subject of research. Hamburg would be an equally fascinating regional study. A good introduction to the city's complicated institutions is Ernst Baasch, *Geschichte Hamburgs, 1814–1918,* 2 vols. (Stuttgart, 1925) while an initial exploration of party history is provided by Carl F. Rode, *Das hamburgische Parteiwesen in Vergangenheit und Gegenwart* (Hamburg, 1919).

INTEREST ORGANIZATIONS

Schorske's bibliography on trade unions is still a valuable one and can be supplemented with Gerhard A. Ritter. Only one additional account of trade-union politics seems worth mentioning: Johann

Fritsch, *Eindringen und Ausbreitung des Revisionismus im deutschen Bergarbeiterverband bis 1914* (Leipzig, 1967).

For the connection between business organizations and politics, Arnold J. Heidenheimer and Frank C. Langdon, *Business Associations and the Financing of Political Parties* (The Hague, 1968) provides a good introduction. A more detailed work, excellent in its analysis of the various political currents in the German business community, is Hartmut Kaelble, *Industrielle Interessenpolitik in der wilhelminischen Gesellschaft* (Berlin, 1967). Also good for the declining participation and influence of individual businessmen in politics is Hans Jaeger, *Unternehmer in der deutschen Politik, 1890–1918* (Bonn, 1967). An East German study which sheds light on the struggle of heavy and light industrialists within the National Liberal party is Helga Nussbaum, *Unternehmer gegen Monopole: Ueber Struktur und Aktionen antimonopolistischer bürgerlicher Gruppen zu Beginn des 20. Jahrhaunderts* ([East] Berlin, 1966). Another work which illumines the struggle between business and labor is Roswitha Leckebusch, *Entstehung und Wandlungen der Zielsetzungen, der Struktur und der Wirkungen von Arbeitgeberverbänden* ([East] Berlin, 1966).

An older work treating the politics of the agrarians and valuable for pin-pointing the participation of groups and parties is Sarah Tirell, *German Agrarian Politics after Bismarck's Fall: The Formation of the Farmers' League* (New York, 1951). A more modern work, which contains some information about the degree of National Liberal involvement in agrarian politics, is Hans-Jürgen Puhle, *Agrarische Interessenpolitik und preussischer Konservatismus im wilhelminischen Reich, 1893–1914* (Hanover, 1966).

Recently Dirk Stegmann, *Die Erben Bismarcks: Parteien und Verbände in der Spätphase des wilhelminischen Deutschlands* (Cologne, 1970), has thoroughly explored the cooperation of all those groups opposed to a liberalization of Germany. His research into the *Sammlungspolitik* highlights movements strongly counteracting the Grand Bloc policy.

BACKGROUND MATERIALS

Two general histories of Germany in this period, helpful for the establishment of the issues and their chronology, are Adalbert Wahl, *Deutsche Geschichte von der Reichsgrundung bis zum Ausbruch des Weltkrieges 1871–1914,* 4 vols. (Stuttgart, 1926–36) and Johannes

Ziekursch, *Politische Geschichte des neuen deutschen Kaiserreiches,* 3 vols. (Frankfurt / Main, 1925–30). Another general history that deals roughly with the same period of time and the same issues as this monograph is Walter Koch, *Volk und Staatsführung vor dem Weltkrieg* (Stuttgart, 1935). A political, sociological approach to the same period is Peter Molt, *Der Reichstag vor der improvisierten Revolution* (Cologne, 1963).

Elections to the Reichstag, with valuable information concerning alliances, are covered by George Crothers, *The German Elections of 1907* (New York, 1941) and Jürgen Bertram, *Die Wahlen zum deutschen Reichstag vom Jahre 1912* (Düsseldorf, 1964). Changes in German electoral patterns are presented by Arthur Dix, *Die deutschen Reichstagswahlen 1871–1930 und die Wandlungen der Volksgliederung* (Tübingen, 1930).

The problem of democratization, so central to the history of the liberals and to this study, receives an interesting introductory treatment from Peter Gilg, *Die Erneuerung des demokratischen Denkens im wilhelminischen Deutschland: Eine ideengeschichtliche Studie zur Wende vom 19. zum 20. Jahrhundert* (Wiesbaden, 1965). A more specific treatment of the problem can be found in Walter Gagel, *Die Wahlrechtsfrage in der Geschichte der deutschen liberalen Parteien, 1848–1918* (Düsseldorf, 1958). For democratic developments on the local level, H. Heffter, *Die deutsche Selbstverwaltung im 19. Jahrhundert* (Stuttgart, 1950), is a mine of information and indispensable for any regional study. Manfred Rauh, *Föderalismus und Parlamentarismus im wilhelminischen Reich* (Düsseldorf, 1973) argues that the democratic Reichstag gradually helped to diminish the powers of the Bundesrat after the turn of the century.

There have been two recent monographs devoted to nationalism in the Kaiserreich. Konrad Schilling, *Beiträge zu einer Geschichte des radikalen Nationalismus in der wilhelminischen Aera, 1890–1900* (Cologne, 1968) supplements the various histories of the Pan-German League and provides a wealth of sociological material for the origins of the Navy and Army Leagues. In a different vein, Elisabeth Fehrenbach, *Wandlungen des deutschen Kaisergedankens, 1871–1918* (Munich, 1969) corroborates Naumann's ideas about the unifying power of the monarchy and describes the role of Wilhelm II in reinforcing this power. Much useful information about the press and its role in the growth of

German nationalism and imperialism can be found in Klaus Wernecke, *Die Wille zur Weltgeltung: Aussenpolitik und Oeffentlichkeit im Kaiserreich am Vorabend des ersten Weltkrieges* (Düsseldorf, 1970). The politics of German defense are explained in Hans Herzfeld, *Die deutsche Rüstungspolitik vor dem Weltkriege* (Bonn, 1923), and the chronology of naval bills can be found in Hans Georg Fernis, *Die Flottennovellen im Reichstag, 1906–1912* (Stuttgart, 1934). The position of the various parties toward imperialism is thoroughly and concisely outlined in Hans Spellmeyer, *Deutsche Kolonialpolitik im Reichstag* (Stuttgart, 1931).

Anyone studying social legislation and financial policy should consult Karl Erich Born, *Staat und Sozialpolitik seit Bismarcks Sturz* (Wiesbaden, 1957) and Edwin R. A. Seligman, *Essays in Taxation,* 10th ed. (New York, 1925). The latter book is still the best account of the history of taxes in Europe and the United States before 1914. For a nonanalytical statement of party positions on tax reform, see Hans Teschemacher, *Reichsfinanzreform und innere Reichspolitik, 1906–1913* (Berlin, 1915). Lastly, a detailed and enlightening study of the Reich's financial history is Peter-Christian Witt, *Die Finanzpolitik des deutschen Reiches von 1903 bis 1913: Eine Studie zur Innenpolitik des wilhelminischen Deutschlands,* vol. 415 of *Historische Studien,* ed. W. Berges et al. (Lübeck and Hamburg, 1970).

Index